A GUIDE TO THE
British Landscape

D0528549

There are also Collins Pocket and Field Guides to:

A GUIDE TO THE

British Landscape

J. R. W. Cheatle

With over 500 drawings by the author

COLLINS
St James's Place, London

William Collins Sons & Co Ltd
London · Glasgow · Sydney · Auckland
Toronto · Johannesburg

First published 1976

© J. R. W. Cheatle, 1976

ISBN 0 00 219240 3

Made and Printed in Great Britain by
William Collins Sons & Co Ltd Glasgow

FOREWORD

by H. C. K. Henderson, B.Sc., M.A., Ph.D.

Professor of Geography, Birkbeck College

It gave me real pleasure to receive an invitation from the author to contribute a brief foreword to this book. It is many years since Mr Cheatle and I first went out together into the field and his interest in field work has been maintained throughout. The present result in the form of this book is a very inclusive guide as to what can be done by personal observation, and it is a real achievement of considerable value to have brought together under one cover such information as a description of various common grasses, a guide to archaeological remains which yield evidence of the prehistory of an area, architecture and agricultural features.

I am sure many schoolmasters will find this book a very valuable aid in their work and I foresee an appreciable market among university and polytechnic students.

CONTENTS

CONTENTS

PHOTOGRAPHS

PREFACE

Today, greater leisure and mobility are enabling more people to enjoy Britain's vast range of topography, but while everyone can appreciate a piece of beautiful scenery without knowing how it came into being and developed – just as they can control a car without detailed knowledge of all its mechanical complexities – more pleasure, satisfaction and advantage are derived from a wider understanding of at least the background and basic principles. Realising this, an ever-increasing number of thinking people are no longer content merely to look, they want to know more about what they see; but the main problem is where to begin, for landscape is such a wide concept that it spreads right across the whole gamut of Arts, Humanities, Sciences and Technologies. Indeed, virtually everything we do, or think of, is reflected in some measure in our landscape. However, most of the information needed in the search for a wider understanding can only be found either superficially in elementary books for schools or buried deeply in extremely advanced specialised works. Unfortunately much of the middle ground has been virtually ignored. This book then is an attempt to bridge the gap and cover the broad spread of the subject, providing identification/information keys to what can be found and basic background material in those areas which cannot be treated in this way. But to begin at the beginning.

What is Landscape? To most the word conjures up a sunlit view of countryside seen from a lofty hill-top; the golds and varied greens of the fields, some dotted with farm animals often seeking the shade of darker tinted trees, and the whole cut by rippling streams and winding lanes linking villages and individual farms. Only on the horizon does a patch of dark haze betray the presence of an industrial town, like the one from which we have escaped all too briefly. Many people think of town and countryside as being distinctly separate entities, but nature knows no arbitrary dividing lines. Both are integral parts of one landscape, sharing the same weather, physical features and biological controls. The main difference lies in that Man's hand is more obvious in urban areas. Although he has changed the rural scene as much, it is far less apparent to our eyes and minds. This dichotomy of landscape into town and countryside is perhaps symptomatic of our age of over-specialisation, in which knowledge is not only separated into watertight compartments, but then sub-divided into smaller and smaller fragments until they have only depth; a process which seems to begin ever earlier in schools, before the children have acquired a real general education, the complete reversal of the eighteenth-century ideal of an all-rounder, the universal man.

Consideration of landscape involves cutting across many of these inter-disciplinary boundaries, even for one small, but unique scene, although the factors can be grouped under two broad headings, Man and Nature. Both have contributed, but while nature works on a geological time-scale of millions of years or a biological one of thousands, man effects vast changes in centuries or even decades. Time is important for nature is still modifying our peaceful and seemingly eternal scenery. What we see is only a stage in a complex series of cycles of change which will themselves be modified long before completion.

In looking at landscape, we begin with geology, which forms its bones and sinews. The rock-forming minerals, the rocks themselves, the fossils they contain and the geological succession tell much of their origins and formation, while physical evolution shows what has happened in geologically recent times and what is still happening today. The section on soils, an altogether neglected aspect of scenery, bridges the gap to vegetation and wild animals. The review of Man's activities begins with prehistory, as many ancient structures figure prominently in interesting scenes, before turning to a brief résumé of the changes produced in Roman and Anglo-Saxon Britain. The period since the Norman Conquest is viewed chiefly through its buildings, which are amongst the more permanent of Man's landmarks, but which so often expressed his thoughts and ideas besides reflecting his progressive settlement of the land, shown in the change of place-names, and the growth of transport. Farming is still the largest land occupier and here emphasis is placed on identification. But, because of the tremendous number of possible combinations and permutations of landscape elements, no attempt can be made to draw the many threads together. This must be done for each highly individual area.

While every attempt has been made to avoid jargon, the use of some technical terms is unavoidable. These have been grouped together in section glossaries, avoiding both the use of frequent footnotes and an over-large general glossary.

Finally, my grateful thanks are due to many kind friends for their help and encouragement, to Professor H. C. K. Henderson for his generous Foreword, to understanding publishers and to many librarians for running to earth a wide range of very varied books and information. However, any mistakes are mine.

J.R.W.C.

SCALE LINES

All drawings of plants and animals are based on a theoretical average but remember that their size can vary as widely as humans. As far as possible all leaves or similar groups of animals are drawn on the same scale, but the scale is indicated by a toothed bar. Those with a single toothed bar show inches and centimetres, while those with a double bar show feet and decimetres (10cms).

PART I

THE LAND

GEOLOGY

Geology, the scientific study of rocks, should be given pride of place in any book about British landscape. In Britain we find rocks of almost every geological age and composition, which have been attacked by a wide variety of physical forces to give the greatest range of scenery within such a small compass in the world, extending from the glaciated peaks and valleys of the North and West to the fertile and rolling Midland Plateau; from the high northern Moors through the low spread of the Fens, to the broad sweep of the Downs and ending in the famous White Cliffs. As a result many fundamental geological discoveries have been made in Britain and, in addition, geology is one of the few scientific fields in which the interested amateur can still make real contributions.

The section begins with a key and composition of the commoner minerals. Then come descriptive keys of major rock types and broad fossil groups, followed by a general survey of the sequence of rocks (Stratigraphy) found in Britain, and a short account of the principal ways in which natural forces have acted upon these to produce such a wide range of landforms. The section ends with a glossary to clarify any unavoidable technical terms.

IDENTIFICATION OF THE COMMON
BRITISH MINERALS

Minerals can be found in a great variety of forms and colours. The only easily determinable and constant characteristics of many minerals are their hardness and streak (the colour of the powdered mineral), which is often quite different from that of the mineral in a mass. First, using the guide below, the approximate hardness is found, taking care the mineral is scratched, not the reference material. If the mineral dust from this is collected on white paper this will show the streak, or the mineral can be rubbed across an unglazed tile (streak plate). The key below will show which table to look at, and the hardness which part of the table. Final identification will depend on the form, colour, lustre, cleavage, fracture and relative 'heaviness' of the mineral.

Approximate Hardness

Minerals of hardness 7 and over are not scratched by quartz, nor easily by a file
Minerals of hardness between 5 and 7 are scratched by quartz, easily by a file but not by a knife.
Minerals of hardness between 3 and 5 are scratched by a knife but not by a copper coin.
Minerals of hardness less than 3 are scratched by copper coin.
Minerals of hardness less than 2.5 can be scratched by most finger-nails. (Check this, as the hardness of finger-nails varies.)
Minerals of hardness 1.0 or less are easily scratched by a finger-nail and have a greasy feel.

Key to Tables

A. The mineral is as hard as quartz (H.7), or harder. Streak, if obtainable, is colourless, white, or nearly so. **Table 1** p. 16
B. The mineral is not as hard as quartz (H. less than 7). See C–F below.
C. The streak and mineral are both white, or nearly so. **Table 2** p. 18
D. The streak is white, or nearly so, but the mineral is distinctly coloured. **Table 3** p. 22
E. The streak is black, lead-black or greenish-black. The opaque mineral has a metallic lustre. **Table 4** p. 24
F. The streak is coloured, but not black; the mineral is coloured. **Table 5** p. 25

Abbreviations

H.	Hardness	Col	Colour(s)	Cl	Cleavage
SG	Specific Gravity	Sys	Crystal System	F	Fracture
St	Streak	L	Lustre	Occ	Occurrence

TABLE I

The mineral is as hard as quartz ($H. = 7.0$) or harder. Streak, if obtainable, is colourless, white or nearly white.

A. *H:*6.5–7.5 *SG:*3.2–4.3 *Col:* shades of red, brownish-red, emerald to pale olive-green: rarely yellowish. *Sys:* cubic. *Forms:* crystals rhombdodecahedra or trapezohedra: also massive, surface often rounded. *L:* vitreous; transparent to opaque. No *Cl. F:* conchoidal to uneven. *Occ.* quite common in metamorphic rocks; also found in crystalline limestones and some igneous rocks.

Garnet

Rhombdodecahedron

Trapezohedron

Garnets showing combinations of rhombdodecahedron and trapezohedron

B. *H:*7.0 *SG:*2.7 *Col:* colourless when pure, often tinged by impurities; white, amethyst, pink, yellow to dark brown, orange or smoky. *Sys:* hexagonal. *Forms:* prismatic crystals capped by pyramids; also massive, nodular or granular. *L:* transparent (usually) to opaque. No *Cl. F:* irregular to conchoidal. *Occ:* essential mineral in acid igneous rocks; granular (sands and sandstones); also in veins and geodes. Distinguished from calcite by its hardness.

Quartz

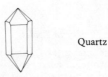
Quartz

Varieties
  i. Colourless. Transparent   Rock Crystal
 ii. Pale pink or rose; colour may fade on exposure, but is restored by moistening with water. Transparent   Rose Quartz
iii. Smoky-brown to smoky-yellow. Transparent to opaque
                                                              Smoky Quartz

C. *H:*7.0 *SG:*2.6 *Col:* white, greys, pale blue or brownish-white, often variegated. *Forms:* cryptocrystalline to wax-like masses; usually nodular, often mammillated or botryoidal; sometimes stalactitic; al may show radiating structure. No *Cl. F:* irregular.

Chalceden Silica

Varieties

i. Shades of darker greys to black. *F:* conchoidal, giving sharp edges; sparks when struck by steel. Irregular nodules, often found in layers of Upper Chalk; river-gravels   **Flint**

ii. Greys, weathering to reddish-browns. *F:* fairly flat. Found usually in limestones other than Chalk and river-gravels   **Chert**

iii. Flat bands of sharply separated colours   **Agate**

iv. As (iii), but with dendrites (tree-like growths) of darker minerals   **Moss Agate**

D. *H:* 7.0–7.5 *SG:* 4.7 *Col:* colourless, grey, pale yellow, greenish or reddish-brown. *Sys:* tetragonal. *Forms:* small prismatic crystals; also rounded grains. *L:* adamantine; transparent to opaque. *Cl:* indistinct. *F:* conchoidal. *Occ:* primary mineral of igneous, especially acidic, rocks; also found in crystalline limestones and metamorphic rocks.   **Zircon**

E. *H:* 7.0–7.5 *SG:* 3.1 *Col:* black, bluish-black, sometimes red, green or blue. *Sys:* hexagonal. *Forms:* long prismatic crystals, broad and narrow prism faces alternate often striated; colours may be zoned along the long axis; also compact or columnar. *L:* vitreous; transparent to opaque. *Cl:* indistinct. *F:* subconchoidal to uneven. *Occ:* accessory mineral of granite and the more acidic rocks.   **Tourmaline**

Tourmaline and (*below*) section showing face sequence

F. *H:* 7.5 *SG:* 3.2 *Col:* pearl-grey, flesh-pink or purplish. *Sys:* orthorhombic. *Forms:* square-section prismatic crystals, flat-topped; also granular or massive; cruciform 'spots' in slates (variety Chiastolite). *L:* vitreous; translucent to opaque. *Cl:* poor, parallel to prisms. *F:* uneven. *Occ:* clayey metamorphic rocks; also an accessory mineral of some granites.   **Andalusite**

G. *H:* 7.5 *SG:* 2.7 *Col:* emerald to pale green, blue, yellow or white. *Sys:* hexagonal. *Forms:* often large prismatic crystals, capped by pyramids, sometimes truncated; also massive. *L:* vitreous to resinous; transparent to opaque. *Cl:* indistinct basal. *F:* conchoidal or uneven; brittle. *Occ:* an accessory mineral of acidic igneous and metamorphic rocks.   **Beryl**

Beryl   Topaz   Olivine

H. *H:* 8.0 *SG:* 3.5 *Col:* rich to pale yellow or greyish; sometimes blue or pink. *Sys:* orthorhombic. *Forms:* usually short prisms, often capped by pyramids which may be truncated; also granular. *L:* vitreous; transparent to translucent. *Cl.* perfect basal. *F:* subconchoidal to uneven. *Occ:* acidic igneous and metamorphic rocks; often associated with tin-bearing rocks and veins.   **Topaz**

I. *H:* 9.0 *SG:* 4.0 *Col:* grey, greenish or reddish. *Sys:* hexagonal. *Forms:* squat, barrel-shaped or double pyramids; also granular. *L:* vitreous to dull; transparent to opaque. *Cl:* none, but basal separation planes common. *F:* conchoidal or uneven. *Occ:* some igneous and many metamorphic rocks, especially contact-metamorphosed shales.   **Corundum**

Corundum: 'barrel' form

TABLE 2

H less than 7; mineral and streak are colourless, white or nearly so.

A. *H:* 1.0 *SG:* 2.7 *Col:* white, pale greens or silvery. *Sys:* monoclinic. *Forms:* usually foliated, massive or granular; tabular crystals rare. *L:* pearly; translucent to opaque; soapy feel. *Cl:* perfect, giving thin flexible, but inelastic sheets. No *F. Occ:* secondary mineral produced by hydration of magnesium-bearing rocks during metamorphism.   **Talc**

B. *H:* 1.5–2.0 *SG:* 2.3 *Col:* crystals colourless; massive, compact or fibrous forms white, grey or pink. *Sys:* monoclinic. *Forms:* lozenge-shaped crystals, often twinned to give 'arrowheads'. *L:* pearly to silky. *Cl:* perfect, giving thin flexible, but inelastic sheets. No *F. Occ:* saline deposits; pyrite-bearing clays; dolomitised limestones.   **Gypsum**

Gypsum crystal: selenite

Varieties
i. Colourless crystals; transparent   Selenite
ii. Light-coloured, fine-grain, compact   Alabaster
iii. Fibrous. *L:* silky   Satin Spar

C. *H:* (crystals) 2.0–2.5 *SG:* 2.6 *Col:* white, when pure; usually
greyish, yellowish or brownish. *Sys:* triclinic. *Forms:* usually soft,
fine, clayey material, easily crumbled under light pressure; crystals
small, pseudo-hexagonal uncommon. *L:* earthy; opaque; greasy
feel. *Occ:* produced by weathering of granitic felspars.   **Kaolin**

D. *H:* 2.0–2.5 *SG:* 2.2 *Col:* colourless when pure, usually tinged
yellowish, reddish or purple. *Sys:* cubic. *Forms:* hollow-faced (inverted stepped pyramids) cubes; octahedra rare; also massive or
granular. *L:* vitreous; translucent; salty taste; may dissolve in
moist air. *Cl:* perfect cubic. *F:* conchoidal; brittle. *Occ:* saline
residues.   **Rock Salt**

E. *H:* 2.0–2.5 *SG:* 2.9 *Col:* thin sheets colourless, or nearly so;
yellow, green, brown to blackish when thicker. *Sys:* monoclinic.
Forms: silvery flakes to squat, pseudo-hexagonal crystals. *L:* pearly;
transparent to translucent. *Cl:* perfect basal, giving thin, flexible
and elastic sheets. No *F. Occ:* essential mineral of acidic igneous
rocks; also some metamorphic ones and as tiny flakes in some
sedimentaries.   **Muscovite**

F. *H:* 2.5–3.5 *SG:* 4.5 'heavy' for a crystal *Col:* colourless or
white; often tinged yellow, red or brown, rarely blue. *Sys:* orthorhombic. *Forms:* tabular crystals; also massive, compact or columnar. *L:* vitreous; transparent to translucent. *Cl:* perfect in three
planes. *F:* uneven; brittle. *Occ:* common vein mineral; associated
with galena, fluorspar, zinc blende, calcite and quartz; also
residual nodules from decayed limestone.   **Barytes**

Barytes

G. *H:* 3.0 *SG:* 2.7 *Col:* colourless or white, often tinged blue,
yellow, red, brown or grey. *Sys:* hexagonal. *Forms:* rhombohedral,
often 'Nailhead' or 'Dogtooth'; also massive, compact, fibrous or
stalactitic. *L:* vitreous to earthy; transparent to opaque. *Cl:* perfect
rhombohedral. *F:* conchoidal; brittle. *Occ:* principal constituent of
limestones; larger crystals found within cavities. May resemble
quartz, but less hard.   **Calcite**

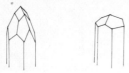

Calcite: *left*, 'dogtooth'; *right*, 'nailhead'

Varieties
i. Colourless, rhombohedral crystals. Transparent   Iceland Spar
ii. Finely fibrous. *L:* silky   Satin Spar
iii. Fine-grain, compact. Opaque. Cream-coloured, often
   speckled. Deposited by limestone waters and streams   Calcareous Tufa

H. *H:* 3.0–3.5 *SG:* 2.9 *Col:* white, often tinged red, blue or grey. *Sys:* orthorhombic. *Forms:* prismatic or tabular; also fibrous, compact or granular. *L:* vitreous; transparent to translucent. *Cl:* perfect, three planes, giving rectangular fragments with pearly lustre. *F:* uneven; often splintery. *Occ:* saline deposits; associated with rock salt and gypsum. Harder than latter, which has only one cleavage plane.   **Anhydrite**

I. *H:* 3.5–4.0 *SG:* 2.9 *Col:* white, often tinged yellow or brown; sometimes pink, green or grey. *Sys:* hexagonal. *Forms:* rhombohedral crystals, often with curved faces ('saddle-backs'); also massive or granular. *L:* vitreous to pearly, dull when massive; opaque. *Cl:* perfect rhombohedral. *F:* conchoidal to uneven; brittle. *Occ:* saline deposits; cavities in limestones; schists; often associated with galena and zinc blende.   **Dolomite**

J. *H:* 3.5–4.0 *SG:* 2.9 *Col:* white, pale grey or yellowish; sometimes greenish or violet. *Sys:* orthorhombic. *Forms:* prismatic crystals, often appear pseudo-hexagonal, and needle crystals; also massive or stalactitic. *L:* vitreous; transparent to translucent. *Cl:* poor basal. *F:* sub-conchoidal; brittle. *Occ:* in beds of gypsum and iron ores; deposited from hot springs. Distinguished from calcite by poor cleavage.   **Aragonite**

Aragonite prismatic crystals

K. *H:* 3.5–4.5 *SG:* 3.0 *Col:* white, greyish or brownish. *Sys:* hexagonal. *Forms:* chalk-like, massive, compact or fibrous; rhombohedral crystals rare. *L:* dull; vitreous on crystals; transparent to opaque. *Cl:* perfect rhombohedral on crystals. *F:* flat to conchoidal. *Occ:* in veins and fracture-zones; metamorphosed magnesium-rich rocks, e.g. serpentine, olivine or talc.   **Magnesite**

L. *H:* 4.0 *SG:* 3.1 *Col:* white, colourless, often tinted blue, green, yellow, pink or purple; may be variegated. *Sys:* cubic. *Forms:* aggregate common; cubic crystals often repeatedly twinned; also massive, compact or granular. *L:* vitreous; transparent to translucent. *Cl:* Perfect octahedral. *F:* conchoidal to uneven; brittle. *Occ:* in veins; often associated with galena, zinc blende and barytes.

Fluorspar

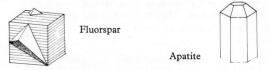

Fluorspar

Apatite

M. *H:* 5.0 *SG:* 3.2 *Col:* white or pale shades of blue, yellowish-green or green. *Sys:* hexagonal. *Forms:* large prismatic crystals, capped by pyramids, often truncated; may have coloured centres and white margins; also massive. *L:* resinous to vitreous; transparent to opaque. *Cl:* poor basal. *F:* uneven; brittle. *Occ:* common accessory mineral in all types of rocks. Resembles beryl, but is much less hard.

Apatite

N. *H:* 6.0–6.5 *SG:* 2.7 *Col:* usually white, flesh or grey; sometimes tinted blue, red, green or yellow. *Sys:* triclinic. *Forms:* prismatic laths of rectangular section; faces marked by fine striations (which distinguish it from orthoclase); also massive. *L:* vitreous; pearly on cleavage. *Cl:* perfect, in two planes at 86°. *F:* conchoidal to uneven; brittle to splintery. *Occ:* primary constituent of many igneous rocks.

Plagioclase Felspar

(The name covers a graded series of six closely related minerals. Field differentiation is very difficult.)

O. *H:* 5.5 *SG:* 4.0–4.5 *Col:* white, greyish, greenish to brownish. *Sys:* hexagonal. *Forms:* usually massive; reniform, botryoidal stalactitic or earthy; crystals rare. *L:* vitreous to pearly; translucent to opaque. *Cl:* perfect rhombohedral. *F:* uneven; brittle. *Occ:* beds or veins; associated with zinc blende, galena, copper and iron ores.

Calamine

P. *H:* 6.0 *SG:* 2.6 *Col:* white, often tinted, red, greyish-green or grey; rarely colourless. *Sys:* monoclinic. *Forms:* prismatic crystals common, often lath-like; also massive. *L:* vitreous to pearly; translucent to opaque. *Cl:* Perfect, two at 90°. *F:* conchoidal to uneven. *Occ:* an essential constituent of the more acidic igneous rocks, where it may be found as large individual crystals (phenocrysts).

Orthoclase Felspar

Orthoclase

TABLE 3

The streak is white, or nearly so, but the mineral is distinctly coloured.

A. *H:* 1.0 *SG:* 2.7 *Col:* paler greens or silvery. *Sys:* monoclinic. *Forms:* usually foliated, massive or granular; tabular crystals rare. *L:* pearly; translucent to opaque; soapy feel. *Cl:* perfect, giving thin flexible, but inelastic sheets. No *F. Occ:* secondary mineral produced by hydration of magnesium-bearing rocks during metamorphism.   **Talc**

B. *H:* 1.5–2.5 *SG:* 2.3 *Col:* pink, grey to whitish. *Sys:* monoclinic. *Forms:* massive, compact or fibrous. *L:* pearly to silky. *Cl:* perfect, giving thin flexible, but inelastic sheets. No *F. Occ:* saline deposits; pyrite-bearing clays; dolomitised limestones.   **Gypsum**

Varieties
  i. Light-coloured, fine-grain, compact   Alabaster
  ii. Fibrous. *L:* silky   Satin Spar

C. *H:* 1.5–2.5 *Col:* 2.7 *Col:* shades of green. *Sys:* monoclinic. *Forms:* usually granular or in scales; sometimes pseudo-hexagonal tabular crystals. *L:* pearly; usually opaque; greasy feel. *Cl:* perfect basal, giving thin flexible, but inelastic plates. No *F. Occ:* alteration product of biotite, hornblende, epidote, etc. in igneous rocks.   **Chlorite**

D. *H:* 2.0–2.5 *SG:* 2.2 *Col:* yellows, greens, browns to blackish when thick. *Sys:* monoclinic. *Forms:* small silvery flakes to squat, pseudo-hexagonal crystals. *L:* pearly; transparent to translucent. *Cl:* perfect basal, giving thin flexible and elastic sheets. No *F. Occ:* essential mineral of acidic igneous rocks; also in some metamorphic ones and as tiny flakes in some sedimentaries.   **Muscovite**

E. *H:* 2.5-3.0 *SG:* 2.7–3.1 *Col:* dark brown or dark green to black. *Sys:* monoclinic. *Forms:* flakes or squat pseudo-hexagonal crystals. *L:* splendent; transparent to nearly opaque depending on thickness. *Cl:* perfect basal, giving thin flexible and elastic sheets. No *F. Occ:* essential constituent of igneous rocks; also in some metamorphic.   **Biotite**

F. *H:* 3.0–4.0 *SG:* 2.5 *Col:* greens to almost black; sometimes red, yellow, brown or variegated. *Sys:* monoclinic. *Forms:* massive; sometimes granular or fibrous. *L:* sub-resinous; often has greasy feel; translucent to opaque. *Cl:* one, indistinct. *F:* conchoidal. *Occ:* alteration product, metamorphic or chemical, of magnesium-rich rocks.   **Serpentine**

G. *H:* 3.5–4.0 *SG:* 4.0 *Col:* usually black or brown; sometimes yellow. *Sys:* cubic. *Forms:* tetrahedra and rhombdodecahedra crystals common, often twinned; also massive or compact. *L:* resinous to adamantine; transparent to opaque. *Cl:* perfect rhombdodecahedral. *F:* conchoidal; brittle. *Occ:* associated with galena in veins, sometimes a metamorphic replacement of calcite in crystalline limestones.   **Zinc Blende**

H. *H:* 3.5–4.0 *SG:* 2.9 *Col:* pale grey, greenish or violet. *Sys:* orthorhombic. *Forms:* prismatic crystals, often pseudo-hexagonal, or needles; also massive or stalactitic. *L:* vitreous; transparent to translucent. *Cl:* poor basal. *F:* sub-conchoidal; brittle. *Occ:* in beds of gypsum and iron ores; also deposited from hot springs. Distinguished from calcite by its poor cleavage.   **Aragonite**

I. *H:* 3.5–4.5 *SG:* 3.8 *Col:* yellow, buff, brownish-red to brownish-black. *Sys:* hexagonal. *Forms:* rhombohedral crystals, often with curved faces; also massive, nodular or granular. *L:* pearly to vitreous; opaque. *Cl:* perfect rhombohedral. *F:* uneven; brittle. *Occ:* in beds or nodular in clays associated with the Coal Measures; sometimes in shales.   **Siderite**

J. *H:* 4.0 *SG:* 3.1 *Col:* blue, green, yellow, purple or pink; may be variegated, when white often present. *Sys:* cubic. *Forms:* aggregates common; simple cubes often repeatedly twinned; also massive, compact or granular. *L:* vitreous; transparent to translucent. *Cl:* perfect octahedral. *F:* conchoidal to uneven; brittle. *Occ:* in veins, often associated with galena, zinc blende and barytes.   **Fluorspar**

K. *H:* 5.0 *SG:* 3.2 *Col:* paler shades of blue, yellowish-green or green. *Sys:* hexagonal. *Forms:* large prismatic crystals, capped with pyramids, often truncated; sometimes with coloured centres and white margins. *L:* resinous to vitreous; transparent to opaque. *Cl:* poor basal. *F:* uneven; brittle. *Occ:* common accessory mineral in all types of rocks. Resembles beryl, but is much less hard.·   **Apatite**

L. *H:* 5.0–5.5 *SG:* 3.5 *Col:* usually brown; also grey, green, yellow or black. *Sys:* monoclinic. *Forms:* wedge- to lozenge-shaped crystals; also massive. *L:* adamantine to resinous; transparent to opaque. *Cl:* good prismatic. *F:* poor conchoidal; brittle. *Occ:* accessory mineral in acidic igneous rocks; also in calcium-rich metamorphic ones.   **Sphene**

M. *H:* 5.0–6.0 *SG:* 3.3 *Col:* dark green to black. *Sys:* monoclinic. *Forms:* squat 8-sided crystals; also massive or granular. *L:* vitreous; translucent to opaque. *Cl:* good, two at right angles. No *F.* *Occ:* intrusive basic igneous rocks and some metamorphic ones.   **Augite**

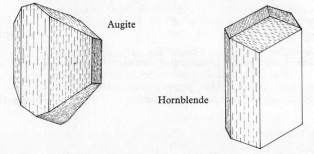

Augite

Hornblende

N. *H:* 5.0–6.0 *SG:* 3.0–3.5 *Col:* greenish-black to black. *Sys:* monoclinic. *Forms:* prismatic crystals, 6-sided in section; also massive. *L:* vitreous; transparent to opaque. *Cl:* perfect, two parallel to prisms, at 120°. *F:* uneven. *Occ:* primary mineral of acidic and intermediate igneous rocks, uncommon in basic ones; common in metamorphosed igneous rocks. **Hornblende**

O. *H:* 6.0 *SG:* 2.6 *Col:* paler shades of red, greyish-green or grey. *Sys:* monoclinic. *Forms:* prismatic crystals common, often lath-like; also massive. *L:* vitreous to pearly; translucent to opaque. *Cl:* Perfect, two at 90°. *F:* conchoidal to uneven. *Occ:* essential constituent of the more acidic igneous rocks, where it is often found as large individual crystals (phenocrysts). **Orthoclase Felspar**

P. *H:* 6.0–7.0 *SG:* 3.3 *Col:* yellowish-green to blackish-green. *Sys:* monoclinic. *Forms:* elongated or tabular crystals; sheaf-like or granular aggregates. *L:* vitreous; transparent to opaque. *Cl:* perfect basal. *F:* uneven. *Occ:* common in metamorphic rocks, including limestones subjected to contact-metamorphism. **Epidote**

Q. *H:* 6.0–7.0 *SG:* 3.2–4.2 *Col:* usually shades of green; sometimes brownish; rarely yellow. *Sys:* orthorhombic. *Forms:* massive, compact or granular; prismatic crystals rare. *L:* vitreous; translucent. No *Cl. F:* conchoidal to uneven. *Occ:* essential mineral of ultra-basic igneous rocks; sometimes found in basic ones. **Olivine**

R. *H:* 6.0–7.0 *SG:* 6.6–7.1 *Col:* black or brown; rarely yellow. *Sys:* tetragonal. *Forms:* tetragonal prisms and pyramids; also massive, fibrous ('woody') or granular. *L:* adamantine, brilliant on pale crystals. No *Cl. F:* sub-conchoidal; brittle. *Occ:* originally veins in acidic igneous rocks, associated with quartz, fluorspar, tourmaline and topaz; also found in placer deposits. **Cassiterite**

TABLE 4

The streak is black, lead-grey or greenish-black. *L:* metallic; opaque.

A. The streak and mineral are black and shiny.
i. *H:* 3.0–4.5 *SG:* 4.5–5.0 *Col:* steel-grey to iron black. *Sys:* cubic. *Forms:* tetrahedral crystals, often twinned; also massive, compact or granular. No *Cl. F:* sub-conchoidal to uneven; brittle. *Occ:* associated with other copper ores, galena, pyrites or zinc blende. **Tetrahedrite**

ii. *H:* 5.0–6.0 *SG:* 4.5–5.0 *Col:* iron-black. *Sys:* hexagonal. *Forms:* scales, thin plates or granular. No *Cl. F:* conchoidal. *Occ:* an accessory mineral of many basic rocks. **Ilmenite**

iii. *H:* 5.5–6.5 *SG:* 5.1 *Col:* iron-black. *Sys:* cubic. *Forms:* octahedra common; also rhombdodecahedra; sometimes massive or granular. *Cl:* poor octahedral. *F:* sub-conchoidal. Strongly magnetic, may show polarity. *Occ:* primary constituent of most igneous rocks; also lenticular masses and sands. **Magnetite**

B. The streak is black, the mineral brass-yellow.

i. *H:* 6.0–6.5 *SG:* 5.0 *Sys:* cubic. *Forms:* cubes, adjacent faces striated at right angles; also massive or nodules with radiating structure. *L:* splendent. No *Cl. F:* conchoidal; brittle. Sparks struck with hammer. *Occ:* secondary mineral in igneous rocks; also veins and nodules.   **Pyrite**

Pyrite

ii. *H:* 6.0–6.5 *SG:* 4.7 *Col:* darkens on exposure. *Sys:* ortho-rhombic. *Forms:* tabular crystals, often repeatedly twinned pro-ducing pseudo-hexagonal forms ('Spear-head' and 'Cockscomb'); also nodules with radiating structure. No *Cl. F:* uneven; brittle. *Occ:* nodules in sedimentaries or as a replacement in limestones.   **Marcasite**

C. The streak is greenish-black; the mineral brassy-yellow, when fresh.
H: 3.5–4.0 *SG:* 4.2 *Col:* rapidly tarnishes, often to iridescence. *Sys:* tetragonal. *Forms:* usually massive; crystals wedge-shaped, often twinned forming cubes. No *Cl. F:* conchoidal to uneven; crumbles when cut with a knife (pyrite cannot be cut). *Occ:* in veins, associated with quartz, pyrite, galena and zinc blende.   **Chalcopyrite**

D. The streak is lead-grey, as is the mineral when fresh.
i. *H:* 2.5 *SG:* 7.5 *Sys:* cubic. *Forms:* cubes, tetrahedra, octahedra or any combination; also massive. *Cl:* perfect cubic, but may crumble when struck or rubbed. *F:* flat. *Occ:* veins in limestones; associated with quartz, barytes and fluorspar.   **Galena**

ii. *H:* 2.5–3.0 *SG:* 5.6 *Sys:* orthorhombic. *Forms:* usually massive; also compact or granular; crystals rare. *Cl:* poor prismatic. *F:* con-choidal. *Occ:* in veins or beds of other copper ores.   **Chalcocite**

TABLE 5

The streak is coloured, but not black; the mineral is distinctly coloured.

A. The streak is red or reddish-brown.
i. *H:* 3.5–4.0 *SG:* 4.0 *Col:* usually black or brown; sometimes yellow. *Sys:* cubic. *Forms:* tetrahedra and rhombdodecahedra common, often twinned; also massive or compact. *L:* resinous to adamantine; transparent to opaque. *Cl:* perfect, rhombdodecahed-ral. *F:* conchoidal; brittle. *Occ:* in veins, associated with galena; often a metamorphic replacement of calcite in crystalline lime-stones.   **Zinc Blende**

ii. *H:* 5.5–6.5 *SG:* 4.5–5.3 *Col:* steel-grey to iron-grey; or dark
red. *Sys:* hexagonal. *Forms:* flattened rhombohedral, crystal;
reniform or botryoidal masses; micaceous or earthy. *L:* splendent to
metallic on crystals and masses; dull or earthy. *Cl:* poor rhombohedral. *F:* uneven. *Occ:* pockets in limestone and associated with
other iron ores.   **Hematite**

  Varieties
    a. Black. Flat rhombohedral crystals. *L:* metallic   Specular Iron
    b. Reniform or botryoidal masses, usually with radiating
       structure   Kidney Ore
    c. Red. Earthy. *L:* dull   Red Ochre

Hematite kidney ore

B. The streak is yellow or yellowish-brown.
i. *H:* 5.0–5.5 *SG:* 3.6–4.0 *Col:* shades of brown, yellow to
yellowish-brown when earthy. *Forms:* stalactitic or mammillated,
often showing radiating structure, or earthy. *L:* sub-metallic to
dull; masses often coated with a black glaze; opaque. No *Cl. F:* uneven; brittle. *Occ:* an alteration product of other iron ores.   **Limonite**

  Varieties
    a. Brownish-yellow. Earthy. Found in swampy areas   Bog Iron Ore
    b. Yellow. Earthy. *L:* dull   Yellow Ochre

ii. *H:* 6.0–6.5 *SG:* 4.2 *Col:* reddish-brown, red, yellowish or
black. *Sys:* tetragonal. *Forms:* prismatic crystal, usually capped by
pyramids; 'knee-shaped' twinning common, or needle-like. *L:*
adamantine; opaque to translucent. *Cl:* poor, prismatic. *F:* sub-
conchoidal to uneven; brittle. *Occ:* accessory of mineral of acidic
igneous rocks; also metamorphic ones derived from them.   **Rutile**

C. The streak and mineral are both blue.
H: 3.5–4.0 *SG:* 3.8 *Col:* darker than streak. *Sys:* monoclinic.
Forms: massive or earthy; sometimes prismatic crystals. *L:* vit-
reous; crystals transparent to opaque; other forms opaque. No *Cl.*
F: conchoidal; brittle. *Occ:* associated with other oxidised copper
ores.   **Azurite**

D. The streak and mineral are both green.
H: 3.5–4.0 *SG:* 3.9 *Col:* different shades of bright green, often
concentrically banded, darker than streak. *Sys:* monoclinic.
Forms: usually massive; mammillated or botryoidal, or nodular;
often show fibrous, radiating structure; crystals rare. *L:* silky on
fibrous structures; others dull. *Cl:* poor, basal. No *F. Occ:* associated with other oxidised copper ores.   **Malachite**

Malachite

COMPOSITION OF MINERALS

Andalusite *Comp:* aluminium silicate, $Al_2O_3.SiO_2$.

Anhydrite *Comp:* anhydrous calcium sulphate, $CaSO_4$.

Apatite *Comp:* calcium fluo-phosphate or chloro-phosphate, $3Ca_3P_2O_8.CaF_2$ or $3Ca_3P_2O_8.CaCl_2$.

Aragonite *Comp:* calcium carbonate, $CaCO_3$.

Augite *Comp:* silicate of calcium, magnesium, iron and aluminium, but somewhat variable.

Azurite *Comp:* hydrated basic copper carbonate, $2CuCO_3.Cu(OH)_2$.

Barytes *Comp:* barium sulphate, $BaSO_4$.

Beryl *Comp:* silicate of beryllium and aluminium, $3BeO.Al_2O_3.6SiO_2$.

Biotite *Comp:* silicate of magnesium, iron, aluminium and potassium with hydroxyl and fluorine.

Calcite *Comp:* calcium carbonate, $CaCO_3$.

Cassiterite (Tinstone) *Comp:* tin oxide, SnO_2.

Chalcedonic Silica *Comp:* a mixture of crystalline silica (quartz) and amorphous hydrated silica (opal).

Chalcocite (Copper Glance) *Comp:* copper sulphide, Cu_2S.

Chalcopyrite (Copper Pyrites) *Comp:* copper and iron sulphide, $Cu_2S.Fe_2S_3$.

Chlorite *Comp:* hydrated silicate of aluminium iron and magnesium.

Corundum *Comp:* aluminium oxide, Al_2O_3.

Dolomite *Comp:* calcium and magnesium carbonates, $CaCO_3.MgCO_3$.

Epidote *Comp:* basic silicate of calcium aluminium and iron.

Fluorspar *Comp:* calcium fluoride, CaF_2.

Galena *Comp:* lead sulphide, PbS.

Garnet *Comp:* $3R''O,R''_2O_3,3SiO_2$, where R'' is calcium, iron (ferrous) or magnesium, and R''' is iron (ferric), aluminium or chromium.

Gypsum   *Comp:* hydrated calcium sulphate, $CaSO_4.2H_2O$.

Hematite (Kidney Ore)   *Comp:* iron oxide, Fe_2O_3; clay and sand impurities may be present.

Hornblende   *Comp:* silicate of aluminium, calcium, magnesium, iron and sodium.

Ilmenite   *Comp:* oxide of iron and titanium, $FeO.TiO_2$.

Kaolin (China Clay)   *Comp:* hydrous aluminium silicate.

Limonite   *Comp:* hydrated iron oxide, $Fe_2O_3.3H_2O$.

Magnesite   *Comp:* magnesium carbonate, $MgCO_3$.

Magnetite (Magnetic Iron Ore, Lodestone)   *Comp:* iron oxide, Fe_3O_4.

Malachite   *Comp:* hydrated basic copper carbonate, $CuCO_3.Cu(OH)_2$.

Marcasite   *Comp:* iron sulphide, FeS_2.

Muscovite   *Comp:* silicate of aluminium and potassium with fluorine and water.

Olivine   *Comp:* magnesium iron orthosilicate, $2(Mg,Fe)O.SiO_2$.

Orthoclase   *Comp:* potassium aluminium silicate, $K_2O.Al_2O_3.6SiO_2$.

Plagioclase   *Comp:* silicate of aluminium with calcium and/or sodium. There are six members of the plagioclase felspar series, the end members of which are albite and anorthite and as these grade into one another, precise classification is difficult without microscopic examination.

Pyrite (Pyrites, Iron Pyrites)   *Comp:* iron sulphide, FeS_2.

Quartz   *Comp:* silicon dioxide, SiO_2.

Rock Salt (Halite, Common Salt)   *Comp:* sodium chloride, $NaCl$.

Rutile   *Comp:* titanium dioxide, TiO_2.

Serpentine   *Comp:* hydrated magnesium silicate, $2H_2O.3MgO.2SiO_2$.

Siderite   *Comp:* iron carbonate, $FeCO_3$.

Smithsonite   *Comp:* zinc carbonate $ZnCO_3$.

Sphene   *Comp:* titanate and silicate of calcium, $CaO.TiO_2.SiO_2$.

Talc   *Comp:* hydrated magnesium silicate, $3MgO.H_2O.4SiO_2$.

Tetrahedrite   *Comp:* sulphide of copper and antimony, $4Cu_2S.Sb_2S_3$.

Topaz   *Comp:* fluo-silicate of aluminium, $Al_2SiO_4F_2$.

Tourmaline   *Comp:* a complex borosilicate of aluminium with tin and magnesium.

Zinc Blende (Blende)   *Comp:* zinc sulphide, ZnS.

Zircon   *Comp:* zirconium silicate, $ZrO_2.SiO_3$.

KEY TO THE IDENTIFICATION OF ROCKS

Rocks are divided into three categories:

SEDIMENTARY ROCKS: The rock is composed of beds, which may vary in colour or content, mostly non-crystalline, and may contain fossils or other rock fragments more or less cemented together.

METAMORPHIC ROCKS: The rocks show banding, foliation or strong cleavage.

IGNEOUS ROCKS: The rocks are completely crystalline, individual crystals may be visible to the naked eye. They sometimes form irregular masses, which may be large or narrow intrusions between, or cutting across, other strata.

Sedimentary Rocks

A Composed of large fragments (over 2mm) in a fine matrix.

a The fragments are irregular, angular or sub-angular, ranging in size from gravel (2mm) to boulders, in a clay matrix. **Boulder Clay (Till)**

b The fragments are well rounded and comprise the major portion of the rock, which is almost uncemented. **Pebble Beds**

c The fragments are well rounded and well cemented in a finer matrix. **Conglomerate**

d The fragments are angular and well cemented in a fine matrix. **Breccia**

e The fragments are angular, consisting of igneous rock, in an ashy matrix. **Agglomerate**

B Composed of medium-sized grains (between 2mm and 0.002 mm).

a The grains are of quartz, angular or sub-angular and coarse. **Grit**

b The grains are of quartz and wholly, or almost wholly, un-cemented. **Sand**

c The grains are of quartz, fairly uniformly graded, often well cemented. **Sandstone**

Varieties:

Fawn to almost white quartz, siliceous cement.	Quartzose Sandstone
Yellow or brown tints due to limonite. } Reddish tints due to hematite. }	Ferruginous Sandstone
Green tint due to glauconite.	Glauconitic Sandstone
Mica present as tiny silvery flakes.	Micaceous Sandstone
A high proportion of felspar is present.	Felspathic Sandstone or Arkose

C Composed of fine-grained material (less than 0.002mm).

a The material is ash-like, usually dark grey to black in colour and often partly consolidated. **Volcanic Ash**

b   Very fine-grained material. The colour varies. It gives off a
    clayey odour when breathed upon. In water it becomes plastic
    and can be moulded.   **Clay**
c   Clay-like. Associated with granite. White when pure, often grey.
    Has a greasy feel but crumbles when pressed.   **Kaolin (China Clay)**
d   Powdery. Often light grey in colour. Crumbles in water without
    forming a plastic mass.   **Fuller's Earth**
e   Grey or greyish to black in colour. Thinly bedded, splits easily
    along bedding plane.   **Shale**
f   Grey, greyish or black in colour. Consolidated, but shows no
    bedding planes. Fracture irregular.   **Mudstone**

D   Effervesces with dilute hydrochloric acid.
a   *H:* 3.0. Colour white, bluish-grey and sometimes yellow, brown
    or black. Fossils may be present and sometimes form the bulk
    of the rock.   **Limestone**
b   White or almost white in colour. Earthy, soft and friable.   **Chalk**
c   *H:* 3.0. White, grey, cream or buff in colour. Small well-
    rounded grains of limestone, about 1–2mm in diameter.
                                                    Oolitic Limestone
d   As (c), but the grains are larger, often reaching the size of a
    small pea.   **Pisolitic Limestone**
e   *H:* 3.5–4.0. Colour yellowish, white or buff. Slight efferves-
    cence only with cold dilute hydrochloric acid but greater along
    a scratch.   **Dolomite**
f   Fine-grained clay-like material, which gives off a clayey odour
    when breathed upon and may form a plastic mass in water.
    Unconsolidated.   **Marl**
g   As (f), but consolidated.   **Marlstone**

E   Dark brown to black in colour. Streak usually black or dark
    brown, sometimes light brown. It may contain plant remains.
a   The streak is light to dark brown. Often dark brown in colour.
    It crumbles very easily and is chiefly composed of vegetable
    matter, but the water content may be high.   **Peat**
b   The streak is light to dark brown. The colour varies from light
    brown to almost black. It can often be crumbled between the
    fingers, and plant remains may be discernible.   **Lignite (Brown Coal)**
c   The streak is black, or nearly so. The colour is dark brown to
    black.

Dark grey to black shale; can be cut with a knife giving splinters that can
be ignited with a match; burns with a smoky oily-smelling flame.
                                                    Bituminous Shale
Dark grey to black; not laminated; fracture conchoidal. Lustreless. Splinters
burn with a long smoky flame.   **Cannel Coal**
Black; fracture cuboidal; lustre pitchy. Soils the hands when handled.
                                                    Bituminous Coal
Black; fracture conchoidal; lustre brilliant. Does not soil the hands; can only
be ignited with difficulty, burning with a non-smoky flame.   **Anthracite**

Metamorphic Rocks

A   The rocks show strong cleavage.

a   A fine-grained rock. Colour varies from blue-grey to almost black, sometimes purple or green. It may show colour-banding at an angle to the cleavage plane.   **Slate**

b   The rock resembles (a) but there is much flaky mica along the cleavage planes.   **Phyllite**

B   Foliation is well marked.

a   Foliation is thin, wavy and continuous.   **Schist**

b   Foliation is coarse, lenticular and discontinuous.   **Gneiss**

c   Foliation is as (b), but large almond-shaped knots are dispersed throughout a finer matrix.   **Augen Gneiss**

Igneous Rocks

Introduction

Always examine the fresh surface of a specimen which you have removed from the bed, NEVER a chance fragment or a weathered surface.

Three factors must be considered when examining igneous rocks:

1   Texture. Igneous rocks are mostly formed by crystallisation and the crystal size depends upon the rate of cooling. In extrusive rocks, the texture is fine-grained or glassy, a result of the rapid cooling. The intrusive rocks have a medium-grained texture because of the slower cooling. Deep-seated or plutonic rocks have a coarse-grained texture, a result of very slow cooling. There may be a difference of texture between the edges of the bed and its centre, especially in thin intrusions.

    Large individual mineral crystals, phenocrysts, in a finer matrix giving a porphyritic texture may be found in many rocks.

2   Field Relationships. In many cases the relationship between the igneous rock and the adjacent rocks can be seen clearly, but it should be noted that: (i) Extrusive rocks only affect the underlying rocks, the heat may have been sufficient to 'bake' them. (ii) Intrusive rocks can affect the beds on both sides of them. (iii) Plutonic rocks may produce changes in the surrounding country rock, contact metamorphism, but the floor and underlying beds are never visible.

3   Composition. When examining a piece of igneous rock, the component minerals should be identified whenever possible (see Key, p. 15) and the presence, or absence, of quartz, orthoclase, plagioclase, the micas, hornblende, augite, olivine and the iron minerals should be noted.

Key to the Identification of Igneous Rocks

A The rock is glassy.

a *Col:* black or dark brown, rarely grey, green or red; may be streaked with darker or lighter tints. *L:* vitreous. *F:* conchoidal, giving sharp transparent edges. Occurs in large masses. *Comp:* granitic. **Obsidian**

b *Col:* black, grey or brown, rarely reddish. *L:* dull to pitchy. *F:* splintery, less smooth than that of glass. *Comp:* varies. **Pitchstone**

c *Col:* black; opaque, edges not transparent. Found on the edges of basalt dykes and sills. *Comp:* basaltic. **Tachylite**

d *Col:* usually light grey, sometimes darker grey to almost black. Vesicular (full of tiny holes). 'Light' in weight. Rough to the touch. *L:* pearly or silky. **Pumice**

B The rock is very fine-grained (microcrystalline), with the individual crystals too small to be identified by the naked eye.

(1) The rock is white, light grey or pink.

a The rock consists of quartz and orthoclase. Biotite and hornblende may be present as accessory minerals. **Felsite**

b As (a), but with phenocrysts of quartz. **Quartz-felsite (Quartz-porphyry)**

c As (a), but with phenocrysts of quartz and orthoclase. **Porphyry**

d *Col:* light grey but may show flow structure. *Comp:* quartz and orthoclase and some micas in the groundmass, usually with small phenocrysts of quartz and orthoclase. **Rhyolite**

e *Col:* white to light grey. Occurs in acidic, rounded lava cones. *Comp:* orthoclase or plagioclase, sometimes with biotite or hornblende but little or no quartz; may contain phenocrysts. **Trachyte**

(2) The rock is dark grey to black.

a *Col:* dark grey to black, weathering to red or brown, not rust-coloured. A dense (heavy) rock, but may sometimes be vesicular, *Comp:* plagioclase, sometimes with biotite, augite or hornblende. **Andesite**

b *Col:* dark grey to black but weathered surfaces may be rust-coloured or greenish. Found in extrusive sheets, frequently showing columnar jointing, with columns divided into short sections by downward curved joints. *Comp:* plagioclase, augite, iron minerals (usually limonite or magnetite). **Basalt**

C The rock is medium-grained.

a *Col:* mainly light grey. *Comp:* plagioclase, usually with biotite or hornblende but with little or no free quartz; phenocrysts of plagioclase showing repeated (lamellar) twinning are generally very plentiful. **Porphyrite**

b *Col:* medium grey. *Comp:* plagioclase (Labradorite), augite and sometimes olivine. Found in minor intrusions, e.g. dykes and sills. May show columnar structure; weathering often produces concentric shells like onion skins. **Dolerite**

D The rock is coarse-grained and the individual crystals can easily be seen and identified.

a *Col:* grey or pink, often found in large masses. *Comp:* always contains three minerals: quartz – glassy; orthoclase – white or pink; and mica (biotite or muscovite) – black; may contain phenocrysts of orthoclase.   **Granite**

b *Col:* pink or light grey. *Comp:* orthoclase and plagioclase in roughly equal amounts – white or pink, biotite – black, and sometimes a little free quartz or hornblende and augite. Exposures rare in Britain.   **Syenite**

c *Col:* dark grey, rarely mottled green or white. Coarser in texture than syenite. *Comp:* plagioclase, hornblende, biotite and augite.   **Diorite**

d As (c), but some quartz is present.   **Quartz-diorite**

e *Col:* dark grey to almost black, very coarse-grained and heavy. Usually found in sheets or large lenses. *Comp:* plagioclase (often large irregular crystals showing lamellar twinning), augite, apatite and an iron mineral (ilmenite or magnetite). Olivine may be present.   **Gabbro**

f *Col:* green, sometimes red or black, often mottled; heavy and with a greasy feel. *Comp:* olivine, which decomposes to ser-p ntine.   **Serpentine Rock**

PRINCIPAL GROUPS OF FOSSILS:
KEY AND CHARACTERISTICS

I Consists of one or more thin, often branched, rod-like bodies (generally crushed flat), which may appear serrated on one, or both, sides. Rarely a mesh of radiating and inter-connected rods.

GRAPTOLITES   Upper Cambrian – Silurian
An extinct form of colonial hydrozoa with a horny skeleton (rhabdosome) supporting many polyps in small cups (thacae) arranged along branches (stipes) on one (uniserial), two (biserial) or rarely four sides. Growth begins from a pointed body (sicula) which marks the proximal end (opposite distal).

The rapid development of Graptolites makes them a convenient stratigraphical index.

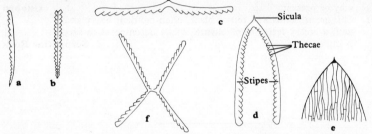

Graptolites: **a,** *Monograptus*; **b,** *Diplograptus*; **c,** *Didymograptus* 'extensiform'; **d,** *Didymograptus* 'tuning-fork form'; **e,** *Dictyonema*; **f,** *Tetragraptus*

II Shows a marked five-fold symmetry.

ECHINOIDERMA   Ordovician – Present
A Generally hemispherical, although somewhat flattened, composed of 5 double rows of small plates (ambulacre), each pierced by one or more pairs of pores, and 5 double rows of large plates (interambulacre). Both types of plates may bear tubercules, but the attached spines are rarely found with the fossil. At the convergence of the ambulacre ('ambs') on the underside, is an opening (peristome) occupied by the mouth in life. This was smaller than the peristome, being surrounded by a membrane and external gills, and was equipped in some types with jaws and pointed teeth (Aristotle's lantern) which protruded through the peristome. Another opening (periproct) was occupied by the anus in life. There are two types of Echinoidea (Echinoids or 'Sea-urchins'):
 (i) Periproct within compact set of 10 plates (apical disc) from which the 'ambs' radiate on the upper surface; peristome central   **Regularia**
 (ii) Periproct lies outside the apical disc; peristome central, or moved forward and may possess a shovel lip   **Irregularia**

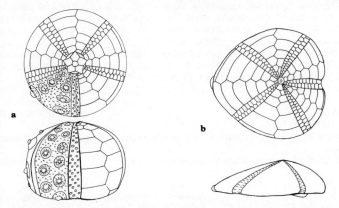

Examples of Echinoidea: **a**, Regularia – *Hemicidaris*; **b**, Irregularia – *Micraster*

B Consists of 5-pointed stars, circular, oval or squarish, bead-like bodies, usually in series, with a central hole, from which radiate grooves. Central hole and/or groove pattern usually show 5-fold symmetry

Crinoid Ossicles ('Stem' or 'arm' segments)

C Ovoid, sometimes rather truncated, composed of rings of 5 plates, 5- or 6-sided   Crinoid 'Calyx'

The **CRINOIDEA** (Crinoids or 'Sea-lilies') are marine animals with a 'root' and 'stem', which solely anchor them to the sea-bed. The 'calyx' has a mouth and anus on its upper surface, surrounding the edge of which are a series of 'arms', often branched.

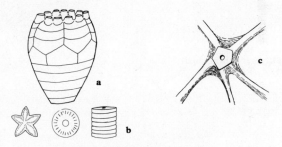

Crinoidea: **a**, 'calyx'; **b**, 'stem' ossicles; **c**, 'root'

III The fossil (corallum) consists of either a horn-shaped individual (simple coral), or a colony (compound coral) or inter-connected tubes (corallites), generally with concave horizontal divisions (tabulae), and usually showing vertical partitions (septa), or partial partitions, directed towards the centre, where they may unite to form a central column (columella). The polyp occupied a cup-shaped depression (calice) at the top of the corallite. A well-marked groove (cardinal fossula) can be seen in the calice floor of some types.

CORAL   Ordovician – Present

Corals can be divided into:

A   Simple or compound corals, with plate-like septa of two, or more different sizes.

(i) No cardinal fossula; septa in multiples of six   Hexacoralla

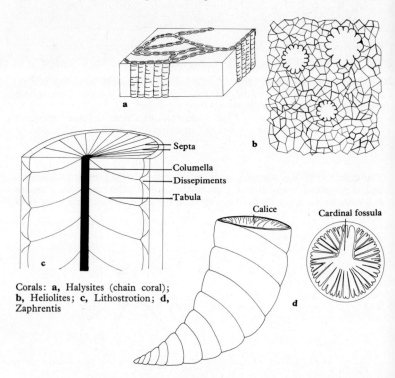

Corals: **a,** Halysites (chain coral); **b,** Heliolites; **c,** Lithostrotion; **d,** Zaphrentis

(ii) Cardinal fossula present; septa in multiples of four   Tetracoralla (Rugosa)

B   Compound corals, usually composed of small tube-like corallites with many tabulae; septa missing or only represented by ridges or spines
                                                                     Tabulata

IV Bivalve (two-part shell), symmetrical about its long axis but the two valves are markedly different. Normally found closed. There are external radiating ribs and concentric growth lines.

BRACHIOPODA
Cambrian – Present

The marine animal attached itself to a rock by means of a muscular 'stalk' (pedicle), which passed between the valves in primitive types but, in more advanced ones, emerged through an opening (delthyrium). This may be closed below by two small triangular (deltidial) plates leaving a circular hole (foramen) just below the 'beak' (umbo) of the larger (ventral) valve. Early types had no teeth, but in later ones these can be seen on the ventral valve and fitted into sockets on the dorsal. The scars of the muscles for opening (diductor) and for closing (adductor) the shell may be seen in both valves. Between the umbo and the hinge-line is a flat, or slightly concave (cardinal) area.

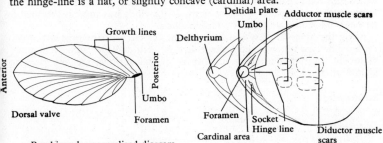

Brachiopoda: generalised diagram

The brachiopoda are divided into four orders, Atremata, Neotremata, Protremata and Telotremata, of which the first two have no teeth (inarticulate) and are usually horny, while the last two have teeth (articulate) and are calcareous. The order Telotremata includes the sub-orders Rhynchonellacea, Terebratulacea and Spiriferacea.

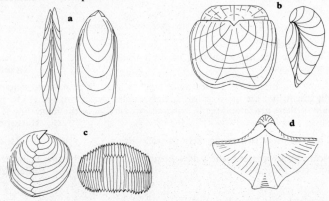

Brachiopoda: **a,** Lingula; **b,** Productus; **c,** Rhynchonella; **d,** Spirifer

V   Two unequal valves (left and right) which are almost mirror images. Neither valve is symmetrical about its long axis. It is usually found open, and often the valves are separated.

LAMELLIBRANCHIA
Cambrian – Present

Lamellibranchs are freshwater or marine animals enclosed in a bivalve shell with the two valves permanently in contact along a straight or curved hinge-line above which the 'beak' (umbo) points forward. Between the umbo and the hinge-line is sometimes a triangular (cardinal) area, where the ligament is attached.

In life the shell was opened by one (monomyarian) or two (dimyarian) adductor muscles, the scars of which can be seen at the ends of the pallial line which runs round parallel to the lower edge of the shell. An indented pallial line indicates the existence of a pallial sinus. If the sinus was present the shell is termed sinupalliate, and if not intergripalliate.

Along the hinge-line are usually a number of teeth, alternating in the two valves. The type number and arrangement of teeth, together with the number of muscle scars and presence or absence of pallial sinus, are important in identification.

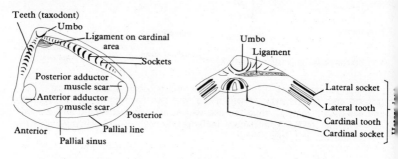

Lamellibranchia: generalised diagrams

Types of Dentition:

a   The hinge-line has a number of short transverse teeth, more or less of similar shape **Taxodont**

b   Below the umbo are 1–3 cardinal teeth, which differ in size, shape and alignment, but are more or less at right-angles to the hinge-line. On either side of these are lateral teeth, lying almost parallel to the hinge-line **Heterodont**

c   There are only two strong teeth in each valve **Isodont**

d   No teeth are present, the valves being held together by the ligament and adductor muscles only **Endentulous**

VI Unchambered univalve (tube) generally coiled into a cone (helicoid) or rarely into a flat spiral (discoid).

GASTROPODA   Cambrian – Present

The shell consists of a number of coils (whorls), in contact with adjacent ones along the suture-line, which progressively increase in size from the apex to the last and largest (the body whorl) and end in the anterior aperture, marked by inner and outer lips. The aperture margin may be entire (holostomatous) or either notched or extended into an anterior or posterior canal (siphonostomatous) while a smooth calcareous coating may have been deposited on the inner lip.

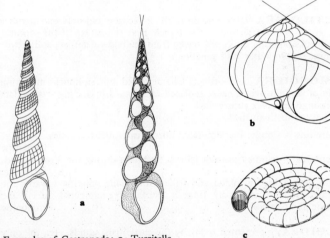

Examples of Gastropoda: **a,** Turritella with section showing solid columella (heavily shaded) formed where the inner parts of the whorls have united; **b,** Natica; **c,** Planorbis with (*below*) transverse section

The axis of the spire (all whorls except the last) may be hollow (perforate) forming a tube (umbilicus) or solid (imperforate) forming a solid pillar (columella).

Externally the shell may be ornamented by spiral or transverse lines, ridges or both with tubercules, sometimes produced into spines, where they intersect.

The coiling is usually clockwise (dextral), looking from the anterior to the apex, rarely anti-clockwise (sinistral).

VII   Univalve (tube), divided by partitions (septa) into chambers and coiled into a flat spiral, sometimes hook-like, rarely a cone.

CEPHALOPODA   Cambrian – Present

The coiling may be tight so that the last whorl almost overlaps and conceals those within (involute), or the smaller inner whorls may form a central shallow depression (umbilicus). The whorls may be ornamented with transverse ribs or may show only radial (growth) lines, sometimes tubercules, while the outer margin (ventral) may bear a longitudinal ridge (keel). Internally a fleshy tube (siphuncle) extended in life from the last chamber (the body chamber) in which the animal lived to the remaining (gas) chambers, passing through funnel-like holes (septal necks) pointing away from the aperture.

The class is divided into three orders:

A   **NAUTILOIDEA** was abundant in the Palaeozoic but only one member exists today. It is characterised by: siphuncle near the centre of the septum; the septal necks pointing backwards away from the body chamber; and simple suture lines, septum/outer wall junction.

B   **AMMONOIDEA** now extinct. Characterised by: siphuncle migrating to margin of septum, septal necks replaced by forward projecting setal collars and increasingly complex suture lines.

Three types are distinguished:

(i)   Suture line is simple. Predominated during carboniferous times.

Goniatitic

(ii)   Suture line is crimped but not frilled. Common during the Trias period.

Ceratitic

(iii)   Suture line is highly folded and frilled with folds pointing towards the aperture (saddle) and away from it (lobes). Predominated during the Jurassic and Cretaceous.   Ammonitic

C   **COLOIDEA,** represented today by the cuttle-fish, squids, etc., the only common fossils are the Belemnites (Mesozoic, becoming abundant in the Cretaceous), which consist of three parts:

(i)   The Guard: a solid conical or cylindrical rod, with a conical cavity (alveolus) at the upper (anterior) end and tapering at the lower (posterior) end.

(ii)   The Phragmacone: a hollow-chambered cone fitting into the alveolus and analogous to the entire ammonite skeleton.

(iii)   The Pro-ostracum: a flat forward projection of the phragmacone, rarely found as a fossil.

VIII   Roughly oval or shield-shaped and shows bilateral symmetry. Divided transversely into a more or less semi-circular head (cephalon) and segmented body (thorax) and tail (pygidium).

TRIOLOBITES   Cambrian – Permian

The head has two longitudinal grooves flanking a raised area (glabella), on either side of which are the cheeks, divided into the fixed (inner) and the free (outer) by a line of weakness (facial suture), which extends from the front of the head (immediately behind the compound eye when present) and backwards or sidewards to the cephalon margin (head-shield), the posterior (genial) angles of which may be either rounded or drawn out (genial spines). Thus the facial suture may either cut the head-shield in front of the genial angle (proparian) or behind it (opisthoparian).

The thorax is composed of articulated segments (usually 2–14), each consisting of a central raised portion (axis) and two lateral members (pleurae) which may be elongated into pleural spines.

The semi-circular to triangular pygidium consists of 1–15 fused trilobed segments, which remain parallel in the fossil unlike those of the articulated thorax. Some genera bear a pygidial spine. The legs and other appendages are rarely found.

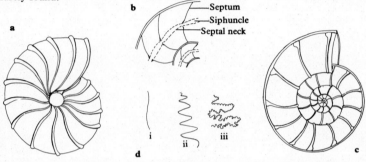

Cephalopoda: **a,** Nautilus; **b,** section; **c,** Ammonite; **d,** types of septal suture lines: i) goniatitic; ii) ceratitic; iii) ammonitic

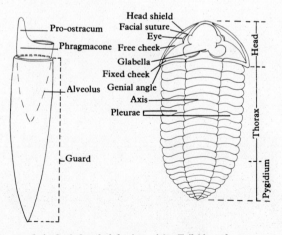

Left, Cephalopoda belemites; right, Trilobita calymene

THE GEOLOGICAL COLUMN

Below is a list of the stratigraphical systems beginning with the most recent and a brief description of their constituent beds, together with the name of the area, or areas, where these beds are best known. In some the regional variations are noted, but in others these variations are so great, even within a small area, that details cannot be given. For a description of these, and a fuller account of all the beds, the relevant British Regional Geological Handbook and the publications of the Geologists' Association should be consulted.

Pliocene

Cromer Beds   East Anglia
3   Upper Freshwater Bed: peat, peaty clay and loams.
2   Forest Bed: deltaic sands and gravels, with clay lenses.
1   Lower Freshwater Bed: peat, peaty clay and loams.

Weybourn Crag   East Anglia
Sand with scattered shells and local patches of shells.

Chillesford Clay   East Anglia
Deltaic shelly clay. Small mica flakes are often present.

Chillesford Sand   East Anglia
Deltaic shelly sand. Small mica flakes are often present.

Norwich Crag   East Anglia
Laminated sands, clays and gravels all of which often contain shells.

Red Crag   East Anglia
Brick-red sands with iron-stained shell fragments.

White or Coralline Crag   East Anglia
White or yellowish-white shelly sands.

Lenham Beds   North Downs, Kent
Beach deposits of sand and rounded flint pebbles on, or in pipes in, the Chalk.

Miocene

Not found in Britain.

Oligocene

Hampstead Beds   Isle of Wight
2   Marine Clays.
1   Black and green freshwater clays with some sands and marls.

Bembridge Marls and Limestone   Isle of Wight
Estuarine muds and marls.
Cream limestone, with thin marl partings.

Osborne Beds Isle of Wight
Freshwater marls and fine-grained sands, with some thin limestones.

Headon Beds Isle of Wight
A series of freshwater, estuarine and marine marls, soft sandstones
and thin bands of limestones and lignites.

Eocene

Barton Sands Isle of Wight
White, grey and yellow sands, clayey at base.

Barton Clays Isle of Wight
Grey clays and multi-coloured sands.

Bracklesham Beds Isle of Wight
Sandy clays and multi-coloured sands.

Bagshot Beds
London Basin | Hampshire Basin
Current-bedded, pale sands with thin pipe-clay seams, and local pebble beds. Finer-grained sands with marine shells to the east of the Lea Valley. | Fluviatile sands with many pipe-clay seams in the lower levels, and fresh-water shells in the higher.

Claygate Beds London Basin
A series of thin beds of sands and clays.

London Clay
London Basin | Hampshire Basin
Stiff, blue-grey clay, weathering to a yellowish-brown. | Silty clay with local spreads of fine sand and pebbles.

Blackheath and *Oldhaven Beds* London Basin
Yellow sands and soft sandstone, with shells and local beds of well-
rounded flint pebbles.

Reading Beds London Basin
Mottled freshwater clays overlying yellowish-white, current-
bedded sandstone. A basal bed of sandy clay containing rounded
flints is sometimes present.

Woolwich Beds London Basin
Interbedded clays and sands, with well-rounded flint pebbles.

Thanet Sands London Basin
Fine-grained marine sands with rounded flint pebbles in the higher
levels.

Cretaceous

Chalk The Weald, North and South Downs
3 Upper Chalk: well-banded, soft, white, almost pure limestone
containing flints throughout. Chalk Rock, a more resistent nodular
form of Chalk, forms the basal bed.

2 Middle Chalk: massive, soft, white, almost pure limestone with few flints. Thin, grey, marl bands occur near the top. Melbourn Rock forms a basal bed of nodular Chalk.

1 Lower Chalk:
    (c) Plenus Marls: thin, greenish-grey marls.
    (b) Chalk Marl: light grey, nearly pure limestone, becoming increasingly grey and marly in the lower levels.
    (a) 'Chloritic' (glauconitic) Marl: greenish sandy marls containing phosphatic nodules.

Upper Greensand   The Weald
Fine-grained sands and sandstones with some clays. Glauconite which gives the green colour is absent in some areas.

Gault   The Weald
Stiff, blue-grey, or greyish, marine clays; marly in upper levels, and sandy with phosphatic nodules at the base.

Lower Greensand   The Weald
4 Folkestone Beds: current-bedded, nearly white, brown or yellow, quartzose sands, with local patches of limestone, pebbles or clay, and irregular beds of ferruginous sandstone (Carstone). Gives sandy heaths.
3 Sandgate Beds: dark, glauconitic sands, sandy clays or clays with seams of 'Fuller's Earth' occurring near Redhill. Near Godalming, the equivalent sandy and shelly limestones are known as the Bargate Beds.
2 Hythe Beds: grey or greenish-grey sands and soft sandstones with chert, or limestone (Kentish Rag) near the coast. Forms a high escarpment e.g. Leith Hill.
1 Atherfield Clay: brown, blue, red or mottled marine clays, sometimes rather sandy, with brown clay ironstones locally.

Weald Clay   The Weald
Thick blue or brown, rarely red or mottled, freshwater clays with thin bands of shelly limestone, sand, sandstone or clay ironstone nodules locally.

Hastings Beds   The Weald
3 Tunbridge Wells Sands: brown, buff or red, quartzose sands, mainly unconsolidated, with thin conglomerates and clays locally. Forms outer ridges of the Ashdown Forest which are covered with heath.
2 Wadhurst Clay: a series of grey and bluish-grey clays and shales, with thin beds of clay ironstone nodules and shelly limestone locally.
1 Ashdown Sands: buff quartzose sandstones, some poorly cemented with frequently greenish-grey or nodular ironstones. Forms central ridges of Ashdown Forest.

Fairlight Clays   The Weald
Partly overlain and partly replaced, by Ashdown Sands. A com-

plicated series of grey and variegated clays and pale shales, silts or
siltstones, with some white sandstones and yellow ironstones.

Jurassic

Purbeck Beds   Dorset Coast
Mainly freshwater limestone with marls and shales above with
thin limestone breccia and fossilised soils containing trunks of
conifers and cycads below.

Portland Beds   Dorset Coast
Well-bedded hard limestone (Portland Stone) above with sands
and sandy marls below.

Kimmeridge Clay   Dorset to Yorkshire Coast
Dark bluish-grey marine clay with thin clayey limestone beds and
locally black bituminous shale.   (Contd. opposite)

Great Oolite Series

Somerset   Bath and South Cotswolds

Forest Marble: false-bedded, shelly limestones with thin interbedded clays
locally replaced by white or buff sands with clay (Hinton Sands).

Bouetti Beds: thin beds of pale marl.	*Bradford Beds:* thin beds of pale coloured clay.
Upper Fuller's Earth Clay: a thick series of greyish clays with thin limestone or marl bands.	*Great Oolite Limestone:* white, cream or pale yellow, hard oolitic limestone (including the 'Bath Stone', and other important building stones), with bands of hard, current-bedded, flaggy limestone in the upper levels.

Fuller's Earth Rock: a rubbly fossiliferous grey limestone.

Lower Fuller's Earth Clay: a series of clays with a thin bed of
Fuller's Earth.

Jurassic (cont.)

Corallian Beds   Dorset to Yorkshire Coast
Calcareous sands and grits, often current-bedded, with lenses of
palish yellow oolites or marls. Forms a low escarpment.

Oxford Clay   Dorset to Yorkshire Coast
Stiff greyish-brown or blue-black marine clays with thin sandy
beds in lower levels. Forms a broad vale.

Kelloway Beds   Dorset to Yorkshire Coast
Thin sands and calcareous sandstones.

Cornbrash   Dorset to Yorkshire
Hard, grey to reddish-brown, flaggy or rubbly limestone with thin
fossiliferous marlstone bands locally. An aquafer, the outcrop is
often marked by a line of villages.

Great Oolite Series

North Cotswold
Forest Marble: false-bedded shelly limestone and clays.

Bradford Clay: a thin pale-coloured clay.

Kemble Beds: buff or cream false-bedded oolitic limestone.

White Limestone: white or almost white limestone mainly oolitic with bands of marl and hard splintery, fine-grained limestone.

Hampden Marly Beds: grey marls with thin interbedded limestones, often shelly.

Minchinhampton Freestones: white current-bedded oolitic freestones.

Stonefield Slates: shelly, oolitic or sandy limestones with thin sandy shale partings.

Fuller's Earth Clay: a fine grey clay.

Northamptonshire
Forest Marble: false-bedded limestone passing downwards into a blue-black or yellow clay (Great Oolite Clay).

Great Oolite Limestone: a fine-grained limestone with bands of impure limestone containing varying amounts of ooliths, sometime rubbly or shelly and cream to blue in colour.

Upper Estuarine Series: a series of buff, bluish, green, grey or black silts and clays with some thin interbedded limestone bands.

Upper Inferior Oolite

South Cotswolds
Zigzag Beds: pale grey limestone, often flaggy with clay partings.

North Cotswold
Chipping Norton Limestone: varies locally from buff hard oolite to flaggy limestone with sands.

Rubbly Beds: white rubbly limestone.

Clypeus Grit: a yellow pisolitite, usually in a buff chalky matrix.

Anabacia Limestone: a white flaggy limestone.

Doulting Stone: a white massive limestone.

Upper Coral Bed: an off-white, crystalline rubbly limestone, often siliceous, with interbedded marls.

Dundry Freestone: a massive, white to buff limestone. Iron-stained limestones and conglomerate.

Upper Trigonia Grit: a coarse greyish sandstone.

Middle Inferior Oolite

Cotswolds
Phillipsiana and Bourguetia Beds: hard shelly limestone.

Northamptonshire
Lincolnshire Limestone: a chemically precipitated, fine-grained limestone varying in colour from almost white to buff and sometimes pink, and in structure from oolite, often with shelly fragments, to mainly calcite crystals.

Wilchellia Grit: a thin greyish-brown iron-stained limestone.

Notgrave Freestone: a hard fine-textured white limestone, locally shelly.

Gryphi Grit: a massive bedded sandy limestone.

Buckmani Grit: a yellow sandy limestone.

Lower Trigonia Grit: a rubbly or conglomeratic fossiliferous limestone frequently iron-stained.

Collyweston Slate: a sandy fissile limestone. Frost-split into roofing slabs.

Snowshill Tilestone: a sandy oolitic limestone.

Snowshill Clay: a stiff dark brown clay.

Harford Sands: pale brown quartz sands sometimes locally well-cemented.

Lower Inferior Oolite

Cotswolds
Upper Freestone: a hard cream oolite with interbedded soft marly bands.

Oolite Marl: a fine conglomerate of ooliths in a white marly matrix.

Lower-Freestone: a pale cream oolite.

Pea Grit: a cream or fawn pisolitic limestone, often coarse or rubbly.

Lower Limestone: cream oolitic limestones, locally conglomeratic.

Northamptonshire
Lower Estuarine Series: a series of clays, silts and sands.

Northamptonshire Sands and Iron-stones: a variable series of sands and yellow or brown ferruginous sandstones, sandy oolitic limestones and ironstones (siderite weathering to limonite).

Upper Lias

South of Bath
Midford and Yeovil Sands:
3 Fine to medium grained pale-coloured sands, with sandy limestone and a few shelly limestone lenses.
2 Blue-grey micaceous marls, with increasingly more fine sands and silts in the upper levels.
1 Blue-grey micaceous marls and pale grey silts, with lenses of impure limestone.

Junction Bed: thin limestone, greyish and sometimes oolithic or conglomeratic above, earthy below.

North of Bath
Scissum Bed: a sandy limestone.

Cephalopod Bed: ferruginous oolitic limestone containing ammonites.

Cotswolds Sand: fine yellow sands.
Upper Lias Clay: a thin clayey limestone.

Middle Lias

Pennard Sands: micaceous silts and fine yellow sands.

Marlstone Rock Bed: shelly ferruginous limestone, sometimes sandy or oolitic. Forms flat platforms in the main scarp.

Middle Lias Marls: soft brownish-yellow sands and marls.

Lower Lias

Lower Lias Clays: a series of marine clays. Forms low damp areas.
Blue Lias: blue-grey clays and shales, often with shelly limestone interbedded and at base.
White Lias: a series of fine-grain, pale grey limestones and mudstones.

Rhaetic

Cotham Beds   Cotham, Nr. Bristol
Cotham Marble: a hard buff fine-textured limestone or calcite
mudstone, often containing dendrites of manganese dioxide.

Westbury Beds   Westbury, Nr. Bristol
3   Pteria contorta Beds: a series of black pyritous shales with thin
beds of limestone and sandstone.
2   Ceratodus Bone Bed: a thin pyritous layer containing coprolites
and the remains of amphibians, reptiles and fishes.
1   Basal Bed: a sandy or conglomeratic bed.

Triassic

KEUPER SERIES

Keuper Marls   West Midlands
Red or reddish-brown, slightly calcareous mudstones, with pale
green streaks or bands locally, one of which usually forms the topmost bed (Tea-Green Marl). Thin beds of pale grey or buff sandstones are found in the lower levels and these cap hills in a flat
landscape.

Lower Keuper Sandstone   West Midlands
3   Waterstones: a series of brown, mainly micaceous, thin sandstones with interbedded thin red marls and shales.
2   Sandstone: evenly-bedded sandstones, usually red-brown but
sometimes brown, yellow or almost white.
1   Basal Beds: conglomeratic reddish sandstones, locally with
breccia, and often showing current-bedding.

Muschelkalk   Not found in Britain

BUNTER SERIES

Upper Mottled Sandstone   West Midlands
A mainly fine-grained, bright red sandstone with a few lighter-
coloured streaks and patches.

Pebble Beds   West Midlands
Well-rounded pebbles, often of reddish quartz, in masses or
scattered throughout a false-bedded, coarse-grained, dark red
sandstone, sometimes locally conglomeratic. A calcareous basal
breccia forms a scarp in the Severn valley.

Lower Mottled Sandstone   West Midlands
Generally a fine-grained, bright red sandstone with local marl
bands and greenish or yellowish streaks or patches. Often forms a
distinct scarp.

Permian

Upper Permian Marl   Sunderland-Nottingham
Red marls containing deposits of gypsum, rock-salt and anhydrite.

Yorkshire and Nottinghamshire | Durham
Upper Magnesian Limestone: slaty grey limestone and calcite mudstone, often magnesia-free. | *Upper Magnesian Limestone:* calcite concretions in a softer yellowish dolomitic matrix.

Middle Permian Marl: a narrow band of red marl, with grey silty bands and increasing amounts of gypsum, rock-salt and anhydrite to the south. | *Middle Magnesian Limestone:* a yellowish-grey dolomitic limestone.

Lower Magnesian Limestone: yellowish dolomitic limestone, sometimes shelly or reef limestone.

Lower Permian Marl: thin grey fossiliferous calcareous mudstones above a basal bed of yellow or blue-grey aerolian sands or sandy breccia.

Carboniferous

The Carboniferous period was one in which conditions repeatedly changed from marine to deltaic to swamp and back again, even within a small area; these were superimposed upon the major changes which first occurred in the Midland Valley of Scotland and northern England before affecting the Yorkshire-Lancashire areas followed by the Midlands and the South. There is, therefore, no 'typical' sequence and only a summary of the main divisions can be given.

Upper Coal Measures

These are almost entirely unproductive, consisting of red or reddish sandstones with some marls, shales or mudstones.

Middle Coal Measures

A rhythmic succession of fireclay, coal, limestone, siltstone and sandstone with interruptions. The coal seams vary from paper thickness to thirty feet but are mostly two to six feet thick and comprise only 2–3% of the whole. In Scotland and the North of England little coal was deposited during this period.

Lower Coal Measures

A rhythmic succession as above, but shales are thicker than the sandstones. Clay ironstones are found in some of the lower levels.

Millstone Grit

A dark coarse sandstone with finer or coarser bands representing deltaic conditions and a few marine shales and clayey limestones. In Scotland and the North many thick coal seams occur often associated with blackband ironstones but elsewhere the seams, if present, are very thin and poor.

Yoredale Beds

These occur in the North only and consist of a series of mainly shales and some sandstones, limestones and thin coals.

Carboniferous Limestone

Thick, massive, well-joined, grey limestone, often horizontally-bedded. Contains little, or no, coal except in the North, where the Lower Limestone Group, which began to be formed towards the end of this period, includes many thick seams.

Lower Limestone Shales

Mainly shales and mudstones, but in the North followed by the coarse Fell Sandstone.

Devonian

Devonian Facies		Old Red Sandstone Facies
UPPER DEVONIAN		
South Devon and Cornwall	North Devon	West Midlands
A series of dark slates, tuffs, phyllites, pillow lavas, ashes and sandstones.	*Pilton Beds:* bluish-grey slates with thin sandstone and limestone bands. *Baggy and Marwood Beds:* green to yellow marine sandstones with some shales and flags. *Pickinell Down Beds:* red, purple, brown and green sandstones with some bands of grey-blue shales.	*Farlow Sandstone Group:* yellow sandstones and grey, sometimes red or purple calcareous sandstones with seams of red marls and conglomerates.
MIDDLE DEVONIAN		
A series of grey slates with some limestone lenses, lavas and tuffs.	*Morte Shales:* glossy slates with occasional calcareous nodules and sandy seams. *Ilfracombe Beds:* series of shales, sandstones, sometimes calcareous, and grits. *Hangman Grits:* Shaly and grit deposits.	

LOWER DEVONIAN

Straddon Grits: red grits and quartzites which form Downs.

Meadfoot Beds: greenish slates with thin sandstone and limestone beds.

Dartmouth Beds: purple to green clayey deposits.

Hangman Grits: Fine-grained red sandstone.

Lynton Beds: blue-grey slates with grit bands and partly decalcified calcareous beds.

Foreland Grits: red and grey grits interbedded with reddish slates.

Brownstones: red marls and brown sandstones with coarse red conglomerate near the top.

Senni (Cosheston) Beds: green-brown or green and dull red sandstones, often micaceous, sometimes flaggy.

Ditton Series: red marls with red and green, often micaceous, sandstones, grits and cornstones.

Silurian

South Wales   Shropshire

DOWNTON SERIES

Red Downtonian: reddish marls and mudstones.

Red Downtonian:
2   Red and grey sandstones and clays.
1   Red, grey or mottled marls, sometimes with thin sandstones or shales.

Grey Downtonian: grey and yellow micaceous flaggy sandstones and grits.

Grey Downtonian:
2   Temeside Shales: greenish-grey or olive-green shales with thin sandstones.
1   Downton Castle Sandstone: massive, yellow sandstone with micaceous flaggy sandstones in the higher levels.

LUDLOW SERIES

Upper Ludlow: green shales and calcareous gritty bands.

Upper Ludlow:
2   Ludlow Bone Bed: a mass of organic fragments cemented by calcite.
1   Whitecliff Flags: calcareous greenish flagstones with shaly partings.

Aymestry Group: dark shales with sandy or mudstone bands.

Aymestry Group:
2   Mocktree Shales: a series of grey mudstones with calcareous concretions.
1   Aymestry Limestone: a well-bedded blue-grey, fossiliferous limestone.

Lower Ludlow: dark shales, flags and mudstones.

Lower Ludlow: grey shales and mudstones passing upwards into thin-bedded flags.

WENLOCK SERIES

Wenlock Group: dark grey shales, flags and mudstones with some calcareous beds.

Wenlock Group:
3   Wenlock Limestone: a resistant, bluish-grey, clayey limestone alternating with thin bands of shale. Forms a scarp, Wenlock Edge.
2   Wenlock Shale: a soft grey shale with shelly calcareous flags.
1   Woolhope Limestone: a blue flaggy limestone with thin shaly partings. Forms a scarp.

LLANDOVERY SERIES

Upper Llandovery:
3   Grey mudstones.

2   Shelly sandstones with inter-bedded shales.
1   Shelly mudstones.
Middle Llandovery: mudstones with calcareous nodules.
Lower Llandovery:
3   Sandstones with shale above and sandy mudstones below.
2   Greenish mudstones.
1   Dark shales with thin sandstones. Conglomeratic at base.

Upper Llandovery:
3   Purple (Hughly) Shales: purple and green mudstones and shales.
2   Pentamerus Beds: shelly limestones and calcareous mudstones.
1   Basal Conglomerate.

Ordovician

ASHGILL (BALA) SERIES

2   Slade and Redhill Beds: olive and grey mudstones, shelly in places, or with inter-bedded thin sandstones.
1   Shoalshook Limestone: grey calcareous mudstones with bands of limestone nodules.

CARADOC SERIES

2   Mydrim Shales: dark blue limestone above and black fossiliferous shales below.

4   Marrington Stage: Whittery Shales, a series of soft shales.
3   Hagley Stage: two groups of volcanic tuffs, breccias and some lavas, separated by soft shales.

1 Mydrim Limestone: an impure limestone with black shaly partings.

2 Aldress Stage: shales above and a coarse calcareous sandstone (Spy Wood Grit) below.
1 Rorrington Stage: shales and flaggy sandstones.

LLANDEILO SERIES

Llandeilo Flags:
2 Hendre Shales: dark grey shales weathering to brown.
1 Llandeilo Flags: calcareous flaggy sandstones and limestone.
Ffairfach Grit: coarse sandstones, sometimes with ash and agglomerates.

Meadowtown Stage: shales with limestone and calcareous flagstones locally.

LLANVIRN SERIES

Mainly black or blue-black shales with inter-bedded bands of tuffs and lavas.

4 Betton Stage: shales and flags.
3 Weston Stage: two series of grits, including volcanic material, separated by flags and shales.
2 Stapeley Volcanic Group: shales with inter-bedded tuffs, breccias and some lavas.
1 Hope Stage: mostly shales with bands of fine volcanic tuff ('china-stone ash') in the middle and upper levels.

ARENIG SERIES

3 Tetragraptus Shales: fine-grained shales, sometimes with lavas.
2 Grey sandy mudstones, sometimes with inter-bedded sandstones, grits and conglomerates.
1 Basal conglomerates.

Mylton Stage:
2 Mylton Beds: hard flags and shales.
1 Stiperstone Quartzite: hard, white or cream, siliceous sandstone, sometimes conglomeratic. Forms high crags.

Cambrian

Harlech Dome, North Wales.

Tremadoc Beds
A succession of grey and grey-blue mudstones, many altered to poorly-cleaved rusty-weathered shales and slates.

Linguella ('Lingula') Beds

4   Dolgelly Beds: a series of soft black shales above, and dark shales and slates below.

3   Festiniog Beds: dark, rusty-weathering shales.

2   Maentwrog Beds: dark, rusty-weathering shales with inter-bedded siliceous bands.

1   Bronllwyd Grits: coarse grits.

Menevian, or Clogau, Shales

A series of black, very fine-grained, cleaved mudstones.

Harlech Series

6   Gamlan Shales: shales and mudstones, with interbedded bands of grits.

5   Barmouth Grits: massive, resistant, coarse-grained, grey-green, grits and conglomerates. Forms high hills.

4   Manganese, or Hafotty, Shales: striped and banded, grey and green mudstones. Manganese occurs in one band, chiefly as manganese garnets.

3   Rhinog Grits: resistant, massive sandstones and grits. Forms high hills of the Harlech Dome.

2   Llanbedr Slates: slates with frequent bands of siltstones, sandstones and grits.

1   Dolwen Grits: coarse grits.

Pre-Cambrian

Pre-Cambrian rocks occur in Scotland, north of the Central Valley, Anglesey and North Wales, and as inliers at Charnwood Forest, Leicestershire, and Longmynd, the Wrekin and the Malvern Hills on the Welsh Marches. They largely consist of a complex of resistant, much-altered igneous and other rocks which frequently form steep-sided, high hills. Because of the absence of fossils, correlation from one place to another is based on lithology.

THE PHYSICAL EVOLUTION OF LANDSCAPE

Introduction

Landscape is in a constant state of evolution but the rate of change is extremely slow, being on the geological time-scale where a million years is considered a short period. Landscape exists in time and space, a product of the type and form of the rocks, of the climate which determines the agents which attack them and, above all, of the length of time the various agents have been at work, which determines the stage of the erosion cycle reached. Vegetation and animal life can modify it in detail, but geology provides the bones and sinews.

Much of the land surface is composed of rocks which were originally laid down in horizontal beds – but the earth's crust is not stable. Although the sudden, but usually relatively small movements produced by earthquakes make news, the majority are of little geological importance when compared with the less spectacular but continuous movements which affect much of the surface. Apart from the very old, dense and extremely stable blocks (shields) of Canada and Russia, and the Deccan of India, these movements cause the surface of the land and the adjacent shallow sea areas to rise or sink slowly, independently of the rise or fall of sea-level; an example is the fall caused by the locking up of immense quantities of water as ice during the Ice Age, when the sea-level was lowered by some three hundred feet, and its subsequent rise as the ice melted.

In addition to the vertical movements, the strata may be compressed laterally to produce structures varying from the great ranges of complex fold mountains, e.g. Alps or Himalayas, to simple arches. In other cases the stresses and strains have become so great locally that cracks (faults) occur, the beds on one side of the fault moving in relation to those on the other. In a few cases faults occur on either side of a block which is either pushed up to form a horst or pushed down leaving a rift valley, e.g. the Midland Valley of Scotland.

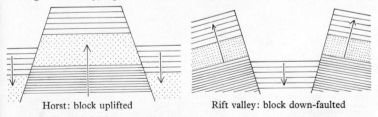

Horst: block uplifted   Rift valley: block down-faulted

Isostasy

The causes of earth movements are not yet fully understood, but one theory is generally accepted as it explains many of the observed facts. This is the Theory of Isostasy, which infers that the earth's crust is very thin in relation to its diameter, is to some extent flexible, and consists of two distinct layers. The less dense upper layer is made up mainly of rocks containing silica and alumina, and is called the *sial* layer (average density 2.4). This 'floats' on the denser lower layer which consists mainly of rocks containing silica and magnesia, and is called the *sima* layer (average density 2.9). At some depth there is a theoretical level at which downward pressures from above are all equal to each other (the level of compensation). This is possible because the sial layer is thin, or completely absent, under the oceans where the sima layer is thick, while beneath the thicker sial layer forming the land masses the sima layer is thinner, and reaches its thinnest under high mountain ranges, where there is a downward projecting 'root' of sial. This is supported by gravity determinations, which show a lack of mass in the region of mountain chains and an excess under the ocean deeps.

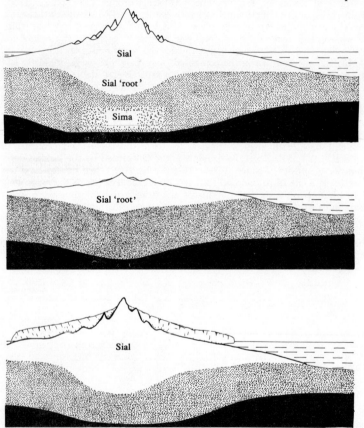

Isostasy: **a,** surface rocks supported by sial layer on denser sima layer; level of compensation is represented by lower edge of drawing. **b,** denudation causes slow uplift of the land mass and a reduction of the sial 'root'. **c,** ice-cap causes depression of land mass and growth of sial 'root'

The whole is in a state of continuous motion. The removal of mass from an area, such as erosion of a mountain region or the melting of a continental ice-cap, causes uplift, while prolonged deposition of sediment or the growth of a continental ice-cap causes a downward movement. However, reaction and movement are so slow that a stable equilibrium is never achieved, as the conditions causing the movements are always in advance of compensatory ones. Thus the rates of change are rarely equal while the conditions which initiated the change may have ceased to be effective, or even have been reversed, before even the initial effects have been counteracted.

Rocks

With the exception of purely organic deposits, all rocks are comprised of minerals, and can be divided into three types: igneous, sedimentary and metamorphic. Igneous rocks are those formed from deep-seated fluid intrusions into the earth's crust, and are further subdivided according to the depth at which they were formed, as shown by the relative size of their constituent crystals:

Plutonic rocks were formed at great depths and usually occurred in large masses, so that cooling took place extremely slowly and are, therefore, composed of large crystals, easily seen and distinguished by the naked eye.

Intrusive rocks were formed at a much shallower depth and in much thinner masses with the result that more rapid cooling occurred, especially on the margins, so that the majority of crystals are small and, although usually seen with the unaided eye, cannot always be distinguished. These sometimes contain a few large crystals (phenocrysts) of one mineral only.

Extrusive, or Volcanic, rocks have been poured out from fissures or vents and cooled so rapidly that the crystals are minute, or entirely absent, when a volcanic glass may be formed.

A second subdivision of each group is based on composition, and especially on the presence or absence of uncombined silica (quartz) and the ferro-magnesium minerals:

Acidic rocks contain crystals of free quartz and more orthoclase than plagioclase felspars (if the latter is present at all) and sometimes mica, biotite or muscovite.

Intermediate rocks contain little or usually no free quartz, plagioclase, but little or no orthoclase, felspar and sometimes biotite, hornblende and possibly a little augite.

Basic rocks contain plagioclase, some hornblende and possibly some olivine, but no free quartz or orthoclase.

Ultra-basic rocks are not common; they contain olivine and possibly some augite or serpentine, but no free quartz or felspars. These are always plutonic and include diorite, peridotite and serpentine.

		Acidic	Intermediate	Basic
Volcanic		Obsidian (gl.)	Trachyte	Tachylite (gl.)
		Pitchstone (gl.)		
		Rhyolite	Andesite	Basalt
Intrusive		Felsite	Porphyrite	Dolerite
		Porphyry		
Plutonic		Granite	Diorite	Gabbro
		Grano-diorite		
		Syenite		

gl. indicates a volcanic glass.

It must be emphasised that these divisions are arbitrary and there is no clear-cut dividing-line. One group merges into the next so that transitional types such as grano-diorite are not uncommon.

Sedimentary rocks are made up either of the weathered fragments of pre-existing rocks, which may themselves have been igneous, sedimentary or meta-morphic and have been transported, or of organic remains or chemical deposits, e.g., peat or gypsum, which have deposited *in situ*. Unlike most igneous rocks, their hardness and resistance to weathering varies from that of the hard lime-stones and the well-cemented sandstones to the soft limestones, clays, un-cemented sands, muds and peat. Sedimentary deposits of very recent geological age, such as alluvium, are termed drift, and these may overlie without con-forming with, and completely conceal the older strata of the solid geology beneath. Most sedimentary rocks contain fossils – the remains, casts or im-pressions of long-dead creatures, plants, etc. – and since living organisms evolve rapidly compared with the geological time-scale, it is possible to cor-relate strata in different areas, or even in different parts of the world.

The metamorphic rocks are derived from either igneous or sedimentary rocks which have been altered by heat, pressure or chemically-rich fluids, acting singly or in combination with the result that new chemical compounds or physical pro-perties are found in the metamorphosed rock, e.g. slate, dolomite.

Igneous Activity

This can be divided into two types: volcanic eruptions in which molten material from within the earth reaches the surface, and intrusions where the molten material was injected into existing rocks below the surface; these may be subsequently exposed by denudation. Although there are no active volcanoes in Britain today, there is ample evidence of both volcanic activity and intrusions in former times.

Volcanic Activity

Volcanoes are openings in the earth's crust, varying in shape from circular to long and very narrow fissures, from which is ejected magma – molten rock containing super-heated steam and other gases which act as a flux and so reduce its melting point. On reaching the surface most of the steam and other gases escape into the air, while the molten lava spreads, baking the underlying rocks before it cools. On the upper surface pumice may be formed by the solidification of light-coloured lava froth, made porous by escaping gases. The spread of lava from fissures is often extensive (e.g. Antrim Plateau, the Giant's Causeway, where basalt sheets are well exposed on the coast), usually as columnar stacks of six-sided slabs, the fractures being caused by stresses set up during cooling. Where eruptions occur from a more or less circular vent, a central cone will be formed. Submarine eruptions are a special case because the lava is in contact with water which cools its surface much more rapidly than land, throwing the lava into a jumbled series of folds. Such lava is termed pillow lava, because the folds resemble a fallen pile of pillows.

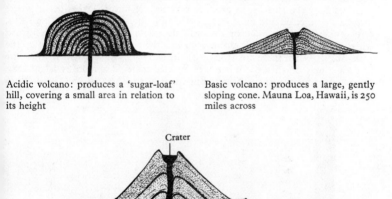

Acidic volcano: produces a 'sugar-loaf' hill, covering a small area in relation to its height

Basic volcano: produces a large, gently sloping cone. Mauna Loa, Hawaii, is 250 miles across

Composite volcanic cone of solidified lava flows, ash and other debris; a new subsidiary cone is developing on the flank

The shape of the cone of a central-type volcano will depend largely on the chemical composition of the magma. Where this is acidic, the lava will be viscous and only flow for a short distance before solidifying, giving rise to a round-topped, steep-sided, 'sugar-loaf' hill; but where the magma is basic, the lava is more mobile and flows further producing the familiar conical form. The centres of these basic cones are often marked by large craters (calderas), formed by subsidence after the level of magma has fallen, and these may contain a lake of molten rock rising through the vent (pipe). Many cones are not composed only of lava. During an eruption, especially after a long period of inactivity, ash and other debris which has collected in the crater and pipe will be ejected together with blobs of lava (bombs) which solidify before reaching the ground. All these may be incorporated into the composite cone. In some cases the quantity of ash will be enormous and if the super-heated steam is rapidly condensed locally, massive mud-flows will cover the surrounding area. Sometimes when an eruption occurs after a plug of solidified lava has sealed the pipe, part of the cone shatters and augments the effect.

Many lavas are weathered to fertile soils, which accounts for the high population density on volcanic slopes, despite the dangers. While the ash is more easily eroded away the solidified plug of lava remaining in the pipe is more resistant and may be left isolated, standing above the surrounding countryside, e.g. Castle Rock, Edinburgh.

Intrusions

Magma may be injected into the earth's crust without producing volcanoes or even reaching the surface, to produce a variety of forms. Dykes occur where magma was injected into more or less vertical fissures in the pre-existing rocks, forcing them apart and cutting discordantly across the strata. Sills are formed where intrusions occurred conformably along the bedding planes, lifting up the rocks above. When these are brought to the surface by subsequent erosion, the landscape may be affected. Where the injected material is more resistant than the country rocks, a sill will stand out either as an edge, e.g. the Great Whin

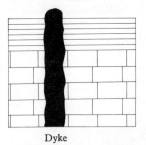

Dyke

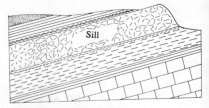

Sill with rocks both above and below affected by heat, unlike lava flows

Sill, Northumberland, possibly capping less resistant strata, or as a 'natural' wall in the case of a dyke. But where it is less resistant sills produce no noticeable feature and dykes only a narrow trough.

Where a block of country rock has been supported from beneath by a magmatic mass which flows away allowing the block to sink repeatedly, the almost vertical concentric fissures produced will be successively infilled, producing ring-dykes. Where the block is forced up by successive injections into the mass supporting it, the concentric fissures will be cone-shaped, originating in the mass; when infilled from below they are called cone-sheets. A very viscous

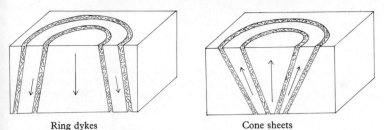

Ring dykes   Cone sheets

intrusion may not spread out as a relatively thin sheet to form a sill, but merely uplift the overlying rocks into a dome producing a laccolith. It will be noticed that while intrusions 'bake' the pre-existing rocks on both sides, volcanic lavas only affect those beneath them.

Laccolith

One igneous formation has long remained the subject of much controversy. These are batholiths, huge, elongated masses of igneous rock, usually granite, with steep sides and extremely irregular domed roofs, which may be exposed by subsequent erosion giving craggy scenery such as that of the tors of Dartmoor.

Batholith. M =metamorphic aureole

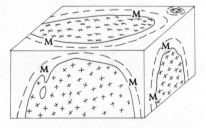

Smaller, elongated masses are known as stocks, and small, more or less circular ones as bosses. The adjacent country rocks above and on the flanks have been metamorphosed for a considerable thickness, forming a metamorphic aureole. Under suitable conditions the granitic orthoclase weathers to china clay (kaolin), e.g. St Austell, Cornwall. Although at first sight batholiths appear to be simple igneous intrusions, their origins remain a subject of dispute. Despite their immense volume there is little sign of displacement of surrounding country rocks above and around them (no basal section has ever been discovered). In addition, doleritic dykes from surrounding rocks have been traced as granitised 'ghosts' in the batholiths, while rocks broken from the roof also show granitisation. These facts, together with the thickness of the metamorphic aureole, have led some geologists to suggest that batholiths are not magmatic intrusions but were generated *in situ* by hot, gas-rich, granitising fluids.

Folds

Although sedimentary rocks are originally deposited in horizontal beds many of these have been uplifted or laterally compressed so that the majority are now inclined at an angle. Each bed exposed at the surface forms a separate outcrop

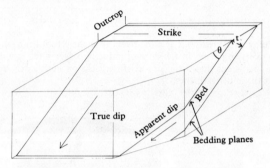

Geological bed. θ = angle of dip; t = thickness of bed

and while the true thickness of the bed is constant, the apparent thickness of any outcrop depends on the slope of the ground and the inclination of the bed. The faces of the upper and lower surfaces of a bed are termed bedding planes, the greatest angle between the bedding plane and the horizontal is the dip, measured with a clinometer, while the horizontal line along the bedding plane at right-angles to the dip is known as the strike. Great care is needed when measuring the dip of any bed, as an exposure along the strike of a vertical section, such as a cliff, gives a horizontal outcrop, and any other exposure, except at right-angles to the strike, gives a false value (apparent dip).

The form of folds can show tremendous variation. These range from single large simple folds producing a raised, more or less circular area (dome) or de-pressed area (basin), to the complex folded mountain systems. Or, on a smaller

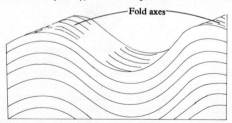

Simple folds: anticline and syncline

scale, are the simple arch (anticline) and trough (syncline), which are folded about a line (fold axis). These may be symmetrical, with the beds which form both sides (limbs) dipping at approximately equal angles, or asymmetrical where

Above, raised beach, Isle of Islay. Evidence of isostasy is clear in the inland cliff which has been smoothed by normal weathering, in marked contrast to the rough and ragged present cliff-line. The extremely flat surfaces both above and below it are characteristic of marine peneplanation, suggesting at least two major uplifts. *Below*, the Great Whin Sill. The Romans took advantage of the resistant outcrop, which forms such a notable feature in the area, to increase the defensibility of Hadrian's Wall.

Above, Land's End, Cornwall. The resistant rocks forming the cliffs have been eroded irregularly and so slowly that prolonged sub-aerial weathering agents have had time to carve both the face and crest very deeply. *Below,* Dunwich, Suffolk. The barely cemented sands are so weak that marine erosion has produced a smooth cliff-line with a gently sloping face, also subjected to wind action. During severe storms, the sea has advanced up to twelve feet locally in a single day.

there is a marked angular difference between the dip of the two limbs. At either end the folds die away where the axis dips into the ground forming pitching folds. Complex folds are sometimes produced where the beds forming

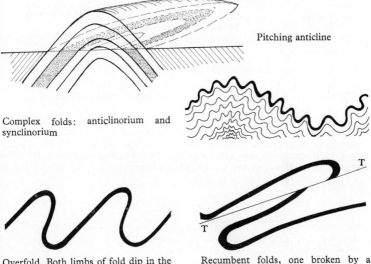

Pitching anticline

Complex folds: anticlinorium and synclinorium

Overfold. Both limbs of fold dip in the same direction

Recumbent folds, one broken by a thrust plane (T) forming an overthrust fold

a fold are themselves folded, producing either an anticlinorium or a synclinorium.

In regions of very intense folding the simple anticline may be folded to such an extent that one limb is turned through the vertical (inclined fold), and if this continues the point will be reached where one limb lies vertically above the other (recumbent fold). Continued pressure may cause the rocks to sheer along a fault plane at a very low angle (sometimes called a thrust plane), so that the fold is broken (overthrust fold).

Faults

When the stresses within a bed or a series of beds become too great a fracture (fault) occurs, with the result that the beds on one side of the fault move in relation to those on the other. Faults are usually divided into three types, but there may be some lateral movement in the first two:

Normal Faults: here the fault is vertical, or nearly so, and the block on the raised (upthrow) side moves away from it so that when the fault is parallel to the strike there is a surface belt below which some beds are not represented.

Reverse Fault: in this case, the angle between the plane of the fault and the vertical (hade) is considerably greater, often more than 45°, and the block on the upthrow side moves towards the fault. Thus, when the fault is parallel to the strike there is a surface belt below which some beds occur twice.

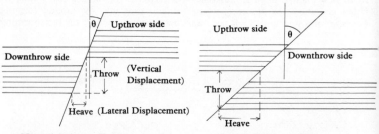

Normal fault. θ = Hade   Reverse fault. θ = Hade

Tear Fault: the fault is usually almost vertical and one block moves horizontally in relation to the other, with little or no vertical displacement (throw).

It should be noted that both normal and reverse faults can produce steep slopes (fault scarps) on the upthrow side of the fault, while tear faults leave far less obvious evidence, except in pre-existing valleys.

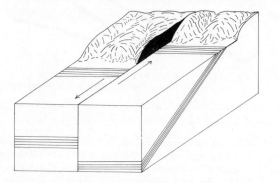

Tear fault

Carving the Land Surfaces

As soon as a land surface is exposed, it is attacked and worn down by a variety of agents and processes. The 'normal' cycle of erosion occurs where running water plays the major role, with river valleys passing successively through stages of youth, maturity and old age, until the area has been worn down almost to a plain (peneplain), with only a few isolated hills (monadnocks) of resistant rock remaining. Other cycles depend on extremely cold conditions giving a glacial cycle, or hot desert conditions, giving an arid one. Evidence that both of these have occurred in Britain can be seen in the rocks. However, irrespective of the type of cycle, the end-product is basically the same. In reality, the final stage of peneplanation is rarely reached, as the length of time needed is so great that either earth movements intervene, producing rejuvenation or submergence, or climatic changes replace one set of agents by another.

During the process of stripping away the rocks (denudation) a great variety of landforms are evolved, depending on the agent, or more usually the agents, at work. Denudation is, therefore, the collective result of weathering, transport and erosion.

Weathering is the disintegration and decay of the surface rocks, with virtually no removal of the rock-waste produced. It is usually divided into:

Mechanical weathering, in which the rocks are broken up by purely physical means, such as frost-shattering; large temperature changes which result in rock-shattering, splitting or exfoliation, where successive layers of rock crack off like the skins of an onion; and sand blasting, caused by wind-borne particles striking the surface.

Chemical weathering, in which a chemical reaction takes place, such as the dissolving of limestone in rainwater containing carbon dioxide, or the hydration of felspars resulting in the formation of clay minerals.

Transport is the removal of rock-waste by running water, ice, the sea, gravity wind and in solution.

Erosion is the destructive process which produces and removes rock-waste thereby lowering the land surface.

Rain and Running Water

Rain falling on land disperses in three ways: some flows directly into streams and rivers (run-off), some soaks down into the ground (ground water), and some evaporates. The proportion accounted for by each process depends on a number of factors. Run-off is greatest where heavy rain falls on bare, steeply

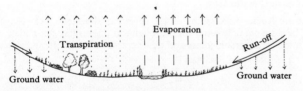

Dispersal of rain-water

sloping, impermeable rocks, possibly carrying away some of the soil with it, or on ground so saturated or waterlogged that it is virtually impermeable. Soakage is important where light rain falls on flat ground or gentle slopes of permeable rocks, especially where vegetation cover is complete. Evaporation is greatest when the temperature is high and the water remains on the surface in areas of impaired drainage or waterlogged soils, but it is aided by the transpiration of plants such as willows, a full-grown tree being capable of transpiring nearly 2,000 gallons a day.

Ground Water Where the rain falls on permeable rocks, it soaks downwards through them, as ink soaks through blotting paper, until it reaches an impermeable layer, where it changes direction, soaking downhill and saturating the lower levels of the permeable layer above the interface. This continues until the base of the permeable bed outcrops or the upper level of saturation (water table) reaches the surface. Here the water oozes out to form a spring, or a series of

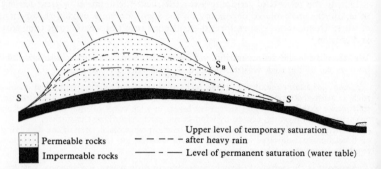

Permeable rocks

Impermeable rocks

- - - - - Upper level of temporary saturation after heavy rain

—— - —— Level of permanent saturation (water table)

Dispersal of rain-water on limestone. S =permanent springs; S_B = temporary spring after heavy rain only

springs (a spring-line). This is a slow process; rain falling on the Downland chalk may take up to nine months to complete its journey.

Below the surface, the height of the water table will vary with rainfall, but in general roughly follows the surface relief. Although the lower levels below the permanent water table are always saturated, heavy or prolonged rain will raise the saturation level temporarily, giving rise to intermittent springs and streams, known as 'bournes' on the south-eastern chalklands, at a higher level than the permanent springs. The existence of springs was important in influencing the location of early settlement.

Limestone Rocks Rain falling on the surface of limestone rocks is a different matter, because not only can it soak through soft porous limestone such as chalk, or down the innumerable joints and other cracks of the harder older limestone,

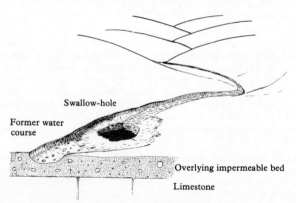

Swallow-hole

Former water course

Overlying impermeable bed

Limestone

Swallow hole in limestone formed after the stream has removed the overlying impermeable boulder clay.

such as that of the Carboniferous period, but, since it has dissolved some carbon dioxide from the air, it behaves as a weak acid, dissolving some of the limestone through which it passes. This is shown by the reversible equation: $CO_2 + H_2O + CaCO_3 \rightleftharpoons Ca(HCO_3)_2$ in which insoluble limestone (calcium carbonate) is converted into soluble bicarbonate; the reaction is reversed when water containing calcium bicarbonate is heated, causing the deposition 'fur' on the inside of kettles and pipes in those districts which take water from limestone areas.

Where streams flow from an area of impermeable rock on to limestone, they may disappear, cascading down enlarged vertical joints or 'swallow holes' (often called 'pot-holes'); where streams flow over a flat limestone surface they may disappear, except in times of flood, without any opening being apparent. In areas where an almost horizontal limestone bed is overlain by an impervious deposit, e.g. boulder clay, a dry stream course will extend below the present swallow hole, and may be marked by a series of swallow holes, each higher one representing a further uncovering of the limestone as the overlying impermeable deposit was progressively removed.

In some areas, especially the Pennines and the Mendips, underground streams have gradually dissolved the limestone along joints and cracks until a very complicated system of horizontal caverns and vertical waterfalls have been formed. In these the water may flow for miles underground, sometimes re-

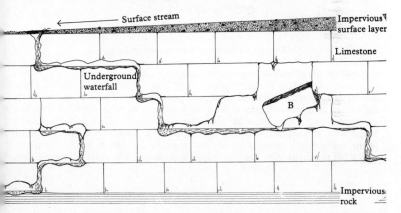

Caves produced by solution and the removal of support of roof blocks. B = fallen block

appearing on the opposite side of the range to its point of entry, while cases are known where two underground streams cross each other, flowing at different levels within the bed. The exploration of underground water courses provides an exciting and adventurous leisure activity for an ever-increasing number of people, but, like other worth-while pursuits, without adequate training and equipment to reduce unnecessary risks it can become extremely dangerous both for the foolhardy and their would-be rescuers.

The narrow vertical and horizontal passages are first formed by solution, but in later stages this is aided by the well-jointed nature of most limestones, so that once the sides and the area beneath a block have been removed, the block falls into the stream where the solution continues more speedily. The removal of successive blocks, by withdrawing basal and lateral support, is largely responsible for the formation of the immense and often lofty caverns, but the process may continue until the cavern roof finally collapses, in part or whole forming a narrow gorge, e.g. Cheddar Gorge, or Goredale (Yorks).

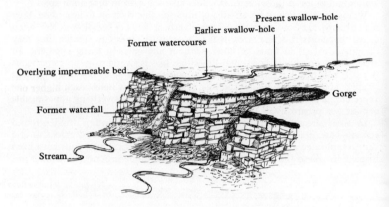

Emergent stream, cavern collapse and gorge

A feature of all limestone caves and passages is the slender icicle-like pendants (stalactites) and their thicker ground-based counterparts (stalagmites). These are formed by water containing calcium bicarbonate seeping down cracks in the cavern roof and hanging, at least for a short time, while some of the water evaporates and forms deposits of calcium carbonate. When it falls, further evaporation and deposition occur on the ground or stalagmite below. If the top of the stalagmite is examined a shallow cup-like depression will be seen, into which fall the drips from the over-hanging stalactite. The splatter of the falling

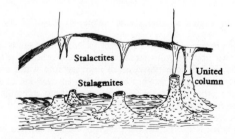

Limestone cave

drop causes greater evaporation so that the ground-based column is thicker. Although the process of deposition is very slow, both stalactites and stalagmites continue to grow until eventually they meet and form a united column.

When an underground stream emerges, it may vary in size from an insignificant stream to a full river flowing out of a cave at the base of the limestone strata, or from an apparently solid cliff face as at Malham Cove (Yorks.), where the outlet is blocked by boulders and gravel through which the water emerges.

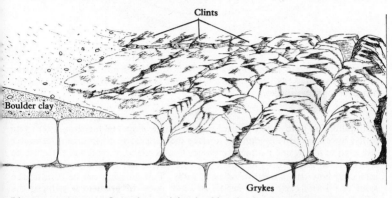

Limestone pavement. Once the overlying boulder clay has been removed, increased solution occurs along the joints

The effects of limestone solution can be seen on the surface as well as underground: where almost horizontal, well-jointed limestone beds are exposed forming a limestone pavement, e.g. Ingleborough, and above Malham Cove (Yorks.). Here the vertical joints have been widened forming grikes which may contain exotic vegetation in their well-sheltered depths, while the formerly flat-topped blocks have become well-rounded clints whose fantastically sculptured surfaces are difficult to cross. Moreover, solution along near horizontal joints may cause the blocks to rock when stepped on, an added and often unexpected hazard.

Artesian Basins

Where a bed of limestone or other permeable rock has been down-folded into a syncline, any rain falling on the exposed portions seeps down into the basin so formed. Where the limestone is sandwiched between two impermeable rocks, the water is unable to escape and the pressure at the bottom of the basin increases until the water table rises to the lowest level of the base of the outcrop. If a well is sunk at the bottom of the valley, the level of water in it will rise above that of the upper surface of the limestone and may possibly reach the surface of any overlying deposits.

London lies in such a synclinal basin with the Chalk, outcropping in the Chilterns to the north and the North Downs to the south and sandwiched between the Gault below and London Clay above. When the fountains were first installed in Trafalgar Square, the pressure of water from a bore-hole was

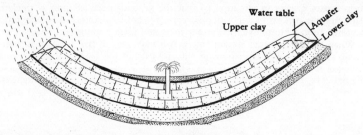

Artesian well

sufficient to operate them without mechanical aid, but now pumps are needed as so much water has been extracted that the water only rises to within about fifteen feet of the surface.

Rivers

Rain falling on newly uplifted land runs down the slope, taking the easiest route to the lowest level. Although the surface may appear to be uniform, rainwater will tend to follow one path in preference to others and erosion will therefore be concentrated along this line at the expense of the surrounding surface as the increased flow cuts a narrow valley or gully. This gullying can be seen on the sides of piles of earth, spoil heaps, etc., but once the gradient is reduced the stream course begins to wind from side to side because of irregularities in its course. Streams formed in this way are called 'consequent streams' because their formation is a direct consequence of the slope. Later, tributaries develop on the slope and sides of the consequent valley; much of the river valley development will then depend on the nature and form of the rocks and the amount of rainfall, although the basic section of the valley is always V-shaped.

Most river valleys show three stages:

Youthful or Mountain course where the fast-flowing river is mainly engaged in down-cutting, so that the valley will be narrow and the course interrupted by many irregularities;

Mature Valley course where the flow has slackened and the river is mainly occupied in widening its valley; here the irregularities are few unless rejuvenation has taken place;

Senile or Plain course where the flow is slow, the valley wide and flat-floored with much deposition and practically no erosion of new material.

At first the entire river course is at the youthful stage, but gradually first the mature and then the senile stages begin to work their way up from the mouth towards the source. Finally, in theory, the whole course should reach the senile stage and the entire basin – the area of land drained by the river system (the main river and its tributaries) – should be reduced to an almost flat surface (peneplain). In reality, however, this rarely happens as there is a change of level, uplifting or tilting of the land which rejuvenates the river system and compels it to begin down-cutting again, or a downward movement which may drown whole or part of the area.

All rivers, whether flowing into the sea or down to some other base-level, cut downwards until the gradient is such that the speed of the current is just adequate to remove its acquired load. Where the gradient is too steep and the force of the current too high, down-cutting occurs, and where the gradient is too gentle deposition takes place. When the gradient is just enough to achieve equilibrium it is said to be graded or to have a graded profile.

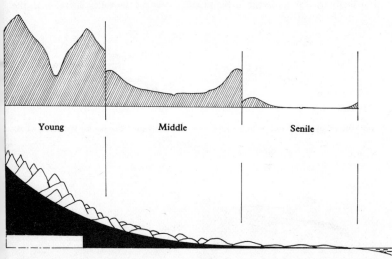

Young   Middle   Senile

Profile of a graded river with transverse sections of young, middle and senile courses

Youthful Stage Streams in the youthful stage are normally fast-flowing and, since a doubling of the speed increases the possible load by its second power, are able to carry a large load of debris which they use almost exclusively to deepen their courses, producing very narrow valleys which often follow lines of natural weakness.

Since this stage is mostly found in areas of resistant rock, lateral erosion due to other agencies is small and the valley sides are steep, and although frost-shattering may be important in supplying debris, it works slowly. The stream transports these pieces of rock which pound the bed as it trundles them along and they collide with other material, knocking off corners and edges to produce the familiar well-rounded, water-borne pebble. Indeed, where there is a sudden change of gradient where, for example, the stream leaves the hills and the speed slackens, the bed may be so thickly covered with pebbles and boulders that in a dry period the water can be heard but not seen; the course is turned into a 'river of stones', which must remain where they are until a storm fills the bed and carries them on the next part of their journey, replacing them with others from the stream's higher reaches.

In this part of its course the gradient often shows many irregularities due to more resistant strata forming barriers across it. These lead to the formation of waterfalls, rapids or lakes which provide a temporary local base-level reducing

the rate of the current and down-cutting above them until they have been removed or, in the case of lakes, infilled.

Mature Course As the gradient lessens so does the speed of the current and
with it the ability to move the stones and boulders it has used to down-cut its
upper course. The force of the running water now predominates and this is
principally used to undercut its banks and so extend the valley laterally. In the

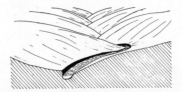

Youthful valley with interlocking spurs

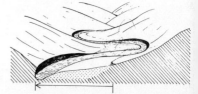

River begins the lateral widening of its
valley

Stream has moved

Spur truncated and a flood plain
beginning to be formed

higher parts of the valley, the river bends are separated by interlocking spurs of
high ground, and it is on these that the attack is most noticeable. The bends
are not fixed for all time, but move slowly downstream and outwards. On any
bend erosion takes place on the outside where the water is deepest and the
current fastest, while deposition occurs on the inside where the water is shallow
above the gentle (slip-off) slope and the current is slowest. The stream under-
cuts its outside bank producing a vertical face along an arc that extends not only
along the side but also forward into the spur, so that the bed moves sidewards
and forwards. The ground on the inside of the bend is left as a low flat area – a
miniature flood-plain of river deposits.

As the process continues, the original spurs are removed as one river bend
follows another down-valley, cutting into the sides of the wide valley and often
reworking its earlier deposits of the flood-plain, which are augmented when
storms cause the muddy flood waters to overflow the banks, and deposit much of
their load as they spread out in a shallow sheet bringing a slackening of speed
with reduction of depth.

When the land is uplifted by earth movement and rejuvenation of the river
takes place, a sudden change of gradient in the stream bed (knick-point) is produced, which gradually migrates upstream. The same effect is produced where
the river, having graded down to some temporary base-level (lake or head of a

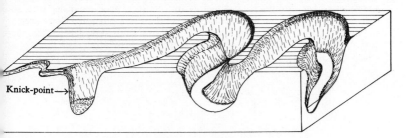

Incised meanders and knick-point eroding headwards

waterfall), breaks through the barrier. In both cases down-cutting restarts and continues until the river has readjusted its profile to that of the level below the obstruction. It is thus possible for a whole series of knick-points to be working headwards at the same time, with successive parts of the course graded down to each in turn.

When rejuvenation occurs after a river has already established a flood-plain, the bends or meanders down-cut and become incised into the deposits.

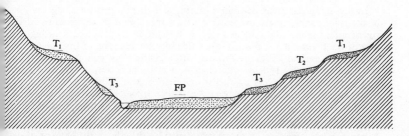

Valley section of the middle course. FP = flood plain; T_1, T_2, T_3 = river terraces

These continue lateral erosion, both during and after the down-cutting. Eventually a new flood-plain is established at a lower level than the old one, the remnants of which remain as river terraces. Where a succession of rejuvenations have occurred, the sides of the valley are marked by a series of river terraces, which are referred to by number or by the altitude at the back. The River Thames gives good examples of this. Not only does it possess a series of terraces, but the difference in height can easily be seen if you compare the land at the northern end of Waterloo bridge, on the 50-foot terrace, with that at the bottom of the ramp of the southern end, on the flood-plain.

Senile Course The senile course proper begins from the point where the river has cut back into its sides to such an extent that the original surface of the ridge-tops (interfluves) have been removed. In this part of the course down-cutting has stopped. The current moves slowly, cutting laterally into terraces and sides of the interfluves, but mainly into its own flood-plain deposits, so that meanders wind sinuously across a broad flat floor, migrating downstream in immense loops, which are sometimes cut off to form ox-bow lakes where the current has taken a short cut across the narrow neck between the two limbs of a meander.

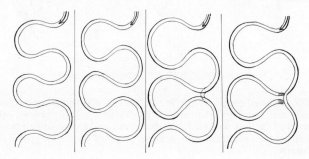

Lower course meanders move downstream, sometimes leaving an isolated 'ox-bow' or 'mort' lake

In low-lying flat areas deposition during flooding is greatest along the line of the river banks, where the water slackens speed as it passes from the deep river course to the shallow flooded area. As a result the bank becomes the highest part of the flood-plain, a process often aided by the planting of trees along the banks, until natural levees are formed with a gentle slope running down from the bank to the flood-plain. The change of slope here may be marked by a minor stream more or less parallel to the main stream. The levees give some flood protection, but may cause the river to deposit material in its own bed, and so raise itself above the level of its own flood-plain, as has happened in parts of the Fens, sometimes with disastrous results.

River Mouth The form of the mouth depends not only on the amount of its load, but also on the strength of its current and the scouring effect of the tides. Where a sinking or drowned valley has a wide mouth with an adequate outflow, an estuary develops and is maintained where the tides are able to assist the flushing out; but where the current flow is insignificant and tides are unable to cope, the estuary will gradually silt up (e.g. Dee Estuary, Chester). This may, in some cases, be assisted by longshore drift (e.g. The Wash). Silting up begins with the formation of sandbanks and mud-flats only uncovered at low tide, but their presence causes a local reduction of current flow, so that once started the process snowballs. Once an area has been built up so that it is above water for most of the day, seeds carried by current, wind or birds bring plant life, which in turn, by trapping and retaining soil particles, gradually helps to develop a salt-marsh which is only covered by very high tides and this the plants can withstand.

Deltas occur where deposition is great, the flow poor and the tides inefficient, but in Britain these conditions are found only in lakes where continuous deposition increases the size of the delta until it may stretch right across the lake.

River Valley and Drainage Patterns

After initial uplift of land the consequent streams drain down towards the sea. Thus a symmetrical dome or volcanic cone gives rise to a radial pattern, while a long anticline produces two sets of streams flowing in opposite directions. In time each stream deepens and widens its valley, so increasing its true drainage area and providing secondary slopes for tributaries. Both the main and tributary streams lengthen their courses upstream by headward erosion, following the line of least resistance, with the result that the pattern of drainage depends on the nature of the rocks and the structures they form.

Where the composition and slope are uniform the pattern resembles the

Dendritic drainage

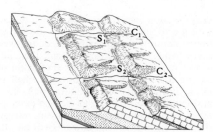

Consequent rivers. C = consequent; S = subsequent

silhouette of a shrub in winter (dendritic), but this is uncommon. A more usual situation occurs where the main stream cuts across ground made up of outcrops of rocks of varying degrees of resistance. Here the tributaries (subsequents) on the weakly resistant rocks (e.g. clays and shales) have a tremendous advantage, as they can cut back headwards and enlarge their valleys quickly. In general, the consequent valleys become narrow and steep-sided where they cross the more resistant rocks, but are broad and gently concave on the weakly resistant ones. Subsequent valleys too depend largely on the strength of the rocks, so that where it lies wholly in the less resistant rock the valley is usually symmetrical, but where the stream has cut down to a more resistant underlying stratum it will tend to move down the dip; thus there is a gentle slope on the up-dip sides and a steep slope which it will continue to undercut on the down-dip side, producing a markedly asymmetrical valley. Further erosion causes the stream to move further down the dip, deepening the valley and heightening the contrast between the two sides until it has graded down to the main stream and deepening ceases.

River Capture Streams not only cut headwards at different rates because of the local differences in the resistance of rocks, but differ also in their drainage areas. Other factors being equal, the stream with the greatest flow will be able to deepen and cut headwards at the fastest rate; the same applies to their tributaries. In time, one tributary will cut so far headwards that it will not only remove the separating high ground between it and the smaller tributary of an adjacent consequent, but will join up with it and continue cutting back along its valley, diverting more and more of its water into its own consequent; this in turn increases the rate of erosion of both. Ultimately, the whole tributary

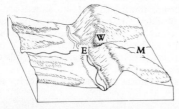

River capture. E = elbow of capture; W = wind gap; M = misfit

valley is taken over and the water from the consequent itself, above its junction with the tributary, is added to the more vigorous subsequent. This is termed 'river capture'; the upper course of the weaker consequent flows down to a sharp bend (elbow of capture) and then into the tributary valley. Below its former junction and now deprived of its former headwaters, it continues down-cutting more slowly and becomes a small stream in an overlarge valley – a misfit. In the course of time it lowers its floor, and a col (wind gap) marks the position of its former floor in the next outcrop of resistant rock below the elbow of capture. Meanwhile a small stream (obsequent) may develop on the higher side of the wind gap, and flow towards the elbow of capture.

Other Drainage Patterns In regions of intense folding the main streams follow the troughs of the folds and only traverse the fold lines along belts of weakness, so that the drainage is largely rectangular with right-angled bends forming a trellis pattern.

Sometimes the drainage pattern appears to be completely unrelated to the existing surface geology. This occurs where the visible surface rocks were once covered by newer sedimentary deposits, which in the course of time have been completely removed. The river system established on the newer strata impressed itself on the underlying rocks which form the present surface as they were grad-ually exposed by denudation, and the pattern had already cut into these before the newer had been completely removed. A good example of this superimposed drainage occurs in the Wye valley between Ross and Chepstow where the river meanders across outcrops of the Coal Measures, Carboniferous Limestone and Old Red Sandstone and back again with complete disregard for the present surface geology.

This should not be confused with antecedent drainage when a river, flowing across an area which is slowly being uplifted, is able to maintain its channel by vigorous down-cutting. This keeps pace with the uplift and so produces a relatively narrow and often steep-sided valley.

Ice and Snow

Today, erosion by ice and snow is on a small scale when compared with the massive works of the ice-caps and valley glaciers of the four glaciations of the

Pleistocene Ice Age. These have left many characteristic glacial landscape features in Britain, especially in the north and west. Frost, however, continues its destructive work.

Frost When the temperature falls below freezing point, water trapped in exposed cracks and crevices turns to ice. But since ice has a greater volume than the same weight of water, the expanding ice, exerting a force of nearly one ton to the square inch, widens and deepens the crack. When the ice melts by day to refreeze at night, the crack will get larger until a rock fragment becomes completely detached and sooner or later falls to the base of the slope, to join other similarly sharp-edged pieces of frost-shattered debris (scree) in forming an extremely unstable heap, commonly seen at the foot of many mountain or rocky slopes, on which movement can be very dangerous.

Valley Glaciers While a light covering of snow containing a great quantity of trapped air insulates the ground beneath from the effects of frost in the same way as the entrapped air in an eiderdown insulates a sleeper, heavy and repeated snowfall has completely different results, as the snow accumulates faster than the summer melting can remove it.

Here, the weight of the overlaying snow compresses the lower layers into ice, expelling much of the entrapped air. Further falls increase the weight on a sloping surface until cohesion is broken and the whole mass slides off as an avalanche into the valley bottom below, just as snow slips off a roof.

Over a long period of time the increasing accumulation of ice and snow in the valley extends further and further. At first it remains stationary, but under the force of gravity and pressure of the mass of ice and snow in the upper valley it begins to move. This is aided by the fact that pressure lowers the melting point of ice, so that the base is lubricated by water in the same way as the pressure of a skater's blade causes the ice beneath to melt, enabling the blade to glide easily over the ice on a thin film of water.

A valley glacier easily removes any loose surface deposits, either pushing them ahead of it or freezing them into its basal surface where, together with rock fragments of all sizes brought down by avalanches and scree falling down crevasses, they are used to gouge and grind away the valley floor, greatly deepening it and producing a U-shaped section. Where the valley is restricted, the glacier, unable to erode laterally, over-deepens the floor to accommodate its bulk – these usually elongated depressions will later be occupied by glacial valley lakes.

The upper surface of a glacier is cut by narrow, but often very deep, cracks (crevasses) caused by the tremendous stresses and strains produced within as it proceeds along the valley, and are often masked by bridges of fresh snow. One

Level of preglacial valley

Scree

Lake

Section of U-shaped glaciated valley

group (marginal crevasses), which occurs throughout the length of the glacier, extends from near the sides diagonally forward towards the centre. These are produced by the differential rates of movement within the glacier, the rate being higher at the centre of the upper surface and lower at the sides and bottom where the flow is retarded by friction. On a bend, pressure ridges are produced on the inner side while transverse crevasses appear on the outer. The latter are produced right across the glacier where the gradient steepens. Where the valley is restricted, the glacier is laterally compressed to produce longitudinal pressure ridges, which are matched by longitudinal crevasses where the valley widens and the glacier spreads out.

When the total amount of snow received by a glacier exceeds that lost, the blunt lower end (snout) continues to slide forward, perhaps for hundreds of feet below the snow line until equilibrium is attained. But where the rate of melting exceeds the snow supply the snout is gently sloping and retreats; i.e. at the end of each summer the snout is found a little further back up the valley.

In addition to crevasses the glacier is marked by a considerable amount of scree from adjacent rock slopes. This tends to form wide lines (lateral moraines) close to the sides. Where tributary glaciers join the main one or where glaciers unite on the same level, the original lateral moraines are then found away from the sides and are termed medial moraines. It is not unusual to see roughly parallel, longitudinal moraines covering the full width of the lower glacier.

Glacial Deposition Features

Much of the load of debris transported by a glacier is deposited around its snout as an untidy line of boulders, gravel, clay and rock-flour to form a terminal moraine. This is especially noticeable where the glacier has remained in equilibrium (still-stand) over a long period. Where the glacier has retreated a series of more or less concentric ridges marks the successive stages of its recession, but a re-advance carries material forward again and destroys the earlier features.

The melt water from the snout may emerge as innumerable streams or as a river from a huge ice-cave, which may possibly extend many hundreds of feet into the glacier. In either case it will carry a heavy load of fine debris, which may be deposited in a lake formed between the snout and a previous terminal moraine, or spread as a gently-sloping outwash fan where it escapes from restriction and slackens its speed.

Long sinuous banks (eskers), mainly of gravel, may indicate either the position of persistent ice-caves during a long period of still-stand, or merely the gradual withdrawal of their outlets as the glacier retreated.

A commonly found deposit consisting of smallish boulders or pebbles in a clay matrix (boulder clay) may either be spread out over the whole area covered by a glacier or remain only in patches. In some places, where there is a heavy deposit of boulder clay, it is not spread out evenly but raised into a series of egg-shaped mounds (drumlins) varying greatly in size, but perhaps averaging 150 feet in height and a third of a mile in length, with their long axes parallel to the line of ice-flow and their blunt ends pointing up-valley, to produce a landscape resembling a basket of eggs, e.g. Craven Lowlands of Yorkshire, and Co. Down. Their origin is obscure, although a few at least are known to have had boulder clay piled up against solid rock cores.

Since valley glaciers were once many miles in length and ice-caps were on a

Above, Grey Mare's Tail Waterfall, near Moffat. Below the waterfall, caused by a knick-point working upstream, is a typical V-shaped upper river valley with interlocking spurs. Some lateral erosion has begun, the stream having cut off the end of the nearest spur, leaving a small flood plain, before swinging in again to undercut its side to produce an earth-slip and a resulting river-cliff. *Centre,* lower river course: large meanders near the mouth of the River Cuckmere, Sussex. Already the stream is beginning to cut through the narrow neck of land between the two lower loops. *Below,* Mawddach Estuary, Merioneth. The stream is wider, but low tide exposes the numerous sandbanks, the larger grading into the flood plain on the far bank. But despite this, the valley is not mature, the resistant rock forming the valley is seen in the foreground outcrop and the tree-clad steep-sided lower spurs.

Above, Borrowdale, a glaciated valley. The flat floor, with its few rocky outcrops contrasts with the steeply-sloping rugged sides, indicating the infilling of a glacial valley lake, giving a fertile alluvial soil. *Below*, Helvellyn, the Lake District, showing the summit and the narrow arête of Striding Edge and the steep-sided corries, the central one being occupied by a lake, Red Tarn.

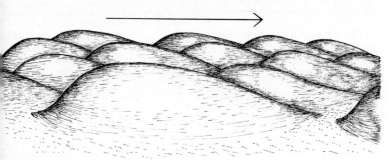

A drumlin tract giving a 'basket of eggs' topography. Arrow shows direction of ice movement

continental scale, it is not surprising to find boulders of a type of rock which is completely foreign to the particular locality. The boulders (erratics) may be slightly eroded after being transported on the top of a glacier, or badly worn and ground down through being rubbed along the valley floor. Such erratics provide valuable evidence as to the routes followed by the moving ice.

Glacial Erosion

In the mountainous upper glacial course, corries (cwms or cirques) form the higher points of interest. These are arm-chair shaped depressions with very steep to near vertical sides and rear walls which originated on gentle or slightly concave slopes which were covered by snow during the glacial periods. The snow and ice protected the lower part but tended to slip down from the upper surface leaving it exposed to frost-shattering so that the depression was cut back. Subsequent snowfalls accumulated at the back, not only removing the frost-shattered fragments but also increasing the pressure at the base of the rear slope and causing the whole mass to slide round, pushing out that at the front. The upper part of the back and sides were again left unprotected so that rearward erosion by frost action, alternating with the grinding and gouging of the base by ice and its load of debris, combined to form this characteristic

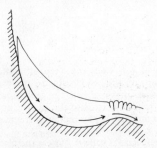

Corrie formation. Arrows show direction of ice movement

Development of multiple corries in a single highland mass

depression. But as there was relatively little pressure or frost action on the front, a rock lip remained which now often holds back a small lake.

Sometimes two corries have each cut back into opposite sides of the same ridge, leaving only a narrow, steep-sided edge (arête) of high ground between them, e.g. Crib Goch, Snowdon, or Striding Edge, Helvellyn. Where more than two corries have cut back into the same rocky mass, several arêtes are produced which often culminate in an isolated, central, pyramidal peak.

The upper end of a glaciated valley is often marked by a sudden deepening where several corries or small tributary glaciers once discharged into a common channel. This 'trough-end' marks the beginning of the glaciated valley proper; above it the tributary glaciers were usually too small to erode their valleys to any significant extent, but from this point we find the typical U-shaped glaciated valley section. Streams from these and other tributary valleys often pour into the main valley as waterfalls; since comparatively little erosion occurred in them they are still graded to the pre-glacial river valley, and there is a considerable difference in height between the two levels. The streams from these 'hanging valleys' make the change in one vertical drop.

Glaciated valley with hanging valleys and valley lake

On the valley floor, low, rather streamlined, rocky outcrops (roches moutonnées) may be seen. These have a gentle slope on the headward side, up which the glacier rode, although exposed rock surfaces may still bear the deep grooves and scratches made by boulders frozen into the underside of the glacier, and a craggy, or stepped, lower face from which the glacier plucked away fragments which froze into it as it passed.

The sea now fills the lower parts of some glaciated valleys. Where the glacier reached the sea, the lower end floated, moving up and down on the tides until it 'calved', the broken pieces floating away as icebergs. But below the point where

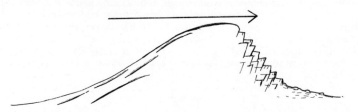

Roche moutonnée. Arrow shows direction of ice movement

it floated out of contact with the valley floor no glacial deepening could occur, so that the entrance of a true fjord is marked by a distinct threshold, e.g. Loch Leven. On the other hand, glaciated valleys which have been submerged in post-glacial times retain their more or less constant gradient and have no threshold.

Ice Dammed Lakes

In addition to those features produced directly by erosion and deposition during glaciation, the Ice Age was also indirectly responsible for changing the courses of many rivers. As the ice retreated, lakes formed between enclosing hills and edges of ice sheets. The pre-glacial River Severn flowed northwards into the present-day Dee Estuary. But during the later stages of glacial retreat a great lake (Lake Lapworth) formed between the Welsh hills and the ice which still covered much of Cheshire and north Shropshire. The great flow of melt water caused the level to rise until it overtopped a weakly resistant clay ridge to the south, and the resulting outflow was easily able to cut a gorge at Ironbridge. By the time that its former course was free of ice the new course had become firmly established. Similar conditions prevailed in the Vale of Pickering in Yorkshire, where North Sea ice blocked the short seaward courses of the rivers and the whole vale was flooded (forming Lake Pickering) until a new channel was cut to the west.

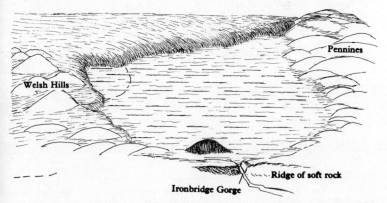

Lake Lapworth. Drainage of preglacial Dee (broken line) blocked by retreating Irish Sea ice

Perhaps the best-known example occurs in Scotland. Glen Roy contained an ice dammed lake, which was lowered in three stages as successively lower cols were uncovered by the retreating ice. Its former shores, during periods of still-stand, are marked by parallel lines, produced by the different deposits on the vegetation, and although these are easily seen at a distance, they are difficult to find on the ground, unless you observe the level of the 'parallel roads' on the opposite side of the glen.

Coasts

The coast-line is not only produced by the interaction of erosive forces on rocks and rock forms, but also indicates more clearly than anything else the effects of the vertical movements of land in relation to sea-level. A downwards movement of land has the same effect on the coast-line as a rise in sea-level; for example, after the last glaciation which covered much of the landmasses of the northern hemisphere, part of the North European Plain was submerged by the North Sea. These vertical movements produce two types of coast-line: those caused by submergence give an indented coast-line because of the drowning of land previously modified by sub-aerial erosion, and are characterised by drowned river valleys (rias) such as those of southern Devon and Cornwall. Those produced by emergence, where the irregularities have been infilled, give smooth outlines with raised beaches and wave-cut platforms left stranded inland, while in extreme cases accordance of the height of hills may mark former marine peneplanation.

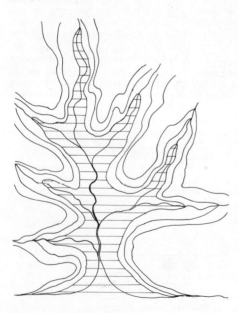

Ria. Former valley land flooded by the sea (hatched)

Waves Normal waves are due to wind sweeping over the sea surface and their height depends on the strength, duration and distance the wind or wave front has travelled over open water (fetch). The wave length, measured from crest to crest, may vary considerably – wind-blown waves may travel into adjacent calm areas, flattening out as a groundswell with wave lengths of over 1,000 feet. In the open sea the wave front passes forward leaving the water relatively undisturbed; indeed, a floating cork would trace a circular path as a wave front passed. Only if the wind were extremely strong or if the water were shallow would its advance be greater than its retreat.

When waves approach land two new factors become important: the beach gradient and the type of waves. Where the slope is steep, the beach and cliff-base receive the full force of the breaking wave so that much of the material carried by the forward movement (swash) of the wave returns under gravity and the pull of the wave's downward run (backwash). Where the slope is gentle, the waves break at some distance from the beach because there is insufficient depth of water to support their swelling crests. The full force of the water therefore goes into the swash, pushing loose material up the beach; when its momentum is expended the slope is too gentle to give much impetus to the backwash, so most of its load remains higher up the beach than it was originally, creating a storm beach of pebbles or deposits of sand which may result in dune formation. In extreme cases, waves may break so far from the beach that they deposit their load in the shallows forming offshore bars.

Inshore waves are of two types: destructive waves have a high frequency and a short wave length producing an almost circular orbital motion. This causes them to plunge steeply, breaking in the backwash of their predecessors with a weak swash; the backwash in contact with the beach is thus virtually uninterrupted and loose material is carried seaward in an endless stream. On the other hand, constructive waves have a low frequency (less than eight per minute) and a long wave length, flattening the orbital motion of the destructive type to an ellipse; these break directly up the beach with a considerable swash, pushing the loose material before them.

Marine Erosion The sea uses a wide range of weapons during the course of its continuous assault on the coast. Besides the sheer physical force of storm waves hurling their immense weight of water on to the shore, the waves themselves are armed with 'tools' ranging from sand and gravel to large boulders weighing many tons which pound away at the cliff-base, meanwhile reducing and rounding themselves. Waves may also trap air in the joints and crevices of rocks and compress it to a tiny fraction of its original volume, before falling back and releasing the air explosively. The surrounding rocks loosen as a result and eventually break up. Under storm conditions many huge waves break each minute, perhaps for several days on end, and the cumulative effect is considerable. Nor is this all, for even on a calm day sea-water continues the attack chemically and by solution.

The sea can only attack land above its reach, such as cliffs, by under-cutting and here it is sometimes aided by land structure. Where the beds dip seawards, the upper beds will tend to slide down, especially when clay forms one of the lowers beds; where the dip is landwards, progress will be much slower. If the rocks are resistant the struggle is a long one, as the battle-scarred cliffs of western Cornwall testify; where the cliff rocks have little resistance, being com-

posed of clays, e.g. Herne Bay, Kent, or of almost uncemented sandstone as at
Dunwich, Suffolk where the sea advanced twelve feet in a single storm, it is a
very different story.

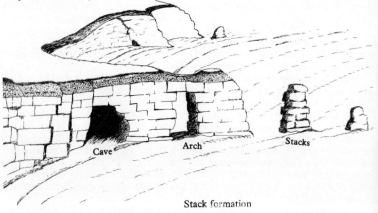

Stack formation

In some rocks, especially limestones, caves may be cut which may be enlarged
under favourable conditions and extended until a section of roof collapses and
a blow-hole is formed, up which the storm waves send bursts of spray. This may
be followed by further roof collapse until the cave becomes a narrow inlet.
Where a band or patch of more resistant rock occurs in a weaker cliff this may
be cut back until only a narrow isthmus remains. This latter may disintegrate
from above, or the sea may cut a cave through it at the weakest point leaving an
arch, until the supporting rocks are eroded and it falls leaving the more resistant
rock standing as an isolated sea-stack.

As the resistant rocks of the cliff are gradually cut back, the worn stump of
strata is left as a wave-cut platform, often only exposed at low water. This too
is subjected to erosion, but it is far less efficient than that at the cliff-base, as
shown by the very gentle overall seaward slope produced mainly by the scouring
of the load carried by the backwash. The platform may be extended seawards
by deposition from the cliff destruction, forming a wave-built terrace. In time, a
combination of these two can reduce the effectiveness of marine erosion by
causing the waves to break before they can fling their full force at the cliff. If the
cliffs are composed of very resistant rock they usually become craggy as the
effects of sub-aerial erosion become dominant; if the rocks are only moderately
resistant they lose their hard outlines and become gently sloping with rounded
tops.

Longshore Drift As waves approach a shore-line at an angle to their forward
movement, they are progressively slowed down by friction in the shallowing
water, thus the wave fronts are refracted towards the beach, running up in lines
apparently almost parallel to it, though at least part of their original motion
remains and pebbles, other beach material and debris are **carried diagonally**

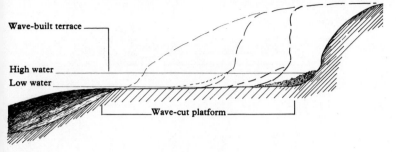

Cliff development

up the beach by the swash of each wave, to return straight down the slope in the weaker backwash. Although each pebble or sand grain is only moved a short distance by every wave which affects it, the total movement is considerable, especially where aided by tidal currents such as those which generally sweep eastwards along the south coast and southwards along the east coast.

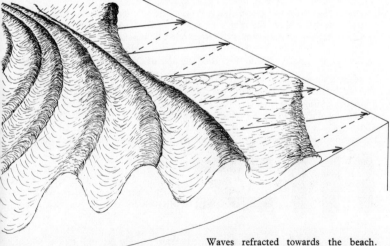

Waves refracted towards the beach. Pebbles are carried *diagonally* up the beach (→) by the breaking waves, and are carried *straight* down (– – –) by the backwash

The results of this movement can be clearly seen at many seaside resorts, where in an effort to stabilise and retain the sandy beach material, which so often forms their chief holiday attraction, solid wooden walls (groynes) have been built from above the high-water mark into the sea. The difference in levels of beach material on the two sides of the groynes may exceed ten feet.

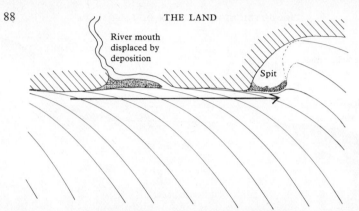

River mouth
displaced by
deposition

Spit

Longshore drift. Arrow shows direction of drift

Where a stretch of relatively straight coast is followed by an inswing of the land at a bay or estuary, material that has been carried along the coast is deposited to form a projecting sand-bar, which is gradually built up until it is above high water and forms a spit. Prolonged longshore drift builds up a considerable area of deposition which is gradually covered by vegetation, e.g. Dawlish Warren in the Exe estuary. The mouths of some of the smaller rivers may also be affected as bars may seriously limit the draught of ships using them, or a spit may be extended until the river must flow parallel to the coast before it reaches a point where it can maintain a channel, e.g. the River Arun at Shoreham harbour, and the River Alde with the long spit of Orford Ness.

Special Coast-Lines The character of coast-lines of submergence is greatly affected by their relationship to the fold-lines. Where the coast cuts across the fold-lines (Atlantic type coast), it forms a succession of hilly headlands or points alternating with sandy bays which extend into the troughs of the valleys, e.g. South-west Ireland. But where the coast is parallel to the fold-lines (Pacific or Dalmatian type of coast), the more resistant beds hold the sea back along a more

a, Atlantic and b, Pacific types of coast where resistant (black) and weak rocks alternate

a   b

or less smooth line, until it breaches the barrier, usually through a cave which is later reduced to an arch after a weakly resistant bed has been reached and partly excavated, e.g. Staire Hole, Lulworth. In time the arch collapses and the way is left open for the sea to excavate a large area of weaker rock between two more resistant ones, e.g. Lulworth Cove. Eventually the outer resistant bed is reduced to a line of elongated island stacks parallel to a new coast-line which is formed by the next bed of more resistant rock.

For fjords and drowned glaciated valleys see p. 82; for rias (drowned river valleys) see p. 84.

GEOLOGICAL GLOSSARY

Accessory minerals. Minerals which may occur in small amounts in a rock without affecting its fundamental character.

Acicular. The mineral is in the form of long needle-like crystals.

Acid igneous rocks. Igneous rocks containing more quartz than orthoclase and characterised by the presence of 'free' quartz crystals. Also called over-saturated.

Aerolian deposits. Deposits of fine-grained, wind-blown material; mainly sands and dusts (loess and volcanic ash) with some pollen grains.

Agglomerate. A sedimentary rock consisting of angular fragments in a fine ash matrix. Normally found around explosive volcanic vents.

Alluvial deposits. Muds, sands and gravels bodily transported by rivers or floods and later deposited when the current slackens speed. Often called alluvium, if of geologically recent origin.

Amphiboles. An important group of dark-coloured minerals (iron-magnesium-calcium silicates), often occurring as laths; the two cleavage planes intersect at almost 120°, as do the prism faces. The most common mineral in this group is hornblende.

Amygdale. Gas cavities in lavas which have been later infilled with a secondary mineral, e.g. agate.

Aquafer (Aquifer). A layer of permeable rock sandwiched between two impermeable ones through which water may soak. The whole is usually tilted or folded synclinally; sometimes refers to any water-bearing rock.

Arenaceous rocks. Sedimentary rocks composed of sand grains either unconsolidated or cemented.

Argillaceous rocks. Sedimentary rocks containing a high proportion of clays or muds.

Arkose. A coarse-grained sandstone or grit containing at least 10% unaltered felspar.

Basic igneous rocks. Igneous rocks which contain no 'free' quartz or orthoclase; usually dark-coloured; also called unsaturated.

Batholith (Bathylith). A very large mass of intrusive igneous rock, commonly granite, dome-shaped but with no known floor.

Bedding planes. The interfaces within a bed of sedimentary rock between successive deposits of similar material; they appear as parallel lines of weakness.

Bladed. Crystals shaped like a knife-blade.

Botryoidal. A mineral form consisting of intergrowing spheres somewhat resembling the surface of a raspberry.

Breccia. A sedimentary rock consisting of angular fragments of other rocks cemented in a fine matrix.

Brickearth. Rock other than clay from which bricks can be made; usually loess.

Calcareous. Sedimentary rocks which contain appreciable amounts of calcium carbonate; they effervesce (fizz) with dilute acid.

Cleavage. The planes along which a mineral splits naturally.

Clints. The well-rounded blocks of limestone pavements surrounded by solution-widened joints (grikes); sometimes unstable or liable to rock owing to solution along the horizontal joints.

Columnar. A form in which the mineral resembles slender columns.

Concretion. A local concentration due to cementation or replacement around a nucleus, the composition of which is different from that of the surrounding sedimentary rock, e.g. flints in chalk.

Cone sheets. A series of dykes in the form of inverted concentric cones, probably due to magmatic pressure from below causing fractures in the overlying rocks which are then infilled by magma, e.g. Skye.

Conglomerate. A sedimentary rock consisting of rounded fragments of any rock cemented in a finer matrix.

Contact metamorphism. The changes in pre-existing rocks caused by an igneous intrusion in the immediate vicinity; it does not usually extend for more than a mile or two.

Cornstone. A rock containing small calcareous concretions etc., found in the Old and the New Red Sandstones.

Corrosion. The abrasive work done by the load of a river or flood in cutting downwards and sidewards.

Country rock. The pre-existing rock of an area, i.e. before it was penetrated by igneous intrusions or mineral veins or changed by metamorphism.

Crags. Shelly and sandy deposits laid down in shallow water during the Pliocene. Found in East Anglia.

Crystals. Bodies bounded by plane surfaces arranged on a definite plan which expresses the internal atomic arrangement.

Crystal systems. All crystals belong to one of the six crystal systems which are defined according to the relative lengths of, and angles between, their crystallographic axes:

Cubic. The three axes are all equal and at right angles.

Tetragonal. The two horizontal axes are equal, but the vertical axis is longer or shorter; all three axes are at right-angles.

Orthorhombic. The three axes all are of different lengths, but all are at right-angles.

Monoclinic. The three axes are all of different lengths; the vertical and one horizontal axes are at right-angles to each other while the third is inclined to the plane containing the other two.

Triclinic. The three axes are of different lengths and none are at right-angles.

Hexagonal. There are four axes: three are of equal length and lie at 120° to each other in the same horizontal plane, while the vertical axis is at right-angles to this plane.

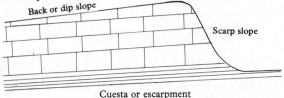

Cuesta or escarpment

Cuesta. A landform due to denudation consisting of a steep scarp slope, capped by more resistant beds which form the more gentle back, or dip, slope.

Current-bedding. A sedimentary structure particularly found in sandy rocks in which the deposits were laid down at an angle to the horizontal, as in the case of sand-dunes or sandbanks. Also known as false bedding.

Deltaic deposits. Sands and clays, possibly with organic remains, deposited in a river delta; characteristically current-bedded.

Dendrites. Tree-like or moss-like markings found on fractures or in inclusions within a mineral or rock; often consists of manganese or iron oxides.

Dip. The maximum angle between the surface of a bed and the horizontal.

Disconformity. A minor break in the sequence of deposition with no angular difference between the upper and lower deposits.

Downthrow. The vertically downward displacement of faulted strata.

Drift. A general term for all superficial deposits especially those of Quaternary age.

Dyke. A sheet intrusion of igneous rock, usually almost vertical, which cuts across the pre-existing beds.

Dynamic metamorphism. The changes produced during orogenic processes which result in structural changes and in the formation of new rocks from the old by low temperature crushing and shearing, or by high temperature recrystallisation.

Enrichment. The secondary concentration of a mineral within a deposit.

Erratic. A glacial-transported rock deposited when the ice melted.

Essential minerals. Those minerals which give a rock its characteristics and by which it is known and named.

Estuarine deposits. Sediments deposited within an estuary. Generally finer-grained and more uniform than deltaic deposits.

Exfoliation. The removal by weathering of successive thin layers of rock, usually under arid conditions.

Extrusive rocks. Fine-grained or glassy igneous rocks formed by the rapid cooling of lavas on the surface of the earth.

Facies. Beds, bed, or part of a bed, having a definite stratigraphical position but of different lithology or fossil content when compared with other deposits of the same stratigraphical position.

Faults. A fault is a fracture in the earth's crust along which a relative vertical or horizontal displacement has occurred. Three terms are used in connection with faults:

Hade. The angle between the plane of the fault and the vertical.
Throw. The relative vertical displacement of strata caused by the fault.
Heave. The relative horizontal displacement caused by the fault.

There are three types of faulting:
Normal. The fault is nearly vertical with the hade to the downthrow side of the fault.
Reversed. The hade, which is usually less than 45°, is to the upthrow side of the fault.
Tear. A line of fracture in which the relative displacement is horizontal, with little or no vertical movement.

Fault scarp. A scarp running along the upthrow side of a fault.

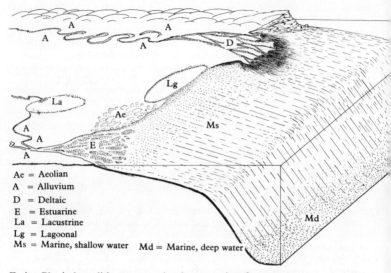

Facies. Physical conditions govern the characteristics of contemporaneous deposits

Ae = Aeolian
A = Alluvium
D = Deltaic
E = Estuarine
La = Lacustrine
Lg = Lagoonal
Ms = Marine, shallow water   Md = Marine, deep water

Fault-line scarp. A steep slope, originally a fault scarp, which has been eroded back until it is more or less parallel to the fault but is no longer on it.

Felspars. The most important group of rock-forming minerals consisting of the silicates of aluminium and varying amounts of those of potassium, sodium, calcium and barium. The identification of the individual felspars is difficult except in thin sections under a geological microscope, as the chemical composition grades from one member of the series into the next, while the physical properties are almost identical. (*Col:* whitish, greyish, or pinkish. *Cl:* two planes at, or nearly at, right-angles. *H:* about 6.0. *SG:* 2.5–3.0.) Orthoclase can be distinguished from plagioclase in hand specimens by the absence of the fine striations caused in the latter by repeated (lamellar) twinning.

The major groups and felspars are as follows:

Orthoclase	
Microcline	Alkali Felspars
Albite	
Labradorite	Plagioclase Felspars
Anorthite	

Fibrous. A mineral form consisting of fine thread-like strands.

Flagstones (Flags). Well-stratified sediments, usually fine-grained sandstones, with shaly partings along which they split.

Fluviatile deposits. The sediments which have been laid down by a river or flood.

Folds. The bending of strata caused by earth movements; the two principal types are: Anticlines in which the fold is arched upwards and the limbs dip away from the axis, and Synclines in which the fold is arched downwards and the limbs dip towards the axis. These folds may be further described as: *Symmetrical:* where the limbs of the fold dip at equal, or nearly equal, angles; *Asymmetrical:* where the limbs of the fold dip at considerably different angles; *Pitching:* where the axis of the fold is inclined to the horizontal, so that the fold enters the ground at an angle; *Complex:* where a major fold consists of a number of minor ones, thus giving either an anticlinorium or a synclinorium. Other types of folding include:

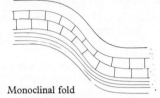

Isoclinal fold

Monoclinal fold

Isoclinal. This occurs in areas of intense folding where both limbs of each of many folds, which may have been partly overturned, dip in the same direction and at almost the same angle.

Monoclinal. In which only one limb has been formed.

Overfold. In which both limbs dip in the same direction but usually at different angles.

Recumbent. In which both limbs dip in the same direction and are almost horizontal.

Foliation. The straight, wavy or contorted, parallel structure in schists, which result from the re-orientation and/or the development of new minerals under great pressures during regional metamorphism.

Fossils. The remains and traces of animals, plants, etc., which are found in sedimentary rocks; these include bones, shells, plant remains, moulds, casts, animal tracks and such inanimate things as rain-pitting and water-ripple marks.

Fracture. The surface characteristics of a mineral broken unnaturally, e.g. by a hammer blow.

The most common types of fracture are:

Conchoidal. The fracture-surface consists of concentric curves, resembling shell growth-lines, diminishing towards the point of percussion, e.g. volcanic glasses, quartz and flint.

Sub-conchoidal. As in conchoidal but far less marked.

Even. The fracture-surface is flat or nearly so, e.g. chert.

Uneven. The fracture-surface is minutely rough.

Hacky. The fracture-surface is composed of jagged edges, like broken cast-iron.

Earthy. The fracture-surface is smooth but irregular, e.g. Chalk.

Ganister. A compact grey rock with a splintery fracture, composed of fine to medium grains of quartz in a siliceous cement. It occurs below coal seams in the Coal Measures.

Geode. The inside of a hollow concretion or nodule, the walls of which are lined with crystals.

Geosyncline. A major structural feature consisting of a long and relatively narrow deep trough, in which a great thickness of sediments were, or are being, deposited.

Grade. An arbitrary description of the size of rock and soil particles measured according to their diameter:

Clay and Mud	less than 0.002mm	Gravel	2–10mm
Silt	0.002–0.02mm	Pebbles	10–100mm
Fine Sand	0.02–0.2mm	Boulders	over 100mm
Coarse Sand	0.2–2mm		

Granular. A form in which the mineral is in grains.

Grikes. The vertical joints, especially in limestone pavements of Carboniferous age, which have been greatly widened by solution. They may contain exotic vegetation

Hardness. The comparative hardness of a substance with reference to Moh's scale of hardness which is purely arbitrary:

1. Talc — Greasy feel.
2. Gypsum — Scratched by finger-nail.
3. Calcite — Scratched by brass or copper pin.
4. Fluorspar — Scratched by knife.
5. Apatite — Scratched by knife with difficulty.
6. Orthoclase — Scratched by file.
7. Quartz — Scratched by file with difficulty.
8. Topaz
9. Corundum
10. Diamond

Hog-back

Hog-back. A cuesta in which both slopes are inclined at the same angle.

Igneous rocks. A general term covering the three types of rock which are of magmatic origin. These are:
Extrusive or Volcanic rocks which have solidified quickly on the surface.
Hypabyssal rocks which solidified more slowly within the earth's crust.
Plutonic rocks which solidified under pressure at great depth.

Inclusion. Any foreign material, including gas, enclosed in other minerals or rocks.

Inlier. An outcrop of older rock completely surrounded by younger rocks.

Interfluve. A subsidiary ridge separating two adjacent river valleys.

Intrusive rocks. Igneous rocks which have been injected into the earth's crust without reaching the surface, but which may later be exposed as a result of denudation.

Iron pan. A hard layer of hydrated iron oxide, found beneath sands, gravels or podzolised soils, which has been formed by the deposition of iron salts leached from the layers above.

Joints. Usually horizontal or vertical breaks in almost any rock produced by stress or twisting; in sedimentary rocks, they are mostly perpendicular to the bedding planes.

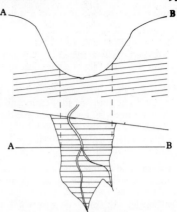

Inlier: section and plan. Older rocks hatched

Laccolith. A convex flat-floored igneous intrusion which has arched up the overlying strata; generally rather thick in comparison with breadth.

Lacustrine deposits. Sediments which have infilled a lake, ranging from pebbles at the edges to muds and clays in the depths.

Lava. Magma which issued from a volcano or fissure and solidified after losing its volatile constituents and cooling.

Lamellar. A form in which the mineral appears as separable leaves or plates.

Leaching. The removal by percolating water of mineral salts or organic matter from a higher to a lower stratum.

Lenticular. Beds or minerals occurring in the form of a double-convex lens or a greatly flattened ball.

Limestone pavement. A horizontal or nearly horizontal outcrop of limestone, usually Carboniferous, divided into rounded blocks (clints) by solution-widened joints (grikes).

Loam. A soil containing approximately equal parts of sand and clay, with some silt.

Lode. A long narrow often twisting vein which is rich in minerals.

Loess. A fine-grained, yellow or buff silty material which originated under arid conditions such as glacial rock-flour or the finer parts of desert sands and was then wind-transported; generally forms thick, unstratified deposits. Where it is suitable for brick-making it is known as brickearth.

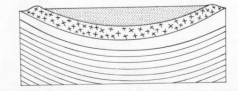

Lopolith

Lopolith. A basin-like lens of intrusive igneous rock, often of considerable extent.

Lustre. The surface shine on a mineral; the most common terms used are:

Metallic   The ordinary shine of a metal.
Sub-metallic   The feeble shine of a metal.
Vitreous   The shine of freshly-broken glass.
Sub-vitreous   The feeble shine of broken glass.
Resinous   The shine of resin.
Pearly   The shine of a pearl.
Silky   The shine of silk, often found on fibrous forms.
Adamantine   The shine of a cut diamond.
Brilliant   Brightly sparkling.
Splendent   Bright, capable of reflecting like a mirror.
Dull   No lustre.

Magma. The mobile igneous mass containing large amounts of gases, including steam, which rises and erupts from volcanic vents and fissures or is injected into pre-existing rocks.

Malleable. Minerals, slices of which can be hammered flat.

Mammillated. A mineral form consisting of large mutually interrupting spherical surfaces.

Marl. A clay or loam deposit (including soil) containing some forms of calcium carbonate.

Marlstone. A consolidated marl.

Mineral. A naturally-occurring element or compound of fixed chemical composition and with definite chemical and physical properties.

Mud. An unconsolidated sedimentary rock of very fine-grained, clay-like material often containing a considerable proportion of water.

Mudstone. An unstratified, fine-grained, clay-like, compact sedimentary rock.

Nodule. Any separate concretionary body.

Non-sequence. A minor break in the stratigraphical sequence with no obvious angular difference between the upper and lower beds.

Off-lap. A succession of conformable beds along the margin of an emerging landmass, in which each bed covers a smaller area than the preceding one.

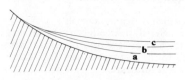

Off-lap

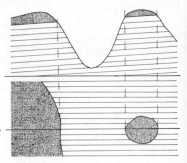

Outlier: section and plan. Younger rocks stippled

Outcrop. The whole of the area over which a rock is visible, or would be visible if there were no soil cover.

Outlier. An outcrop of younger rock completely surrounded by older rock.

Overlap. A conformable sequence of beds in which each bed extends beyond the boundary of the one beneath it; found on the margin of a sinking landmass.

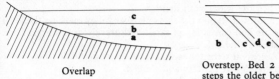

Overlap

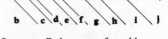

Overstep. Bed 2 unconformably oversteps the older beds b – j

Overstep. An unconformable bed which lies across the edges of dipping beds of older rocks, thus overstepping each in turn.

Overthrust. A reversed fault of low hade, often nearly horizontal, in which one rock mass may be pushed for a considerable distance, sometimes many miles, over another as a result of earth movements.

Permeable. Rocks which may or may not be porous, but through which water can pass, e.g. through the joints in granite.

Phacolith. A small lenticular igneous mass which occupies either the crest of an anticline or the trough of a syncline; its form is produced by folding after intrusion.

Phacolith

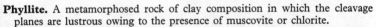

Phyllite. A metamorphosed rock of clay composition in which the cleavage planes are lustrous owing to the presence of muscovite or chlorite.

Pillow lava. Folded lava which has solidified under water; resembles a series or jumbled heap of pillows.

Plug. The nearly cylindrical mass of solidified lava which occupies the vent of a dormant or extinct volcano.

Pneumatolysis. The process by which minerals are formed or altered by hot fluids during magmatic intrusions.

Porous. Rocks with spaces (pores) between the particles; most, but not all, are permeable.

Pothole. A circular depression worn in solid rock in a water course by stones swirled round by the current; also used, in a non-geological sense, for a swallow hole.

Pyroxenes. A large and important group of minerals consisting of iron, magnesium and other silicates which are found in igneous rocks; distinguished by the angle between the two cleavage planes, or prism faces, which is nearly 90° (120° for amphiboles). The most common member is augite.

Radiating structure. A form in which long fibres or crystals diverge from a central point.

Ragstone. A coarse hard sandstone which breaks up into thick slabs.

Regional metamorphism. The total of all the changes due to metamorphism effective over a large area, as opposed to the local effects of contact meta-morphism.

Reniform. A kidney-shaped form of a mineral, e.g. kidney iron ore.

Ring dyke. An almost vertical dyke or series of dykes which form a rather irregular ring and become wider with depth.

River terrace. An almost flat step in the side of a river valley marking the level of a former flood-plain and consisting of sands and gravels; if more than one are present the highest is the oldest.

Rudaceous rocks. A general term for sedimentary rocks consisting mainly of the larger grade material, e.g. pebbles and shingle.

Secondary minerals. Minerals formed as a result of the alteration of pre-existing minerals, e.g. kaolin from the orthoclase in granite.

Silification. The process by which silica cements a rock after deposition or replaces existing minerals or organic material which often retain their original structure.

Sill. A concordant sheet of igneous rock resulting from the injection of magma between layers of pre-existing rocks; the thickness varies considerably but is small in relation to the area.

Stellate. A mineral form in which radiating crystals form a star-shape.

Streak. The name given to the colour of the powder of a mineral.

Strike. The horizontal direction at right-angles to the direction of the dip of a rock and in the same plane.

Subsoil. An intermediate layer grading upwards into soil and downwards into bedrock.

Swallow hole. A small saucer-like hollow in limestone regions through which a stream enters the ground and begins its underground course.

Tabular. A mineral form showing broad flat surfaces.

Tufa. Porous or compact, rarely concretionary, deposits of calcium carbonate found around springs and hot springs.

Tuff. A sedimentary rock composed of angular, often vesicular, fragments of lava in a finer matrix, sometimes ashy; may contain rounded masses of igneous rocks together with pieces of country rocks.

Ultrabasic rocks. Dark-coloured igneous rocks containing a high proportion of ferromagnesium minerals such as amphiboles or pyroxenes, but no free quartz and little or no felspars.

Unconformity. A major break in the stratigraphical sequence caused by non-deposition or erosion, usually with a marked angular difference between the beds above and those below.

Upthrow. The relative upward vertical displacement of faulted strata.

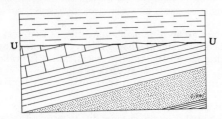

Unconformity (U—U)

KEY TO THE IDENTIFICATION OF SOILS

A Rub the soil sample between the fingers:
It is:
1	predominantly gritty	B
2	predominantly sticky	C 1
3	predominantly silky	C 2
4	sticky or silky and also gritty	C 3
5	NOT sticky, silky or gritty; NOT black	**Loam**
6	NOT sticky, silky or gritty; black or very dark, will mark paper	**Peat** ... D

B Predominantly gritty. Try to mould the soil sample into a thin roll:

1 The sample cannot be so moulded but does not mark the skin. **Sand**

The individual grains are:
i	of the size found on a sea-shore	**Medium Sand**
ii	larger than (i)	**Coarse Sand**
iii	smaller than (i)	**Fine Sand**
iv	hardly visible to the naked eye	**Very Fine Sand**

Note: these subdivisions can be applied in all cases where sand is present.

2 A thin roll can be formed, but the soil marks the skin:

The roll breaks when bent double **Loamy Sand**
The roll does not break when bent double:
   a The surface can be polished with the thumb **Sandy Clay**
   b The surface cannot be so polished **Sandy Loam**

C Roll soil sample into a ball and polish it with your thumb.
1 Sample is sticky; can be balled and polished:
   Ball very resistant to deformation **Clay**
   Ball fairly resistant to deformation **Clay Loam**
2 Sample is silky; can be balled but not polished:
   Ball fairly resistant to deformation; silky **Silt**
   Ball has little cohesion and probably crumbles **Silty Loam**

	Ball feels smooth; fairly resistant to deformation	**Silt Loam**
3a	Sample is sticky and gritty; can be balled and polished	**Sandy Clay Loam**
3b	Sample is silky and gritty; can be balled but not polished	**Sandy Silt Loam**
D	Not sticky, silky or gritty; black or very dark in colour:	
	Sample is firm, coherent and tough, but not plastic; plant structures may be visible; often spongy.	**Fibrous Peat**
	Sample may appear fibrous, but is soft becoming almost paste-like under pressure.	**Pseudo-fibrous Peat**
	Sample is plastic when wet and powdery or granular when dry; no plant structures remain.	**Amphorous Peat**

SOILS

Introduction

We are inclined to take soil for granted though it is in fact of fundamental importance and just as much an integral part of landscape as are the hills and valleys. On it depend both vegetation and animal life; beside reflecting climatic and vegetational changes, it also records its own misuse, which can be ruinous if allowed to continue unchecked.

Soils are composed of *mineral material* derived from the parent rock (whether drift or solid) in the form of particles in one or more grades (sand, silt or clay); *humus* formed by decomposition of organic debris, and *air and water*. Plants are supported and supplied with the essential inorganic foods and water by the soils in which they grow.

Pure mineral soils do exist and are known as 'Skeleton Soils'; they consist of gravels, shingle, scree and blown sand, but provide little or no nourishment for any except the lowest forms of life (mosses and lichens), which assist weathering processes to break down and hold the mineral particles, while their remains provide the initial humus necessary for more advanced plants to begin colonising the area. These in turn die, decay and so add further humus to the soil. The time factor is, therefore, an important one and the immature soils found in parts of the Highlands, which were still covered by valley glaciers some 6,000 years ago, contrast with the mature soils of parts of southern England, which have had hundreds of thousands of years to develop.

Soil Texture

The mineral or inorganic part of the soil is a mixture of stones and particles of sand, silt and clay (for size ranges see p. 94) each with different properties and degrees of chemical activity.

Soil Constituents

Sand grains consist of chemically inert silica and their irregular shapes allow both air and water to pass easily through the spaces (pores) between them.

Silt particles are usually more chemically complex, but are also usually inert. However, their smaller size reduces the pores and they may block the pores between larger particles.

Clay particles are minute and have a large surface area in relation to their volume. They are also both chemically active (taking part in base exchange) and colloidal, possessing the power to absorb water which causes them to swell and produce a sticky mass, though they shrink on drying out to give an almost brick-hard lump. In excessively acid conditions the particles clot (flocculate) to form an 'acid' clay which is completely unsuitable for most plants, while in excessively alkaline conditions the clots break up (deflocculate).

Calcium is the usual base in British clays, thus allowing the formation of a crumb structure; but if the calcium is replaced by sodium, as when the land is seriously flooded by sea-water, a very sticky impervious mass is formed, which needs treatment with gypsum to replace the lost calcium before the land can again be cultivated. On the heavy clays under cultivation, crumb formation is aided by the addition of lime and humus, often in the form of farmyard manure.

Humus consists of dead organic remains on or in the soil, which have been attacked chemically or by fungi and, principally, by certain bacteria; these break down the complex substances into chemically simpler ones which other plants can absorb through their roots. In addition, humus increases the water retentive power of the soil, which is particularly important on porous soils containing a high proportion of sand, and helps in the formation of a 'weathering complex' in which complicated chemical reactions occur in aqueous solution. Finally, the more slowly decomposing material helps to open up the soil, aiding both aeration and drainage. Earthworms greatly assist in the mixing of humus from the surface with the mineral material of the lower levels, but are adversely affected by excessive acidity and are not found in soils of pH greater than 4.5.

Humus may be divided into *Fresh humus*, which has not yet decomposed and retains its structure, and *True humus*, which is dark-coloured, shows little or no trace of its original structure, and is mixed with partially decomposed material and decomposition products.

Surface humus is found in two forms, mild humus (mull) and raw humus (mor). Mull is formed under favourable conditions of moderate temperature, rainfall, and good aeration where there are nitrates and essential minerals available, i.e. under deciduous woodlands, giving leaf-mould. Mor is formed under less favourable conditions of low temperatures, a lack of basic ions, especially calcium, giving an acid soil in which earthworms are scarce or absent, i.e· heaths, moors and under coniferous forests.

Air and water are two soil constituents which are frequently overlooked, but their presence and free passage through the soil is one of the prime factors in cultivation. Not only is air necessary for the existence and successful function- ing of many beneficial bacteria and other soil organisms, but its exclusion can lead to chemical changes in the soil itself. Water affects both the soil and any crop grown in it. In excess it can cause waterlogging with all its accompanying evils, whilst a lack of water may cause a decrease of yield, wilting or a total crop failure and can cause a breakdown in crumb structure within the soil. Here the operative factor is not the annual rainfall but the effective water supply, taking into account both the seasonal distribution (since soil already saturated cannot take up more water, which is therefore lost as run-off) and the ability of the soil to retain water. A soil with good water retentive powers like loam, having absorbed larger amounts of water is less affected by a short period of drought than a sandy soil which retains little.

Crumb Structure

Under favourable conditions, soil particles collect together to form irregularly shaped porous 'crumbs', each about $\frac{1}{8}$ inch in diameter and almost a miniature soil in itself, and yet with adequate space between them to allow a good circula- tion of air and water. This structure is largely dependent on the presence of sufficient humus and is particularly common under grass – especially lucerne – but it can be destroyed by overheating, drying or by heavy rain which breaks down the surface crumbs so that their constituent particles 'glaze' the surface, effectively sealing it against the free passage of air and restricting the further percolation of water. The establishment and maintenance of these crumbs is one of the major objects of cultivation.

Soil Classification

Both the forms of weathering and the vegetation are largely dependent upon climate, so that it is not surprising to find that the world (zonal) soils are more closely related to climatic and natural vegetational regions than to the minera- logical composition of the parent rocks. In Britain, only two of these zonal soils are found:

Podzols   These are heavily leached soils in the wettest areas, or very light (sandy) soils, covered by coniferous forests or heaths, where the raw humus accumulates on the surface producing acids which remove the bases, if any, from the upper (A) horizon together with the sesquioxides, leaving a bleached silvery-grey sand. Below this is a darker (B) horizon containing the precipitated humic compounds, and still lower are the coarse-grained redeposited iron oxides, which may form a more or less continuous 'iron-pan'. The excess acidity of the soil prevents the activity of earthworms, which would otherwise aid the dis- persal of the surface humus.

Brown Earth Soils   Here there is less leaching than in podzols due to lower rainfall, higher evaporation or better water retention. Although soil may not be rich in bases, neither is it extremely acid. Under natural vegetational cover of deciduous forests or scrub, the humus is quickly converted into leaf-mould, a mild humus, and mixing occurs with the help of abundant earthworms. Because

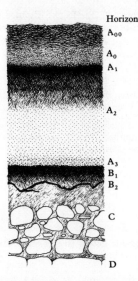

Horizon
A_{00}
A_0
A_1
A_2
A_3
B_1
B_2
C
D

Podsol: a leached soil (see page 104)

of the lack of acidity leaching of the sesquioxides of iron and aluminium does not take place.

Some pedologists recognise a third type, the Grey-brown Podzolic Soils, but this is usually regarded as intermediate between the other two types.

Soil Series

Just as biological orders are subdivided into genera, so the zonal soils are broken down into Soil Series and here the parent mineral rock plays a critical role.

A soil series is a group of soils which are alike in the following essentials:

Natural drainage.

Geology, both of the parent rock and the underlying strata. The effect of the former is obvious as it determines chemical composition, but the rocks immediately beneath the soil, either solid or drift, have a marked effect on drainage and rate of weathering, which can alter the characteristics of the soils. A resistant rock such as granite weathers slowly and drainage is restricted to lateral flow within the soil above it, unless the granite has been subjected to stresses and strains producing joints down which water can pass. In contrast, on poorly-cemented sandstones water is able to percolate easily downwards, whilst where the underlying rocks are impervious and near to the surface, both water and roots are prevented from penetrating downwards by a permanently waterlogged layer.

Topography. This is especially important in respect of: (a) aspect, in that a south-facing slope receives more sun than a north-facing one, providing always that the slopes are not so steep and the valleys so narrow that sunlight cannot reach them; (b) altitude, which not only affects the form of weathering and the temperature, which in turn affects the rate of vegetation growth and decay, but also the amount and seasonal distribution of rainfall; (c) effective distance from the sea, that is the distance covered by the rain-bearing winds, and the character of the ground over which they pass.

The colour of the surface soil.

The manner of formation. The soil may have been developed mainly from rocks on that site, or may have been deposited by water, ice or wind.

Soil profile. This is a vertical section from the surface down to underlying unaltered rock. It is usually broken up into a number of more or less horizontal layers, or horizons, which usually differ in one or more of the following: composition, colour, texture.

Soil

Horizon

A_{00}	*Raw Humus*, uncompressed, fresh organic debris (leaves, etc.), largely undecomposed. No mixing with mineral soil.	
A_0	*Humus*, from organic debris, mainly decomposed, or at least partially so, but the more resistant structures may still be discernible. Usually some mixing with mineral soil.	
A_1	*Mineral soil* darkened by incorporated humus. The thickness varies considerably. Some leaching of soluble salts may occur.	The A horizon is characterised by the presence of humus from organic residues, and by leaching, which results in a greyish tinge becoming progressively more pronounced.
A_2	*Light-coloured;* humus and sometimes iron and aluminium oxides (the sesquioxides) have been leached out.	
A_3	*Transition to B horizon*	
B_1	*Darker-coloured layer* containing redeposited humic material.	The B horizon is characterised by the deposition of soluble material leached out from A horizon and the surface humus.
B_2	*Any sesquioxides* (oxides of iron and aluminium) leached out from above are deposited and may form 'iron-pan'.	
B_3	*Transition to parent material*	
C	*Parent rock*, partly weathered and broken up by root actions, etc.	The parent rock is not strictly a part of the soil profile.
D	*Unaltered parent rock*	

Some pedologists classify both C and D horizons as C horizons, but the matter is of rather academic interest only.

Soil reaction. This is a measure of soil acidity or alkalinity, and is expressed as numbers on the pH scale, where a pH value of 7 indicates a neutral soil, while lower values show increasing acidity, and higher ones increasing alkalinity.

Prevailing climate. This is important in two major factors, temperature and rainfall. Here seasonal variation must be considered as well as the annual figures, because while two places may have the same total rainfall, if it all falls during a period when growth is restricted by low temperature, then little may be available during the growing period. In the same way, average temperatures can produce incorrect conclusions, as soils developed in areas with very cold winters and hot summers are quite different from those in areas where there is a more equitable climate. Plant growth is normally restricted to the period when the temperature exceeds 42°F, and in places where the minimum temperatures are greater than this growth can continue throughout the year.

While all members of a soil series are alike in all eight respects, soils can vary considerably in texture, and it is on texture that soil types (soils in the everyday conversational sense) depend.

Soil Types

These are named after the constituent, or constituents, which gives the soil its characteristic texture and other properties, but not necessarily the constituent that forms the greatest proportion of the soil. Thus a 'clay' may contain less than 40% of clay-sized particles.

Sandy Soils. These are mainly large particles, containing at least 45% fine and coarse sand and rarely more than 10% clay, with the result that they have little coherence but ample pore space which allows the easy penetration of air, water and roots. This combined with their poor water retention may cause crops to 'burn' in a dry summer, while any minerals or humus are rapidly washed down by draining water. For this reason these soils are often described as 'hungry', and constant manuring is necessary to increase the available plant food and water retention. An old method of improving sandy soils was by 'marling', the spreading and ploughing in of large quantities of clay, but this was always expensive and was only practical if the clay outcropped nearby.

As these soils warm up rapidly in spring, they are suitable for market gardening, especially where the permanent water table is not far below the surface.

Under natural conditions, or in coniferous plantations, calcium is rapidly leached out, leading in turn to an increase in acidity and the leaching of iron and aluminium oxides and their redeposition at lower levels gives a typical podzol.

Heath (*Erica*) and Heather (*Calluna*) are common vegetation where the land is not grazed, but these are replaced by short grasses, with Sweet Vernal Grass (*Anthoxanthum odoratum*) and Ragwort (*Senecio jacobaea*) when repeatedly grazed, while Sessile Oaks (*Quercus petraea*), Wavy Hair Grass (*Deschampsia flexuosa*) and Sheep's Sorrel (*Rumex acetosella*) are found on the more acid soils.

Clay Soils. These contain at least 35% clay-sized particles, as well as a high proportion of other fine-grained material, with the result that the pores are small and the movements of air and water are restricted. In addition, clay particles take up water with an increase in volume, producing a sticky mass; claylands are thus liable to 'puddle' in wet weather, sealing the surface so that they can neither be grazed nor worked when wet. The particles contract on drying out, and in hot sun deep cracks are left between brick-hard lumps. Although unfavourable to many plants because of poor aeration, they are rich in minerals and with improved drainage, which has ranged from the old ridge and furrow system to modern tile and mole drains, together with the spreading of lime and artificial or farmyard manure before early ploughing, the soil texture is considerably improved, while the crumb structure is less likely to disintegrate. The use of powerful crawler tractors and other modern equipment, with the improved seed varieties has made profitable arable farming possible, but much clayland is still put down to permanent grass and clover for cattle pasture.

The old description of 'cold' or 'late' soils referred to the slowness with which soil temperature rose in the spring, while in the days of horse-drawn ploughs the tenacity of the clay was shown by such terms as 'two-horse' or 'eight-horse' land, indicating the size of the plough team needed.

The natural vegetation of the claylands was chiefly Oak forest (*Quercus robur*) with Ash and some Thorn.

Silty Soils.   These are favourable to many plants since they contain a considerable proportion of medium-sized particles. Characteristics are intermediate between those of sands and clays, but with far less tendency to 'puddle' or 'bake' than the latter.

Loamy Soils.   These are a mixture of sand, silt and clays, and combine the coherence and water retentive powers of clays with the aeration, drainage, response to fertilisers and ease of working of sands, to produce the best soil for all-round farming. Although they cannot be worked when wet, the excess moisture drains away quickly. Lime and other basic minerals may be leached out once the deciduous forest cover has been removed, and replacement is necessary, especially if the rainfall is heavy.

Special Soils

Calcareous Soils.   Contain calcium carbonate ($CaCO_3$) as powder or as small lumps, but since it is soluble in water containing dissolved carbon dioxide, e.g. rainwater, the surface soils may show calcium deficiency due to solution. Thus soil reaction can vary from alkaline to neutral, or even to acid, while the colour varies from whitish to grey on the Chalk, and from brown to reddish when the underlying rocks are of other limestones.

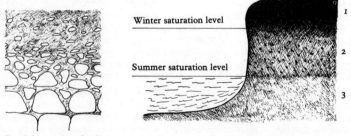

Rendzina: a dwarf soil   Gley: a riverside soil

Winter saturation level

Summer saturation level

1

2

3

Rendzinas. Found on steep limestone slopes, especially Chalk, and consist of a dark, stable, humus-rich A horizon that is constantly saturated with calcium carbonate, washed down from the higher levels, and which may be present as free particles or as small lumps. There is little or no leaching. The B horizon is absent, as rainwater either runs off quickly or percolates the underlying limestone.

Gley Soils (also known as Glei, Meadow or Riverside Soils).   Occur where the water table is comparatively near the surface and there is a marked difference between the summer (minimum) and the winter (maximum) levels, so that some levels of the soils are alternatively waterlogged and drained. They are found on valley floors beside a lake or water course, or where the soil is underlain by a relatively impervious rock. Three distinct levels or zones can usually be distinguished:

1. A dark brown or black upper level containing abundant humus and decomposing organic matter, above the higher saturation level.
2. A lighter brown or grey layer, sometimes with a faint blue tinge, mottled red or orange due to the alternating oxidation when aerated and reduction under waterlogged conditions of iron compounds.
3. A bluish-grey lower layer, below the permanent saturation level, in which all the iron compounds have been reduced to the ferrous state.

   A special case is the Surface Water Gley (*pseudoglei*), where a shallow soil is underlain by an impervious rock, such as heavy boulder clay, but where no permanent water table exists. These soils are rarely more than six to eight inches deep, and dark greyish-brown and heavy in texture, passing into a lighter coloured, red- or orange-mottled, lower layer, which lies directly on the impermeable rock. The whole soil is characterised by a marked prismatic structure passing upwards.

Waterlogged Soils

A   Mineral Soils

Swamp.   The soils are just above summer (dry season) water level. In Britain, it is chiefly covered by tall grasses, sedges and rushes.

Marsh.   This occurs where the water table is normally at about ground level. As the land level is raised by deposition drying out begins and grasses and herbs begin to compete with the marsh plants, increasing retention of alluvial deposits, further raising the level so that the area becomes grassland (water meadow). This is followed by invasions of Willows, Birch and Alder. A further rise in level due to accumulated humus allows the establishment of damp oakwoods.

B   Organic Soils

Peat is formed in areas of high rainfall, where the partially decayed plant remains are waterlogged and continue to accumulate in the absence of air. Succeeding generations of plants grow on top of the compressed remains of earlier ones, building up a considerable thickness. If the upper layers dry out due to a change in physical conditions, the plants cannot survive and are replaced by a different group, while the peat itself may disintegrate.

Peat Bog.   This occurs where the peat is strongly acid and structures are usually well-preserved. Two layers may be distinguished, an upper dark brown, fibrous recent layer and an older black lower layer.

Peat bogs can be divided into (a) Hill bogs, which form on elevated flat or gently sloping areas of very high rainfall, but where drying winds may sometimes partially dry out the surface, and (b) Low bogs, which are found at low altitudes of low rainfall, where the underlying rocks are impervious or the drainage is otherwise impeded.

The vegetation varies from Sphagnum Moss, Cotton Grass (*Eriophorum* spp.), Sundew (*Drosera* spp.), Bog Asphodel (*Narthecium ossifragum*) and Sedges (*Carex*) on the wettest parts, through Cotton Grass and Deer Grass (*Scirpus cespitosus*) to *Molinia, Calluna* and Bilberry (*Vaccinium myrtillus*) on the driest.

Fen Peat. This is found where the water entering waterlogged peat is alkaline, as a result of flowing through calcareous or basic rocks. The humic acid in the peat has been neutralised and the fen peat thus gives a neutral to alkaline reaction. It is dark, usually black, in colour and often sooty in appearance, lacking any structure although it may contain some vegetable fragments.

The vegetation largely depends upon the depth of water with Reedswamp, characterised by the Common Reed (*Phragmites*) being succeeded by 'Carr' (fen scrub) with Creeping, White and Crack Willows, Alder, Buckthorn and Bog Myrtle (*Myrica gale*). This is followed in turn by Common Buckthorn and Guelder Rose (*Viburnum opulus*), while Hawthorn is frequently found. In East Anglia, Saw Sedge (*Cladium mariscus*) is found during the transition from swamp to fen and along the stretches of open water.

Raised Bogs. Where fen peat continues to develop, the surface will eventually be raised above the level of the alkaline waters; this is a raised bog with Sphagnum Moss and other acid peat plants replacing the fen peat vegetation, though the acidity is usually less than that of the true peat bog.

The vegetation of the raised bogs commonly includes Narrow Cotton Grass (*Eriophorum gracile*) and *Erica tetralix* at the wetter hollows, while Crowberry and Common Cotton Grass (*Eriophorum angustifolium*) are found at the higher levels. *Calluna* may be present in the driest areas.

Valley Bogs. These are found in small depressions on heaths, etc. where the drainage is impeded. In high rainfall areas of the North and West, they also occur in obstructed courses of streams which drain acid rock areas, but these are usually less acid than true peat bogs. The vegetation usually includes the Soft, or Common, Rush (*Juncus effusus*) and Sedges.

Blanket Bogs. These occur in areas of high rainfall, damp air and impeded drainage, covering large areas of Western and Highland Scotland, Ireland, the Pennines and the Dartmoor plateau. Acidic in character, they owe their name to the large area they cover.

The vegetation varies considerably with Sphagnum on the wettest areas, Cotton Grass and Deer Grass on the less wet and *Molinia* present, at least, on the edges. *Calluna* is common on the drier areas. In the South Pennines Tufted Cotton Grass (*Eriophorum vaginatum*) is dominant.

TREES AND SHRUBS

Introduction

The natural vegetation over much of the British Isles consists of woodland, and although the great deciduous woods were cleared long ago many trees remain, often giving the impression from some vantage point that the ground is still more wooded than it really is. Perhaps only the salt-marshes and heaths retain something of their true natural vegetation. The tree-planting of landowners and the Forestry Commission was once mainly geared to commercial needs, but now a greater variety of trees is being planted including some deciduous types.

Despite the many conflicting demands on land, some areas have retained their character and beauty, a fact recognised by some planning authorities, the National Parks Commission, the Nature Conservancy, private bodies and, most important of all, by an increasingly aware public, whose interest in the natural world has been stimulated by mass-communication media, the Wildlife Movement and the creation of 'nature trails'.

In a general book of this type it is not possible to deal with every species for there are over 1,250 different species of trees and shrubs growing in Britain and to deal with any except the more common would demand a whole book. This section therefore consists of an identification key and descriptive notes.

Key to the more common British trees and shrubs

Summary of Key

1.0 Low bush, *h:* under 2′; upper stems erect or ascending.
    1.1 *Ls:* small, linear, entire.
    1.2 *Ls:* ovate to obovate, leathery, hairless, almost sessile.
2.0 Many-spined, dense-topped, dark green, *ES*.
    A. Spines branched.
    B. Spines unbranched.
3.0 Trees with woody needle-like, linear or scale-like ls.
    3.1 *Ls:* needle-like, sheathed in pairs.
    3.2 *Ls:* narrowly linear to needle-like, single, spirally arranged on leading shoots, appear 2-ranked on older ones.
    3.3 *Ls:* needle-like, in whorls of 3.
    3.4 *Ls:* narrowly linear, spirally arranged on leading shoots, clusters from bosses on older ones.
    3.5 *Ls: opp*, linear, single on leading shoots, scale-like on older ones.
4.0 *Ls:* compound.
    4.1 *Ls:* trefoil.

4.2 *Ls:* palmate.

4.3 *Ls:* pinnate.

5.0 *Ls:* simple, markedly lobed.

   5.1 *Ls:* palmately lobed.

   5.2 *Ls:* pinnately lobed.

6.0 *Ls:* simple, *opp.*

7.0 *Ls:* simple, *alt.*

   7.1 *Ls:* toothed, long-stalked.

   7.2 *Ls:* short-stalked, entire or rarely partly minutely or vaguely toothed.

   7.3 *Ls:* short-stalked, toothed.

Abbreviations

Alt	Alternate
D	Deciduous
E	Evergreen
Fl(s)	Flower(s). Followed by month of flowering
h	Height, normally in feet
Lf, Ls	Leaf, Leaves
Opp	Opposite
S	Shrub
Stip	Stipules, stipulate
T	Tree
var	Variety
Fr	Fruit

1.0 Plant a low bush, less than 2′ high; upper stems erect or ascending.

   1.1 *Ls:* small, linear, entire. *Fls:* July–Sept.; terminal spikes. Small round seed capsules.

   A. *Ls: opp,* arranged in 4 rows; almost scale-like, keeled; closely cover new shoots. Lower stems form brown mat. *Fls:* small, purplish-pink, 4 petals, 4-lobed calyx, short stalk; in thin spikes. Acidic heaths and moors. **Heather (Ling)**, p. 145

   B. *Ls:* in whorls of 3. *Fls:* small, ovoid, mouth constricted, petals united.

      i. *Ls:* narrow, blunt; dark green; hairless. *Fls:* bright purple. Drier heaths and moors. **Scottish (Bell) Heather**, p. 145

      ii. *Ls:* rounded apex, smooth; green, white below; fringed with long hair. *Fls:* rose-red, one-sided spike. Sandy heaths Dorset to Cornwall. **Fringed Heath**, p. 145

   C. *Ls:* in whorls of 4, apex blunt.

      i. *Ls:* margins recurved; bright green; hairless. *Fls:* pinkish-purple or white, bell-shaped, in long spikes usually tipped by leafy tuft. Restricted to moors at the Lizard. **Cornish Heath**, p. 146

    ii. *Ls:* green, white below; fringed with long hair. Stems
       and foliage downy. *Fls:* rose-pink, ovoid, in dense
       spikes. Damp peaty soils.   **Cross-leaved Heath,** p. 145

1.2 *Ls: alt,* ovate to obovate, leathery, hairless, almost
    sessile. Many erect, branching stems and creeping
    rhizomes. *Fls:* April–July. $\frac{1}{4}''$, pink. *Fr:* $\frac{1}{4}''$, globular
    berry. Acidic soils.
  A. *DS:* green, hairless twigs. *Ls:* $\frac{1}{2}$–$1''$, round toothed; glossy
    green; closely net-veined. *Fls:* solitary, drooping, axil-
    lary, flask-shaped, calyx not lobed. *Fr:* black.   **Bilberry,** p. 146
  B. *ES:* yellowish-green, warted twigs. *Ls:* $\frac{1}{2}$–$2''$, entire or
    minutely toothed outer half; glossy dark green, paler
    below. *Fls:* bell-shaped, 1–4 fls. in axillary racemes.
    Fr: red.   **Cowberry,** p. 147

2.0 Many-spined, dense-topped, dark green *ES.* Stamens all
    united.
  A. Spines branched, stems furrowed and often bare brown
    below. *Ls:* compound, 3-ld on young shoots, reduced to
    minute scales on others. *Fls:* $\frac{3}{4}''$, bright yellow, solitary, in
    lf-axils, 2-lobed calyx. $\frac{1}{2}''$ seed pod persists till spring.
    Heaths, light acid soils.

    i. *h:* 6′. Erect, deeply furrowed, stout stems and spines.
      Fls: Jan.–June. Calyx very hairy, bracts conspicuous.
              Gorse (Furze, Whin), p. 140

    ii. *h:* 3′. Erect, stiff spines; stems striated. *Fls:* July–
      Nov. Calyx hairy, bracts minute. Wetter acidic soils.
                Summer Gorse, p. 141

    iii. Rarely over $18''$. Striated stems, prostrate or straggling
      slender weak spines. *Fls:* July–Nov. Calyx almost
      hairless, bracts minute. Drier acidic heaths.
                Dwarf Gorse, p. 141

  B. Spines unbranched. *ES h:* 6–$18''$. Straggling or ascend-
    ing spiny stems; young shoots 4-angled. *Ls: alt,* $\frac{1}{4}''$ ovate,
    usually pointed, hairless; dark to bluish green. *Fls:* $\frac{1}{4}''$,
    bright yellow, solitary in lf-axils near ends main branches;
    2 calyx lobes fringed. Seed pod $\frac{1}{2}''$, pointed both ends.
                Needle Furze, p. 140

3.0 Trees with woody, needle-like, linear or scale-like ls.
  3.1 *E:* needle-like ls. sheathed in pairs, mainly on short
    lateral shoots. *Fls:* April. Catkins, males clustered at base,
    females terminal. Minute green cone matures to woody
    cone by Nov. second year.

    a. *h:* 80′. Trunk divides well above ground, stout
      horizontal branches, pyramidal crown. *Ls:* $5''$, dark

green, often curved, stiff, in dense spirals along
shoots. *Fls:* ovoid catkins on new shoots; male
yellow, basal; female reddish, terminal. Ovoid
pointed cones $3 \times 1''$, glossy tawny-brown. Most soils;
tolerant of wind, planted as shelter for other trees.
Austrian Pine, p. 126

b. As (a), but form more pointed and narrower, branches
thinner and shorter, less foliage. *Ls:* 4–6″, soft, bend
at a touch.   **Corsican Pine,** p. 126

c. *h:* 80′. Pyramidal when young, lower branches die off,
by maturity foliage restricted to flattened spheres at
trunk and upper branch ends. Bark becomes rough,
wide fissures separate large plates. *Ls:* $2\frac{1}{2}''$, straight,
stiff, grooved above; bluish-green. *Fls:* May. Cat-
kins; male $\frac{1}{2}''$, yellow, globular; female $\frac{1}{4}''$, ovoid,
pinkish. Conical cone $3 \times 1''$, pale brown, knobbly,
often in clusters of 3.   **Scots Pine,** p. 127

3.2 *Ls:* narrowly linear to needle-like, single, spirally arranged on leading shoots, appear 2-ranked on older ones.

A. *Ls:* 2 white bands below; no lf-pegs; lf-scar conspicuous. *ET h:* 120′. Pyramidal crown, branches whorled.
Fls: April–May. Catkins; male $\frac{1}{2}''$, yellow, cylindrical,
on last year's growth; female green, terminal.

i. *Ls:* 1″, glossy dark green, apex notched, rigid; lf-scar
round. *Fls:* female ovoid, erect, with projecting
bract. Cone $6 \times 2''$, erect, ovoid wide scales. Planted
on moist soils.   **Silver Fir,** p. 124

ii. *Ls:* 1″, light green, paler below, soft, grooved above;
lf-scar elliptical. Large branches, feathery foliage.
Cone $3 \times 1''$, ovoid, pendulous. Planted on sandy
soils.   **Douglas Fir,** p. 127

B. *Lf:* rises from peg on older shoots, which persists after
lf-fall; lf-scar conspicuous, 4-sided, raised. *Fls:* May.
Catkins on new shoots; male yellow or reddish, axillary;
female green or purple, terminal. Large, pale brown cone,
pendulous. *ET h:* 100′

i. *Ls:* $\frac{3}{4}''$, bluntly pointed, dark green, 4-sided each
bearing bluish-grey lines. Pointed crown, loses
lower branches in forest. Cone $5 \times 2''$, rich cream,
apex tapered. Planted sheltered, deep moist soils.
Norway Spruce, p. 126

ii. *Ls:* 1″, flat, sharply pointed, keeled; bluish-green,
silvery-grey below. Cone $4 \times 1''$, apex blunt, pale
cream.   **Sitka Spruce,** p. 126

c. *Ls:* ¾″, linear, pointed; dark green, paler below. *ET h:* 40′. Stout trunk of many fused stems, numerous spreading branches; dense ragged crown. Reddish-brown bark, flaking. *Fls:* April. Single sex tree. Male globular, 6–14 stamens, underside twigs; female bud-like, axillary. *Fr:* ¼″, scarlet fleshy cup, contains 1 seed. Wild on limestone soils, planted in churchyards.   **English Yew,** p. 123

3.3 *Ls:* needle-like, in whorls of 3s, ½″, sharp-pointed; green, central bluish-white stripe above, slightly keeled below. *Fls:* May. Minute catkins. *Fr:* ¼″, globular green berry, turning blue-black. *ES* or *T:* form varies with soil and exposure.   **Common Juniper,** p. 125

3.4 *Ls: alt*, narrowly linear, spirally arranged on leading shoots, clusters from bosses on older ones; bosses persist after lf-fall. *Fls:* March. Catkins.

A. Tall *DT*. Conical crown, single tapering trunk; straight, slender, drooping branches and twigs. *Fls:* small; male yellow discs, solitary; female red or purple, broadly cylindrical, erect.

   i. *Ls:* 1½″, bright green, soft, 20–30 in clusters, widely spaced. Cone 1½ × 1″, ovoid, rough, brown; scales not recurved. Twigs yellowish-brown. **European Larch,** p. 125

   ii. *Ls:* 1½″, bluish-green, blunt, 2 white bands below, clusters 40 +, crowded at ends of long shoots. Twigs reddish-brown. Cone 1 × 1″, globular, brown, scales recurved when ripe. Usually in plantations.   **Japanese Larch**

B. Tall *ET*. Pyramidal when young, foliage later restricted to fan-like masses at ends of trunk and major stout branches. *Fls:* Autumn. Male 2″, cylindrical, erect; female ½″, ovoid, purple, erect. Cones large, barrel-shaped, erect, purplish turning brown; central axis persists. Ornamental.

   i. Branches horizontal, twigs straight. *Ls:* 1″, on upper side of older shoots; green to greyish-green. *Fls:* Male in long terminal clusters. Cone 4 × 2″, ends flattened.
   Cedar of Lebanon, p. 124

   ii. Branches and twigs drooping. *Ls:* 1½″, sharply long-pointed; greenish-grey. Cone 4 × 3″, ends taper to points.   **Deodar (Indian Cedar),** p. 124

3.5 *E Ls: opp*, 1″, linear; single on new shoots, scale-like on older; often appear white-edged, closely pressed to stem

in 4 ranks. Tall cylindrical tree, branches much-divided
towards ends. Catkins; male red, drooping, cylindrical,
on last year's growth; female minute, pale blue, on old
shoots. Cone $\frac{1}{2}''$, spherical, 8 non-overlapping scales.
Ornamental.   **Lawson Cypress,** p. 123

4.0 *Ls:* compound.
  4.1 *Ls:* trefoil.
    A. *DS h:* 6′. Erect, much-branched, dark green stems;
sharply ascending, 4-angled twigs. No spines. *Ls alt,*
stip. *Lflts:* $\frac{1}{2}''$, lance to obovate, pointed, entire; dark
green, silky below; almost sessile. *Fls:* May. 1″, bright
yellow, solo, axillary, 2-lobed green calyx, all stamens
united, long style, spirally coiled. Seed-pod 1–2″, black,
hairy fringe when ripe. Sandy heaths or siliceous soils.

Broom, p. 140

4.2 *Ls:* palmate; lflt size decreases from central lflt; green,
paler below.

    a. *DS:* long, trailing, prickly and sharply-angled stems.
Ls: alt, 3–5 lflts, 3–5″, ovate, shortly-pointed,
sharply toothed. Lf and lflt stalks long and prickly.
Fls: July–Sept. 1″, pink or white, in few-fld racemes.
Fr: compound, fleshy, black berry, each sphere 1-
seeded. Hedgerows and waste. **Bramble (Blackberry),** p. 137

    b. *DT h:* 80′. Stout trunk; huge, dense crown; long
ascending branches. *Ls: opp,* 5 lflts, 10″ downwards,
obovate to oblance, small point, coarsely double-
toothed. Long lf-stalk, lflts (almost) sessile. *Fls:* May.
$\frac{3}{4}''$, white, tinged purple at base, upright panicles
('candles'). *Fr:* prickly green husk, contains 1–3
shiny, rich brown nuts. Largely ornamental.

Common Horse Chestnut, p. 143

4.3 *Ls:* pinnate; lflts dark green, paler below; sessile or nearly
so.
  A. *Ls: alt.*
    i. *DT h:* 30′. Straight trunk, slender ascending branches.
Ls: long grooved stalk; 11–17 equal lflts, 2″, lance,
finely toothed; curved veins, hairy below at first.
Fls: May. $\frac{1}{2}''$, white, in dense flat corymbs. *Fr:* Aug.
Round, red berry $\frac{1}{4}''$, yellow flesh. Usually on hill-
sides.   **Mountain Ash (Rowan),** p. 136

    ii. *DT h:* 80′. Ascending branches form broad crown,
thick smooth grey twigs, contain chambered pith.
Ls: long tapering stalk; 5–9 lflts, terminal much the
largest, basal very small, ovate, entire; aromatic when
bruised. *Fls:* May. Male drooping catkins, green,

many stamens, axillary, last year's growth; female erect, solo or small clusters, terminal. *Fr:* 2″, smooth, ovoid, green, contains 1 wrinkled nut. Prefers deeper southern soils.   **Common Walnut,** p. 132

B. *Ls: opp.* long tapering stalk; lflts pointed, finely toothed.
   i. *DS* or *T h:* 20′. 2–3 irregular main stems, ascending branches; thick grey twigs, white pith core. *Ls:* 5–9 lflts, terminal larger, 1–3″, ovate to lance. *Fls:* May. ¼″, creamy, 5–parted, terminal, in large, flat-topped cymes. *Fr:* round black berry ½″, 4–8 seeds. Waste and scrub on alkaline soils.   **Common Elder,** p. 147

   ii. *DT h:* 90′. Round crown, ascending branches. *Ls:* May. Stalk grooved. 7–13 lflts 3″, lance. *Fls:* April. Minute, no petals, greenish-yellow, in loose panicles, 2 purple stamens or red stigma. Seed near notch of twisted wing; persists till spring. Usually limy damp soils.   **Common Ash,** p. 148

5.0 *Ls:* simple, markedly lobed.
  5.1 *Ls:* palmately lobed, *opp.*
  A. *Ls:* 5-lobed, veins to points of lobes and teeth, heart-shaped. Long-stalked. *Fls:* May. 5-lobed calyx, 8 stamens, yellow anthers; 1 pistil. *Fr:* 2-winged seed.

   i. *DT h :*30′, also *S* in southern hedgerows. Oval crown; twigs shortly hairy. *Ls:* 3″, deeply-cut, rounded lobes, a few rounded teeth; dull green, shortly hairy below; stalk-sap milky. *Fls:* May. ¼″, greenish, erect clusters; no petals. Prefers open, dry, basic soils.
               Common Maple (**Field Maple**), p. 142

   ii. *DT h:* 70′. Large open crown, stout spreading branches; smooth twigs, hairless. *Ls:* 6″, rounded lobes, deeply-cut, a few sharply-pointed teeth; pale yellowish-green, hairy tufts in vein axils below; stalk-sap milky. *Fls:* April. ½″, yellowish, erect corymbs; 5 petals. Prefers dry, limy soils. Resistant to sea-salt and wind.   **Norway Maple,** p. 143

   iii. *DT h:* 90′. Large dense crown, wide-spreading branches often droop; smooth stiff twigs hairless. *Ls:* 6″, wedge-cut lobes, pointed, sharply toothed; dark green, greyish below; stalk-sap clear. *Fls:* May. ¼″, yellow-green, dense drooping panicles; 5 narrow petals. Prefers deep, moist soils. Tolerates sea-salt and wind.   **Sycamore,** p. 143

B. *Ls:* palmately lobed, *alt.*
   i. Hedgerow *DS*, or small *T* with foliage almost to

ground. Twisted stems and twigs, spiny. *Ls:* 1–2″, ovate, narrowly lobed nearly to midrib; dark green, paler and downy in vein axils below; short-stalked, lf-like stipules. *Fls:* May–June. $\frac{3}{4}$″, white, flat corymbs; 5 petals, 5 sepals, 1 style. *Fr:* $\frac{1}{2}$″, ovoid, hard-cased, red berry ('Haw'), 1-seed. Common, often 'laid' as a hedge.   **Hawthorn (Quick),** p. 138

ii. As (i), but less spiny, lobes reach less than halfway to midrib. *Fls:* 2–3 styles. *Fr:* berry 2–3 seeded. Midlands and south.   **May,** p. 138

iii. *DT h:* 40′. Broad crown, spreading branches; young twigs woolly. *Ls:* 3″, ovate, 5–9 triangular lobes, sharply toothed, veins to points, rounded base; green. *Fls:* May. $\frac{1}{2}$″, white, in flat clusters, 15–25 stamens. *Fr:* $\frac{1}{2}$″, ovoid, brownish berry. Local; woods on heavier clays.   **Wild Service Tree,** p. 139

iv. *DT h:* 90′. Large crown, long clean bole in open. Bark: smooth, flakes, showing yellowish-green patches. *Ls:* 5–9″, ovate, 5 broad and shallow lobes, coarsely toothed; green, green-grey below; long-stalked. *Fls:* May. $\frac{1}{2}$″, 2–3 bristly balls, purple styles. *Fr:* globular, burr-like. Widespread, often planted in city streets.   **London Plane,** p. 137

v. *DT h:* 60′. Large spreading crown. Pale grey bark, smooth. Young twigs felted. *Ls:* April. 3″, broadly ovate, 5-lobed, rounded base; glossy dark green, densely white to greyish felted below; veins to points; long-stalked. *Fls:* Feb. Drooping catkins; male (rare) 2–3″ red; female 1″, 2 slender stigmas. *Fr:* dry splitting capsule; ripe July, seeds in white cottony fibres. Warmer soils, mainly southern England.

White Poplar, p. 127

5.2 *Ls: alt,* pinnately lobed.
A. *DT h:* 90′. *Fls:* April–May. Male yellowish drooping catkins, 4–12 stamens; female small inconspicuous, solo or small spikes.

i. Stout trunk, many long, heavy and twisted stems and branches give large rounded crown. *Ls: stip,* 4″, ovate, rounded lobes; green, greyish below; small auricles ('ears') at base. Stalk short, $\frac{1}{2}$″. *Fr:* acorn 1″, bluntly ovoid, scaly cup covers $\frac{1}{3}$; slender stalk 1–3″. Woods, widespread.   **English Oak,** p. 135

ii. Open pyramidal crown, long drooping branches; twigs downy. *Ls:* 5″, narrowly ovate, lobes unequally triangular, points sharp, few irregular teeth, rough

above; dark green, greyish-green below. Stalk under
$\frac{1}{2}''$. Long persistent stipules. *Fr:* acorn, bristly cup
covers $\frac{1}{2}$, sessile. Prefers deep dry soils. **Turkey Oak,** p. 135

  iii. Open, narrower crown; twigs downy. *Ls:* 5", ovate,
deep rounded lobes; dark green, greyish downy below.
Stalk over $\frac{1}{2}''$. Acorn, ovoid, pointed, sessile clusters;
scaly cup covers under $\frac{1}{3}$. Woods on poorer soils of
old siliceous rocks. **Durmast Oak (Sessile Oak),** p. 136

6.0 *Ls:* simple, *opp.*

  A. Much-branched shrubs or small trees. *Ls:* ovate. *Fls:*
May. Small, in axillary clusters. Found on calcareous
soils.

    i. *D:* many 4-angled twigs, green and smooth. *Ls:* 1–3",
pointed, minutely toothed, veins curve forward; dull
green; short stalk. *Fls:* greenish-white, 4 spreading
petals alt. with 4 lobes of calyx, 4 stamens in fleshy
disk, yellow anthers, central pistil. *Fr:* July. 4-lobed
red berry; orange flesh. South of Scottish Highlands.
Common Spindle Tree, p. 142

    ii. *D:* slender stems, with almost perpendicular hairless
twigs, usually with terminal spine. Grey bark becomes
rough, flakes showing orange. *Ls:* 2", pointed, finely
toothed, 2–3 pairs veins follow lf outline; dull green.
Longish slender stalk. *Fls:* yellowish-green on last
year's growth, floral parts in 4s; sexes on separate
trees. *Fr:* bluish-black, globular berry, $\frac{1}{4}''$. Local,
woods and scrub.
Common Buckthorn (Purging Buckthorn), p. 142

    iii. *E:* slender stems and branches; yellowish-green,
4-angled twigs. *Ls:* 1", entire, leathery; dark green,
paler below; almost sessile; persists many years. *Fls:*
greenish-white; male 4 stamens; female top of cluster,
3 stigmas. *Fr:* small, woody, 3 2-horned valves. Local
beechwoods and scrub. **Common Box,** p. 141

7.0 *Ls:* simple, *alt.*

  7.1 *Ls:* toothed, long-stalked.

    A. Tall *DT. Ls:* pointed, unequal heart-shaped base, finely
and sharply toothed; dark green, paler below. *Fls:* June.
$\frac{1}{4}''$, greenish-yellow, 5 petals; in clusters from long, strap-
shaped bract. *Fr:* $\frac{1}{4}''$, yellowish-green nut. Prefers calcareous soils.

      i. *h:* 80'. Rather pointed crown, branches ascend
sharply; young twigs downy. *Ls:* 2", roundish,
sometimes wider than long; axillary tufts below. *Fls:*
erect or spreading 3–10-fld clusters, 5 stamens.

Fr: not noticeably ribbed. Scattered England and
Wales.   **Small-leaved Lime,** p. 144

ii. *h:* 90′. Round crown, spreading branches; young
twigs hairy. *Ls:* 3–5″, broadly ovate; downy below.
Fls: drooping, 2–5 fld clusters, usually 3; more than
5 stamens. *Fr:* 3–5 strong ridges. Welsh Marches
and Humber–Mersey to Scottish Highlands.
                                          Large-leaved Lime, p. 145

iii. *h:* 100′. Rather pointed crown, lower branches arch;
young twigs hairless. *Ls:* 3–4″, broadly ovate; pale
hairy axillary tufts below. *Fls:* 4–10 fld clusters,
drooping, long-stalked; 5 or more stamens. *Fr:* 3–5
weak ridges. South of Scottish Highlands.
                                          Common Lime, p. 145

B. *Ls: stip,* 2½″, ovate to triangular, pointed, leathery, 3–7
pairs of veins parallel to base; dark green; slender stalk.
Foliage scanty. Bark peels in paper-thin strips. *Fls:* Catkins: female, April with ls, cylindrical, on short shoots;
scale 3-lobed; male autumn, axillary, 2 stamens, persist
till spring. *Fr:* minute winged nut. Woods and heaths.

i. *DT h:* 60′. Slender single trunk, drooping branches;
hairless warted twigs. Silvery-grey bark, becoming
marked by dark horizontal 'cuts': basally black and
fissured into raised rectangles. *Ls:* long pointed,
sharply double-toothed. Dry soils.   **Silver Birch,** p. 133

ii. *DT h:* 60′, or *DS.* Divided at base into several stems,
ascending and spreading branches; slender dark
brown twigs downy but not warted. Nearly white
bark, darker basally. *Ls:* sharply and more evenly
toothed. More tolerant of damp soils than (i).
                                          White Birch, p. 132

C. *DT:* slender branches. *Fls:* March, before ls, drooping
catkins; fl with cup-like disk; sexes on separate trees.
Fr: dry splitting capsule, seeds in white cottony fibres.

i. Broad open crowns, spreading branches. Suckering
freely. Smooth, grey bark, except basally on old
trees. *Ls: stip,* 1–4″, roundish to ovate, 10 or less
uneven teeth. *Fls:* 4–12 stamens.

a. *h:* 50′. Twigs hairless. *Ls:* sometimes wider than
long, coarsely blunt toothed; greyish-green. Much
flattened slender stalk causes lf to tremble in least
breeze. *Fls:* 2–4″, scales hairy, divided over half;
anthers red; thick stigmas purplish. Commoner
in the north and west.   **Aspen,** p. 128

b. *h:* 90′. Twigs white, hairy. Bark often marked by
black diamonds. *Ls:* base heart-shaped to rounded,
shallowly toothed; shiny dark green, white felted
below. *Fls:* scales divided less than halfway; thin
purplish stigmas. Damp woods, south of Humber-
Mersey   **Grey Poplar,** p. 127

ii. *h:* 90′. Dark grey or brown bark becomes deeply
fissured, with large round swellings. *Ls,) stip:* 4″,
triangular to roundish, slender pointed, many
(20 +) shallow rounded teeth, translucent border;
dark green, hairless.

a. Broad open crown, often asymmetrical, spreading
branches arch downwards. Wetter soils in south
and central Britain and north-west. **Black Poplar,** p. 128

b. Slender erect branches, very close to trunk give a
columnar outline. Planted for shelter and landscaping.   **Lombardy Poplar,** p. 128

7.2 *Ls:* simple, *alt*, entire or rarely partly minutely or
vaguely toothed.

A. *DS:* long slender stems; often coppiced. *Ls: stip* long,
narrow, tapering to a point. *Fls:* March, before ls. Fens,
marsh and stream-sides. Cultivated for basket-making.

i. *h:* 20′. Pliant, yellowish stems, hairy at first. *Ls:*
5–8″, narrowly lance, finely pointed, margins wavy,
entire; dark green, white felted below; midrib
prominent. *Fls:* dense, ovoid catkins; male 1–2″,
fluffy, brown-tipped scales; 2 stamens, yellow anthers; female 2 long tapering styles. **Common Osier,** p. 130

ii. *h:* 15′. Loose straight stems, glossy twigs, purplish
shading to olive. *Ls:* 2–4″, narrowly ovate to obovate,
rarely minutely toothed near apex; green, bluish-
green below; hairless. *Fls:* erect catkins, scales black-
tipped; male cylindrical, 1 forked stamen, purple
anthers; female ovoid, hairy, 2-lobed stigmas.
                                    Purple Osier, p. 131

B. *DS:* rarely small *T. Fls:* March, before ls, short stalked
catkins, erect at first; male ovoid, two short stamens,
yellow anthers. Common, marsh- and stream-sides.

i. Spreading, long, straight branches; dark twigs,
downy at first. *Ls:* small persistent *stip*, 2–3½″, ovate
to obovate, small bent point; grey-green, grey-felted
below at first, although a few rusty-coloured hairs
may persist in vein-axils. *Fls:* scale apex black;
female two long styles, bifid yellow stigmas. Most
common East Anglian fens.
                      Common Sallow (Grey Willow), p. 130

ii. Erect stems; twigs downy. *Ls: stip* 3″, ovate, small
twisted point, wrinkled, net-veined; dark green,
downy below. *Fls:* dense; male 1½″, fluffy ('Pussy
Willow'), stamens protrude; female two-lobed stigma.
Drier sites than most willows.
Great Sallow (Goat Willow) p, 129

iii. Many spreading branches; slender angular brown
twigs, soon hairless. *Ls:* 2 large persistent ear-shaped
stip. 1–2″, ovate to obovate, wrinkled, veins deeply
impressed; dull green, grey-felted below. *Fls:* Male
¾″; female ½″, two blunt stigmas. Damp acidic soils.
Eared Sallow (Round-eared Willow), p. 129

c. *DT h:* 100′. Broad rounded dense crown, when solitary
trunk divides into several straight ascending stems;
slender widespreading branches droop. *Ls: stip* 1–4″,
ovate, pointed, 5–9 pairs parallel veins, young margins
hairy; bright green, paler below, hair tufts in vein-axils.
Fls: May. Male ½″, purplish-brown, long-stalked tassels;
female green-brown, solo or in 3s, surrounded by bracts.
Fr: four-lobed bristly husk, contains two smooth
triangular brown nuts. Southern half Britain, forms
conspicuous 'hangers' on Chalk.   **Common Beech,** p. 134

d. As (c), but ls are coppery-red.   **Copper Beech,** p. 134

e. *ET h:* 70′. Compact crown to ground level, short
branches. *Ls: stip* 3″, ovate to lance, pointed, margins
sometimes scooped; grey-green, downy below. *Fls:* June.
Catkins on new shoots; male drooping clusters; female
axillary, single or small inconspicuous spikes. *Fr:* ½″, cup
covers over half acorn, single or small clusters; almost
sessile. Sandy soils southern half England and coasts
E. Scotland.   **Holm Oak,** p. 135

7.3 *Ls:* simple, *alt.*, toothed, short-stalked.
a. *Ls:* 3″, ovate with long triangular spiny teeth on lower
branches, sometimes entire on upper ones, leathery;
glossy dark green, paler below. *ET h:* 40′. Compact
pyramidal or cylindrical; retains branches to ground.
Fls: May. ½″, greenish-white, in few-fld clusters on old
shoots. Sexes on separate trees. *Fr:* globular red berry,
3–4 stones. Woods, hedges and scrub, except wet soils or
extreme north.   **Holly,** p. 141

b. *Ls: stip* narrowly ovate tapering to slender point, finely
toothed. *Fls:* April, before ls. Dense cylindrical catkins,
short styles, 2-lobed yellow stigmas. Stream- and marsh-
sides.

i. *DT h:* 70′. Narrow pyramidal crown, ascending branches, ends droop; often pollarded. White rootlets. *Ls:* 2–4″, hairy both sides, dense below; dull green. *Fls:* yellow scales; 2 yellow stamens. Richer damp soils. **White Willow,** p. 129

ii. As (i), but branches erect. *Ls:* less hairy: bluish-green. **Cricket-bat Willow,** p. 129

iii. *DT h:* 70′. Broad crown, often pollarded; stout trunk, nearly erect branches; glossy twigs, easily snap off at base. Red rootlets. *Ls:* 3–6″ becoming hairless; glossy green above, paler below. *Fls:* drooping; scales yellowish; male 2″, on short stalk, 2 yellow-tipped stamens; female 1–3″, narrow. South of Scottish Highlands. **Crack Willow,** p. 131

iv. *DT h:* 40′. Long slender yellowish branches droop almost to the ground. *Ls:* 3″, hairless; green, bluish-green below. *Fls:* erect, 2″, 2 stamens united, purplish or red anthers. Ornamental. **Weeping Willow,** p. 131

c. *Ls:* heart-shaped base, lobes unequal.
DT h: 100′. *Ls: stip,* broadly oval, double-toothed, rough above; dark green, hairy below. *Fls:* Feb., before ls. Small, red, erect, in dense cluster in previous year's lf-scar. *Fr:* 1″, circular, flat-winged seed.

i. Massive straight trunk, a few large spreading branches; multi-domed crown. *Ls:* 2–3″, 10–12 pairs parallel veins. **English Elm,** p. 136

ii. Rounded open crown, trunk divides near base into a few large branches. *Ls:* 3–7″, larger basal lobe overlaps stalk, 12–18 pairs parallel veins; stalk less than ⅛″. **Wych Elm,** p. 136

d. *DT h:* 60′. Oval fluted trunk, gently ascending branches. *Ls: stip* 1–3″, ovate, pointed, rounded or tapering base unequal, sharply double-toothed, wrinkled; glossy dark green, midrib hairy below. *Fls:* April. Many cylindrical catkins; male greenish, drooping from 1-year growth; female erect on new shoots. *Fr:* minute green nut at base of 3-lobed bract. Woods and hedges, especially sandy clays south-east England. **Common Hornbeam,** p. 133

e. *DS:* many branched stems; often coppiced. *Ls: stip* 2–4″, rounded, slender-pointed, slightly unequal heart-shaped base, unevenly and sharply double-toothed, somewhat hairy at first; dull green. *Fls:* Jan.–April, before ls. Few-fld catkins; female bud-like, red protruding stigmas; male autumn, cylindrical drooping ('lamb's tails'), bright yellow anthers. Woods and scrub. **Common Hazel,** p. 133

F. *DT h:* 15′, or *DS.* Rigid black twigs ending in stout thorns. Many twisted branches. *Ls: stip* 1–1½″, oval, sharply toothed; dark green, thinly hairy below. *Fls:* May, before ls. ½″, white stars, solo or paired; 5 petals, 5-lobed calyx. *Fr:* ½″, blue-black fleshy berry, 1 round stone. Hedges, woods and scrub.   **Blackthorn (Sloe),** p. 138

G. *DT h:* 35′. Dense crown or large shrub depending on soil and exposure. *Ls:* 3–5″, ovate, to broadly oval, double-toothed, 9–11 pairs straight veins; green, white-felted below. *Fls:* May. ½″, in loose flat clusters. *Fr:* ½″, globular red berry. Calyx persists. Woods and scrub on calcareous soils.   **Whitebeam,** p. 139

H. *DT h:* 70′. Oval crown, or shrub, with many ascending twisted branches. *Ls: stip* 4″, roundish to obovate, flattened or notched apex, tapering base, irregularly and coarsely toothed; glossy green, paler and hairy axil tufts below. *Fls:* Feb., before ls. Short catkins; male red scales, 4 stamens; female erect, ovoid, covered red-brown bracts, 2 styles. *Fr:* 1″, woody cone. Empty cone persists till spring. Damp, non-acid soils.   **Common Alder,** p. 132

I. *DT h:* 90′. Massive trunk sub-divides into several stout stems. Wide crown, branches arch, ends sag. *Ls:* 5–9″, lance to oblance, pointed, straight veins to sharply even teeth; glossy dark green. *Fls:* June. Erect slender catkins; male 10–20 stamens, golden anthers; female few at base. *Fr:* green husk with branched prickles, 1–3 deep brown nuts. Neutral soils everywhere; oldest in Ross-shire.

Sweet Chestnut (Spanish Chestnut), p. 134

Family Taxaceae

ENGLISH YEW *Taxus baccata*
Description. *ET:* 40'. A very short trunk, consisting of many fused stems in older trees. Numerous spreading branches form a low ragged rounded crown. *Bark:* reddish-brown, thin, peels off in long flakes. *Ls:* spirally arranged, but twisted and flattened to appear two-ranked on all except the young shoots. $\frac{3}{4}''$, linear, rounded at apex, glossy dark green, paler green below. Almost stalkless. *Fls:* March–April. Sexes usually on different trees: males $\frac{1}{4}''$, round, 6–14 stamens, on the undersides of twigs; females minute, green, bud-like, in the leaf-axils. *Fr:* a round fleshy scarlet cup, $\frac{1}{4}''$, containing a yellow-green nut.
Distribution. Wild on limestone soils, especially on the Sussex and Hampshire Downs; also planted in churchyards.

English Yew

Lawson's Cypress

Family Cupressaceae

LAWSON'S CYPRESS *Chamaecyparis lawsoniana*
Description. *ET:* 100'. Tall slender cylindrical. Trunk and much of the short horizontal branches visible. Branches much divided towards flattened leafy ends. *Bark:* brown, thick, often with vertical fissures. *Ls:* opp., young ls, 1", needle-like, green. Adult ls scale-like, closely pressed to the stem hiding it completely, green with white edging. *Fls:* sexes on different trees; catkins: male red, cylindrical, at twig ends; females $\frac{1}{4}''$, green, spherical. *Fr:* spherical woody cones, $\frac{1}{2}''$, only eight scales, all pressed closely together but not overlapping.
Distribution. Mostly in gardens and parks. The most common cypress.

Family Pinaceae

SILVER FIR   *Abies alba*
Description.   *ET:* 120′. A tall narrow pyramidal crown, with a straight tapering trunk and whorled branches almost from ground level when young, later
with a clean bole up to 70′ in forests. Smooth grey twigs.   *Bark:* light grey,
smooth, becoming darker with vertical fissures.   *Ls:* spirally arranged on young
shoots, but twisted and flattened into two ranks on older ones. 1″, needle-like,
apex notched, dark glossy green above, silvery-white below.   *Fls:* April–May.
Males ¾″, yellow, cylindrical; females pale green, ovoid, erect, with projecting
bracts.   *Fr:* erect ovoid cones, 6″ × 2″, with wide woody scales, green changing
to reddish-brown. Central axis remains on the tree after scales fall.
Distribution.   Planted in parks and plantations. Flourishes on most soils.

Silver Fir

Deodar

Cedar of Lebanon

DEODAR (Indian Cedar)   *Cedrus deodara*
Description.   *ET:* 100′. Pyramidal, with a light spire, trunk and bases of
branches visible. Spirally arranged branches and leading shoots droop.   *Bark:*
dark brown, rough, deeply furrowed. Branches smooth.   *Ls:* spirally arranged
on leading shoots, in clusters on older ones. 1½″, needle-like, pointed, dark
green.   *Fls:* sexes on different trees: males 2″, cylindrical, erect; females ½″,
purple, ovoid, erect.   *Fr:* erect ovoid cones, 4″ × 3″, purple when young,
becoming brown. Seeds fall when ripe leaving the central axis on the tree.
Distribution.   Parks and gardens.

CEDAR OF LEBANON   *Cedrus libani*
Description.   *ET:* 80′. Short clean bole 8′, divides into several stems, from
which the branches arch outwards. Often pyramidal when young, becoming
flat-crowned, with the foliage in fans at the branch ends. Twigs smooth.

Bark: brown to dark grey, thick, rough and deeply furrowed. *Ls:* spirally arranged around the young shoots, and in rosettes on the upper side of older twigs. 1″, needle-like; dark green. *Fls:* sexes on different trees: male catkins 2″, cylindrical, in long erect clusters at twig-ends; females ½″, purple, ovoid and erect. *Fr:* erect barrel-shaped cones, 5″ × 3″, purple when young, becoming purple-brown. Development may take three years.

Distribution. Gardens and parks.

COMMON JUNIPER *Juniperus communis*

Description. *ES:* 1–15′, less commonly *ET:* 20′. Shape varies with exposure and soil, ranging from a shapely tree, mainly on the sheltered limestone soils of south-east England, to a low straggling shrub on exposed hillsides in Scotland. *Bark:* red-brown, scaly, flakes off. *Ls:* whorled in threes, ½″, needle-like, sharply pointed, green with central bluish-white stripe above, slightly keeled below. *Fls:* May–June. Catkins: males ¼″, ovoid, solitary, females minute in leaf-axils. *Fr:* an almost spherical fleshy berry, ¼″, green the first year, turning blue-black, with a greyish bloom.

Distribution. S.E. England, Scotland and Ireland.

Common Juniper

European Larch (old shoot)

EUROPEAN LARCH *Larix decidua*

Description. *DT:* 90′. Pyramidal, with a straight tapering trunk, and graceful downward-curving slender branches. Drooping yellowish-grey hairless twigs. *Bark:* brown, thick, rough, often flaking. Deeply fissured at base. *Ls:* spirally arranged, single on leading shoots; in tufts of 20–30, which rise from small bosses, on older twigs. 1″, needle-like, soft, bright green. Deciduous. *Fls:* March–April. Small catkins: males round or cylindrical, yellow, at the end of shoots; females ¾″, round, purple, erect. *Fr:* an ovoid cone, 1½″, rough, black and woody.

Distribution. Mainly in plantations, especially on sandy soils.

COMMON SPRUCE (Norway Spruce) *Picea abies*

Description. *ET:* 100′. A pointed crown with a delicate spire. Branches whorled. In forests, older trees lose lower branches. *Bark:* reddish-brown, smooth, becoming scaly. *Ls:* spirally arranged, pointing in all directions on young shoots, but usually twisted to appear two-ranked on older ones. ¾″, four-sided, needle-like, dark green, with bluish-grey lines on each face. The peg, from which the ls grow, remains on the twig after the ls fall. *Fls:* April–May. Male catkins appear in the leaf-axils, yellow tinged with pink; females 2–4″, green or purple, terminal. *Fr:* hanging cones, 5″ × 2″, pale brown, almost cylindrical with the apex tapering. Seeds ripen in one year. The cone falls whole.

Distribution. Mostly in plantations in sheltered areas with deep moist soils.

SITKA SPRUCE *Picea sitchensis*

Description. *ET:* 120′. The trunk has little taper. Clean bole up to 40′ in forest. Main twigs opp., stiff, yellowish-brown, hairless. *Bark:* greenish-grey, scaly. *Ls:* radially arranged, 1″, linear, sharp-pointed, stiff, bluish-green on one side, silvery-grey on other. Small pegs remain after ls fall. *Fls:* April–May. Male catkins in leaf-axils at the ends of shoots, yellow or red; females terminal, green or purple. *Fr:* hanging cones, 4″ × 1″, blunt-ended, pale brown.

Distribution. Mostly in plantations, in sheltered areas.

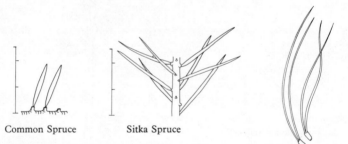

Common Spruce   Sitka Spruce

Austrian Pine

AUSTRIAN PINE *Pinus nigra*

Description. *ET:* 80′. A heavy crown, with long stout horizontal branches. Light brown twigs covered with long narrow plates. *Bark:* brown, rough and deeply fissured. *Ls:* sheathed in pairs, 5″, needle-like, often twisted or curved in young trees, very stiff, do not bend at a touch, glossy dark green. *Fls:* catkins: males in clusters at the base of a shoot; females ovoid at end of young shoots. *Fr:* pointed ovoid cones 3″ × 1″, woody, glossy tawny-yellow. Usually horizontal.

Distribution. Planted in shelter belts for land or other trees, as it is tolerant of high winds.

var. *maritima*, Corsican Pine, crown narrower, branches thinner and shorter, with less foliage. *Ls:* 6″, needle-like, soft, bend at a touch.

SCOTS PINE *Pinus sylvestris*

Description. *ET:* 80′. Pyramidal when young, crown of older trees restricted to flattened spheres at ends of trunk and main branches. Lower branches die off. *Bark:* red-brown, smooth when young, becoming rough with large plates, separated by wide fissures, when mature. *Ls:* sheathed in pairs, 2½″, needle-like, straight, stiff, grooved above, convex below, bluish-green. *Fls:* April–May. Catkins: male ½″, pale yellow, erect, clustered at base of shoots; females ¼″, pinkish-brown, ovoid, at end of young shoots. *Fr:* a conical cone, 3″ × 1″, woody and knobbly, on thick stalks, often in clusters of three.

Distribution. Grows well even on most poor soils, except heavy clays.

Scots Pine

Douglas Fir

DOUGLAS FIR *Pseudotsuga menziesii*

Description. *ET:* 120′. Tall pyramidal, large feathery branches in whorls. Lower branches die off. *Bark:* darkish grey, smooth on young trees, becoming thicker and furrowed. *Ls:* spirally arranged on younger shoots, imperfectly arranged in two ranks on older shoots. 1″, needle-like, grooved, light green above, paler below with two white bands. *Fls:* catkins: males ½″, cylindrical in axils of previous year's ls; females ¼″, green, terminal, on short twigs. *Fr:* oval cones, 3″ × 1″, woody, hanging.

Distribution. Flourishes in deep sandy soils.

Family Salicaceae

WHITE POPLAR *Populus alba*

Description. *DT:* 60′. Branches spread horizontally giving a broad crown. Twigs white-felted. *Bark:* pale grey, smooth. *Ls:* alt., stipulate, 3″, broadly ovate, 3–5 palmately lobed; green slightly hairy above, dense white-felted below. Long flattened stalk. *Fls:* Feb.–April. Male catkins 2–3″ (rarely seen in Britain), female 1″, with two slender yellow stigmas. *Fr:* a dry seed capsule, opens July. Long, white cotton-like fibres attached to seeds.

Distribution. On warmer soils, principally in S. England.

GREY POPLAR *Populus canescens*

Description. *DT:* 90′. Long clean bole. Compact crown. Branches ascending. *Bark:* whitish-grey, smooth, becoming vertically fissured at base. *Ls:* alt., stipulate, 4″, roundish to ovate, shallowly and unevenly toothed, or shortly lobed, shiny dark green above, coated thinly with white or grey hair below. Long-stalked. *Fls:* March. Male catkins drooping, female four wedge-shaped purple stigmas. *Fr:* A dry splitting capsule.

Distribution.   Mostly in S. and E. England.

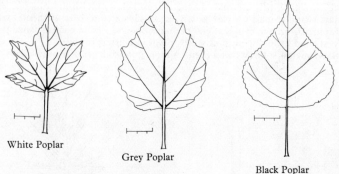

White Poplar

Grey Poplar

Black Poplar

BLACK POPLAR   *Populus nigra*

Description.   *DT:* 90′. A broad, very open crown, often asymmetrical. Spreading branches arching downwards. Twigs cylindrical and hairless. *Bark:* dark grey, deeply diagonally furrowed, with many rough swellings on the trunk. *Ls:* alt., stipulate, 4″, triangular to almost circular, slender-pointed, rounded base, shallow rounded teeth, clear translucent border, dark green, hairless. Long, laterally flattened stalk. *Fls:* March–April. Male catkins 2–3″, drooping, many stamens with dark red anthers; females shorter, erect, with reddish stigmas. *Fr:* a dry capsule, splitting in May to reveal seeds covered with long white cotton-like fibres.

Distribution.   Uncommon. Found on wetter soils in S. and E. England.

LOMBARDY POPLAR   *Populus nigra* var. *italica*

Description.   *DT:* 90′. Slender branches grow upwards close to the trunk, giving a tall, very narrow outline. Twigs smooth. *Bark:* dark grey, deeply and spirally furrowed. *Ls, Fls, Fr:* as Black Poplar, but there are very few, if any, female trees in Britain.

Distribution.   Mostly planted for shelter belts or landscaping.

ASPEN   *Populus tremula*

Description.   *DT:* 50′. Open crown, slender branches with drooping ends. Grey-brown twigs, hairless. *Bark:* grey, smooth, becoming rougher. *Ls:* alt., stipulate, 1–4″, roundish, sometimes wider than long, shortly pointed, unevenly and coarsely blunt-toothed, dark green above, light grey below, hairless. The long flattened stalk allows the leaf to tremble in the least breeze. *Fls:* Feb. Male catkins, 2–4″, drooping, hairy scales, reddish anthers; females small, with purplish stigmas. *Fr:* a dry splitting capsule, with the seeds enclosed in long fluffy cotton-like fibres.

Distribution.   Common on most moist soils.

Above left, Gaping Ghyll Cavern. The water falls some 360 feet before reaching the floor of the 110 foot high cavern. *Right,* Goredale. Goredale Scar was caused by faulting which left the Carboniferous Limestone on the upthrow side. The gorge was caused by the collapse of the cavern roof after it had been weakened by solution and the lateral widening. *Below,* Gaping Ghyll, a swallow-hole. The stream flowing from the left has cut through the impermeable boulder clay to the Carboniferous Limestone beneath and then eroded a vertical shaft. Now, except after heavy rain, the limestone has been uncovered for some distance and the stream disappears before entering the shaft several feet below the lip.

Above, The Strid, Wharfdale, a pothole. The Strid, near Bolton Abbey, is a narrow and very deep channel cut through a band of hard rock, submerged after heavy rain. Potholes are caused by the current swirling stones round a depression, widening and deepening it into a cauldron shape. Many geologists consider this is a major factor in rivers cutting their way through resistant rock strata.

Centre, Wenlock Edge. The gently dipping alternate beds of hard and soft rock have produced a series of escarpments, or cuestas, and broad vales. Much of the higher scarp slopes are tree-clad, increasing the contrast between the two sides of the asymmetrical valleys.

Below, Lulworth, Dorset. Much folded strata on the east side of Stair Hole. The sea has already broken through the hard beds of rock which form the coast line by gorging out a cave, and it is now attacking the softer rock behind.

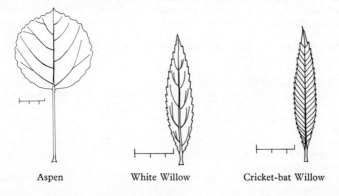

Aspen   White Willow   Cricket-bat Willow

WHITE WILLOW   *Salix alba*
Description. *DT:* 80′. Open pyramidal crown. Frequently forks near the ground. Branch ends droop. Often pollarded. Twigs covered with silky hair. Rootlets entering the water are white. *Bark:* greyish-brown, deeply fissured and closely ridged. *Ls:* alt., stipulate, 2–4″, narrow lance, finely toothed; smooth or thinly hairy, dull green above, densely white silky hairy below. Short-stalked. *Fls:* April–May. Yellow catkins: males 1–1½″, erect, two stamens; females smaller, with two yellow bifid stigmas. *Fr:* a dry splitting capsule.
Distribution. Common on riversides and other damp places.

CRICKET-BAT WILLOW   *Salix alba* var. *coerulea* (*S. coerulea*)
Description. *DT:* 90′. Branches ascend fairly sharply giving a conical shape. Twigs olive-green. *Bark:* grey, thick, deeply and closely furrowed. *Ls:* alt., stipulate, 3″, narrow lance, finely toothed, a little downy at first, becoming hairless in late summer, dull green above, blue-grey below. Short-stalked. *Fls:* May. Yellow, erect catkins: males 1–2½″, two stamens, females smaller.
Distribution. Common on riverside sites in parts of S. England.

ROUND-EARED WILLOW   *Salix aurita*
Description. *DS:* 3–5′. Wide-spreading, straggling or prostrate branches. Reddish-brown twigs, hairy at first. *Ls:* alt., two large ear-shaped stipules at leaf-stalk base, 1–2″, ovate to obovate, vaguely toothed, wrinkled, dull green above, grey downy below, veins deeply impressed. Short-stalked. *Fls:* April. Erect catkins: males ¾″, scales dark tipped, two stamens, almost stalkless; females ½″, two blunt stigmas. *Fr:* a dry splitting capsule.
Distribution. Throughout Britain on damp acidic soils, up to 2,500′.

GOAT WILLOW   (Sallow)   *Salix caprea*
Description. Often *DS*, sometimes *DT*: 20′. Erect stems or trunk. Twigs slightly hairy at first. *Bark:* grey, smooth, becoming irregularly fissured. *Ls:* alt., stipulate, 3″, broadly ovate or roundish, small twisted point, vaguely

toothed or entire, wrinkled, dark green above, pale grey-felted below. Short-stalked. *Fls:* March-April. Erect catkins; males 1½″, fluffy, two protruding stamens; females ¼″, flask-shaped, hairy, two-lobed stigmas. *Fr:* a dry splitting capsule.
Distribution. Common on drier sites than most willows, e.g. lowland hedge-rows and waste ground.

GREY WILLOW *Salix cinerea*
Description. *DT* or *S:* 10′. Spreading branches. Blackish twigs, covered with pale cotton-like hair. *Bark:* grey, roughly fissured. *Ls:* alt., stipulate, 2–3½″, narrowly ovate to oblance, vaguely toothed or entire; dull grey and slightly hairy above, grey-felted below. Veins prominent. Short-stalked. *Fls:* March–April. Erect catkins: males 1″, two stamens with yellow anthers; females small, ovary hairy, two long styles with bifid yellow stigmas. *Fr:* a dry splitting capsule.
Distribution. Common near streams, especially around the marshes and fens of E. England.

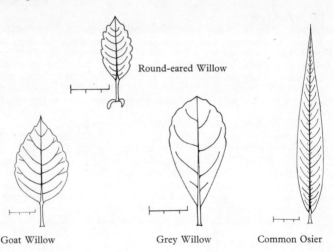

Round-eared Willow

Goat Willow   Grey Willow   Common Osier

COMMON OSIER *Salix viminalis*
Description. *DS:* 20′. Usually coppiced for its long slender pliant yellowish annual shoots, which are densely hairy when young. *Ls:* alt., lance-shaped stipules, 5–10″, linear to tapering lance, entire, midrib prominent; dark green above, silvery silky hair below. Short-stalked. *Fls:* March–April. Erect cat-kins: males ovoid, fluffy, with brown-tipped scales, two yellowish stamens; females flask-shaped ovaries, two long tapering stigmas. *Fr:* a dry splitting capsule.
Distribution. Widespread in lowlands along streams and marshes. Cultivated for basket-making.

CRACK WILLOW   *Salix fragilis*
Description.   *DT:* 70′. Stout bole with spreading branches forming a broad
rounded crown, but often pollarded. Glossy hairless twigs, easily snapped off at
base. Rootlets entering water are red or reddish.   *Bark:* grey-brown, rough
with widely-spaced ridges.   *Ls:* alt., stipulate, 3–6″, narrowly lance, tapering
base, distinctly toothed, glossy green above, paler (sometimes bluish-grey)
below, adult ls hairless. Short-stalked.   *Fls:* April–May. Long drooping
catkins: male 3″, at the end of a short stalk, scales greenish-yellow, two stamens;
females narrow, smooth flask-shaped ovaries, short style ending in a two-lobed
stigma.
Distribution.   Streamsides and marshy ground throughout Britain, but less
common in the north.

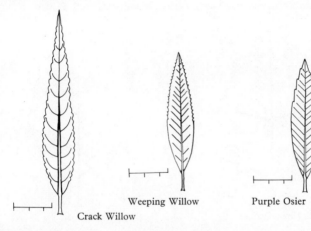

Weeping Willow   Purple Osier

Crack Willow

WEEPING WILLOW   *Salix alba* 'Tristis'
Description.   *DT:* 40′. Long slender branches droop almost to the ground.
Bark: yellowish, smooth.   *Ls:* alt., stipulate, 3″, narrowly ovate, long tapering
point, tapering base, finely toothed; green above, bluish-grey below; adult ls
hairless. Short-stalked.   *Fls:* March–April. Erect catkins, 2″: males two stamens,
females hairless flask-shaped ovaries.   *Fr:* a dry splitting capsule.
Distribution.   Planted in riverside gardens and parks.

PURPLE OSIER   *Salix purpurea*
Description.   *DS:* 4–15′, rarely a tree. Loose straight slender branches,
rather glossy. Glossy twigs purple-tinted, rarely yellowish.   *Ls:* alt., but
nearly opp., stipulate, 2–4″, narrowly lance, entire or minutely toothed near
the apex, green above, slightly bluish-grey below, adult ls hairless. Short-
stalked.   *Fls:* April. Erect catkins: males 1″, narrowly cylindrical, with dark-
tipped scales, two stamens (united) with purplish or reddish anthers; females,
¾″, ovoid, shortly hairy flask-shaped ovaries, two-lobed stigmas.
Distribution.   Streamsides in lowland Britain, less common in the north.
Cultivated for basket-making.

Family Juglandaceae

COMMON WALNUT *Juglans regia*

Description. *DT:* 80′. A broad crown formed of slightly arched ascending branches, sometimes twisted. Clean bole only some 20′. *Bark:* ashy-grey, smooth at first, becoming rugged with vertical furrows forming a network. *Ls:* alt., compound, pinnate; leaflets 2″, roundish, entire; green. Fragrant when bruised. Common stalk long; five, seven or nine leaflets. Short-stalked. *Fls:* May. Drooping catkins: male green with many stamens on old twigs; female solo, or in small clusters, with two fleshy stigmas on young twigs. *Fr:* 2″, ovoid husk, green at first, later turning brown, containing one wrinkled nut.

Distribution. Rarely found wild. Prefers deep dry soil in S. Britain.

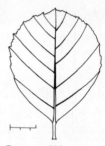

Common Walnut   Common Alder

Family Betulaceae

COMMON ALDER *Alnus glutinosa*

Description. *DT:* 70′, or *DS.* Many ascending twisted branches. Twigs clammy and hairless. May have a short clean bole when a tree. *Bark:* black, rough. *Ls:* alt., stipulate, 4″, obovate to roundish, tapering from base, irregularly and coarsely toothed, rounded or notched at apex, parallel-veined; glossy dark green above, paler below. Young ls hairy. Short-stalked. Remains on twigs long after other ls. *Fls:* Feb., before ls. Shortish catkins: males erect, later drooping, red scales, four stamens; females erect, fleshy scales covered by red-brown bracts, two styles. *Fr:* 1″, woody cone, ripe in October. Empty cones remain throughout winter.

Distribution. Streamsides and damp places throughout Britain, but not on acid soils.

WHITE BIRCH *Betula pubescens*

Description. *DT:* 60′, or *DS.* Divided from base into several trunks. Branches spreading and ascending. Downy twigs not warted. *Bark:* silvery-grey, peels off in paper-thin layers, brown below. Smooth, becoming darker and furrowed with age at base. *Ls:* alt., stipulate, $2\frac{1}{2}''$, ovate, pointed, finely and sharply toothed, less than seven pairs of parallel veins, straight base parallel to these. Long slender stalk. *Fls:* April. Catkins: females on short stalks; males appear in autumn in leaf-axils of long shoots and remain throughout the winter. *Fr:* a minute winged nut.

Distribution.   Scotland and Ireland, often on damp peaty soils, up to 2,000'.

SILVER BIRCH   *Betula verrucosa   (B. pendula)*

Description.   *DT:* 60', or *DS.* Slender trunk. Drooping twigs warted and hairless. May be a shrub in exposed areas.   *Bark:* smooth, brown on saplings, becoming silvery-white. May peel off in paper-thin layers.   *Ls:* alt., stipulate, $2\frac{1}{2}''$, ovate to triangular, long-pointed, sharply double-toothed, less than seven pairs of parallel veins, straight base parallel to these, leathery, dark green turning golden then pale brown. Long slender stalk. *Fls:* April. Female catkins appear at the end of short stalks, males in leaf-axils of long shoots in autumn and remain throughout the winter.   *Fr:* a small oblong cone. Seeds are minute nuts with delicate pairs of wings.

Distribution.   Sandy and acidic soils. Requires plenty of light.

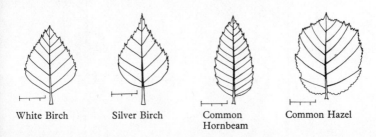

White Birch   Silver Birch   Common   Common Hazel
                                          Hornbeam

COMMON HORNBEAM   *Carpinus betulus*

Description.   *DT:* 60'. Trunk fluted, often oval in section. Slender branches point upwards.   *Bark:* light grey, smooth, may become rougher and darker with age.   *Ls:* alt., stipulate, 3'', narrowly ovate, slender-pointed, sharply double-toothed, parallel-veined, base almost equal-sided, wrinkled, glossy dark green above, rough below. Short-stalked.   *Fls:* April. Male catkins drooping, cylindrical, from axils of previous year's shoots; females cylindrical, erect at first, at end of young shoots.   *Fr:* a minute nut at the base of a three-lobed leaf-like bract.

Distribution.   S. and S.E. England, especially on heavy soils.

COMMON HAZEL   *Corylus avellana*

Description.   *DS:* rarely a tree, 20'. Many-branched. Downy reddish twigs. If a tree, the trunk is narrow and irregular.   *Bark:* brown, smooth, downy, darkens with age. Trunk, if present, furrowed.   *Ls:* alt., stipulate, 2–4'', roundish, slender pointed, heart-shaped slightly unequal base, unevenly toothed, often slightly lobed, hairy. Short-stalked.   *Fls:* April. Female catkins, very small, bud-like, with red protruding stigmas; male cylindrical, drooping, ap-

pear in the autumn ('lambs' tails').   *Fr:* one-seeded nuts, $\frac{3}{4}''$, in clusters, each enclosed in a leafy cup.
Distribution.   Throughout Britain.

Family Fagaceae
SWEET CHESTNUT (Spanish Chestnut)   *Castanea sativa*
Description.   *DT:* 100'. Massive short bole divides into several huge limbs which form a large broad crown. Branches horizontal, ends sag. Stout twigs hairless, except when young.   *Bark:* Brown, smooth on saplings, becoming greyer and deeply furrowed, often with a slight spiral twist.   *Ls:* alt., stipulate, 9'', lance, straight veins end in sharp even teeth, dark glossy green above. Short-stalked.   *Fls:* June–July. 5'', slender, yellow catkins rise from leaf-axils; usually female at base, with five stigmas.   *Fr:* Prickly husk, contain 1–3 reddish-brown nuts.
Distribution.   S. England, in warm nearly neutral soils.

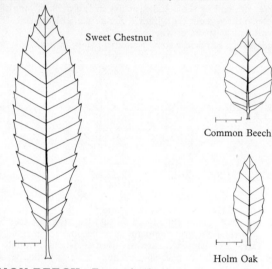

Sweet Chestnut

Common Beech

Holm Oak

COMMON BEECH   *Fagus sylvatica*
Description.   *DT:* 100'. Broad rounded crown. In forests clean bole 50–60'. but, when solitary, the trunk divides into several separate tall straight boughs, Slender drooping branches spread widely and may reach the ground.   *Bark:* pale grey, smooth.   *Ls:* alt., stipulate, 3'', ovate, entire, wavy margin, hair fringed when young, 5–9 pairs of lateral veins, dark glossy green above. Stalked.
Fls: April–May. Male purplish-brown, drooping, with yellow anthers, on long stalks; female green, bristly, surrounded by bracts, in pairs.   *Fr:* four-part, thick, bristly, woody husk containing two smooth triangular nuts.
Distribution.   Southern England. Forms conspicuous copses ('hangers') on Chilterns.

   var. *cuprea*, Copper Beech, ls coppery-red.

HOLM OAK (Evergreen Oak)   *Quercus ilex*
Description.   *ET:* 70′. Massive deep green crown, extending to ground as lower branches are retained. Twigs downy.   *Bark:* dark grey to black, nearly smooth, scaly.   *Ls:* alt., stipulate, 3″, oval to lance, entire, margin scooped, or finely and sharply toothed, dark green above, grey-green downy below. May resemble spineless Holly. Short-stalked.   *Fls:* April–May. Short catkins: male in drooping clusters; female small and inconspicuous.   *Fr:* a nut (acorn), ½″, single or in small clusters on very short stalk. Cup covers over half the acorn.
Distribution.   Prefers dry sandy soils.

TURKEY OAK   *Quercus cerris*
Description.   *DT:* 110′. Open crown with long drooping branches and twigs giving a pyramidal shape.   *Bark:* dark grey, widely spaced deep furrows.   *Ls:* alt., stipules long and persistent, 5″, narrowly ovate, pinnate lobed, teeth of lobes triangular; dark green above, greyish-green below. Short-stalked.   *Fls:* April–May. Male catkins 3–4″, drooping; female small and inconspicuous.   *Fr:* a nut (acorn), ½″, the cup covering half the acorn is covered with narrowly bristly scales. Stalkless.
Distribution.   Adaptable. Prefers deep dry soils.

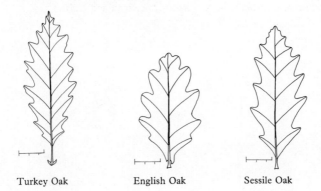

Turkey Oak   English Oak   Sessile Oak

ENGLISH OAK   *Quercus robur*   (*Q. pedunculata*)
Description.   *DT:* 80′. Short bole 25′, divides into many heavy twisted branches giving a large round spreading crown when solitary.   *Bark:* dark grey, thick, deeply and closely furrowed.   *Ls:* alt., stipulate, 4″, ovate, entire, rounded lobed, dark green above, greyish below, hairless. Small lobes or 'ears' at junction with very short stalk.   *Fls:* April–May. Male catkins 2–3″, yellow, drooping; female erect, reddish, with three styles, on short stalks.   *Fr:* a nut (acorn), 1″, ovoid, in small clusters, on long slender stalk. Short scaly cup covers less than a third of the acorn.
Distribution.   Widespread throughout lowland Britain.

SESSILE OAK (Durmast Oak)   *Quercus petraea*   (*Q. sessiliflora*)
Description.   *DT:* 80′. Short bole. Large spreading open crown. Branches only slightly twisted. Twigs downy.   *Bark:* dark grey, thick, rough, deeply furrowed in open network pattern.   *Ls:* alt., stipulate, 5″, ovate, deeply lobed, lobes rounded; dark green above, greyer and downy below; rounded or tapering base, no 'ears'. Stalk usually longer than ½″.   *Fls:* April–May. Male catkins 3–4″, drooping, female small and inconspicuous.   *Fr:* a nut (acorn), pointed, in small close clusters. Cups cover less than a third of the acorn. Stalkless.
Distribution.   In most parts of lowland Britain, especially on poorer soils of the older siliceous rocks.

Family Ulmaceae

WYCH ELM   *Ulmus glabra*
Description.   *DT:* 120′. Broad rounded open crown, with spreading branches bending downwards. Thick forked twigs, hairy when young.   *Bark:* greyish, rough, deeply fissured.   *Ls:* alt., stipulate, 3–7″, ovate to obovate, slender-pointed, base unequal, double-toothed, parallel-veined, rough dull green above, hairy below. Almost stalkless.   *Fls:* Feb.–March, before ls. ¼″, red, long bell-shaped, edges cut into lobes, finely fringed, in clusters, four stamens with pink anthers, two styles.   *Fr:* 1″ flat circular wing, with the seed in the centre.
Distribution.   Mainly in N. England, Scotland and Ireland.

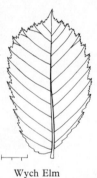

Wych Elm

Common Elm

COMMON ELM   *Ulmus procera*
Description.   *DT:* 120′. A massive straight tree, with a few large spreading branches and many smaller ones giving a dense many-domed crown. Twigs corky and hairy.   *Bark:* greyish, rough and deeply fissured. Saplings rough. *Ls:* alt., stipulate, 2–3″, broadly ovate, short-pointed, double-toothed, parallel-veined, rough green above, paler hairy below. Short-stalked, but the unequal base does not overlap it.   *Fls:* Feb.–March, before ls. Small, reddish, erect, in small dense clusters, in the axil of previous year's leaf-scar.   *Fr:* ½″, flat circular wing, notch nearly reaches the seed.
Distribution.   The warmer parts of England.

Family Platanaceae

LONDON PLANE *Platanus acerifolia*
Description. *DT:* 90'. When in the open, the trunk reaches well up into the large open crown with a considerable length of clean bole. In towns it is often severely cut back. *Bark:* brownish-green, smooth, often peels off in large thin flakes, leaving pale yellowish-green patches. *Ls:* alt., stipulate, 5–9", ovate palmately five-lobed, lobes broad and shallow, coarsely toothed, sometimes downy at first, becoming shiny green. Long-stalked. *Fls:* May. ½", dense globular catkins, usually two on a stalk, males brownish-yellow, females reddish. *Seeds:* globular, burr-like.
Distribution. Widespread. Often found in city streets.

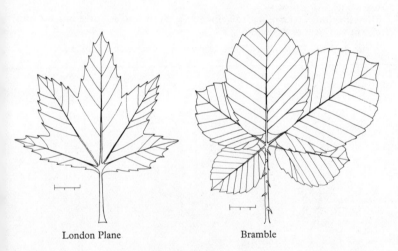

London Plane   Bramble

Family Rosaceae

BRAMBLE (Blackberry) *Rubus fruticosus*
Description. *DS:* height variable. Long trailing, sometimes climbing or erect, stems often prickly or bristly. *Ls:* alt., stipulate, compound, digitate; three or five, rarely seven, leaflets, each 3–5", ovate, short-pointed, sharply toothed; dark green above, paler, sometimes grey, below. Some varieties hairy. Long-stalked. *Fls:* July–Sept. 1", white or pink, in few-flowered clusters. Five sepals and petals, numerous stamens. *Fr:* a compound black berry, consisting of a mass of small one-seeded spheres.
Distribution. Found throughout Britain, in hedgerows and on waste land. Very tolerant and exists in numerous varieties.

SLOE (Blackthorn)   *Prunus spinosa*
Description.   *DT* or, often, *DS:* 15′. Much branched, dense crown. Branches and twigs twisted. Black twigs rigid, with many stout thorns.   *Bark:* black and smooth.   *Ls:* alt., stipulate, 1½″, ovate to lance, distinctly and sharply toothed, green, thinly hairy below. Short-stalked.   *Fls:* March–April. ½″, white stars, singly or in pairs. Five petals, five-lobed calyx, 15–20 stamens.   *Fr:* a fleshy berry, ½″, bluish-black or black, containing one round stone.
Distribution.   Hedgerows and natural woods, also found wild at low altitudes.

COMMON HAWTHORN   *Crataegus monogyna*
Description.   *DT* or *S:* 30′. Large crown beginning near ground level, trunk twisted. Stems and twigs bear spines.   *Bark:* brown, rough. Twigs smooth. *Ls:* alt., 1–2″, ovate, 3–5 deeply cut lobes (often nearly to midrib), veins extend to lobe angles; dark green; downy in vein-axils below. Short-stalked.   *Fls:* May–June. ¾″, white, in branched clusters. Five spreading petals, five sepals, ten stamens, one style.   *Fr:* a red berry ('haw'), ½″, ovoid, usually containing one stone.
Distribution. Common in hedgerows as a shrub, also as a tree in most soils, except very acid or dry ones.

var. *praecox*, Glastonbury Thorn, flowers in summer and winter.

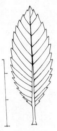
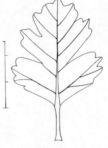

Sloe or Blackthorn   Common Hawthorn

May

MAY   *Crataegus oxyacanthoides*
Description.   *DT:* 15′. Large round crown, with few spines on the stems. *Bark:* brown, rough. Twigs smooth and hairless.   *Ls:* alt., 2″, ovate, shallowly lobed, veins extend to lobes and to the angles between them, dark green, hairless. Short-stalked.   *Fls:* May–June. ½″, white or pink, in branched clusters. Five spreading petals, 2–3 styles, pink anthers.
Distribution.   Chiefly found in S.E. and Central England.

WHITEBEAM   *Sorbus aria*
Description.   *DT* or *S:* 30′. Varies considerably in size according to soil and
exposure. All except the lowest branches bend upwards.   *Bark:* grey, becoming brownish and smooth. Twigs shiny dark brown.   *Ls:* alt., 4″, ovate, double-
toothed, smooth dark green above, densely white-felted below, strongly marked
straight-veined. Short downy stalk.   *Fls:* May–June. ½″, white, in loose flat
clusters.   *Fr:* a red berry, ½″, almost round, spotted. Calyx persistent.
Distribution.   Usually found on calcareous soils in the southern half of
England and Wales.

Whitebeam   Wild Service Tree

Rowan

MOUNTAIN ASH (Rowan)   *Sorbus aucuparia*
Description.   *DT:* 30′. Straight clean bole. Slender spreading branches point
upwards fairly sharply.   *Bark:* smooth, grey, horizontally lined when old.
Ls: alt., compound, pinnate, 11–17 leaflets, each 2″, lance, finely and sharply
toothed, dark green above, paler below, veins curved. Midrib and veins hairy
when young. Leaflets stalkless.   *Fls:* May–June. ½″, white or creamy, in dense
clusters. Stalks may be covered with greyish hair.   *Fr:* a round bright red
berry, ¼″, yellow flesh inside containing few seeds.
Distribution.   Mostly found in hilly districts, but will grow at altitudes up t
2,500′.

WILD SERVICE TREE   *Sorbus torminalis*
Description.   *DT:* 40′. Broad crown.   *Bark:* dark grey, rough. Twigs
brown, woolly when young.   *Ls:* alt., 3″, ovate, 7–9 sharply pointed triangular
lobes, sharply toothed, with straight veins extending to the lobe points, green,
changing to crimson and orange in autumn. Long slender stalk.   *Fls:* May
½″, white, in flat branched clusters.   *Fr:* a brownish ovoid berry, ½″.
Distribution.   Not common. Wild in woods and copses, usually on heavy
soils, in the south and Midlands.

Family Leguminosae

Sub-family Papilionaceae

COMMON BROOM *Cytisus scoparius* (*Sarothamnus scoparius*)
Description. *DS: 6′.* Much branched. Stems erect, green, long, angular and
ribbed. Twigs sharply ascending. *Ls:* alt., stipulate, compound with three
leaflets, each $\frac{1}{2}''$, lance, entire, green, silky below. Very short-stalked. May be
sessile and simple near stem tip. *Fls:* May. 1″, bright yellow, solitary, resemble Sweet Pea; all stamens united. *Seeds:* 2″, green pods, becoming black,
flattened, with hairy margins.
Distribution. Sandy and other well-drained soils throughout Britain.

NEEDLE FURZE (Petty Whin) *Genista anglica*
Description. *DS: 2′* or less. Low straggling shrub with dark green, spiny,
ascending stems, mostly unbranched. *Ls:* alt., $\frac{1}{2}''$, narrowly ovate or lance,
usually pointed, entire, smooth greyish-green. Very short-stalked. *Fls:* May–
June. $\frac{1}{4}''$, bright yellow, in terminal racemes. *Seeds:* smooth linear-oblong
pods, $\frac{1}{2}''$, narrowing at both ends.
Distribution. Common on well-drained soils of Britain, except in the
extreme north.

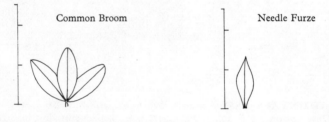

Common Broom   Needle Furze

GORSE (Furze or Whin) *Ulex europaeus*
Description. *ES: 6′.* Dense topped, often bare below. Young stems furrowed, dark green, becoming rough and pale brown. Very spiny. *Ls:* simple,
usually reduced to minute scales. *Fls:* Jan.–June. $\frac{3}{4}''$, golden yellow, solitary,
on short hairy stalks. Calyx very hairy, bracts at base conspicuous. *Seeds:*
brown pods, $\frac{3}{4}''$, hairy when ripe, containing seeds.
Distribution. Common on heaths and moorlands, except in the extreme
north.

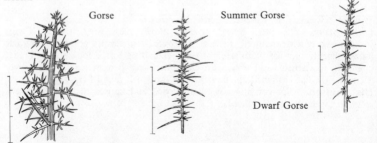

Gorse   Summer Gorse

Dwarf Gorse

SUMMER GORSE   *Ulex gallii*
Description.   *ES:* 3'. Erect, many strong spines, dark green above, often bare below.   *Ls:* simple, often reduced to minute scales.   *Fls:* July–Dec. ¾", golden yellow. Bracts at base minute.   *Seeds:* pod ½", appearing in spring.
Distribution.   Found on acid heaths and hillsides in Ireland and many western parts of England and Wales; also S.W. Scotland.

DWARF GORSE   *Ulex minor*
Description.   *ES:* 1'. Creeping green and furrowed stems with many thin spines.   *Ls:* simple, reduced to minute scales.   *Fls:* July–Dec. ¾", bright yellow, solitary. Calyx almost hairless, bracts at base minute.   *Seeds:* a green pod, ½".
Distribution.   Common on heaths in S.E. England.

Family Buxaceae

COMMON BOX   *Buxus sempervirens*
Description.   *ET* or *S:* 6–20'. Slender branches. Twigs yellowish-green, four angled.   *Bark:* grey, rough.   *Ls:* opp., 1", ovate, entire or notched end, leathery, glossy dark green above, paler below. Almost stalkless. Remain on the tree for several years.   *Fls:* April–May. Small, greenish-white, in axillary clusters. Female flower uppermost in centre of each cluster.   *Fr:* a woody, three-valved capsule, with three horned cells, each containing one or two black seeds.
Distribution.   Favours calcareous soils, in the southern half of England.

Common Box   Holly: **a,** lower leaves; **b,** upper leaves

Family Aquifoliaceae

HOLLY   *Ilex aquifolium*
Description.   *ET:* 40'. Compact, retains branches and ls to ground level. *Bark:* smooth and grey.   *Ls:* alt., 3", ovate, usually with large spiny teeth and wavy margins, glossy green above, paler below. Spines may be absent on the ls on upper branches.   *Fls:* May. ½", greenish-white, in few-flowered clusters. Floral parts in fours. Usually unisexual, sexes on different trees.   *Fr:* a round red berry, ¼", containing two or more stones. Poisonous. Remains on the tree throughout the winter.
Distribution.   Found in all except the most northerly parts of the British Isles.

Family Celastraceae

SPINDLE TREE *Euonymus europaeus*
Description. *DT* or *S:* 15'. Much-branched, often a shrub. Twigs usually
four-angled, green and smooth. *Bark:* green when new, becoming smoother
and greyer. *Ls:* opp., 3", narrowly ovate or lance, pointed, minutely toothed,
dull green. Short-stalked. *Fls:* May. ¼", greenish-white, in branched axillary
clusters. Floral parts in fours. *Fr:* a four-lobed fleshy red berry, containing
four bright orange-covered seeds.
Distribution. A common plant on limestone soils in England; also found in
S. Scotland and Ireland.

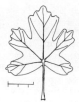

Spindle Tree   Common Buckthorn   Common Maple

Family Rhamnaceae

COMMON BUCKTHORN *Rhamnus cathartica*
Description. *DT* or *S:* 20'. Much branched, with slender stems and smooth
hairless twigs, often ending in a spine. *Bark:* smooth, grey, becoming darker
and rougher. May flake showing orange inner bark. *Ls:* opp., or almost so,
2", ovate, finely toothed, yellowish-green, smooth. Veins follow leaf outline.
Longish, slender stalk. *Fls:* May–June. ½", yellowish-green or white, in leaf-
axil clusters or racemes. Floral parts in fours. Unisexual. *Fr:* a bluish-black
berry, ½", round, containing four small stones.
Distribution. Common in Central and S. England on alkaline and calcareous soils, also on the East Anglian fens.

Family Aceraceae

COMMON MAPLE (Field Maple) *Acer campestre*
Description. *DT:* 30', also frequently *DS* in southern hedgerows. Round
crown. Twigs corky. *Bark:* pale brown and rough, becoming slightly fissured
with age. *Ls:* opp., 3", five rounded deeply-cut palmate lobes, sometimes with
a few rounded teeth; dull green, turning red or orange. Long stalk with milky
sap. *Fls:* May. ¼", yellow to greenish-yellow, in upright terminal clusters.
Petals often absent, eight stamens. *Seeds:* horizontally winged, both at right-
angles to the stalk.
Distribution. Prefers a dry stony soil, but is very tolerant.

NORWAY MAPLE *Acer platanoides*

Description. *DT:* 70′. Large round open crown. Stout ascending and spreading branches. The brown twigs are streaked with grey. *Bark:* brownish-grey, fairly smooth, often developing short shallow fissures. *Ls:* opp., 6″, five rounded, deeply-cut, palmate lobes, coarsely and sharply toothed, pale yellowish-green turning vivid yellow in autumn, hairless except for vein-axil tufts below. Veins extend to lobe points. Long stalk with milky sap. *Fls:* April–May. ½″, yellow, in erect clusters. *Seeds:* long (1½–2″) narrow-winged curving almost horizontally.

Distribution. Planted for windbreaks. Resistant to sea-salt and wind. Prefers a dry limy sandy soil.

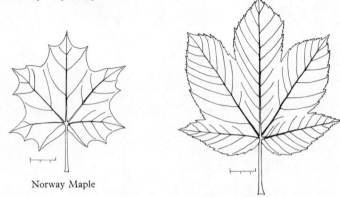

Norway Maple

Sycamore

SYCAMORE *Acer pseudoplatanus*

Description. *DT:* 90′. Stout clean bole of 50′ not uncommon. Develops a large dense crown when solitary. Branches at wide angles, with tips tending to droop. Lower branches almost horizontal. Stiff straight twigs green and smooth. *Bark:* greenish-grey and smooth when young, becoming purplish and rougher. *Ls:* opp., 6″, five pointed, wedge-cut, palmate lobes, coarsely double-toothed all round, base heart-shaped, dark green above, grey below. Long stalk with clear sap. *Fls:* April–May. ¾″, yellowish-green, in long drooping many-flowered panicles. *Seeds:* two wings curving away at less than 90°.

Distribution. Prefers deep moist soils, but is tolerant. Resistant to sea-salt

Family Hippocastanaceae

(Formerly included in the family Sapindaceae)

COMMON HORSE CHESTNUT *Aesculus hippocastanum*

Description. *DT:* 80′. Stout cylindrical trunk, but clean bole usually less than 20′. Huge dense crown. Long ascending branches droop in their middle lengths, but the tips turn upwards. *Bark:* smooth, brown-grey, becoming greyer and fissured, sometimes with a slight spiral twist. *Ls:* opp., compound,

digitate, leaflets of different sizes, 9″ downwards, obovate or oblance, coarsely
double-toothed, green. Compound ls have long stalks, leaflets almost stalkless.
Fls: May. ¾″, white, tinged with yellow or red, in upright panicles. Four petals,
five-lobed bell-shaped calyx, seven stamens.   *Fr:* a thick green outer husk, 1½″,
with many prickles, containing one, rarely two or three, large shiny rich brown
nut or nuts.
Distribution.   Usually planted in parks and gardens for ornament.

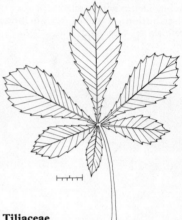

Common Horse Chestnut

Family Tiliaceae

SMALL-LEAVED LIME   *Tilia cordata*
Description.   *DT:* 70′. Crown somewhat pointed. Branches ascend sharply.
Twigs hairy.   *Bark:* grey, smooth, becoming furrowed with age.   *Ls:* alt., 2″,
roundish, sharply pointed, sharply and finely toothed, base heart-shaped, lobes
rather unequal, green, smooth except for brown tufts in vein-axils below. Long-
stalked.   *Fls:* June-July. ¼″, yellowish, erect, in 5–10 fl. clusters, from a large
green strap-shaped bract.   *Fr:* a yellowish-green round nut, ¼″, dry, smooth
and woody.
Distribution.   S. and Central England.

Small-leaved Lime

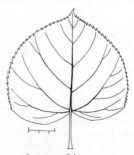

Common Lime

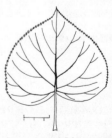

Large-leaved Lime

Top left, Cirrus. High thin clouds of separate fibres but, as here, may end in up-turned, denser hooks. *Right,* Altocumulus. A layer usually broken into rounded masses which may vary from widely-scattered to an almost continuous sheet. *Centre left,* Stratocumulus. A layer of rounded masses or rolls. Here the thin edges are merging but the variable depth of cloud is still clearly seen, as is the irregularly rounded base. *Right,* Cumulus. Large clouds of considerable depth, becoming more closely packed. While the upper margins are loose and rather fluffy, the bases are flattened and dense. *Bottom left,* Fair weather Cumulus. The clouds are scattered but of considerable depth. The rounded upper margins are very loose and fluffy but the bases are much flatter. *Right,* Cumulonimbus. Here is the common anvil form with a veil of false cirrus around the upper margin. A striking sight from a distance, but below it appears heavy, often with intense rain or hail.

Above left, Burnham Beeches, near Slough. An old 'natural' woodland with ground, field and shrub layers of vegetation between the trees of all ages, from the gnarled old ones in the foreground to the saplings and shoots behind. *Right,* pinewood. The edge of a man-made pine plantation. All the trees are of one species and of the same age. The closely-planted trees block out the light so that there is little other vegetation except beside the track. *Below,* Frensham Common, Surrey. A typical southern heath with heather and scattered birch on the light, sandy soil, which has already begun to be eroded along the footpath.

LARGE-LEAVED LIME   *Tilia platyphyllos*
Description.   *DT:* 100′. Round crown. Twigs covered with long hair when young.   *Bark:* grey, thin, nearly smooth, becoming closely-ridged with age.   *Ls:* alt., 4–5″, roundish to ovate, sharply-pointed, sharply toothed, heart-shaped base, lobes unequal, green, few scattered hairs above, downy or hairy below. Long-stalked.   *Fls:* July. ¼″, greenish-yellow, drooping, usually in three-fl. clusters, from a large green strap-shaped bract.   *Fr:* a yellowish-green round nut, ¼″, dry and ridged.
Distribution.   S. and Central England, including the Welsh borderland.

COMMON LIME   *Tilia vulgaris*   (Hybrid *T. platyphyllos* × *T. cordata*)
Description.   *DT:* 80′. Crown somewhat pointed. 50′ clean bole in woods, but much less when solitary. Twigs smooth.   *Bark:* Grey, thin, nearly smooth when young, rougher with age.   *Ls:* alt., 4″, roundish, sharply pointed, finely and sharply toothed, heart-shaped base, lobes unequal, green, smooth except for pale tufts in vein-axils below. Long-stalked.   *Fls:* June–July. ¼″, yellowish-white, in long-stalked drooping clusters, from a large green strap-shaped bract.   *Fr:* a pale yellow round nut, ¼″, dry, slightly ridged and downy.
Distribution.   S. and Central England and Wales.

Family Ericaceae

HEATHER (Ling)   *Calluna vulgaris*
Description.   *ES:* 1½′. A low, much branched shrub, the lower stems forming a brown mat.   *Ls:* opp., minute, scale-like, in four rows, keeled.   *Fls:* July–Sept. Small, purplish-pink, short-stalked, in slender terminal clusters. Corolla deeply divided into four lobes and shorter than the calyx, both persistent.   *Seeds:* enclosed in small round dry capsules.
Distribution.   Heaths and moors.

FRINGED HEATH   *Erica ciliaris*
Description.   *ES:* 1′. A low straggling shrub, with downy shoots.   *Ls:* whorls of three, ¼″, linear, oval ended, green above, white below, smooth, but fringed with long hairs.   *Fls:* June–Oct. ½″, rosy-red, bell-shaped, terminal spikes in the axils of upper ls.   *Seeds:* enclosed in small dry capsules.
Distribution.   Rare. Confined to Dorset and parts of Devon and Cornwall.

SCOTTISH HEATHER (Bell Heather)   *Erica cinerea*
Description.   *ES:* 1′. A low shrub with spreading or erect shoots.   *Ls:* whorls of three, ¼″, narrow needle-like, blunt-ended, with leafy shoots in axils; dark green and smooth.   *Fls:* July–Sept. Small, bright purple, ovoid, in terminal spikes.   *Seeds:* enclosed in small dry capsules.
Distribution.   Widespread on heaths and moors, especially in the drier areas.

CROSS-LEAVED HEATH   *Erica tetralix*
Description.   *ES:* 1′. A low straggling shrub, with greyish hairy stems.   *Ls:* whorls of four, ¼″, linear, blunt-ended, arranged in the form of a cross, green above, white below, fringed with long hair.   *Fls:* June–Sept. Small, pink, ovoid, in dense terminal clusters; ovary hairy.   *Seeds:* enclosed in small dry capsules.
Distribution.   Damp peaty soils throughout Britain.

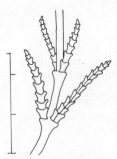

Heather

Fringed Heath

Scottish Heather

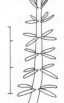

Cross-leaved Heath

Cornish Heath

CORNISH HEATH *Erica vagans*
Description. *ES:* 1–2′. A low shrub with spreading or erect shoots. *Ls:* whorls of four or five, ¼″, linear, needle-like, blunt-ended, margins recurved; bright green; hairless. *Fls:* August–Sept. Small, pinkish-purple or white, bell-shaped, in long terminal spikes. *Seeds:* small dry capsules.
Distribution. Rare. Believed restricted to heathland around the Lizard, Cornwall.

BILBERRY (Whortleberry) *Vaccinium myrtillus*
Description. *DS:* 2′ or less. Spreading stems, flanged or angled, hairless. *Ls:* alt., ½–1′, ovate, round-toothed, bright green, hairless. Veins distinct. Short-stalked. *Fls:* April–June. ¼″, pale pink, round, in pairs or solitary. Corolla not deeply divided, ovary 4–5 celled. *Fr:* a berry, ¼″, black with a bluish bloom. Ripe July onwards.
Distribution. Abundant, especially on peaty soils. Found at altitudes of up to 3,500′, but rarely exceeds 6″ on exposed mountain slopes.

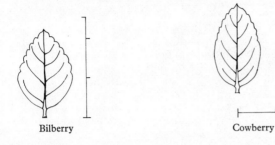

Bilberry   Cowberry

COWBERRY *Vaccinium vitis-idaea*

Description. *ES:* ½′. A low creeping shrub. Sprawling yellowish-green stems, warted and hairless. *Ls:* alt., 2″, ovate, entire or minutely toothed on outer half, leathery, dark green above, pale below, hairless. Very short stalk. *Fls:* May–June. ¼″, pink, bell-shaped, in crowded racemes. *Fr:* a bright red berry, ¼″.

Distribution. Peaty moorland slopes of Scotland, N. England and Ireland.

Common Elder

Family Caprifoliaceae

COMMON ELDER *Sambucus nigra*

Description. *DT:* 20′, or sometimes a low *DS*. Trunk or main stem is generally rough and crooked, other irregular stems form hard tubes with a readily extractable pith core. Twigs corky. *Bark:* light grey, fissured when old. *Ls:* opp., compound, pinnate, 5″; five, seven or nine leaflets, each 1–3″, ovate to lance, pointed, toothed, short-stalked, dark green' *Fls:* June. ¼″, creamy-white, in large, flat-topped, branched clusters (4–8″ in diameter). Corolla a short tube, with five petal-like lobes spreading horizontally. *Fr:* a purplish-black round berry, ½″, containing a few small flattened stones.

Distribution. Found on waste and scrubland, particularly on the chalk.

Common Ash

Family Oleaceae

COMMON ASH   *Fraxinus excelsior*
Description.   *DT:* 90'. Crown round or oval. Clean bole 20–30', with forked growth above this. Branches curve upwards.   *Bark:* pale grey, smooth, becoming rough and fissured.   *Ls:* opp., compound, pinnate; 7–13 leaflets, each 3", lance, evenly toothed, dull green above, paler below. Common stalk grooved, leaflets sessile.   *Fls:* April–May, before ls. Small, greenish-yellow, inconspicuous, in loose panicles, two dark purple stamens.   *Fr:* one seed in a twisted narrow oblong wing, notched at seed end. Remains on tree for most of the winter.
Distribution.   Especially found on calcareous or deep loamy soils.

GRASSES, SEDGES AND RUSHES

Introduction

These plants form a major natural group and, although ignored by many people or merely considered to be intrusive weeds, are an important part of the floral landscape. Grasses receive most consideration as they are not only the most numerous, but also of the greatest economic value, and while the structure of sedges and rushes are generally similar, differences are noted here in the appropriate pages and, in particular, in the Key to Tables of Grasses, Sedges and Rushes, p. 151.

Grasses may be annuals, biennials or perennials and consist of roots, stems, leaves and flower-heads. The roots are mostly fine and are often surprisingly long, while some perennials have greenish to purplish, leafy, short-lived, surface creeping stems (stolons), which root at the tip and nodes to produce new, and later separate, plants. Other perennials may have white to brown, longer-living, underground stems (rhizomes), with new shoots arising from buds in the axils of the scale-like leaves.

All shoots consist of more or less cylindrical, hollow stems, interrupted at intervals by blocks (nodes), which are marked externally by darker ridges and sometimes slightly swollen. Solitary leaves rise from the nodes and consist of a lower cylindrical section (sheath) surrounding the stem and usually split for part or the whole of its length (sometimes with the margins overlapping) on the side opposite to the free section (blade). The base of the blade may extend as two claw-like projections (auricles) across the upper edge of the sheath. On the inside of the blade/sheath junction there is normally a small outgrowth of tissue (ligule), although in some species it is represented by a fringe of hair.

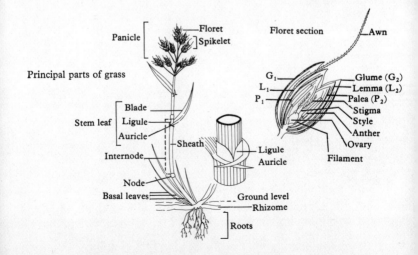

The flower-head consists of a main axis bearing either branches with stalks (pedicels) bearing the scale-encased flowers (spikelets), or stalkless spikelets

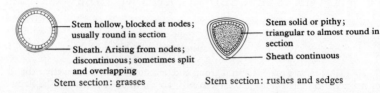

Stem hollow, blocked at nodes; usually round in section

Sheath. Arising from nodes; discontinuous; sometimes split and overlapping

Stem section: grasses

Stem solid or pithy; triangular to almost round in section

Sheath continuous

Stem section: rushes and sedges

attached directly to the axis and forming a spike. Generally the spikelets consist of a pair of basal scales (glumes), and one or more florets, each consisting of a pair of outer scales (lemmas) and a pair of inner scales (palea) around the flower. The glumes, or other scales, may bear a stiff bristle (awn). The flower is made up of the male parts (stamens), each consisting of a stalk (filament) and a terminal body (anther) which contains the pollen, and the female parts consisting of a generally rounded, and sometimes hairy, body (ovary), containing one or more ovules which develop into the seed and one or more stalks (stigma) with terminal pollen-collecting organs (styles). The stigma and style together form the pistil.

Abbreviations

Bl.	Blade(s)	L.	Lemma(s)
c.	About	Pan.	Panicle
Fl.	Flower(s)	Sh.	Sheath(s)
Fld.	Flowered	Spklt.	Spikelet(s)
Flg.	Flowering	St.	Stem(s)
Fls.	Flowering Time	Subequal.	Almost equal
Gl.	Glume(s)	'	Feet
Infl.	Inflorescence	"	Inches

Key to Tables of Grasses, Sedges and Rushes

1. The hollow stem is noded and usually cylindrical. Except in a very few young plants, the sheaths are split for part or the whole of their length and the margins may overlap. Flowers do not have a 6-leaved perianth – ring of sepals (calyx) and petals (corolla).   GRASSES (Gramineae)   **Table 1** p. 151
2. The solid or pithy stem is not noded and varies in section from markedly triangular to almost circular. The sheaths do not split, always forming a complete tube around the stem.
   a. Each flower does not have a 6-leaved perianth.
                                SEDGES (Cyperaceae)   **Table 2** p. 153
   b. Each flower has a complete 6-leaved perianth
      i Hairless plants, with many seeded-capsules
                             TRUE RUSHES (Juncus)   **Table 3** p. 154
      ii Hairy plants, with 3-seeded capsules
                          WOODRUSHES (Luzula)   **Table 4** p. 154

TABLE I : GRASSES

1.0 Ligules are a dense fringe of hairs.
   1.1 Inflorescence is a raceme of 3–6 spikes.
                            Townsend's Cord-grass, p. 188
   1.2 Inflorescence is a panicle.   **Common Reed,** p. 187
                                    Heath Grass, p. 155
                            Purple Moor-grass, p. 155
2.0 Ligules are membranous.
   2.1 Inflorescence is a spike or spike-like.
   A. Inflorescence is one-sided. Spikelets 1-fld. arranged in a double row.   **Mat-grass,** p. 188
                            Stiff Sand-grass, p. 162
   B. Spikelets arranged in 2 rows on opposite sides of axis:
      1-fld.
      i. 'Pen-nib' spikelets fit closely into deep hollows of stiff jointed axis.   **Sea Hard-grass,** p. 188
      ii. Spikelets free, edge fits into curves of wavy axis.
                                    Rye-grasses, p. 160
      iii. Spikelets free; spike-like racemes.   **False Bromes,** p. 171
      iv. Spikelets free, edge broadside to axis.   **Couches,** pp. 171–3
   C. Spikelets in alternating pairs, 3–6 fld., size decreasing upwards.   **Lyme Grass,** p. 173
   D. Spikelets arranged in alternating 3s; central fertile floret and 2 smaller sterile laterally.   **('Wild') Barleys,** pp. 174–5
   E. Spikelets of two types in crowded clusters on short branches; sterile, of up to 18 narrow bracts, predominate.
                            Crested Dog's-tail, p. 166

F. Spikelets densely crowded on all sides of axis.
  i. Panicle slender. Spikelets small, 1–fld.
    a. Panicle cylindrical, compact. Glumes equal, keeled, margins united basally. **Fox-tails,** pp. 185-6
    b. Panicle stiff. Glumes equal, hair-fringed keels end in awn-points. **Timothy Grass,** p. 184
                                                     Cat's-tails, pp. 183-5
  ii. Spikelets large, crowded, 2–fld, often silvery. Blades mostly basal, rolled. **Early Hair-grass,** p. 180
  iii. Spikelets flattened, 3–fld. Sheaths bearded at blade-junction. Blades flat, broad at base, tapering.
                                                     Sweet Vernal Grass, p. 187
  iv. Spikelets large, 1–fld. Lemmas blunt, keels end as minute points. Ligules long, pointed. Blades long, rolled, close-ribbed. Coastal dunes. **Marram Grass,** p. 180
  v. Spikelets silvery-blue, glistening. Lemma nerves end in awn-points. Sheaths keeled, many at base. Stem blades small. Basic moorlands. **Blue Moor-grass,** p. 168
  vi. Panicle erect, cylindrical or lobed below. Spikelets flattened, 2–3 fld. Glumes equal first floret. Blades bristle-like. **Crested Hair-grass,** p. 175

2.2 Inflorescence is NOT a spike or spike-like.
A. Densely tufted. Spikelets small 1–fld.
  i. Branches clustered, much divided in outer half; almost erect; but spreading, at least during flowering.
                                                     Bents, pp. 181–3
  ii. Panicle branches long and fine, only spreading during flowering. **Wood Small-reed,** p. 181
  iii. Panicle branches clustered, often downspreading, each bear few scattered spikelets. **Wood Millet,** p. 186
B. Panicle branches unequally paired. **Fescues,** pp. 157–61
C. Spikelets multi-flowered, awned.
  i. Panicle nodding. Spikelets large, single, drooping at ends of long branches. **Wild Oats,** p. 176
  ii. Panicle nodding; clustered branches long and very slender. Spikelets, small, 2–fld. Lemmas bearded basally. **Hair-grasses,** pp. 179–80
  iii. Panicle almost erect. Spikelets small, flattened, 2–fld. Blades flat and broad. **Yorkshire Fog,** p. 178
                                                     Creeping Soft-grass, p. 178
  iv. Panicle branches bear few spikelets. **Cocksfoot,** p. 165
                                                     Barren Brome, p. 169
                                                     Oat-grasses, pp. 175–8
  v. Awn equals length of lemma. **Soft Brome,** p. 169
                                                     Slender Brome, p. 170
                                                     Meadow Brome, p. 170
  vi. Lemma terminal awn short. **Upright Brome,** p. 168
                                                     Hairy Brome, p. 168
D. Spikelets multiflowered, awnless.
  i. Spikelet axis ends in a club-like mass of sterile

lemmas ringed by 1–6 fertile ones. **Melicks,** p. 167
ii. Reed-like. Glume equals spikelets. **Reed Canary Grass,** p. 187
iii. Spikelets flattened. Glume shorter than first floret.
Meadow-grasses, pp. 163–5
iv. Panicle trembles; long, slender branches. Spikelets drooping. **Common Quaking Grass,** p. 166
v. Panicle stiff, one-sided; short, rigid branches.
Fern Grass, p. 162
vi. Aquatic or semi-aquatic. Glume shorter than first floret. **Sweet-grasses,** p. 156
Salt-marsh-grasses, pp. 161–2

TABLE 2: SEDGES

1.0 Stems slender. Leaves narrow V-section. Flowers globular, 1″, white silky mass. Damp moors.
i. Leaves sharply-pointed, prominent mid-rib.
Common Cotton-grass, p. 189
ii. Leaves basal, bristle-like, few on stem.
Hare's-tail Cotton-grass, p. 189
2.0 Inflorescence a cluster of spikes with leafy bracts around each.
A. One elongated bract overtops inflorescence.
i. Stems triangular, edges sharp. Brackish water.
Sea Club Rush, p. 190
ii. Stems average 6′ tall, thick, tapering. Inflorescence may appear lateral. Freshwater margins.
Common Bulrush, p. 190
B. Aquatic, floating or submerged. Slender-based, erect stems thicken above, branched, each with a terminal panicle. Long narrow leaves grouped on stems.
Floating Club Rush, p. 190
3.0 Terminal inflorescence has many small blackish bracts overtopping the flowers. Damp basic soils. **Black Bog Rush,** p. 190
4.0 Stems markedly triangular, stout.
A. Fairly tall to tall. Inflorescence a male terminal and several female spikes below.
i. Inflorescence erect, dense. Leaves almost bristle-like, on lower stem only. **Great Panicled Sedge,** p. 192
ii. Inflorescence in densely crowded alternate clusters. Outer bract of lowest cluster leaf-like. **Fox Sedge,** p. 192
iii. Spikes crowded, 2″, cylindrical. Leaves long, overtop inflorescence, mid-rib prominent. **Cyperus Sedge,** p. 193
iv. Tall. Leaves long, sharp-edged, mid-rib prominent. Spikelets long-pointed. Bracts long, leaf-like.
Great Marsh Sedge, p. 193
v. Tall. Leaves long, sharp-pointed, keeled. Ligules long. **Lesser Marsh Sedge,** p. 194
vi. Tall. Leaves long, flat, broad. 3 distinct parallel ribs down stem. Female spikes 6″, drooping.
Great Pendulous Sedge, p. 194

B. Stems short. Leaves narrow, re-curved; only on lower
   stem.   **Sand Sedge,** p. 192

5.0 Stems slender, leaves only on lower.
- i. Leaves almost bristle-like. Flowers small, chestnut-
  brown, widely scattered.   **Flea Sedge,** p. 192
- ii. Male terminal spike brown, lower female round,
  green.   **Round-headed Sedge,** p. 193
- iii. Spikes scattered. Long leaf-like bract.   **Loose Sedge,** p. 195
- iv. Male spike nodding, 3–4 female loose, drooping.
  Woodlands.   **Pendulous Wood Sedge,** p. 195

TABLE 3: RUSHES

1.0 Many-fld terminal inflorescence appears lateral, being overtopped by an elongated bract in line with the stiff stem.
Densely tufted perennials. Rhizomes.
- A. Leaves absent or rare.
  - i. Stems bear many fine striations when fresh. White
    pith continuous. NO leaves. Sheaths basal, scale-
    like, reddish to brown.   **Soft Rush,** p. 195
  - ii. Stem marked by a few prominent ridges. Pith inter-
    rupted. Sheaths basal, brown to blackish. Leaves
    rare.   **Hard Rush,** p. 195
  - iii. Many prominent stem ridges especially just below
    inflorescence. Pith continuous. A few basal leaves.
            Common Rush, p. 195–6
- B. Leaves and at least the lowest bracts end in stiff prickly
  points.
  - i. Flowers reddish-brown. Overtopping bract leaf-like.
            Great Sharp Sea Rush, p. 196
  - ii. Flowers straw-yellow. Overtopping bract needle-like.
            Lesser Sharp Sea Rush, p. 196

2.0 Inflorescence clearly terminal. Leaves and bracts NOT
prickly pointed.
- A. Leaves stiff, V-sectioned, interrupted by many cross-
  partitions.   **Jointed Rush,** p. 197
- B. Leaves basal, bristle-like, NOT partitioned.   **Heath Rush,** p. 197

TABLE 4: WOODRUSHES

Stems erect, slender, dark green. Sheaths and leaves, basal only,
all fringed by long white hair.
- A. Panicle chestnut to yellowish-brown. Long pointed leaf-
  like bracts.   **Field Woodrush,** p. 197
- B. Loose cyme dark chestnut. Small tapering bracts.
          Common Hairy Woodrush, p. 198
- C. Compact cyme on widespread branches. Small leaf-like
  bracts.   **Great Hairy Woodrush,** p. 198

DESCRIPTIVE NOTES

Commoner British grasses

PURPLE MOOR-GRASS *Molinia caerulea*
Description. A densely and compactly tufted perennial, often forming large tussocks. *Stems:* 6–36″, (tallest where best sheltered), erect, slender to fairly stout, stiff, 1-noded near the club-shaped base, smooth. *Sheaths:* rounded, usually smooth, sometimes hairy towards blade-junction. *Ligules:* a dense fringe of short hair. *Blades:* 4–18″, flat, narrow, tapering to a long, fine point, smooth or rarely slightly hairy above; green withering to pale yellow ribbons. *Panicles:* 2–16″, erect, very variable, ranging from dense and almost spike-like to very open and loose; green, becoming a distinctive bluish-purple; long, slender branches, smooth to minutely rough; pedicels vary in length. *Spikelets:* awnless, lance to oblong, 1–4 flowered; glumes lance, pointed, unequal to almost equal; lemmas larger lance, pointed. *Fls:* July–Sept.
Distribution. Very common on hills, moors and heaths throughout the British Isles, up to about 4,000′.

HEATH GRASS *Sieglingia decumbens*
Description. A densely tufted perennial. *Stems:* 4–20″, erect to almost prostrate, stiff, slender, 1–3 noded, smooth. *Sheaths:* rounded, hairless except for fine spreading hairs at blade-junction. *Ligules:* a dense fringe of short hair. *Blades:* 2–10″, flat, narrow, blunt or sharply pointed, stiff, sparsely hairy to hairless, rough upwards. *Panicles:* 1–3″, narrow, compact to loose; erect or spreading branches, each bearing 1–3 spikelets. *Spikelets:* awnless, elliptical to oblong, plump, 4–6 flowered; purplish or green; glumes lance, pointed, almost equal, bluntly keeled; lemmas broadly ovate, closely overlapping. *Fls:* June to August.
Distribution. Common on acidic moors and heaths and pastures throughout the British Isles.

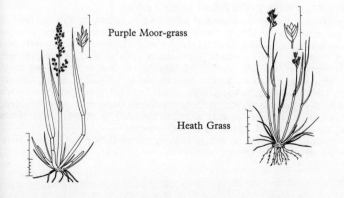

Purple Moor-grass

Heath Grass

FLOATING SWEET-GRASS *Glyceria fluitans*

Description. An aquatic perennial with creeping rootstock, forming loose patches or tufts in shallow water. *Stems:* up to 40″, erect or spreading, sometimes ascending from a prostrate or floating base, where it may root at the nodes, few nodes above water, slender to rather stout, smooth, soft to spongy. *Sheaths:* keeled, tubular except for a small slit at apex, loose-fitting, hairless; green or purple. *Ligules:* long (up to ½″), lance to oblong. *Blades:* 2–10″, flat or folded, abruptly pointed, broad-based; palish green; may float on water. *Panicles:* 4–20″, almost erect, curved or nodding, usually contracted unless flowering, sparingly branched below; branches usually paired, with the longer having 1–4 spikelets, the shorter only one; pedicels short. *Spikelets:* awnless, narrowly oblong, 8–16 flowered; green or purplish; glumes elliptical, blunt, unequal; lemmas larger, elliptical, blunt or pointed. *Fls:* May–August. Anthers purplish.

Distribution. Common in still or slow-moving waters throughout the British Isles, locally plentiful; also found sometimes on land beside still water.

Floating Sweet-grass   Plicate Sweet-grass

PLICATE SWEET-GRASS *Glyceria plicata*

Description. An aquatic perennial with creeping rootstock, forming tufts or loose patches. *Stems:* 12–30″, rising from prostrate, branched bases, where it roots at nodes, unbranched above, slender to fairly stout, smooth, soft and spongy. *Sheaths:* entire, except for a short split at apex, keeled, rough. *Ligules:* up to ½″, oblong, whitish. *Blades:* 2–12″, flat or folded, up to ½″ wide, both sides rough or almost smooth above. *Panicles:* 4–18″, usually broadly lance to oblong, loose; slender, rough branches, spreading, lower often clustered 2–5; pedicels short. *Spikelets:* awnless, cylindrical, 7–16 flowered; green or purplish; glumes broadly elliptical, markedly blunt, unequal; lemmas larger, broadly elliptical, blunt. *Fls:* June–August.

Distribution. Frequent in wet or swampy places throughout British Isles becoming rare in N. Scotland.

REED SWEET-GRASS *Glyceria maxima*

Description. An aquatic perennial, spreading by stout rhizomes to cover considerable areas. *Stems:* 36–100″, erect, stout, smooth, but sometimes rougher towards the panicle. *Sheaths:* tubular, at first, keeled, sometimes with a reddish-brown band and rough towards the blade-junction, hairless. *Ligules:* up to ¼″, blunt, or with a small central point. *Blades:* 12–24″, flat, broad, hairless, rough on thickened margins and sometimes beneath; usually show cross-veining. *Panicles:* 6–15″, broadly ovate to oblong, usually open and loose, sometimes becoming contracted and dense; green; branches much-divided and clustered, rough. *Spikelets:* awnless, narrowly ovate to oblong, slightly compressed, closely 4–10 flowered; glumes broadly ovate, keeled, of unequal width; lemmas broadly ovate, blunt. *Fls:* July–August.

Distribution. Common throughout the lowlands of Britain on the banks of still, or slow-moving waters and areas frequently flooded.

Reed Sweet-grass   Meadow Fescue

MEADOW FESCUE *Festuca pratensis*

Description. A bright green perennial, often forming large tussocks. *Stems:* 18–48″, erect or slightly spreading, fairly slender to stout, 2–4 noded, smooth. *Sheaths:* rounded, smooth. *Ligules:* short. *Blades:* 5–18″, flat, narrow, tapering to a fine point, narrow auricles, rough margins and sometimes above, glossy beneath. *Panicles:* 4–15″, almost erect to nodding, lance to ovate; green to purple; short, angular branches in unequal pairs with the shorter bearing 1–2 spikelets. *Spikelets:* awnless, cylindrical to lance, 5–14 flowered; glumes lance, pointed, slightly unequal; lemmas ovate to lance, pointed. *Fls:* June–August.

Distribution. A valuable grazing grass on rich, moist soils. Common in most parts of Britain, but rare in N. Scotland.

TALL FESCUE *Festuca arundinacea*

Description. A tufted perennial, sometimes in large, dense tussocks. No rhizomes. *Stems:* 18–72″, erect, stout, 2–5 noded, smooth or rough **towards**

panicles; bases often enclosed in whitish scale-like sheaths. *Sheaths:* rounded, smooth or slightly rough, hairless except at blade-junction. *Ligules:* small. *Blades:* 4–24″, flat, up to ½″ wide, stiff, tapering to a fine point, only margins rough, hairless except for margins of narrow auricles. *Panicles:* 4–12″, erect or nodding, lance to ovate, loose; green to purple; spreading, rough, angular branches, usually in unequal pairs, both bearing many spikelets, lower bare and undivided. *Spikelets:* awnless, lance to oblong, closely 3–10 flowered; glumes lance, pointed, unequal; lemmas lance to ovate, pointed sharply. *Fls:* June–July.

Distribution. Common throughout the British Isles. The taller forms appear on heavy, damp, lowland soils, the shorter on the drier calcareous ones.

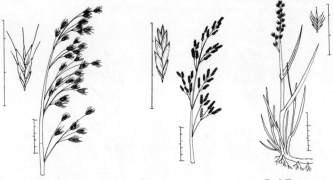

Giant Fescue   Tall Fescue   Red Fescue

GIANT FESCUE *Festuca gigantea*
Description. A loosely tufted, hairless perennial. *Stems:* 18–60″, erect, stout, 2–5 purplish noded. *Sheaths:* rounded, smooth or lower part rough, reddish. *Ligules:* short. *Blades:* up to 24″, flat, tapering to a fine point, narrow spreading auricles; usually drooping, smooth and glossy, but margins rough and sometimes above. *Panicles:* 2–16″, nodding, lance, loose; axis and branches stout, angular; branches usually in unequal pairs (rarely threes), bare and undivided below. *Spikelets:* awned, lance to oblong, 3–10 flowered; glumes lance, pointed, unequal; lemmas larger, lance to ovate, pointed, bearing a fine, rough terminal awn. *Fls:* July–August.

Distribution. Common in damp shady woods and hedgerows, especially in S. England and Wales, decreasingly frequent northwards.

RED FESCUE (Creeping Fescue) *Festuca rubra*
Description. A perennial with slender rhizomes or stolons, forming loose to dense patches. *Stems:* 6–36″, erect or spreading, slender and wiry, 2–3 noded, smooth. *Sheaths:* rounded, tubular when young, soon splitting. *Ligules:* very short. *Blades:* 1–16″, basal bristle-like, tightly inrolled, blunt or abruptly pointed; stem blades open nearly flat, narrow, with small auricles; green or greyish-green; smooth beneath. *Panicles:* 1–6″, erect or nearly so, lance to

oblong, loose and open, later contracting; green, purple or reddish; roug h angular branches usually in unequal pairs. *Spikelets:* awned, small, lance to oblong, 3–9 flowered; glumes lance, pointed, very unequal; lemmas larger, lance, pointed, bear a fine terminal awn. *Fls:* May–June.

Distribution. A very common pasture grass at all altitudes throughout the British Isles, ranging from coastal dunes (usually the greyer forms) to lowland, heaths and mountains.

SHEEP'S FESCUE *Festuca ovina*
Description. A densely tufted perennial, without rhizomes. *Stems:* 2–24″, erect, angular, very slender, stiff, 1–2 noded, smooth or rough towards panicle. *Sheaths:* rounded, smooth, split almost to base. *Ligules:* short. *Blades:* 1–8″, bristle-like, tightly rolled, blunt, rough towards tip, stem blades shorter than basal; short, rounded auricles; green to greyish-green. *Panicles:* 1–5″, erect, narrowly lance to oblong, dense, but rather one-sided; green to purple; axis rough and angular, branches almost erect. *Spikelets:* awned, lance to oblong, 3–9 flowered; glumes lance, pointed, unequal; lemmas lance, pointed, with a short, fine, terminal awn. *Fls:* May–July.

Distribution. A common pasture grass throughout the British Isles, may be dominant on hills and mountains.

Sheep's Fescue   Fine-leaved Sheep's Fescue

FINE-LEAVED SHEEP'S FESCUE *Festuca tenuifolia (F. ovina* ssp. *tenuifolia)*
Description. A densely tufted perennial, without rhizomes. *Stems:* 4–16″, erect, very slender, stiff, 1–3 noded, smooth or rough near panicle. *Sheaths:* rounded, split to base, smooth to slightly rough. *Ligules:* very short. *Blades:* 1–10″, hair-like, tightly infolded, blunt to finely pointed, smooth to rough; bright to dark green; small, rounded auricles. No stem leaves. *Panicles:* 1–4″, erect, contracted, fairly dense, often one-sided; green, yellowish-green or purplish; short branches, erect or nearly so. *Spikelets:* awnless, oblong, 3–8 flowered; glumes lance, pointed, rather unequal; lemmas lance, finely pointed. *Fls:* May–June.

Distribution. Common on acidic heaths, moors and open woodlands throughout the British Isles.

PERENNIAL RYE-GRASS *Lolium perenne*
Description. A loosely to rather densely tufted, hairless perennial. *Stems:* usually 12–24″, (but locally 6–36″), erect or bent below, slender, 2–4 purplish noded, smooth. *Sheaths:* rounded, smooth, tinged pink or purple when young, basal persistent. *Ligules:* short. *Blades:* 1–10″, rolled when young, opening flat, up to ¼″ wide, smooth and glossy, sometimes slightly rough above. *Spikes:* 2–12″, straight or nearly so, stiff, spikelets alternate on opposite sides, almost own length apart; green to purplish. *Spikelets:* awnless, stalkless, oblong, closely 4–14 flowered; glumes bluntly lance, lower absent except in terminal spikelet; lemmas oblong, blunt to pointed. *Fls:* May–August.
Distribution. A very common and valuable agricultural grass for hay and grazing throughout the British Isles; also found on roadsides and waste.

Perennial Rye-grass   Italian Rye-grass

ITALIAN RYE-GRASS *Lolium multiflorum*
Description. An annual or biennial, tufted or solitary. Hairless. *Stems:* 12–40″, erect or slightly spreading, slender to fairly stout, 2–5 noded, smooth or rough towards spike. *Sheaths:* rounded, smooth to somewhat rough. *Ligules:* short. *Blades:* 2–10″, tightly rolled, when young, opening flat up to ½″ wide, finely pointed, smooth and glossy, or rough above. *Spikes:* 4–12″, erect or nodding, slender to fairly stout, with stalkless spikelets alternating on opposite sides almost own length apart; green to purplish. *Spikelets:* awned, oblong, compressed, 5–15 flowered; glumes narrowly oblong, lower present in terminal spikelets; lemmas oblong, blunt or minutely double-toothed, tipped with long straight awn. *Fls:* June–August.
Distribution. Commonly cultivated throughout the British Isles for hay and pasture; also found wild.

SQUIRREL-TAIL FESCUE *Vulpia bromoides*
Description. A loosely tufted or solitary annual. *Stems:* 2–24″, erect or rising from a bent or prostrate base, often branched near base, slender, stiff, 2–4 noded, smooth and glossy. *Sheaths:* rounded, smooth. *Ligules:* very small. *Blades:* ½–6″, flat or rolled and bristle-like, narrow, flaccid to fairly stiff, rough on margins and at finely pointed tip, downy above. *Panicles:* ½–4″, stands well above topmost sheath, erect or slightly nodding, lance to narrowly oblong, fairly loose to compact, one-sided, rarely reduced to 1 spikelet; green to purplish; short branches, erect or almost so. *Spikelets:* awned, oblong to wedge, 5–10 flowered; glumes lance, finely pointed, upper twice length of lower; lemmas lance, tapering to long, fine terminal awn. *Fls:* May–June.
Distribution. Quite common on drier soils throughout the British Isles; locally common.

Squirrel-tail Fescue

Reflexed Salt-marsh-grass

Common Salt-marsh-grass

REFLEXED SALT-MARSH-GRASS *Puccinellia distans*
Description. A tufted perennial. *Stems:* 4–24″, erect, spreading or prostrate, slender, 2–4 noded, smooth, hairless. *Sheaths:* rounded, smooth. *Ligules:* ovate, short. *Blades:* 1–4″, flat, or rolled, abruptly pointed or blunt, narrow, minutely rough above; greyish- or whitish-green. *Panicles:* 1–7″, ovate to pyramidal, loose and open; stiff, rough, clustered branches, bare and undivided below, erect at first, but spreading downwards (reflex) later. *Spikelets:* awnless, narrowly oblong, 3–9 flowered; glumes ovate, blunt, unequal; lemmas broadly ovate, blunt. *Fls:* June–July.
Distribution. Frequent on muds, sands, gravels and salt-marshes around shores of the British Isles; occasionally in river meadows and waste.

COMMON SALT-MARSH-GRASS *Puccinellia maritima*
Description. A densely tufted perennial with creeping stolons, rooting at nodes and forming a compact turf. *Stems:* 4–32″, erect, spreading or prostrate, slender to rather stout, 2–4 noded, smooth. *Sheaths:* rounded, smooth.

Ligules: fairly short, ovate to blunt.   *Blades:* 1–8″, folded or rolled, opening flat, narrow, abruptly pointed or blunt, smooth except on nerves above. *Panicles:* 1–8″, linear to ovate, usually narrow, dense, stiff; green or purplish; short, rough branches, usually erect, especially after flowering.   *Spikelets:* awnless, more or less cylindrical, 3–10 flowered; glumes lance, to ovate, very unequal; lemmas longer than glumes, broadly ovate.   *Fls:* June–July.
Distribution.   Very common on grassy salt-marshes, mud-flats and in brackish water around British coasts.

FERN GRASS   *Catapodium rigidum*
Description.   A tufted or solitary, hairless annual.   *Stems:* 1–10″, erect or spreading, very slender, rigid, 2–5 noded, smooth.   *Sheaths:* rounded, smooth. *Ligules:* ovate, thin, toothed margin.   *Blades:* 1–4″, inrolled or flat, narrow, finely-pointed, only rough on fine nerves; green or purplish.   *Panicles:* ½–3″, linear to ovate, usually one-sided, dense to rather loose, rigid; green or purplish; short branches and main axis rigid, three-angled, smooth.   *Spikelets:* awnless, narrowly oblong, 3–10 flowered; glumes lower elliptical to almost triangular, upper lance; pointed, unequal width; lemmas ovate, blunt, larger than lower glume.   *Fls:* May–June.
Distribution.   Common on dry stony or calcareous soils, banks, walls and sand-dunes throughout the British Isles, locally abundant in southern England.

Fern Grass   Stiff Sand-grass

STIFF SAND-GRASS   *Catapodium marinum*
Description.   A tufted or solitary, hairless annual.   *Stems:* 1–7″, erect, spreading or prostrate, often branched at base, slender, rigid, few noded, smooth with broad, glossy ribs.   *Sheaths:* rounded, ribbed, smooth.   *Ligules:* bluntly ovate.   *Blades:* ½–4″, flat or rolled, narrow, minutely rough above, smooth beneath; dark green.   *Panicles:* ½–3″, spike-like, rigid, branches and pedicels minute or absent; axis angular in front, flattened behind; green or purple. *Spikelets:* awnless, lance to oblong, arranged in two rows on one side of axis, overlapping or touching, 4–12 flowered; glumes lance, unequal width; lemmas longer than glumes, ovate to elliptical, blunt.   *Fls:* May–July.
Distribution.   A frequent grass on sand, shingle or rocky places around British coasts.

ANNUAL MEADOW-GRASS *Poa annua*

Description. A loosely to compactly tufted, hairless annual. *Stems:* 2–12″, erect to prostrate, sometimes rooting at nodes, very slender and weak, 2–4 noded, smooth. *Sheaths:* smooth, compressed, topmost longer than blade. *Ligules:* usually tall, ovate, thin and silvery. *Blades:* ½–6″, flat, or folded at first, weak, transversely wrinkled, smooth, margins minutely rough; bright green. *Panicles:* ½–5″, ovate to triangular, usually open and loose; pale to bright green, sometimes tinted reddish or purple; paired or single, spreading branches, bare and undivided below. *Spikelets:* awnless, ovate to lance, closely 3–10 flowered; glumes lance to ovate, pointed, unequal width; lemmas elliptical, blunted, as long as glumes. *Fls:* all the year, except during severe winters.

Distribution. Common on cultivated grasslands, hills and waste at all altitudes throughout the British Isles. Grown for hay, pastures and lawns.

Annual Meadow-grass

Wood Meadow-grass

WOOD MEADOW-GRASS *Poa nemoralis*

Description. A loosely tufted, hairless perennial, with creeping rhizomes. *Stems:* 6–36″, erect or basally spreading, slender, 3–5 noded, smooth. *Sheaths:* rounded, smooth, topmost shorter than blade. *Ligules:* absent or very short. *Blades:* 2–5″, flat, narrow, finely or abruptly pointed, weak. *Panicles:* 1–6″, usually nodding, narrowly lance to ovate, very loose and open; green to purplish; long, spreading, hair-like branches in clusters, bare and undivided below, minutely rough. *Spikelets:* awnless, ovate, compressed, 1–5 flowered; glumes lance, pointed, keeled, equal or almost so; lemmas ovate, pointed, keels and margins fringed with fine hair. *Fls:* June–August.

Distribution. Common in woods and other shady places throughout the British Isles.

NARROW-LEAVED MEADOW-GRASS *Poa angustifolia* (*P. pratensis* ssp. *angustifolia*)

Description. A compactly tufted perennial with slender, wiry rhizomes and stolons. *Stems:* 8–24″, erect, rarely spreading at base, slender, stiff, two-noded below mid-point, smooth. *Sheaths:* rounded, smooth or minutely rough, basal ones keeled. *Ligules:* very short. *Blades:* 1–12″, basal bristle-like or folded, abruptly pointed, narrow, bluntly keeled; stem-blades wider, smooth, or sometimes slightly rough. *Panicles:* 1–3″, erect or nodding, lance to narrowly triangular, loose to rather contracted; purplish or green; spreading, hair-like branches, usually in clusters of 3–5, unequal, minutely rough, bare below. *Spikelets:* awnless, ovate, to oblong, compressed, closely 2–5 flowered; glumes

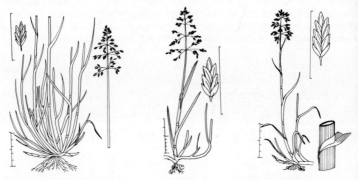

Narrow-leaved Meadow-grass   Meadow Grass   Flattened Meadow-grass

ovate, pointed, keeled, unequal but similar; lemmas ovate, blunt or pointed. *Fls:* May–June.

Distribution. Frequent on rough hill grasslands, especially on chalk and limestone, but rare in Scotland.

MEADOW GRASS   *Poa pratensis*

Description. A loosely to compactly tufted perennial, with slender rhizomes. *Stems:* 5–36″, erect or bent below, sometimes prostrate, slender to rather stout, 2–4 noded, smooth. *Sheaths:* smooth, hairless or sparsely downy, lower compressed, topmost longer than the blade. *Ligule:* short and truncated. *Blades:* 1–12″, flat or rolled, narrow, abruptly pointed or blunt, smooth to rather rough. *Panicles:* 1–8″, pyramidal to oblong, erect or nodding; green, purplish or greyish; mainly undivided, hair-like branches in spreading clusters of 3–5, unequal. *Spikelets:* awnless, ovate, closely 2–5 flowered; glumes ovate, pointed, unequal; lemmas lance, pointed, cottony hairs on keel and marginal nerves. *Fls:* May–June.

Distribution. Very common in most habitats and altitudes throughout tne British Isles.

FLATTENED MEADOW-GRASS   *Poa compressa*

Description. A loosely tufted or scattered perennial, with long creeping rhizomes. *Stems:* 4–20″, erect, or ascending from bent or prostrate base, slender, flattened, stiff, wiry, 4–6 noded, smooth. *Sheaths:* oval, compressed, smooth, topmost equals length of blade. *Ligules:* short, blunt *Blades:* 1–5″, folded or flat, narrow, usually stiff, rough, or often smooth beneath, mostly on lower half of stem; bluish-green. *Panicles:* ½–4″, narrowly ovate to oblong, contracted and dense, rarely spreading and loose; green, yellowish-green or purple; short, angular, undivided branches, clustered or paired, with spikelets to base. *Spikelets:* awnless, lance or ovate, closely 3–10 flowered, compressed; glumes lance to ovate, pointed, equal or nearly so; lemmas ovate, blunt, keeled. *Fls:* June–August.

Distribution. Widespread throughout the British Isles, except N. Scotland; locally abundant, especially on stony places.

ROUGH MEADOW-GRASS *Poa trivialis*
Description. A fairly loosely tufted perennial, with leafy stolons. *Stems:* 8–36″, erect, or rising from a bent or prostrate base, slender to rather stout, 3–5 noded, smooth and hairless. *Sheaths:* rough, slightly keeled. *Ligules:* long (up to ½″), pointed. *Blades:* 1–8″, folded when young opening flat, abruptly pointed, rough, or smooth and glossy beneath. *Panicles:* 1–8″, ovate, erect or nodding, open and loose to contracted and dense; green, purplish or reddish; fine branches, mostly in 3–7 clusters, undivided in lower parts. *Spikelets:* awnless, ovate, compressed, closely 2–4 flowered; glumes lance, pointed, unequal, with reduced keels; lemmas ovate, pointed, larger than glumes. *Fls:* June–July.

Distribution. Very common in meadows and lowland pastures throughout Britain.

Rough Meadow-grass

Cocksfoot

COCKSFOOT *Dactylis glomerata*
Description. A densely tufted, coarse perennial with markedly compressed vegetative shoots. *Stems:* 6–48″, usually erect, or bent at base, slender to rather stout, 3–5 noded, smooth to rough. *Sheaths:* tubular at first, but soon splitting, keeled, rough, hairless to sparsely short-haired. *Ligules:* long (up to ½″) ovate, torn. *Blades:* 4–18″, infolded when young, opening flat, up to ½″ wide, sharply pointed; greyish- or bluish-green. *Panicles:* 1–8″, erect, ovate,

with dense oval masses at ends of long, stiff, bare, angular branches, often spreading horizontally when in flower, otherwise ascending, one-sided. *Spikelets:* awned, oblong to wedge, 2–5 flowered; purplish or yellowish: glumes lance, finely pointed, hairy on keels, very unequal; lemmas larger than glumes, lance, finely pointed, with short, stiff terminal awn. *Fls:* May–September.

Distribution. A very common agricultural grass, grown for hay and pasture throughout the British Isles; also found wild.

CRESTED DOG'S-TAIL *Cynosurus cristatus*

Description. A compactly tufted perennial. *Stems:* 6–30″, erect, fairly stiff, 1–3 noded, smooth. *Sheaths:* rounded, close-fitting, smooth. *Ligules:* very short, blunt. *Blades:* 2–6″, flat, narrow, tapering to a fine point, smooth and shining, but rough at apex above. *Panicles:* 1–6″, spike-like, erect, narrow, dense, stiff; green, sometimes tinged with purple; minute branches. *Spikelets:* shortly awned, fertile and sterile mixed in same dense clusters; fertile oblong or wedge, 2–5 flowered; glumes narrowly lance, pointed, keeled, nearly equal; lemmas ovate, blunt, tipped with a short, stiff awn; sterile ovate, flattened, consist of up to 18 narrow, pointed bracts; these almost mask the fertile ones. *Fls:* June–August.

Distribution. A very common agricultural and wild grass, found at altitudes of up to 2,000 feet throughout the British Isles.

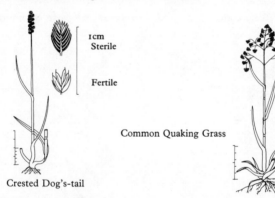

1cm
Sterile

Fertile

Common Quaking Grass

Crested Dog's-tail

COMMON QUAKING GRASS *Briza media*

Description. A loosely tufted or solitary perennial, with short rhizomes. *Stems:* 6–24″, erect, stiff, slender, 2–3 noded, smooth. *Sheaths:* tubular at first, soon splitting, hairless. *Ligules:* short, sharply truncated. *Blades:* 1–6″, flat, narrow, sharply pointed to blunt, rough on margins, hairless; green. *Panicles:* 2–6″, roughly pyramidal, very loose and open; long, spreading, slender branches and long, curving, hair-like pedicels. *Spikelets:* awnless, ovate, laterally compressed, hang downwards, closely 4–12 flowered; usually purplish and shiny; glumes broadly ovate, blunt, spread horizontally, concave, equal or almost so; lemmas similar in size and form to glumes. *Fls:* June–August.

Distribution. Frequent on most soils throughout the British Isles, but rare in N. Scotland.

WOOD MELICK *Melica uniflora*

Description. A perennial with slender, whitish rhizomes, forming loose patches. *Stems:* 8–26″, erect, rarely spreading, slender, smooth. *Sheaths:* appear tubular, close-fitting, loosely covered with short, downward-pointing hairs, or hairless, apex drawn out into a bristle-like projection opposite blade. *Ligules:* short. *Blades:* 2–8″, flat, narrow, hairy above, rough beneath and on margins. Many stem leaves. *Panicles:* 2–8″, erect, ovate, very loose; few long, spreading, slender branches, mostly undivided below, each bear 1–6 spikelets on upper half, usually well separated. *Spikelets:* awnless, oblong or gaping, erect, each consists of one fertile and 2–3 sterile lemmas; glumes lance, pointed, unequal width; purplish to brown; fertile lemmas ovate, blunt, concave; green; sterile lemmas oblong, blunt, club-like, two-thirds size of fertile one. *Fls:* May–July.

Distribution. Common in woods and other shady places throughout the British Isles; locally abundant.

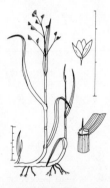

Wood Melick　　　　　Mountain Melick

MOUNTAIN MELICK *Melica nutans*

Description. A loosely clustered or solitary perennial, with slender rhizomes. *Stems:* 8–20″, erect or spreading, slender, slightly angular, minutely rough near inflorescence. *Sheaths:* appear tubular, slightly 4-angled, minutely rough, lower ones purplish. *Ligules:* very short, blunt. *Blades:* 1½–8″, rolled when young, opening flat, sparsely short-haired above, minutely rough below; bright green; lower ones much reduced. *Racemes:* 1–6″, slightly nodding, one-sided, on curved, hair-like pedicels. *Spikelets:* awnless, ovate or gaping, solitary, rarely paired, consist of 2–3 fertile lemmas and a terminal club-like mass of smaller sterile lemmas; glumes ovoid, blunt, equal or almost so; fertile lemmas ovate, blunt, slightly larger than glumes. *Fls:* May–July.

Distribution. Found in wood margins and other shady places, especially on calcareous soils or limestone cracks, not common, but locally abundant. Distributed throughout the British Isles, except S. England.

BLUE MOOR-GRASS *Sesleria caerulea (S. albicans)*
Description. A tufted perennial, with short, slender rhizomes. *Stems:* 4–18″ erect, slender, wiry, frequently noded near base, smooth. *Sheaths:* keeled, smooth, many at base. *Ligules:* very short. *Blades:* 2–8″, mostly basal, firm, smooth, but margins and keels rough; flat or folded, fairly narrow, parallel-sided, abruptly pointed; stem blades much reduced, if present. *Panicles:* ¼–1½″, spike-like, ovoid to cylindrical, dense; bluish- to silvery-grey, glistening; with short ovate bracts sheathing base. *Spikelets:* shortly awned, ovoid, 2–3 flowered; glumes lance, pointed, equal or almost so; lemmas lance, 3–5 toothed tip, shorter than glumes, nerves especially central, project as awn-points. *Fls:* April–May. Purple anthers.
Distribution. Locally common on limestone hill pastures in N. England, Ireland and southern Scotland.

Blue Moor-grass   Upright Brome

UPRIGHT BROME *Bromus erectus (Zerna erecta)*
Description. A densely tufted perennial. *Stems:* 18–40″, erect or slightly spreading, stiff, slender to stout, 3–4 noded, smooth, usually hairless. *Sheaths:* tubular at first, soon splitting, rounded, lower sometimes sparsely hairy, upper usually smooth. *Ligules:* very short. *Blades:* 6–12″, inrolled or flat, upper flatter and broader than basal, margins sometimes hairy. *Panicles:* 4–6″, erect or nodding, loose to rather dense; purplish, reddish or green; short, clustered, almost erect branches, each bearing 1–4 spikelets. *Spikelets:* awned, narrowly lance, slightly compressed, 4–14 flowered; glumes narrowly lance, finely pointed, keeled; lemmas narrowly lance, pointed, tipped with a short, fine awn. Orange to reddish anthers. *Fls:* May–June.
Distribution. Common on well-drained soils, especially chalk and limestone, in S. England.

HAIRY BROME (Wood Brome) *Bromus ramosus (Zerna ramosa)*
Description. A loosely tufted perennial. *Stems:* 18–72″, erect, slender above, thickish at base, 3–5 noded, downy. *Sheaths:* tubular at first, soon splitting, rounded, with stiff reflexed hairs, upper sometimes hairless. *Ligules:* long,

round, firm.   *Blades:* 6–24″, flat, lower broad, upper narrow, drooping, sparsely hairy, narrow auricles; dark green.   *Panicles:* 6–15″, nodding or drooping, loose and open; green or purplish; wiry, hair-like branches, usually paired, undivided below, rough; pedicels longish.   *Spikelets:* awned, narrowly oblong, compressed, 4–11 flowered; purplish or greenish-grey; glumes narrowly oblong, pointed, unequal; lemmas lance, pointed, tipped with a fine awn.   *Fls:* July–August.

Distribution.   Common in shady or partly shady areas on moist soils, especially in woods and hedgerows, throughout the British Isles.

Hairy or Wood Brome   Barren Brome

BARREN BROME   *Bromus sterilis*   (*Anisantha sterilis*)
Description.   A loosely tufted or solitary annual or biennial, with creeping rootstock.   *Stems:* 6–36″, erect or spreading, slender to rather stout, 3–5 noded, smooth, hairless.   *Sheaths:* tubular at first, soon splitting, rounded, lower often with soft, reflex hairs.   *Ligules:* pointed, toothed.   *Blades:* 2–10″, flat, soft to firm, downy, rough, lower ones soon wither; dark greenish to purple.   *Panicles:* 2–10″, nodding, very loose and open, sometimes represented by one spikelet; long, wide-spreading, slender branches, unequal and rough, each bearing one spikelet.   *Spikelet:* awned, oblong, becoming gaping, compressed, 4–10 flowered; pale green tinged with purple, becoming greyish; glumes lance, pointed, very unequal; lemmas narrowly lance, pointed, tipped with a long, terminal awn.   *Fls:* May–July.
Distribution.   A common weed found on waste, roadsides and hedgerows throughout lowland Britain, except in N. Scotland.

SOFT BROME   (Lop Grass)   *Bromus mollis*
Description.   A loosely tufted or solitary annual or biennial.   *Stems:* 4–36″, erect or spreading, slender to fairly stout, 2–5 noded, usually shortly hairy at nodes, sometimes downy.   *Sheaths:* tubular at first, soon splitting, rounded, softly hairy to hairless.   *Ligules:* short, toothed, hairy.   *Blades:* 2–8″, flat, finely pointed, soft, shortly hairy or downy; greyish-green.   *Panicles:* 2–5″, erect, somewhat loose, contracting during flowering; grey-green or purplish;

short, clustered branches, minutely hairy, bearing 1–5 spikelets; pedicels shorter than spikelets. *Spikelets:* awned, narrowly lance, closely 6–15 flowered, downy; glumes lance to ovate, pointed, unequal width; lemmas obovate, apex may be notched, keeled, slightly bent awn arises from just below apex. *Fls:* May–July.

Distribution. Very common in lowlands throughout the British Isles.

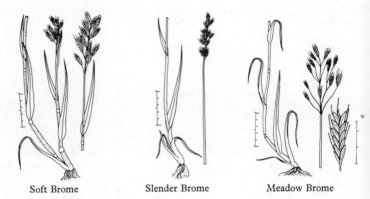

Soft Brome   Slender Brome   Meadow Brome

SLENDER BROME   *Bromus lepidus*

Description. A loosely tufted or solitary annual or biennial. *Stems:* 4–32″, erect or ascending from a bent or prostrate base (where rooting at nodes may occur), slender, 2–6 noded, sometimes downy between vertical ribs. *Sheaths:* tubular at first, soon splitting, usually softly and shortly hairy, especially lower ones. *Ligules:* short, toothed. *Blades:* 2–8″, flat, finely pointed, softly hairy; green. *Panicles:* 1–4″, erect or nodding, lance, opening in flower, later dense; bright green or tinged purple; clustered, short branches bear 1–3 spikelets. *Spikelets:* awned, lance to oblong, spreading later, 3–11 flowered; glumes lance to ovate, pointed, unequal width; lemmas obovate, apex notched, a short, rough awn rises from near the apex. *Fls:* May–July.

Distribution. Frequent in waste and cultivated land throughout the British Isles.

MEADOW BROME   *Bromus commutatus*

Description. A loosely tufted or solitary annual or biennial. *Stems:* 12–42″, usually erect, slender to rather stout, 3–5 noded, smooth, downy. *Sheaths:* tubular at first, soon splitting, downy, especially lower ones. *Ligules:* short, becoming ragged, hairless. *Blades:* 3–12″, flat, finely pointed, rough, thinly hairy; green. *Panicles:* 2–9″, nodding, loose, later drooping to one side; green or purplish; clustered, unequal, fine branches bear 1–4 spikelets; pedicels long. *Spikelets:* awned, lance to oblong, 4–10 flowered; glumes lance, pointed, unequal; lemmas broadly ovate, apex notched or blunt, a fine straight awn rises just below apex. *Fls:* May–July.

Distribution. Widespread on moist lowland soils throughout the British Isles.

SLENDER FALSE BROME (Wood False Brome) *Brachypodium sylvaticum*

Description. A compactly tufted perennial. *Stems:* 12–36″, erect or spreading, slender to rather stout, 4–5 noded, smooth, hairless except at, or sometimes near, nodes. *Sheaths:* rounded, or upper keeled, hairy (sometimes reflexed). *Ligules:* truncated, sometimes ragged. *Blades:* 4–14″, flat, constricted at base, broadening, tapering to a fine point, often soft and drooping, usually loosely hairy; green, sometimes slightly yellowish. *Racemes:* 2–8″, spike-like, usually nodding and loose, 4–12 spikelets overlap and alternate on opposite sides of slender axis; pedicels minute; green. *Spikelets:* awned, narrowly cylindrical, 7–16 flowered; glumes narrowly lance, sharply pointed, unequal, hairy; lemmas narrowly lance, sharply pointed, hairy, tipped with a fine straight awn, longer than lemma. *Fls:* June–August.

Distribution. Common in woods and shady places throughout the British Isles.

Slender (Wood) False Brome   Chalk False Brome   Bearded Couch

CHALK FALSE BROME (Tor Grass) *Brachypodium pinnatum*

Description. A loosely to compactly tufted perennial, with wiry, scaly rhizomes. *Stems:* 12–40″, usually erect, slender to rather stout, stiff, 2–3 noded, smooth, may be downy at first. *Sheaths:* rounded, smooth, sometimes downy, especially lower. *Ligules:* blunt. *Blades:* 4–18, flat or inrolled, erect, rough, sparsely and shortly hairy. *Racemes:* 2–9″, spike-like, erect to slightly nodding, with 3–15 overlapping spikelets alternating on opposite sides of the slender axis; pedicels minute; green to yellowish. *Spikelets:* awned, narrowly cylindrical, 8–22 flowered; glumes narrowly lance, pointed, unequal; lemmas lance, pointed, tipped with a short straight awn. *Fls:* June–August.

Distribution. Common on chalk and limestone, sometimes locally abundant, in S. England; infrequent elsewhere.

BEARDED COUCH *Agropyron caninum*

Description. A loosely tufted perennial, without rhizomes. *Stems:* 12–40″, erect, occasionally bent below, slender, 2–5 noded, smooth, hairless except at, or near, the nodes, bright green. *Sheaths:* rounded, closely fitting, smooth, lower only occasionally downy. *Ligules:* short. *Blades:* 4–13″, flat, broad, finely pointed, finely nerved, rough, sometimes hairy above. *Spike:* 2–9″, curved or nodding, slender; green sometimes tinged with purple; axis slender and rough. *Spikelets:* awned, lance to oblong, erect, arranged alternately in two rows on opposite sides of axis, 2–6 flowered; glumes narrowly lance, sharply pointed, almost equal, sometimes tipped with short awns; lemmas lance, sharply pointed, tipped with a flexible awn, sometimes longer than lemma. *Fls:* June–August.

Distribution. Widespread in woods and shady places throughout the British Isles, but rare on N. Scottish mainland.

TWITCH (Couch-grass) *Agropyron repens*
Description. A tufted perennial, with long, wiry rhizomes, which sometimes forms large patches. *Stems:* 12–48″, erect or bent at base, slender to fairly stout, 3–5 noded, smooth. *Sheaths:* rounded, smooth, usually hairless, but lower may be downy. *Ligules:* minute. *Blades:* 2–16″, flat, finely pointed, with short spreading auricles, soft to stiff, smooth or rough below, loosely or thinly hairy; dull green, sometimes bluish or greyish. *Spikes:* 2–10″, erect, stiff, slender, loose to compact, overlapping spikelets arranged alternately in two rows on opposite sides of slender axis, or dense, green, rarely bluish-green. *Spikelets:* awned, oblong to wedge, 3–8 flowered; glumes narrowly lance, pointed or blunt, equal or nearly so; lemmas lance, blunt or pointed, minutely awned. *Fls:* June–August.

Distribution. A widespread weed found throughout the British Isles.

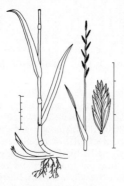

Twitch or Couch-grass

Sea Couch

SEA COUCH *Agropyron pungens*
Description. A tufted perennial, with long, wiry rhizomes, often forming large patches. *Stems:* 8–42″, erect or ascending from a bent base, slender to stout, stiff, 3–4 noded, smooth and hairless. *Sheaths:* rounded, smooth. *Ligules:* minute. *Blades:* 3–14″, flat or tightly inrolled, sharply pointed, stiff, smooth below, strongly marked prominently ribbed above, rough on ribs and margins; bluish-green or greyish-green; short, spreading auricles. *Spikes:*

1½–8″, erect, stiff, slender to stout, spikelets overlap by at least half length and arranged alternately in two rows on opposite sides of rough axis. *Spikelets:* awnless, ovate, 3–10 flowered; glumes lance, keeled, equal or nearly so; lemmas lance, blunt or pointed, keeled. *Fls:* June–August.

Distribution. Common, sometimes dominant, on dunes and salt-marshes in S. and E. England and Wales, and S. Eire.

SAND COUCH-GRASS *Agropyron junceiforme*

Description. A loosely tufted, or matted, bluish-green perennial, with many long, wiry rhizomes. *Stems:* 8–24″, erect or spreading, slender to rather stout, brittle, few-noded above, base smooth. *Sheaths:* rounded, overlapping, smooth basal often whitish. *Ligules:* minute, truncated. *Blades:* 4–14″, often rolled, finely pointed, smooth below, prominently broad ribs above, thickly downy. *Spikes:* 2–7″, erect, straight or curved, stout, easily snapped above spikelets; axis smooth. *Spikelets:* awnless, elliptical to wedge, 3–8 flowered, arranged alternately in two rows on opposite sides of axis, own length or less apart; glumes lance, blunt, keeled, equal or nearly so; lemmas lance, blunt, keeled. *Fls:* June–August.

Distribution. Frequently found on coasts around the British Isles, only a few feet above highwater.

Sand Couch-grass

Lyme Grass

LYME GRASS *Elymus arenarius*

Description. A bluish-grey perennial, with long, thick rhizomes, forming large tufts or patches. *Stems:* 24–80″, erect or spreading, stout, few-noded, smooth. *Sheaths:* rounded, ridged, smooth. *Ligules:* very short, minutely hairy. *Blades:* 8–30″, flat or inrolled, broad, very sharply pointed, rigid, shortly hairy on ribs, narrow, spreading auricles. *Spikes:* 6–14″, up to 1″ wide, stiffly erect, spikelets usually paired alternating on opposite sides of the axis; bluish. *Spikelets:* awnless, long (up to 1¼″), oblong to wedge, 3–6 flowered, overlapping; glumes narrowly lance, sharply pointed, equal or nearly so, rigid, hairy, especially on keel; lemmas lance, pointed, decreasing in size upwards, covered with dense, soft, short hair. *Fls:* June–August.

Distribution. Widespread around coasts of the British Isles, locally abundant on east and north. Used to bind loose dune sand, sometimes in conjunction with Marram Grass.

MEADOW BARLEY   *Hordeum secalinum*
Description. A green or greyish-green tufted perennial. *Stems:* 8–25″, erect or ascending from a bent base, slender, stiff, 3–5 noded, smooth. *Sheaths:* rounded, lower downy, upper smooth and hairless. *Ligules:* very short. *Blades:* 2–6″, flat or rolled, narrow, rough, or smooth beneath, sparsely hairy to hairless, very short, spreading auricles. *Spikes:* ¾–3″, erect, dense, spikelets in threes alternating on opposite sides of the slender main axis. *Spikelets:* awned, consist of large central fertile, bisexual florets (lemma awn longer than glumes) and two sterile, smaller florets (awns shorter than glumes); all glumes are bristle-like, equal and awned; fertile lemmas broadly lance, tipped with a long, straight awn; sterile lemmas narrowly lance, tipped with a short awn. *Fls:* June–July.
Distribution. Common on grassy lowlands of the British Isles, but rare in N. Scotland.

Meadow Barley   Wall Barley

WALL BARLEY   *Hordeum murinum*
Description. A loosely tufted or solitary annual. *Stems:* 8–30″, erect or ascending from a bent base, slender to rather stout, 3–5 noded, smooth. *Sheaths:* rounded, lower downy, upper smooth. *Ligules:* minute. *Blades:* 1–8″, flat, finely pointed, narrow spreading auricles, loosely hairy or hairless, rough. *Spikes:* 2–7″, erect or leaning, dense, compressed; green or tinged purple. *Spikelets:* awned, in threes, alternating on opposite sides of axis, middle bisexual floret flanked by two smaller sterile ones; all glumes bristle-like shortly hairy, and stiffly, long awned; all lemmas narrowly lance, tipped with long, stiff awns (that of the fertile lemma being the longest). *Fls:* May–July.
Distribution. Common and widespread throughout the British Isles, especially near buildings.

SEA BARLEY *Hordeum marinum*
Description. A loosely tufted or solitary annual. *Stems:* 5–16″, erect or ascending from a bent base, slender, stiff, 3–4 noded, smooth. *Sheaths:* rounded, smooth, or lower downy. *Ligules:* minute. *Blades:* ½–3″, flat, tapering to a fine point, often with small to minute auricles, stiff, minutely hairy or hairless; bluish-green. *Spikes:* 1–3″, oblong, erect, dense; green or purplish. *Spikelets:* awned, in threes, alternating on opposite sides of main axis, consisting of a large, bisexual, stalkless floret, and two lateral, barren florets on short stalks. Central floret: glumes bristle-like, terminating in a long, straight, fine awn; lemmas ovate, smooth, terminating in a long, straight awn. Lateral floret: glumes bristle-like, dissimilar (upper winged), rough, tipped by a long, straight, rough awn; lemmas lance, tipped with short, straight awns. *Fls:* June–July.
Distribution. Widespread on salt-marsh margins and coasts of England and Wales; locally common; rare in Scotland.

Sea Barley   Crested Hair-grass   Yellow (Crested) Oat-grass

CRESTED HAIR-GRASS *Koeleria gracilis* (*K. cristata*)
Description. A compactly tufted perennial, with slender, wiry rhizomes. *Stems:* 4–20″, erect, or slightly curved at base, slender, 1–3 noded, downy, especially towards panicles, or hairless. *Sheaths:* tubular at first, rounded, lower downy or hairy, basal may be brownish. *Ligules:* very short. *Blades:* 2–8″, usually inrolled (bristle-like) or flat, narrow, bluntly pointed, finely hairy to hairless; green to grey-green. *Panicles:* ¼–4″, spike-like, erect, narrow, very dense, sometimes lobed below; silver-green to purplish, shining. *Spikelets:* awnless, wedge to oblong, 2–3 flowered; glumes narrowly oblong, pointed, very unequal; lemmas lance, pointed. Yellow anthers. *Fls:* June–July.
Distribution. Common on dry grasslands, especially on calcareous and sandy soils, up to about 2,000 feet throughout the British Isles.

YELLOW OAT-GRASS (Crested Oat-grass) *Trisetum flavescens*
Description. A loosely tufted perennial, with stolons. *Stems:* 8–30″, erect, stiff, slender, sometimes hairy about the 2–5 nodes or smooth. *Sheaths:* rounded, lower often downy or hairy. *Ligules:* very short. *Blades:* 2–6″, flat, narrow, tapering to a fine point, often hairy above, slightly rough to smooth and hairless beneath. *Panicles:* 2–6″, usually erect, oblong to ovate, fairly loose;

usually yellowish, rarely green, purplish or variegated, glistening, becoming dull; fine, loosely divided branches in clusters. *Spikelets:* awned, oblong to wedge and gaping, 2–4 flowered; glumes lance, pointed, very unequal; lemmas narrowly lance, tipped with two short bristles or teeth, fine, bent awn rises from the centre of the back. *Fls:* May–July.

Distribution.   Common on grassland or hill pastures, especially on calcareous soils of England and Wales; rare in Scotland and Ireland.

COMMON WILD OAT   *Avena fatua*

Description.   A very variable, solitary or tufted annual. *Stems:* 12–40″, erect or bent at base, stout, 3–5 noded, smooth. *Sheaths:* rounded, basal often loosely hairy. *Ligules:* variable length, blunt or torn. *Blades:* 4–18″, flat, broadening rapidly from base, then tapering to a fine point, rough; bright green. *Panicles:* 4–16″, nodding, pyramidal, open and loose; green; widespreading, fine, clustered branches; pedicels unequal. *Spikelets:* awned, narrowly ˏoblong or gaping, drooping, 2–3 flowered; glumes lance, pointed, equal or nearly so; lemmas lance, tipped with two short teeth, often bearded, stout bent awn rises from centre of back. *Fls:* June–September.

Distribution.   Common weed on arable and waste, often abundant among cereals, throughout the British Isles.

Common Wild Oat   Winter Wild Oat

WINTER WILD OAT   *Avena ludoviciana*

Description.   A solitary or tufted annual. *Stems:* 24–72″, erect, or bent at base, stout, 2–4 noded, smooth. *Sheaths:* rounded, basal slightly hairy. *Ligules:* long, blunt to pointed. *Blades:* 6–24″, flat, broadening from base, then tapering to a fine point, firm, rough and hairless on both sides. *Panicles:* 6–18″, nodding, pyramidal, very loose; green; spreading, clustered branches. *Spikelets:* awned, lance to ovate, later gaping, drooping, 2–3 flowered; glumes lance, pointed, equal or nearly so; lemmas lance to ovate, pointed, tipped with two short teeth, bearded at base, stout, bent awn rises from ce ntre of back   *Fls:* June–August.

Distribution.   An arable weed, fairly common in the southern half of England, reported to be spreading.

MEADOW OAT-GRASS   *Helictotrichon pratense*
Description.   A densely tufted perennial, with creeping rootstock.   *Stems:* 12–30″, erect, slender, 1–2 noded near base, smooth.   *Sheaths:* rounded or keeled upwards, smooth, or minutely rough.   *Ligules:* pointed, upper long. *Blades:* basal 2–12″, stem shorter, often flattening, margins minutely rough, blunt or abruptly pointed, stiff; bluish-green above.   *Panicles:* 2–5″, erect, narrow; green or purplish; erect, short branches, paired or solitary, with 1–2 spikelets.   *Spikelets:* awned, oblong, 3–6 flowered; glumes lance, pointed, unequal; lemmas narrowly oblong, two short teeth at tip, bent and twisted awn rises from centre of back.   *Fls:* June–July.
Distribution.   Common on dry chalk and limestone soils, but found throughout the British Isles.

Meadow Oat-grass   Hairy Oat-grass

HAIRY OAT-GRASS   *Helictotrichon pubescens*
Description.   A loosely tufted perennial, with short rhizomes.   *Stems:* 12–30″, erect or bent at base, rather stout, 2–3 noded, smooth.   *Sheaths:* tubular at first, soon splitting, lower downy or loosely hairy, upper usually smooth; green or purple.   *Ligules:* long, pointed or blunt.   *Blades:* lower 2–12″, upper shorter, folded when young, later flat, pointed or blunt, downy or softly hairy, often becoming hairless.   *Panicles:* 2–8″, erect or nodding, lance to oblong; green to purplish; fine, clustered branches bear 1–3 spikelets.   *Spikelets:* awned, oblong, loosely 2–3 flowered, axis long hairy; glumes narrowly lance, pointed, unequal; lemmas narrowly lance, tip four-toothed, long bent and twisted awn rises from centre of back   *Fls:* May–July.
Distribution.   Common on lowland pastures and other grasslands, especially on damp calcareous and basic gravelly soils, throughout the British Isles.

TALL OAT-GRASS   (False Oat-grass)   *Arrhenatherum elatius*
Description.   A loosely tufted perennial, with short yellowish roots.   *Stems:* 30–60″, erect or slightly bent at base, stout, usually smooth, but sometimes hairy at 3–5 nodes.   *Sheaths:* rounded, usually smooth.   *Ligules:* short.   *Blades:*

4–18", flat, finely pointed, minutely rough or sparsely hairy. *Panicles:* 4–12", erect or nodding; green or purplish, shining; unequal, rough, clustered branches. *Spikelets:* awned, oblong or gaping, usually two-flowered; glumes lance, pointed, very unequal; lemmas ovate, tipped with two short teeth, long twisted and bent awn rises from the lower half. *Fls:* June–August.

Distribution. A very common grass on rough grasslands, rocky slopes and waste, found throughout the British Isles, but not where the ground is too wet or acidic.

Tall (False) Oat-grass   Yorkshire Fog   Creeping Soft-grass

YORKSHIRE FOG *Holcus lanatus*
Description. A loosely or compactly tufted perennial. *Stems:* 8–32", erect, sometimes bent at base, slender to stout, 2–5 noded, usually downy. *Sheaths:* rounded, hairy or downy. *Ligules:* short, truncated. *Blades:* 2–8", flat, narrow base broadening, then tapering to a fine point, downy on both sides; greyish-green to green. *Panicles:* 1–8", erect or nodding, ovate, very dense to fairly loose; whitish-green, pale green, pinkish or purple; whorled, hair-like, closely divided branches. *Spikelets:* minutely awned, oblong or gaping, two-flowered; glumes ovate, stiffly hairy on upper margins and keels, unequal, short, awn tipped; lemmas ovate, keeled, unequal, the smaller (upper) has a short hooked awn which rises just below the blunt apex. *Fls:* May–September.

Distribution. A very common grassland weed found throughout the British Isles, especially on rough hill pastures and waste; may be grazed when young.

CREEPING SOFT-GRASS *Holcus mollis*
Description. A perennial with tough rhizomes, forming compact tufts or loose mats. *Stems:* 8–36", spreading or erect, beards of reflex (downward pointing) hairs at 4–7 nodes, otherwise hairless, smooth. *Sheaths:* rounded, hairless, lower sometimes downy. *Ligules:* short. *Blades:* 2–8", flat, broad at base tapering to a fine point, shortly hairy to hairless, usually rough; greyish-green. *Panicles:* 2–5", erect to nodding, narrowly ovate, compact to loose; whitish pale green or purplish; usually erect, unequal, hairy branches; pedicels variable. *Spikelets:* awned, oblong, flattened, two-flowered; glumes lance to ovate, pointed, stiffly hairy on nerves and keels, unequal width; lemmas ovate, lower blunt but fringed with short hairs, upper more pointed, and a bent awn rises just below the short hair-fringed apex. *Fls:* June–August.

Distribution. Common in woods and other shady places throughout the British Isles.

TUFTED HAIR-GRASS *Deschampsia caespitosa*
Description. A densely tufted perennial forming large tussocks. *Stems:* 12–80″, erect or slightly bent at base, fairly slender to stout, stiff, 1–3 noded, smooth. *Sheaths:* rounded or faintly keeled, usually smooth. *Ligules:* long and narrow. *Blades:* 4–24″, flat, sharply pointed to rather blunt, stiff, rough on margins and coarse ribs above, smooth beneath; green. *Panicles:* 4–20″, erect or nodding, ovate to oblong, loose; green, silvery, yellow, purple or variegated in these colours; long, very thin, spreading, clustered branches, rough and bare below. *Spikelets:* awned, lance to oblong, loosely scattered or clustered, two-flowered; glumes lance, pointed, unequal width; lemmas truncated lance, toothed or jagged apex, with a fine, straight awn rising from near the base. *Fls:* June–August.
Distribution. A common weed on wet or poorly drained clay soils throughout the British Isles.

Tufted Hair-grass

Wavy Hair-grass

WAVY HAIR-GRASS *Deschampsia flexuosa*
Description. A loosely to densely tufted perennial, sometimes with slender rhizomes. *Stems:* 8–20″, erect or bent at base, slender, 1–3 noded, smooth. *Sheaths:* rounded, hairless, upper rough. *Ligules:* short, blunt or truncated. *Blades:* 3–9″, tightly inrolled, rough towards sharply pointed or blunt apex, mostly basal; green. *Panicles:* 2–6″, nodding, very open and loose; long, spreading, wavy, hair-like branches, much divided above; long pedicels. *Spikelets:* awned, oblong to wedge, 2–5 flowered, silvery, purplish or brownish; glumes ovate, pointed, keeled, almost equal; lemmas ovate to lance, blunt, apex small-toothed or jagged, a long bent awn rises from near the base. *Fls:* June–July.
Distribution. Common throughout the British Isles, especially on acidic, peaty or damp soils; found up to about 4,000 feet.

EARLY HAIR-GRASS *Aira praecox*

Description. An annual found solitary or in small many-stemmed tufts. *Stems:* 2–8″, erect, spreading or prostrate, very slender, 2–3 noded, smooth. *Sheaths:* rounded, smooth and hairless. *Ligules:* blunt, fairly short. *Blades:* up to 2″, inrolled, narrow, blunt, smooth or minutely rough, mostly basal, hairless. *Panicles:* spike-like, narrowly oblong, compact; silvery, purplish or pale green; minute branches erect. *Spikelets:* awned, ovate to oblong, crowded, two-flowered; glumes lance, pointed, keeled, equal, shiny; lemmas lance, apex double-toothed, a yellowish-brown, bent awn rises from the lower half. *Fls:* April–June.

Distribution. Common on acidic and drier soils throughout the British Isles, up to 2,000 feet.

Early Hair-grass   Silvery Hair-grass

SILVERY HAIR-GRASS *Aira caryophyllea*

Description. An annual in few- to many-stemmed tufts or solitary. *Stems:* 2–16″, erect, or spreading, very slender, 2–3 noded in lower half, smooth. *Sheaths:* rounded, minutely rough upwards, hairless. *Ligules:* pointed and toothed. *Blades:* ¼–2″, inrolled, slender, blunt, minutely rough, hairless; greyish-green. *Panicles:* ½–4″, ovate, very loose; main axis often wavy; fairly long, hair-like branches, bare at base, often repeatedly divided into threes. *Spikelets:* awned, ovate, in loose clusters, two-flowered; silvery, sometimes tinged with purple; glumes lance, pointed, equal, slightly rough on keel; lemmas lance, finely two-toothed apex, a bent awn rises from near the base. *Fls:* May–June.

Distribution. Common throughout the British Isles, especially on dry gravelly or sandy soils, heaths, etc.

MARRAM GRASS *Ammophila arenaria*

Description. A compactly tufted perennial, with stout rhizomes and a mass of fine roots. *Stems:* 20–48″, erect or spreading, fairly stout, stiff, few-noded, smooth. *Sheaths:* rounded, smooth, overlapping, loose. *Ligules:* narrow, pointed, sometimes long. *Blades:* 8–24″, flat or tightly inrolled, sharply pointed, stiff, densely hairy and close-ribbed above, smooth beneath. *Panicles:* 3–4″, spike-like, cylindrical tapering above; whitish-green; minute branches erect. *Spikelets:* awnless, narrowly oblong or gaping, one-flowered; glumes narrowly lance, pointed, equal or almost so; lemmas lance, blunt, keeled. *Fls:* July–August, when the yellow anthers are prominent.

Distribution. Common on coastal sand-dunes around the coasts of the British Isles, where it is valuable in consolidating otherwise shifting sand.

Marram Grass   Wood Small-reed

WOOD SMALL-REED (Bush Grass) *Calamagrostis epigejos*

Description. A tufted or tussocky perennial, with rhizomes. *Stems:* 24–80″, erect, slender to fairly stout, 2–3 noded, slightly rough near panicles, otherwise smooth. *Sheaths:* rounded, smooth, hairless, close-fitting. *Ligules:* long, becoming torn and jagged. *Blades:* 6–28″, flat, tapering to a long, fine point, rough, closely nerved; dull green. *Panicles:* 6–12″, erect, lance to oblong, dense; green to purplish-brown; long, fine branches, rough; pedicels very short. *Spikelets:* awned, narrowly lance, or gaping, densely clustered, one-flowered; glumes narrowly lance, equal or nearly so, two or three times length of lemmas, rough on keels; lemmas oblong, two fine teeth and central short awn at apex, base surrounded by erect, fine, white hairs. *Fls:* June–August.

Distribution. Quite common in damp woods, hedgerows and fens, especially on heavy soils, in England; infrequent to rare elsewhere.

BRISTLE-LEAVED BENT *Agrostis setacea*

Description. A densely tufted perennial, growing singly or forming a dense mat. *Stems:* 6–24″, erect or bent at base, very slender, stiff, 2–3 noded, rough at nodes and towards the panicles. *Sheaths:* rounded, slightly rough, basal straw-coloured, hairless. *Ligules:* narrow, pointed, sometimes torn. *Blades:* 2–8″, bristle-like, finely pointed, thin, minutely rough, hairless; green to greyish-green. *Panicles:* 1–4″, erect, narrowly lance, dense and almost spike-like, but spreading during flowering; purplish to green; short, divided, clustered branches, minutely rough; pedicels short. *Spikelets:* awned, lance, one-flowered; glumes lance, pointed, long, almost equal; lemmas truncated ovate, two-thirds size of glumes, outer nerves project as points at apex, a fine, longish awn rises from near the base. *Fls:* June–July.

Distribution. Locally common on dry sandy or peaty soils in S. England and Glamorgan.

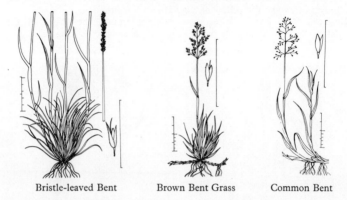

Bristle-leaved Bent   Brown Bent Grass   Common Bent

BROWN BENT GRASS *Agrostis canina* ssp. *montana*
Description. A densely tufted perennial, with slender, scaly rhizomes. *Stems:* 6–24″, erect or bent at base, slender, 1–2 noded, smooth, rarely minutely rough above. *Sheaths:* rounded, smooth, hairless. *Ligules:* pointed or torn. *Blades:* 1–6″, flat, narrow, tapering to a fine point, minutely rough on both sides, or smooth below, hairless; green to greyish-green; mostly basal. *Panicles:* 1–8″, narrowly pyramidal or ovate, fairly close and dense except during flowering; green, purplish or brown; hair-like, clustered branches, almost erect, undivided below; pedicels short. *Spikelets:* usually awned, narrowly lance, closely clustered, one-flowered; glumes lance, pointed, equal; lemmas ovate, truncated, 4–5 nerves project as short points, a fine, bent awn rises from near the base. *Fls:* June–August.
Distribution. Common throughout the British Isles, especially on heaths, hill pastures and other acidic soils.

COMMON BENT *Agrostis tenuis*
Description. A loosely to densely tufted perennial, with short rhizomes and sometimes stolons. *Stems:* 4–30″, erect or spreading, slender, 2–5 noded, smooth. *Sheaths:* rounded, smooth, hairless. *Ligules:* short and squat. *Blades:* ½–6″, flat, finely pointed, smooth to minutely rough, hairless; green. *Panicles:* ½–8″, ovate to pyramidal, erect or nodding, usually loose and open; green or purplish; spreading, hair-like, clustered branches, divided in outer half only; pedicels short. *Spikelets:* awnless, narrowly lance, one-flowered, single or in pairs; glumes lance, pointed, equal or almost so; lemmas ovate, truncated, shorter than glumes. *Fls:* June–August.
Distribution. Very common on heaths, moors and acidic soils throughout the British Isles at all altitudes.

BLACK BENT (Red Top) *Agrostis gigantea*
Description. A loosely tufted perennial, with tough rhizomes. *Stems:* 16–40″, erect or bent at base, rooting and branching at lower nodes, slender to stout, 3–6 noded, smooth. *Sheaths:* rounded, smooth or minutely rough,

hairless. *Ligules:* blunt and toothed. *Blades:* 2–8″, flat, sometimes rolled when young, strongly nerved above, firm, minutely rough; dull green. *Panicles:* 3–10″, ovate, erect, open and loose; green or purplish; spreading, clustered branches, much-divided above, rough. *Spikelets:* awnless, lance to oblong, pointed, one-flowered; glumes lance, pointed, equal; lemmas ovate to oblong, blunt, two-thirds length of glumes. *Fls:* June–August.

Distribution. A common weed throughout the British Isles, especially in lowland woods, rough grassland and hedgerows.

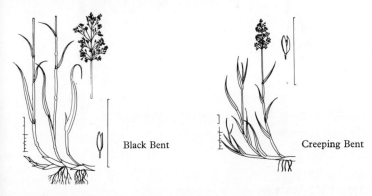

Black Bent   Creeping Bent

CREEPING BENT   *Agrostis stolonifera*
Description. A tufted perennial, spreading by leafy stolons – but no rhizomes – to form a close turf. *Stems:* 6–20″, erect or rising from a bent or almost prostrate base, rooting at lower nodes, slender, 2–5 noded, smooth. *Sheaths:* rounded, usually smooth, hairless. *Ligules:* rounded or torn. *Blades:* ½–4″, flat, sometimes rolled when young, finely pointed, minutely rough, hairless; green, greyish- or bluish-green. *Panicles:* ½–5″, narrowly pyramidal to oblong, contracted except during flowering, often dense and lobed; green, whitish or purple; closely divided, short, clustered branches; pedicels short. *Spikelets:* awnless, lance to oblong, densely clustered, one-flowered; glumes lance, rough on keels, almost equal; lemmas ovate, truncated or blunt. *Fls:* July–August.

Distribution. A very common grass throughout the British Isles, occurring on many types of soil – from salt-marsh to chalk and clays – up to about 2,500 feet.

SMALLER CAT'S-TAIL   *Phleum nodosum* (*P. bertolonii*)
Description. A loosely to compactly tufted perennial, sometimes with leafy stolons. *Stems:* 4–20″, erect or rising from a bent or prostrate base, slender, stiff, 2–6 noded (basal 1–2 internodes short and often swollen), smooth. *Sheaths:* rounded, smooth, lower black or darkish brown, upper green and loose-fitting. *Ligules:* pointed or blunt and torn. *Blades:* 1–4″, flat, broad base, tapering to a fine point, minutely rough on margins and sometimes on nerves; green to greyish-green. *Panicles:* ½–3″, spike-like, narrowly cylindrical, blunt, dense; pale or whitish-green, sometimes tinged purple; pedicels minute. *Spikelets:* shortly awned, oblong, tightly packed and somewhat flattened, one-flowered; glumes oblong, truncated, equal, white hair-fringed keels terminate in

short awns; lemmas very broadly ovate, truncated, two-thirds length of glumes.
Fls: June–August.
Distribution.   Common on hills and old pastures on most soils throughout
the British Isles.

Smaller Cat's-tail   Timothy Grass

TIMOTHY GRASS   *Phleum pratense*
Description.   A loosely to densely tufted perennial.   *Stems:* 12–40″, erect or
bent at base, stout, 3–6 noded (lower 1–3 internodes often short and swollen),
smooth.   *Sheaths:* rounded, basal turning darkish brown, hairless.   *Ligules:*
long and blunt.   *Blades:* 4–18″, flat, taper to a fine point, rough on margins and
towards apex or all over; green to greyish-green or bluish.   *Panicles:* 2–7″,
spike-like, narrowly cylindrical, blunt, dense; greyish-green to purple; pedicels
minute.   *Spikelets:* awned, oblong, closely packed, one-flowered; glumes
oblong, truncated, equal, hair-fringed keels terminate in rigid, short awns;
lemmas very broadly ovate, blunt, two-thirds length of glumes.   *Fls:* June–
August.
Distribution.   A common grass grown for hay and grazing throughout the
British Isles; most frequent in the moist lowland soils; also found wild.

SAND CAT'S-TAIL   *Phleum arenarium*
Description.   A solitary or tufted, hairless annual.   *Stems:* 1–6″, rarely up to
12″, erect or bent at base, very slender, stiff, 1–4 noded below middle, smooth.
Sheaths: rounded, smooth, lower pale green to nearly white, upper somewhat
inflated.   *Ligules:* pointed.   *Blades:* ¼–3″, flat, tapering to a point, closely
nerved, margins sometimes minutely rough, otherwise smooth; pale to whitish-
green.   *Panicles:* ¼–2″, spike-like, narrowly cylindrical, rounded to blunt apex,
tapering base, very dense; pale to whitish-green, sometimes tinged with purple;
pedicels minute.   *Spikelets:* awned, lance to oblong, closely overlapping, one-
flowered; glumes lance, pointed, upper keels hair-fringed and terminate in very
short awns; lemmas broadly ovate, truncated or jagged, one-third length of
glumes.   *Fls:* May–July.
Distribution.   Common on sand-dunes around the coasts of the British Isles,

where it binds the sand, appearing after Marram in the succession; rare on inland sandy soils.

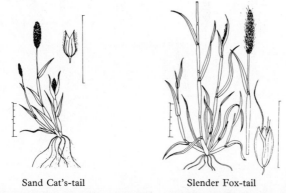

Sand Cat's-tail   Slender Fox-tail

SLENDER FOX-TAIL (Black Grass)   *Alopecurus myosuroides*
Description. A loosely to compactly tufted, hairless annual. *Stems:* 6–30″, erect or bent at base, slender, few-noded, smooth. *Sheaths:* rounded, smooth; upper loose-fitting, sometimes tinged with purple. *Ligules:* blunt or jagged. *Blades:* 1–6″, flat, fairly wide, tapering to a fine point, rough on both sides or smooth beneath; green to bluish-green. *Panicles:* 1–5″, spike-like, very narrow, dense, blunt apex; pale or yellowish green or purple; pedicels minute. *Spikelets:* awned, narrowly lance to oblong, closely packed, flattened, one-flowered; glumes lance, pointed, equal, lower third of margins united, keels narrowly winged; lemmas broadly ovate, blunt, lower third of margins united, long, fine basal awn. *Fls:* June–August.
Distribution. A common arable and grassland weed scattered throughout the British Isles, locally abundant in S. England.

MEADOW FOX-TAIL (Common Fox-tail)   *Alopecurus pratensis*
Description. A loosely to compactly tufted perennial. *Stems:* 12–40″, erect or bent at base, usually rather stout, few noded, smooth, hairless; green, paler above. *Sheaths:* rounded, hairless, basal dark brown. *Ligules:* blunt. *Blades:* basal up to 16″, upper mostly shorter, finely pointed, rolled when young becoming flat, minutely rough, hairless. *Panicles:* 1–4″, spike-like, cylindrical, rounded apex, very dense; green or yellowish-green, rarely purplish; pedicels minute. *Spikelets:* awned, lance, flattened, one-flowered; glumes narrowly lance, equal, margins united at base, keels fringed with fine hair; lemmas ovate, pointed, keeled, a long straight awn rises from near the base. *Fls:* April–July.
Distribution. A very common grass throughout the British Isles, especially in moist, lowland soils.

MARSH FOX-TAIL (Floating Fox-tail)   *Alopecurus geniculatus*
Description. A perennial with the stem sometimes creeping or floating. *Stems:* 6–18″, rising from a bent or prostrate base, often rooting at lower nodes, slender, variably noded, smooth; often whitish-green in ascending parts. *Sheaths:* rounded, hairless, upper loosely fitting. *Ligules:* long, blunt. *Blades:*

Meadow Fox-tail   Marsh (Floating) Fox-tail

1–5″, flat, fairly sharply pointed, minutely rough on nerves above, smooth beneath, hairless; green or greyish-green. *Panicles:* ½–3″, spike-like, cylindrical, rounded apex, dense, green, sometimes tinged blue or purple; pedicels minute. *Spikelets:* awned, oblong, closely packed, one-flowered; glumes narrowly oblong, blunt, shortly hairy on keels, margins united at base, equal; lemmas ovate, truncated, a long awn rises from near the base. *Fls:* June–August.

Distribution.   Common throughout the British Isles in ponds and other wet or moist places.

WOOD MILLET   *Milium effusum*
Description.   A loosely tufted, hairless perennial. *Stems:* 18–60″, erect or bent at base, slender to moderately stout, 3–5 noded below middle, smooth. *Sheaths:* rounded, smooth. *Ligules:* pointed or torn. *Blades:* 4–12″, flat, broad at base, almost parallel-sided, sharply pointed, smooth, or rough on nerves above; dull green. *Panicles:* 4–16″, oblong, nodding, very loose; pale green; long, spreading or reflexed, clustered branches, undivided for much of

Wood Millet   Sweet Vernal Grass

their length; pedicels shortish. *Spikelets:* awnless, ovate, one-flowered; glumes ovate, pointed, equal; lemmas broadly ovate, blunt, shiny. *Fls:* May–July.

Distribution. Fairly common throughout the British Isles; locally abundant in Beech and Oak woods on clay or calcareous soils, especially in the south.

SWEET VERNAL GRASS *Anthoxanthum odoratum*

Description. A tufted perennial. *Stems:* 5–30", erect or somewhat spreading, slender to fairly stout. 1–3 noded, smooth. *Sheaths:* rounded, smooth, bearded at leaf-junctions, otherwise hairless or sparsely hairy. *Ligules:* blunt or jagged, upper sometimes pointed. *Blades:* 5–12", flat, broad at base, tapering gradually to a fine point (often longest and broadest in damp places), hairless to sparsely hairy; green. *Panicles:* ½–5", spike-like, narrowly oblong, sometimes lobed below, generally dense; green to purplish; branches and pedicels very short to minute. *Spikelets:* minutely awned, lance, flattened, three-flowered (lower two barren); glumes lance, pointed, keels extend as short points, very unequal; fertile lemmas ovate, smooth, awnless, brown, about half length of larger glume; sterile lemmas oblong, truncated, hairy, about half size of larger glume, a long, bent awn rises from the base. *Fls:* April–July.

Distribution. Very common on heaths, moors and other grassland throughout the British Isles.

REED CANARY GRASS *Phalaris arundinacea*

Description. A large, hairless perennial, spreading by extensive rhizomes. *Stems:* 20–72", erect, or rarely bent at base, stout, 4–6 noded, smooth. *Sheaths:* rounded, smooth. *Ligules:* long (up to ½"), blunt, later becoming jagged. *Blades:* 4–15", flat, broad at base, tapering gradually to a fine point, firm, rough towards apex; green to whitish-green. Dead blades are retained throughout the winter. *Panicles:* 2–10", lance to oblong, lobed, dense, but rather looser below; pale green or purplish; erect branches spread during flowering, very closely divided and rough; pedicels very short. *Spikelets:* awnless, oblong or gaping, densely crowded, flattened, one-flowered; glumes lance, pointed, keeled, equal or almost so; fertile lemmas broadly lance, pointed, silky hairy, becoming glossy below; sterile lemmas narrowly lance, pointed, keeled, hairy. *Fls:* June–August.

Distribution. A common grass beside water and in wet places throughout the British Isles.

COMMON REED *Phragmites communis*

Distribution. Usually an unbranched perennial, spreading by short rhizomes and stolons. *Stems:* 18–120" (with an average of 6–7 feet), erect, stout, rigid, smooth. *Sheaths:* rounded, close-fitting and overlapping, smooth. *Ligules:* represented by dense fringes of short hairs. *Blades:* 8–24", flat, broad (up to 1¼"), but base contracted where it breaks off in winter; greyish-green. *Panicles:* 6–14", obovate, erect, dense and purplish-brown at first, becoming nodding, loose and greyer; much-divided, smooth, erect branches; pedicels short. *Spikelets:* awnless, lance, 2–6 flowered (lowest sterile); axis covered with silvery hairs; glumes lance, pointed, very unequal; fertile lemmas very narrowly lance, finely pointed, surrounded with long, white, silky hairs; sterile lemmas lance, pointed, smooth. *Fls:* August–October.

Distribution. Common in swamps, fens and other shallow waters throughout the lowlands of the British Isles. Collected for thatching and packing.

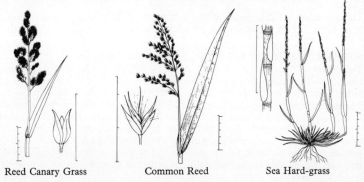

Reed Canary Grass   Common Reed   Sea Hard-grass

SEA HARD-GRASS *Parapholis strigosa*
Description. A solitary or loosely tufted annual. *Stems:* 6–16″, usually ascending from a bent base, or spreading, loosely branched, very slender, few- to many-noded, smooth and often shiny. *Sheaths:* rounded, smooth, lower loosely fitting. *Ligules:* very short, blunt or minutely toothed. *Blades:* ½– 2½″, flat or rolled, pointed, margins and nerves above rough; greyish-green or green. *Spikes:* 1–8″, straight or almost so, very slender, stiff; green or purplish; smooth, jointed axis, deeply hollowed where the spikelets fit closely, alternating in two rows on opposite sides, horizontal joints break easily. *Spikelets:* awnless, narrowly oblong, sharply pointed, one-flowered; glumes narrowly lance, pointed, equal; lemmas ovate, pointed to blunt, almost as long as glumes. *Fls:* June–August.
Distribution. Common around the coasts of the British Isles, locally abundant on salt-marshes and mud-flats; also found on damp, heavy soils near the sea.

MAT-GRASS *Nardus stricta*
Description. A densely tufted perennial with short rhizomes. *Stems:* 4–15″, erect, slender, wiry, one-noded near base, smooth. *Sheaths:* rounded, smooth, basal ones crowded, short and pale, the lowest whitish and leafless. *Ligules:* very short. *Blades:* 2–12″, tightly rolled (bristle-like), sharply pointed, very stiff, erect at first, later spreading towards the horizontal; greyish-green to green. *Spikes:* 1–4″, erect, very slender, one-sided, with axis projecting about ¼″; green to purple. *Spikelets:* awned, narrowly lance, in two rows on one side of the axis, overlapping, one-flowered; glumes, usually only lower is present, lance, very small; lemmas narrowly lance, pointed, tipped with a short awn, keeled. *Fls:* June–August.
Distribution. Common on poor acidic soils of heaths, moors and upland pastures throughout the British Isles, especially in the north and west.

TOWNSEND'S CORD-GRASS *Spartina townsendii*
Description. A clump-forming perennial, with soft, fleshy rhizomes. *Stems:* 15–50″, erect, stout, very stiff, smooth and hairless. *Sheaths:* rounded, smooth, overlapping. *Ligules:* represented by a dense fringe of hair. *Blades:* 6–18″

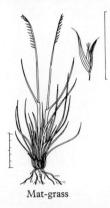

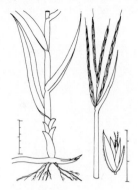

Mat-grass   Townsend's Cord-grass

flat or rolled, finely pointed, stiff, closely ribbed above; yellowish-green to
bright green. *Inflorescence:* usually 3–6 spikes forming a raceme. *Spikes:* up
to 9″, stiffly erect, dense; smooth, triangular axis terminating in a bristle about
1½″ long. *Spikelets:* awnless, narrowly lance, arranged in two rows on one side
of the axis, closely overlapping, one-flowered; glumes lance, pointed, keeled,
downy, very unequal but similar; lemmas lance, pointed, keeled, downy above.
Fls: June–October.
Distribution. Common on tidal mud-flats and spreading along southern
coasts of England, where its extensive root-system stabilises and binds the mud.

Sedges

COMMON COTTON-GRASS *Eriophorum angustifolium*
Description. The stems rise at intervals from creeping rootstock. *Stems:*
12″, slender, almost cylindrical; yellowish-green. *Ls:* few. Long, narrow,
triangular section, gradually taper to a sharp-point, strongly marked midrib.
Upper sheaths loose. *Fls:* terminal cluster of 2–7 brown spikelets, inner
stalkless, outer ones drooping on fine smooth branches of different lengths.
Open May–June, dazzling white, or faintly mauve, fluffy mass of long silky
bristle hairs.
Distribution. Common on bogs, acid fens, moors and damp sites throughout
the British Isles.

HARE'S-TAIL COTTON-GRASS *Eriophorum vaginatum*
Description. Often forms dense tussocks. *Stems:* 12–20″, slender, rising
from basal tuft of bristle-like leaves; upper part deep green. *Ls:* stem usually
leafless, but lower part encased in loose yellowish-green sheaths. Stem blades,
if present, short, triangular section, pointed or blunt. Basal leaves numerous,
bristle-like, triangular section. *Fls:* some stems barren, others bear long
flower-head of greenish-brown spikelets. Enlarged bristles resemble dense,
globular (1″), cotton-like mass. June onwards.

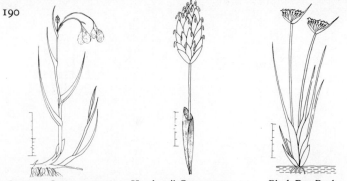

Common Cotton-grass   Hare's-tail Cotton-grass   Black Bog Rush

Distribution. Common on marshy or boggy ground, especially with Sphagnum Moss, which it completely replaces if the area is excessively burnt or grazed.

BLACK BOG RUSH *Schoenus nigricans*
Description. Rush-like, rising from branched rootstock, with long fibrous rootlets. *Stems:* 8–24″, erect, rigid, nearly cylindrical, some barren. *Ls:* no stem leaves, but leaves from rootstock clasp stem base. Very short, thin, rigid; dark green. Sheaths are dark brown to blackish. *Fls:* terminal, V-shaped, compact, spikelets 5–10 flowered, stalkless; numerous, small, blackish bracts considerably overtop panicle.
Distribution. Fairly common on bogs and damp places on calcareous and basic soils.

FLOATING CLUB RUSH *Scirpus fluitans*
Description. Grass-like, floating or submerged, but upper half may be erect above the surface. *Stems:* very slender at base, often twisted, thickening above, with thickish branches, each bearing a small terminal panicle. *Ls:* long, narrow, pointed, grouped at intervals along stems. Close sheaths. *Fls:* a small terminal spike; yellowish-green. July–August.
Distribution. Found locally throughout the British Isles, especially on edges of slow-moving waters.

SEA CLUB RUSH *Scirpus maritimus*
Description. Arises from creeping rootstock forming large tufts. *Stems:* 12–36″, very rough, triangular section, with sharp edges. *Ls:* long, triangular section, keeled, sharp-pointed, very rough on margins; shiny, dark green. *Fls:* large, reddish-brown, oval spikelets, densely crowded and almost stalkless, or loosely branched; glumes awned. One or more large bracts overtop the panicle. June–August.
Distribution. Salt marshes, tidal rivers and brackish water.

COMMON BULRUSH *Scirpus lacustris*
Description. Arises from thick, creeping rootstock. *Stems:* 36–100″, thick

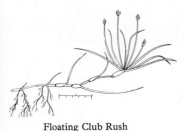

Floating Club Rush

Sea Club Rush

at base, gradually tapering, erect; green to yellowish-green. *Ls:* restricted to base, usually two or three short leaves, sometimes one, but rarely more, long, broad leaf, tapering to a point, all sheathed at the base; deep green. *Fls:* a large head of several clusters of bright reddish-brown spikelets on long branches. One bract at base of panicle elongated and continuous in line with the stem, making the panicle appear lateral instead of terminal. July–September.
Distribution. Found throughout the British Isles, on deep soils on the margins of freshwater lakes, streams and swampy ground.

WHITE BEAK SEDGE *Rhynchospora alba*
Description. *Stems:* 9–14″, slender, smooth, triangular section, branched on one side only, each branch bearing a terminal panicle; dark green. *Ls:* long, narrow, tapering; found on same side as branches; dark green tinged with yellow. Close sheaths, lower ones often leafless. *Fls:* terminal, abruptly V-shaped, crowded cluster, erect, pointed spikelets; pale straw-coloured. Bracts as long as panicle. July–September.
Distribution. Fairly common on bogs, acid moors and heaths, especially in hilly areas throughout the British Isles.

Common Bulrush

White Beak Sedge

GREAT PANICLED SEDGE   *Carex panicula*

Description. Forms large elevated tussocks. *Stems:* 18–72″, stout tapering to slender, triangular section. *Ls:* long (sometimes longer than stem), broad, channelled at base, very rough margins, three prominent longitudinal ribs. Fairly close sheaths. A cluster of short leaves around the base. *Fls:* erect, dense compound spike, 4–5″ long, composed of many spikelets. June–July.

Distribution. Found throughout the British Isles at water-edges, wet and shady places, marshes and soft bogs. Most common in S. England.

Great Panicled Sedge

Flea Sedge

FLEA SEDGE   *Carex pulicaris*

Description. Arises in tufts from creeping rootstock. *Stems:* 6–10″, very slender, leafy below, naked above; grey-green. *Ls:* only found on lower stem. Thin, almost bristle-like, shorter than stem; grey-green. *Fls:* terminal, small, widely separated, rich chestnut-brown, oblong spikelets, ¼″; male above. May–June.

Distribution. Widespread, but localised on wet areas, including pastures, throughout the British Isles.

SAND SEDGE   *Carex arenaria*

Description. Stems arise from thick creeping rootstock. *Stems:* 5–12″, triangular section, leafy below, rough and naked above. *Ls:* restricted to lower half of stem. Narrow, sharp-pointed, curl back; shiny, bright green. Short sheaths; yellowish-green. *Fls:* terminal spike (2″) formed of separated, pointed, pale brown, oblong spikelets, with a very slender, sharply-pointed, leaf-like bract. May–September.

Distribution. Common on coastal sands of S.E. England, and sometimes inland.

FOX SEDGE   *Carex vulpina (C. otrubae)*

Description. *Stems:* 24–36″, stout, erect, rough, triangular section, with very sharp and sometimes ragged edges. *Ls:* arise from base. Long, broad, gradually tapering to a fine point, rough, triangular section, very sharp edges; bright green. Close sheaths sometimes slightly yellowish. Ligules up to ¼″ long. *Fls:* several densely crowded clusters of stalkless spikelets arranged alternately on stem; greenish-yellow, becoming brown when ripe. Outer bract of lower cluster is narrow, pointed and leaf-like. May–July.

Slow worms, The lighter female is on the left.

Adders. The female is on the right.

Smooth snake.

Grass snake basking on a sunny bank.

Above, Brown Rat. *Below,* Black Rat.

Distribution. Found throughout the British Isles in meadows and roadsides. Fairly common in the south, but rare in the extreme north.

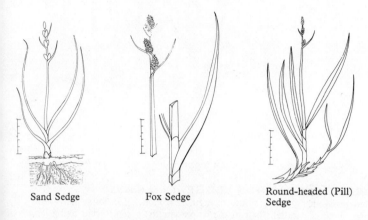

Sand Sedge   Fox Sedge   Round-headed (Pill) Sedge

ROUND-HEADED SEDGE (Pill Sedge) *Carex pilulifera*

Description. Stems arise from creeping rootstock to form broad, rather loose tufts. *Stems:* 6–12″, slender, rough above, erect but droop after flowering. One stem, sometimes with one or more branches arising from the root. *Ls:* very narrow at base, broadening in centre, sharply-pointed, flexible. Confined to lower stem. *Fls:* a few clusters of stalkless spikelets; male terminal, brown, pointed; female below, round, greenish. One bract of lowest cluster often elongated and sharp-pointed. May–June.
Distribution. Found on marshes, moors, damp places and acid heaths throughout the British Isles.

CYPERUS SEDGE *Carex pseudocyperus*

Description. *Stems:* 24–36″, stout, rough, triangular section. *Ls:* spring from whole length of stem. Long (overtop panicle), broadening in centre, long-pointed, midrib very marked; green to pale green or yellowish-green. Close sheaths. Ligules ½″ long. *Fls:* slender, erect, terminal male spike. Several closely crowded, cylindrical (2″), pale green female, on long drooping branches. Prickly appearance of females due to long beak. May–June.
Distribution. Found throughout the British Isles, but very localised on watersides, peat and bogs.

GREAT MARSH SEDGE *Carex riparia*

Description. Stems arise from widely creeping rootstock. *Stems:* 36–60″, stout, rough, triangular section, sharp edges. *Ls:* long, broadening in centre, long tapering point, very sharp edges, midrib prominent; green above, yellowish-green below. Sheaths close-fitting. Ligules ½″ long. *Fls:* crowded, terminal male spike, brown; females below, cylindrical, on short stalks, brownish-green. All spikelets long-pointed. Long, leaf-like, sharply-pointed bracts. May–July.
Distribution. Fairly common along watersides, throughout the British Isles, but less frequent in N. Scotland.

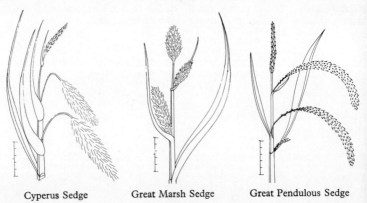

Cyperus Sedge   Great Marsh Sedge   Great Pendulous Sedge

GREAT PENDULOUS SEDGE *Carex pendula*
Description. 36–72″, stout, triangular section. *Ls:* long, flat, wide (1″), three distinct parallel ribs run the whole length; green. Occur along length of stem. *Fls:* terminal male spike, nearly erect, pale reddish-brown; several long (6″), drooping cylindrical female ones below, green to fawn, with long, leafy bracts. May–June.
Distribution. Found throughout the British Isles, except N. Scotland, in damp, shady places, especially on heavy clays.

LESSER MARSH SEDGE *Carex acutiformis*
Description. *Stems:* 24–36″, stout, triangular, section, with very sharp edges, rough. *Ls:* very long, broad, tapering to a sharp point, very sharp rough edges, strongly keeled; green to grey-green. Ligules ½–1″ long. *Fls:* terminal male spike, sometimes two or three, erect, pale green; female spikes below, compact, brownish-green. All spikelets elliptical and stalkless. May–June.
Distribution. Common throughout the British Isles, except N. Scotland, on watersides, marshes and wet meadows.

Lesser Marsh Sedge   Loose (Distant) Sedge   Pendulous Wood Sedge

LOOSE SEDGE (Distant Sedge)   *Carex distans*
Description.   Arises in tufts from fibrous rootstock.   *Stems:* up to 24″, very slender, erect.   *Ls:* narrow, flat, tapering to a sharp point; shiny green or greyish-green.   *Fls:* terminal, erect, cylindrical male spike, light brown; a few widely-spaced, small, oblong, pale yellowish-brown female spikes, largely hidden by a long, narrow, leaf-like bract. May–July.
Distribution.   Found throughout the British Isles, usually near the sea, in wet places or by brackish water; also locally inland on calcareous fen.

PENDULOUS WOOD SEDGE   *Carex sylvatica*
Description.   *Stems:* 12–18″, very slender.   *Ls:* mostly around the stem base, long, narrow, drooping, soft and silky to the touch.   *Fls:* terminal male spike, slightly nodding, compact, pale brown; 3 or 4 female spikes below, drooping, slender, cylindrical, rather loose, pale green. May–June.
Distribution.   Fairly common in neutral to acid woodland soils throughout the British Isles, except in N. Scotland.

Rushes

SOFT RUSH   *Juncus effusus*
Description.   Creeping perennial rootstock sends up numerous stems, which form densely matted circular tufts.   *Stems:* 12–24″, soft, pliant, tapering to a sharp point, 40–90 fine striations when fresh, almost cylindrical; pale green. White pith continuous.   *Ls:* none, but there are a few short, brown, basal, scale-like sheaths.   *Fls:* apparently lateral, two-thirds up bare stem, but truly terminal, globular, loosely branched cluster of greenish-brown flowers. One bract has become elongated to form the 'stem' above. June–August.
Distribution.   Very common on marshes, wet pastures or waste throughout British Isles.

HARD RUSH   *Juncus inflexus* (*J. glaucus*)
Description.   Black perennial creeping rootstock gives off stems, which form dense tufts.   *Stems:* 12–18″, erect, rigid, 12–18 prominent ridges; dull grey-green. Pith not continuous.   *Ls:* rare, if present, much reduced. Stem base

Soft Rush

Hard Rush

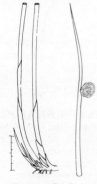

Common Rush

enclosed by short purplish sheaths. *Fls:* apparently lateral, two-thirds up
bare stems, but truly terminal, one bract has become elongated to form 'stem'
above. Widely spreading, long, divided branches, with yellowish-green flowers,
sometimes tinged with brown. June–August.

Distribution.   Fairly common on watersides, wet meadows and moist wastes,
especially on stiff, non-acid soils throughout the British Isles.

COMMON RUSH   *Juncus conglomeratus*

Description.   A number of rigid stems rise from creeping rootstock. *Stems:*
12–30″, rigid to the touch, almost cylindrical, with numerous ridges, prominent
below the flower-head; greyish-green. Pith continuous. *Ls:* none. Stem bases
are sheathed with brown scales. *Fls:* apparently lateral, but really terminal,
one bract has become elongated to form 'stem' above. Globular, very compact,
brown flowers, on short branches. May–July.

Distribution.   Common on watersides and wet ground throughout Britain.

GREAT SHARP SEA RUSH   *Juncus acutus*

Description.   Forms huge tussocks. *Stems:* 48–72″, stout, stiff, erect,
tapering to a very stiff point, rough, almost cylindrical; green. *Ls:* long,
sharply-pointed, rough, very sharp edges. *Fls:* a few inches below their top,
fertile stems bear a cluster of large, pale green spikelets on long, slender, spreading branches. From the base of the cluster two unequal, large, leaf-like, pale
green bracts ascend, the larger being more or less in line with the stem. June–
August.

Distribution.   Found locally near brackish water and among sand-hills of
S. British Isles.

Great Sharp Sea Rush

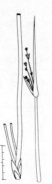

Lesser Sharp Sea Rush

Jointed Rush

LESSER SHARP SEA RUSH   *Juncus maritimus*

Description.   Many stems, forming large tufts, arise from perennial creeping
rootstock, the long fibrous roots of which greatly assist the consolidation of
marshy or muddy soils. *Stems:* 12–24″, stiff, tough, slender, almost cylindrical,
tapering to a sharp point. Pith continuous. Some barren stems occur. *Ls:* none,
but straw-coloured, sharply-pointed sheaths may be found at stem bases.
Fls: almost terminal, loose, on long, slender, almost erect branches. Spikelets

pale green to pale brown. A long, needle-like bract overtops the panicle and is in line with the stem. July-August.

Distribution. Common on salt-marshes and muddy or sandy stretches of tidal rivers of S.W. British Isles.

JOINTED RUSH   *Juncus articulatus*

Description. Stems arise from very fibrous, creeping rootstock. *Stems:* 12–24″, erect, rather slender, somewhat flattened; slightly bluish-green. *Ls:* stiff, narrow, tapering to a sharp point, channelled, with cross partitions at ½″ intervals; slightly bluish-green. Loose-fitting, pale green sheaths. *Fls:* large, very widespreading, terminal panicle. Small, loose clusters of sharply-pointed, chestnut-brown spikelets on long, slender, much-divided branches, with long sharply-pointed, leaf-like bracts. June–August.

Distribution. Common throughout the British Isles on moist pastures, ferns, woodland hollows and watersides.

HEATH RUSH   *Juncus squarrosus*

Description. Prominent in thick tufts in heath paths and other disturbed areas. *Stems:* 8–12″, two or more stems rise from the centre of tuft; flowering stems rigid, erect, somewhat flattened. *Ls:* a cluster of rigid, short, bristle-like leaves spring directly from the thick rootstock, sometimes drooping; yellowish-green. *Fls:* a terminal panicle of large, glossy, brown to reddish-brown flowers, on short branches, somewhat distantly arranged, largely on one side of the stem, which is clasped by large, pointed yellowish to reddish-brown bracts. June–August.

Distribution. Abundant throughout the British Isles on acid moors and heaths; requires little water.

FIELD WOODRUSH   *Luzula campestris*

Description. The creeping rootstock throws off a number of short stems. *Stems:* 3–10″, erect, slender, hairy; dark green. *Ls:* long, broad at base, tapering to a sharp point, hairy margins; dark green. Most arise direct from rootstock, but one or two may spring from stem. *Fls:* terminal male stalkless spikelet. A

Heath Rush

Field Woodrush

few clusters of reddish-brown spikelets of varied length, slender branches; long hairy, leaf-like, pointed bracts. Conspicuous yellow anthers. March–May.

Distribution. Common throughout the British Isles in relatively dry pastures and woodlands, especially at higher elevations, up to 3,000′.

GREAT HAIRY WOODRUSH *Luzula sylvatica*

Description. Once established in large tussocks, it quickly covers the ground with a mat which excludes most other plants. *Stems:* 12–30″, lower in exposed places, taller in woodland; smooth, slender and erect. *Ls:* long, broad, tapering, sometimes sharply-pointed, many distinctly marked parallel veins, fringed with long, white hairs; glossy dark green. The majority are sheathed to the lower stem, but smaller ones may occur above. *Fls:* terminal, very wide-spreading, compact clusters of chestnut-brown flowers, with conspicuous yellow anthers, on long slender, much-divided branches. One or more small leaf-like, sharply-pointed, hairy bracts. May–June.

Distribution. Found throughout the British Isles, except in E. Midlands and East Anglia, in drier places than most rushes and especially in Sessile Oak-woods.

Great Hairy Woodrush

Common Hairy Woodrush

COMMON HAIRY WOODRUSH *Luzula pilosia*

Description. *Stems:* 8–12″, erect, slender; dark green; arise from short root-stock with slender runners. *Ls:* form a tuft at or near the base of stems. Lance-shaped, fringed with fine white hairs; dark bluish-green. A few leaves are rarely sheathed a little way up the stem. *Fls:* terminal. Long, slender branches spread widely in all directions bearing small green to brown spikelets, singly, or in pairs, on separate stalks. Small tapering bracts. March–June.

Distribution. Common throughout the British Isles in woody and shady places.

VEGETATION GLOSSARY

Achene. A small, dry, one-seeded, non-splitting fruit.

Alternate. Of leaves, branches, etc., where one is located on the opposite side of the stem to those immediately next to it.

Annual. A plant which completes its entire life-cycle in one year.

Anther. The pollen-bearing head of the stamen.

Apex. The topmost part. In leaves, the point at the opposite end of the midrib to the stalk.

Auricle. A small ear-like outgrowth at the base of a leaf, or at the junction of leaf-blade and sheath of some grasses.

Awl-like. A slender projection tapering evenly from base to apex.

Awn. A stiff bristle-like projection often found on the glumes and lemmas of some grasses.

Axil. The angle between two adjacent parts of a plant, especially a leaf stalk and the stem or between the midrib and another vein of a leaf.

Axillary. Of, or in, an axil.

Bark. The hard protective layer found on the outside of woody plants.

Base. The bottom part. In leaves the side, or part, near the point of attachment; in tree-trunks, the part at, or near ground level.

Berry. A fleshy, non-splitting fruit containing many seeds.

Biennial. A plant which takes two years to complete its life-cycle.

Blade. The usually flat part of a grass leaf above the sheath (its junction with the stem).

Bole. The part of a tree-trunk between ground level and the first branch.

Bract. A modified leaf-like structure, usually small, found at the base of a leaf, flower, cone-scale, etc.

Branch. An outgrowth from the main stem of a plant, which it resembles, and usually nearer to the horizontal.

 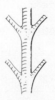

Alternate   Opposite   Whorled

Leaf and twig arrangements

Burr. A seed container which is covered with minute hooks.

Bush. A low dense woody plant with all stems ascending at, or very near, ground level.

Callus. A hard projection at the base of the spikelets of some grasses, which later forms seed units.

Calyx. The outermost whorl of a flower, which consists of sepals, usually green, that may be separate or fused. These completely enclose the bud.

Capsule. A hard dry splitting pod containing many seeds. It is formed from a compound ovary.

Carpel. One or more female reproductive parts of a flowering plant, consisting of a stigma and one or more ovaries. It usually enlarges after fertilisation to become a fruit.

Catkin. A hanging or erect spike of small unisexual petalless flowers, which are usually stalkless.

Cluster. Two or more flowers, leaves or fruits originating from the same point.

Collar. The junction of the sheath and blade of grass; usually whitish, yellowish or purplish.

Compound leaf. A leaf consisting of two or more leaflets, each with its own base and sometimes its own stalk.

Cone. The woody fruit of coniferous or softwood trees.

Cone (Common Spruce)   Coppiced Chestnut

Coppice. The cropping of poles raised by cutting back some deciduous trees near ground level.

Corolla. The petals of a flower considered together.

Corymb. A flat-branched cluster of flowers, each with individual stalks of different lengths. The outer flowers open first.

Crown. The form or outline of tree foliage.

Culm. The stem of a grass.

Cyme. A branched cluster of flowers in which the central flower on the main axis opens first.

Deciduous. Plants which lose their leaves in the autumn, or a falling off of seeds when ripe.

Digitate. A compound leaf in which the leaflets all arise from the same point on the common stalk.

Downy. Covered with short fine hair.

Drupe. A fleshy non-splitting fruit containing a hard stone, which encloses a single seed.

Entire. The leaf margin is without teeth or lobes.

Evergreen. Plants which bear leaves throughout the year, or leafless plants where the stems or some other part remain green.

Felted. Covered with dense short fine hair.

Floret. The flower of grasses.

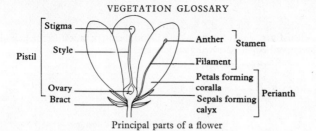

Principal parts of a flower

Flower. The reproductive part of a flowering plant. It consists of the receptacle, sepals, petals, stamens (bearing anthers) and ovaries (with styles bearing stigmas).

Corymb

Cyme

Raceme

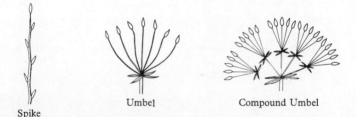

Spike

Umbel

Compound Umbel

Fruit. The seed containing structure formed from a fertilised ovary.

Glabrous. Smooth, not covered with hair.

Glaucous. Bluish-green, often owing to a white wax or to a thick white skin covering the green parts of a plant.

Glume. Two usually empty bracts found at the base of the spikelets of some grasses.

Grain. The bare seed of grasses.

Habitat. The environment inhabited naturally by an animal or plant.

Herb. A plant without woody stems and therefore with no persistent parts above ground.

Husk. The scales (glumes and lemmas) which cover the grain of grasses.

Hybrid. A plant arising from the cross-breeding of two distinct species.

Inflorescence. The flowering part of a plant or the arrangement of a flowering cluster.

Keel. A projecting ridge on the back of a leaf or a seed.

Lance. A leaf-form which is longer than broad, being broadest in the basal half, and the curved edges narrowing at base and apex.

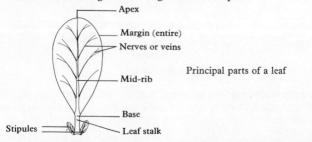

Apex

Margin (entire)

Nerves or veins

Mid-rib   Principal parts of a leaf

Base

Stipules   Leaf stalk

Leaf. The green organ of plants in which photosynthesis takes place.

Lance

Linear

Awn-like

Needle

Oblance

Obovate

Ovate

Sharply pointed:
margin toothed or
serrated

Margin lobed

Palmate lobed

Palmate compound

Pinnate compound

Leaf-axil. The angle between the leaf-stalk and the stem.

Leaflet. The separate green blades of a compound leaf.

Lemma. The lower of the two bracts enclosing a grass flower.

Ligule. A short ribbon or strap outgrowth at the junction of sheath and blade of grasses.

Linear. Long and very narrow, with almost parallel sides.

Lobe. A division of the leaf margin, which does not reach the midrib.

Midrib. The central and largest vein of a leaf, running up the entire length of the leaf from base to apex.

Monoecious. Having flowers of both sexes on the same plant.

Needle. The linear woody leaves of coniferous plants. Long and narrow with almost parallel sides, sometimes cylindrical.

Nerve. The slender veins or ribs of leaves, etc.

Nut. A dry non-splitting one-seeded hard fruit.

Oblance. A leaf form which is longer than broad, but the curved edges narrow towards the base more than at the apex, so that it is broadest in the upper half. An inverted lance.

Obovate. An egg-shaped leaf form with the broadest part in the upper half. An inverted ovate form.

Opposite. Pairs of leaves, branches, etc., with one arising on either side of the stem and at the same level.

Ovate. An egg-shaped leaf form, in which the curving margins narrow more towards the apex than the base, so that the basal half is the broadest.

Ovoid. Egg-shaped, of fruit, etc.

Palea. The upper of the two bracts enclosing a grass flower.

Palmate. Leaflets of a compound leaf originating from the same point, but spreading outwards like the fingers of a hand.

Palmately lobed. Lobes of leaves arranged palmately, as are the main ribs.

Panicle. A branched cluster of flowers, consisting of a main stem, with the flowers on stalks, which may themselves be branched. The whole forming a rough pyramid, with the oldest flowers at the base.

Perennial. A plant which lives for many years.

Persistent. Not falling, remaining in place.

Petal. One of the generally brightly coloured parts of the corolla, or second outermost ring of flower parts.

Pinnate. The leaflets of a compound leaf arranged on either side of a common stalk.

Pistil. The female reproductive part of a flower, consisting of style and stigma.

Plant association. A group of plants which occur together under specific conditions.

Plant succession. The sequence in which plant associations follow one another on barren soil, or where conditions have changed, culminating in a climax vegetation.

Pollard. To cut back trees at above head height, thus restricting the size of the crown.

Pollen. The minute particles produced by the stamens and carried by wind or insects to the stigmas.

Prickle. A thin sharp almost cylindrical structure developed from a surface hair.

Prostrate. Lying on or creeping along the ground.

Raceme. A flowering cluster, consisting of a main stem with unbranched side-shoots, each carrying a flower. The newest flower is at the top.

Recurved. Bent backwards or downwards.

Rhizome. An underground stem from an established plant, with buds in the axils of scale-like leaves.

Rib. The main vein of a leaf.

Runner. A prostrate or trailing stem which puts down roots at nodes as well as producing stems at the same points.

Runner or stolon

Sheath. The lower part of a grass leaf which surrounds the stem.

Shrub. A tallish woody plant with all stems ascending, but rarely more than 20 feet high.

Spike. A stem with stalkless flowers at intervals, giving a tall narrow outline. The term is sometimes also used for any long narrow raceme.

Spine. A modified shoot, bearing flowers or leaves, which does not increase the length of the stem.

Stamen. The male reproductive part of a flower, consisting of anthers and supporting stalk (filament).

Stigma. The receptive organ at the extreme end of the style which catches and retains the pollen.

Stipule. An outgrowth at the base of the leaf-stalk.

Style. The part of a flower which connects the stigma and the ovary.

Toothed. Leaves having small projections on their margins.

Trunk. The main stem of a tree, usually vertical or nearly so.

Tuft. A cluster of stems, especially of grasses.

Umbel. A flowering cluster, in which the flower stalks arise from the same point. The oldest flower is on the outside.

Vegetation. A general term covering all forms of plant life found within an area.

Vegetation, climax. The final plant association of a succession.

Vegetation, natural. The plant life of an area before interference by man.

Whorls. A group of three or more leaves, branches, etc., which arise from the same level on the stem.

WILD ANIMALS

Introduction

With man's increasing control of the landscape, the effects of wild animals have correspondingly declined, but their part cannot be ignored. This becomes obvious either when their numbers reach pest proportions, as can happen locally with Rabbits, Rats and Mice, and Coypu, or when introduced species escape, as was the case with Grey Squirrels, Musk Rats and, more recently, Mink. The position of wild animals in our ecology is not static, but constantly evolving to meet the twentieth century changes in land use. Animals are always interesting in their own right and knowledge of them contributes to an understanding of the natural scene as a whole.

The short key below is for speedy reference to the main animal groups. The main key contains more information for identification of species while the notes further amplify this. For each, the length (head and body) and tail are given in inches, except where there is no distinct tail when total length is given and for the deer, where the height at shoulder is noted. Colours, with variations and characteristic bodily form are followed by brief notes on habitat, types of food, numbers and birth month of young and general distribution, whether purely local, Great Britain (England, Wales and Scotland), or British Isles (including Ireland).

Short Key

Key to the identification of wild animals

1. Animal scaly, legless. Usually hibernates Oct.–March.

a. Length 30–48″. Background colour olive-green, olive-brown or olive-grey; back marked by two rows of small black dots, flanks by nearly vertical black bars; underside chequered black or grey and white. Two large yellow or orange patches just behind the long blunt and narrow head. **Grass Snake,** p. 231

b. Length 18–26″. Colour variable, mostly shades of olive, brown or darker greys. Back bears characteristic darker zigzag line, rarely modified into a series of dots or a straight line. Dark bars on head form **X** or **Λ**. **Viper,** p. 232

c. Length 15–22″. Colour usually a shade of brown, grey or reddish; back marked by pairs of black, red or brown spots or cross-bars. Upper head brown with black neck-patch. Scales smooth. **Smooth Snake,** p. 232

d. Length 10–14″. Colour variable, coppery to yellowish-brown, yellowish-green or grey; dark lines run down the flanks and backs of females. Scales smooth. **Slow Worm,** p. 230

e. As (d), but with light blue to ultramarine spots or bars. **Blue-spotted Slow Worm,** p. 231

2. Animal small, 4-legged, without fur; head blunt.

a. Body 2½″, tail 2½″. Colour variable: often yellowish-brown; also reddish, greenish or greyish-brown; three dark lines, or series of irregularly-shaped spots, along back and flanks; undersides orange or red, spotted black (males) or pale colours, spotted grey (females). **Common Lizard,** p. 230

b. Body 3½″, tail 3½″. Light brown or grey above, undersides cream; lower flanks may be purplish-brown (females) or greenish (males); a series of irregularly-shaped dark brown spots, with white centres, line the back and either flank. Head brown; throat white. Body heavier and legs shorter than (a). **Sand Lizard,** p. 230

3. Upper body spine-covered. Body 9–11″, tail 1″. Spines ¾–1″, dark brown to black with white tips and bases. Yellowish- or greyish-brown fur on head and below. Head pointed, neck very short. **Hedgehog,** p. 211

4. A small, furry animal with a hairy, long and pointed snout extending well beyond mouth; external ear not visible; teeth tipped orange. 3-hour activity cycle.

a. Body 3½″, tail 2¼″. Coat dark to slate-grey above, white or grey below; colours sharply divided. Snout broad; small white ear-

tufts. Tapering, flattened tail fringed by stiff silvery hairs.
Feet brown.   **Water Shrew,** p. 213

b. Body 3″, tail 1½″. Silky coat dark reddish-brown above, grad-
    ing into yellowish or light grey below. Whiskered snout is long
    and flexible. Hairy tail is dark above, lighter below.
                                               Common Shrew, p. 212

c. Body 2″, densely haired tail 1½″. Silky coat light reddish-
    brown above, pale to yellowish-grey below; sharply divided.
    Snout and tail relatively longer and thicker than Common
    Shrew.   **Pygmy Shrew,** p. 212

5. Animal resembles (4), but has a triangular head, large prominent rounded ears and all white teeth. Body 3″, thin tail 2″, with
sparse white hairs. Coat reddish-brown above, pale grey below.
                                               Scilly Shrew, p. 213

6. The black-furred animal has a pointed muzzle, imperceptible
neck and cylindrical body. Body 6″, erect tail 1″. Eyes hidden; no
external ear. Fore-limbs end in broad, shovel-like and outward-
facing feet.   **Mole,** p. 211

7. Small furry animal, rounded head, blunt muzzle, furred tail.
Ears short and rounded, but do not project above head outline.

a. Length 4″, tail 2″, tufted end. Coat reddish-brown above;
    white, yellow or fawn below. White whiskers 1″. **Bank Vole,** p. 216

b. Length 4″, tail 1½″. Coat yellowish-brown to greyish-brown
    above, fawn to pale grey below. Head bluntly oval; short ears
    just visible.   **Short-tailed Vole,** p. 217

c. Length 4½″, tail 2″. Coat dark reddish-brown above, greyish
    below. Found in most Orkney islands.   **Orkney Vole,** p. 217

d. Length 7½″, tail 4″. Coat dark brown to reddish, often sprinkled
    with dark grey above; yellowish-brown to brownish-grey
    below. Ears just reach head outline.   **Water Vole,** p. 217

8. Small, furry animal with pointed muzzle; large, prominent
eyes; ears project above head outline; practically hairless tail at
least three-quarters length of head and body.

a. Length 2¼″, tail 2″, scaly and pensile. Coat greyish-brown in
    young, becoming increasingly brownish-red; white below;
    sharply divided. Ears short and rounded.   **Harvest Mouse,** p. 219

b. Length 3½″, tail 3½″. Coat brown grading to yellowish-brown
    on flanks, white below; sharply divided. Often has a yellowish
    chest-spot. Oval ears.   **Long-tailed Field Mouse,** p. 218

c. Length 4″, tail 4¼″. Coat yellowish-brown above, white below,
    with a yellow or yellowish-brown collar in front of fore-legs.
    Ears oval.   **Yellow-necked Field Mouse,** p. 219

d. Length 3″, tapering tail 3″, scaly-ringed and flexible. Coat grey
    to brownish-grey above, grading into paler to silvery-grey ›
    below.   **House Mouse,** p. 220

e. Length 7½″, tapering tail 8½″, scaly-ringed. Coat usually
    smooth and glossy blue-black sprinkled with grey above, dark
    grey below. Lightly built.   **Black Rat,** p. 220

f. Length 9″, thick tail 7½″, scaly-ringed. Coat coarse and shaggy,
    brown to grey-brown above, paler below. Heavily built.
                                                        Brown Rat, p. 220

9. Small arboreal animal with a bushy tail at least three-quarters
the length of head and body.

a. Muzzle shorter than mice, larger and more rounded head;
    rounded ears project above head outline. Long whiskers.
    Nocturnal. Hibernates in winter.
    i. Length 3″, tail 2½″. Coat grey (especially in young) to
        reddish-brown above, white below, sometimes becoming
        yellowish rearwards.   **Dormouse,** p. 221
    ii. Length 7″, squirrel-like tail 7″. Coat grey tinged with
        brown above, whitish below. Eyes encircled by dark hair.
                                                        Edible Dormouse, p. 221

b. Pointed muzzle and ears. Hind legs much longer and stronger
    than fore. Diurnal. Nest (drey) bulky mass in tree-fork.
    i. Length 8″, laterally flattened tail 7″. Coat brownish-red
        above and tail; greyish in winter; dark spinal stripe; white
        below. Long ear tufts.   **Red Squirrel,** p. 215
    ii. Length 10″, tail 8″, often feathered. Coat grey above; spinal
        stripe reddish; white below. No ear tufts.   **Grey Squirrel,** p. 216

10. Medium-sized animal with long pointed ears, often erect.
Short tail. Hind legs much longer and stronger than fore.

a. Length 16–18″, upturned tail 2″, showing white underside
    when moving. Coat yellowish-brown, buff and various greys
    to black above, white below. Ears shorter than head. **Rabbit,** p. 213

b. Ears black-tipped; loping gait. Solitary.
    i. Length 20–26″, tail 4″, downturned when moving, showing
        black median stripe above. Summer coat sandy-brown
        sprinkled with black above, becoming darker reddish in
        winter; cheeks and chest yellowish-brown; belly white.
        Ears longer than head.   **Brown Hare,** p. 214
    ii. Ears shorter than head, upper ear-back black. Short tail all
        white. Upper coat lighter in winter. Mountain Hare (two
        species):
        A. Length 18–23″, tail 2½″. Coat smoky-brown to smoky-
            grey (giving 'blue' impression at a distance), white in
            winter.   **Scottish Hare,** p. 214

Above left, Harvest Mice. *Right,* Long-tailed Field Mouse. *Below left,* Dormouse. *Right,* House Mouse.

Top left, Edible Dormouse. *Right*, Water Vole. *Centre left*, Water Shrew. *Right*, Short-tailed Field Vole. *Bottom left*, Bank Vole. *Right*, Common Shrew.

B. Length 18–23″, tail 3″. Coat grey-brown to russet, much
lighter in winter.   **Irish Hare,** p. 215

11.   Medium-sized; erect pointed ears on top of the head; bushy
tail.

a.   Length 22–28″, tail 12–18″, generally white-tipped. Coat
brownish-red, back darker; greyish below. Ear-backs and
lower legs often black. Sharply pointed muzzle, long legs.
                                                Fox, p. 222

b.   Length 20–24″, cylindrical tail 9–12″, marked with black rings
and tip. Coat yellowish-grey to yellowish-brown, marked clear
black stripes. Legs ringed black. (Domestic tabby markings
less regular or sharp.)   **Wild Cat,** p. 225

12.   Medium-sized; rounded ears do not project above head outline. Scaly tail, almost hairless. Hind feet webbed.

a.   Length 16–20″, tail 8–11″. Long shaggy coat dark brown,
sometimes reddish-brown, greyish below. Muzzle squarish.
                                                Coypu, p. 221

b.   Length 12″, tail 7″, laterally flattened. Coat dark brown above,
lighter below. Broad flattened head. Feet and tail fringed with
stiff hairs.   **Musk Rat,** p. 218

13.   Rough black to dark grey coat. Head marked by broadening
white bands from tapering muzzle, either side the eyes to short,
pointed, white tipped-ears. Short legs. Length 30–36″, tail 4″. **Badger,** p. 225

14.   Medium-sized. Slim, streamlined and elongated body.
Rounded ears lie close to the head.

a.   Length 7–9″, tail 2″. Coat bright reddish-brown above merging into white or cream below. Short legs. Inquisitive, often
stands on hind legs to see more. Bounding gait. **Weasel,** p. 224

b.   Length 10–14″, tail 5″, tipped with permanent black tuft.
Coat reddish-brown above, cream below, sharply separated.
Entire coat may turn white in winter, especially northwards.
Long neck. Short legs.   **Stoat,** p. 223

c.   Length 13–17″, tail 5–8″. Coat reddish-brown; small white
spot on chin or throat. Many mutations. Vicious. **Mink,** p. 224

d.   Length 14–18″, tail 7″. Coat black, often sparse showing buff
underfur. Creamy patches on muzzle, brow and throat. Ears
white-edged.   **Polecat,** p. 224

e.   Length 16–20″, tail 9–14″. Coat rich brown, back darker, grey
below; creamy patch on throat and upper chest, but no face
markings. Head broadly triangular. Largely arboreal, but also
hunts on the ground.   **Pine Marten,** p. 223

f. Length 26–35″, thick tapering tail 14–18″. Coat rich brown above, lighter to silvery-grey below and on cheeks. Broad muzzle, flat head; short rounded ears barely visible. Short legs, webbed feet. **Otter,** p. 225

15. Deer. Females slightly smaller and do not have antlers.

a. Shoulder (stag) 48″, broad tail 6″. Antlers up to 42″ in length, upper end main horn (beam) branched with brow and 3 lateral tines; fully developed in 5 years; cast March. Summer coat reddish- to golden-brown, rarely fawn or grey, becoming brownish-grey in winter. Rump patch white to yellowish. **Red Deer,** p. 227

b. Shoulder (stag) 34″, white tail 4″. Simple 4-tined antlers 22″ long, cast April. Coat light reddish-brown to fawn, with white spots above, grey-brown in winter; lighter below. White rump patch, edged with black. **Sika Deer,** p. 229

c. Shoulder (buck) 35″, tail 7″, black above, white sides and below. 2-tined antlers 28″ long, upper end of beam flattened into broad curved plate, several small points along rear edge; cast May. Coat buff to light reddish-brown, sprinkled with prominent white spots above; becoming greyish-buff in winter; yellowish below. Rump white, edged black. **Fallow Deer,** p. 227

d. Shoulder (buck) 28″, very short tail. Upright 3-point antlers 8″; grown by May; cast Nov. Coat bright reddish-brown above, greyer and longer in winter; lighter below. Rump patch white. **Roe Deer,** p. 227

e. Small, very short tail; crouching stance. 2-tined erect antlers on long hairy pedicles. Upper canines in both sexes project tusk-like. Muntjac Deer (two species, hybrid reported):
  i. Shoulder 22″. Coat reddish-brown to yellowish-brown above, lighter below. No neck stripe. **Indian Muntjac,** p. 228
  ii. Shoulder 18″. Coat dark reddish-brown above, lighter below. Dark stripe at nape of neck. Ear-backs dusky. **Chinese Muntjac,** p. 228

f. Shoulder 21″, short tail. No antlers, but both sexes have protruding tusk-like canines. Coat reddish-brown to fawn; speckled black above; darker in winter. Head and ears buff, white round eyes and inside ears. **Chinese Water Deer,** p. 229

16. Seals. Marine animals. Body streamlined; fore-limbs modified as flippers. Cows a tenth smaller than bulls.

a. Total length (bull) 68–78″. Coat grey with blackish spots above, lighter below. Nostrils almost meet below in **V**; whiskers broadly divergent. **Common Seal,** p. 226

b. Total length 90–100″. Coat variable; bulls usually rusty-black, cows grey to fawn; both mottled. Nostrils separated below **V** ; whiskers almost drooping. **Atlantic Seal,** p. 226

WILD ANIMALS: DESCRIPTIVE NOTES

Order INSECTIVORA

This order, which shows many primitive features, is comprised of small, mainly nocturnal mammals, which burrow for protection. It has a world-wide distribution. Six species are found in Britain.

Family Erinaceidae

HEDGEHOG *Erinaceus europaeus*
Description: body length 9–11″, tail 1″. Upper body covered with dark brown to black spines ¾–1″ long, with white tips and bases; yellowish- or greyish-brown fur covers the snout and underparts; both the pointed head and the neck are extremely short; the fore and hind feet have five-clawed toes and five pads on the soles. **Habitat:** woods, parkland, gardens and heathland, where it sleeps by day in sheltered places, emerging to hunt at dusk; usually hibernates from October until March. **Food:** snails, slugs, insects, larvae and worms; sometimes mice, rats, frogs, lizards, snakes, berries, acorns and fruit. **Enemies:** gypsies, foxes and badgers. **Breeding:** litter of 3–7 born in May or June; sometimes a second litter between July and September. **Distribution:** widely distributed throughout Britain, except in the mountainous areas.

Hedgehog

Family Talpidae

MOLE *Talpa europaea*
Description: body length 6″, tail 1″. Dark grey fur, which will lie or 'set' in any direction, usually appears black; unusually long pointed skull is joined by an imperceptible neck to the cylindrical body; eyes are almost hidden in the fur, and the external ear is only indicated by a slight ridge; strong forelimbs are set well forward, and the broad shovel-like forefeet, equipped with strong claws, are turned outwards; hindlimbs are less well developed. **Habitat:** soft

Mole

ground, but not bare mountains or sand. Spends almost all its time below ground in a network of tunnels at depths of $\frac{1}{4}''$ to 18″. The excavated soil is pushed to the surface where it forms ridges over shallow tunnels, or mole heaves (mole-hills) over the deeper ones. The heart of the network is the fortress, a mound about 3′ across containing a chamber 6–8″ wide.   **Food:** earthworms, sometimes slugs and insects; seems to follow a three-hour activity cycle of hunting, feeding and sleeping; any excess worms are stored alive.   **Enemies:** buzzards, weasels, herons, owls, foxes and badgers.   **Breeding:** one litter, averaging 3–5, born in May or June.   **Distribution:** found where there are earthworms at altitudes up to 2,500′, but not in Ireland, the Outer Hebrides, Orkneys, Shetland or the Isle of Man.

Family Soricidae

COMMON SHREW *Sorex araneus castaneus*
Description: body length 3″, hairy tail $1\frac{1}{2}''$. Silky fur is dark reddish-brown above, usually shading to yellowish-grey or light grey below; long flexible snout extends beyond the mouth and bears whiskers; a scent gland on either flank between the limbs is its sole protection; teeth are tipped red or orange. **Habitat:** its small runways may be found in the hedge-bottom, ditch-side or among leaf debris in copse or wood. In summer it ranges into rough pasture, where it can hide under the grass stalks.   **Food:** insects, snails, woodlice, grasshoppers, etc. Activity appears to be on a three-hour cycle.   **Enemies:** cats, owls, other birds of prey, stoats, vipers and other shrews.   **Breeding:** breeding season is from May to September, usually with two litters of 4–8 in each; nest is a loosely woven grass ball.   **Distribution:** throughout Great Britain, up to an altitude of 1,000′, but not in Ireland, Orkneys, Shetland, Isle of Man or the Scillies. A sub-species *S.a. granti*, found on the island of Islay, has grey flanks.

PYGMY SHREW (Lesser Shrew) *Sorex minutus*
Description: body length 2″, tail $1\frac{1}{2}''$. Silky fur is light reddish-brown above and dirty white to yellowish-grey below, with the colours sharply separated. Although more lightly built than the Common Shrew, the snout is relatively longer and thicker, tail is thicker and more hairy, and forelimbs are shorter, teeth are tipped red or orange.   **Habitat:** as Common Shrew; widespread where

Pygmy Shrew

Water Shrew

Common Shrew

Scilly Shrew

there is ground cover; uses the runways of other small animals.   **Food:** insects, woodlice, etc. Appears to have a three-hour cycle of activity.   **Enemies:** owls, cats, stoats, vipers and other shrews.   **Breeding:** usually two litters of between two and eight are born between April and October.   **Distribution:** wooded areas throughout the British Isles; the only shrew found in Ireland.

WATER SHREW   *Neomys fodiens bicolor*
Description: body length 3–4″, tail 2–3″. Fur is slate-grey above, fairly sharply separated from the white to grey underparts; concealed ears have a small tuft of white hairs; underwater, the body may appear silvery because of air trapped in the fur; snout is relatively short and broad; broad brown feet and the long tapering tail are fringed on the lower side by stiff hairs; teeth are tipped red or orange.   **Habitat:** shallow but often extensive burrows in stream-banks, seldom swimming more than a few feet from the bank. Sometimes found in woods near a stream.   **Food:** whirligig beetles, water gnats, caddis worms and larvae; sometimes snails, small crustaceans, young frogs and small fish.   **Enemies:** owls.   **Breeding:** two litters of 3–8 are usual. One in May or June and the other in September. The young are independent at 5–6 weeks.   **Distribution:** Great Britain at altitudes of up to 1,000′, but not in Ireland nor any of the islands except Anglesey.

SCILLY SHREW   *Crocidura suaveolens cassiteridum*
Description: body length 3″, tail 1½″, thin with a few long white hairs. Fur is reddish-brown above, dirty white or ash-grey below; head is triangular, ears are large and prominent, teeth are all white.   **Habitat:** prefers heathland, but is found in all parts of the Scillies.   **Food:** sandhoppers and other insects.   **Breeding:** little known. They are believed to have two litters a year.   **Distribution:** found only in the Scilly Islands.

Order LAGOMORPHA

Rabbits and hares were originally regarded as members of the Order *Rodentia*, but have now been assigned to an order of their own on palaeontological evidence.

Family Leporidae

RABBIT   *Oryctolagus cuniculus*
Description: body length 16–18″, upturned tail 2″, white below. Fur is yellowish-brown and various shades of grey above, and whitish below; ears are long and erect; eyes are prominent; hind legs are longer and stronger than the forelegs, soles of the feet are covered with a thick coat of hair, which gives a good grip on rocks.   **Habitat:** open woodlands, hedgerows and grassland. Prefers sandy heaths for digging burrows. Most live in burrows, but a few live on the surface. Normally gregarious and nocturnal.   **Food:** grass and other herbaceous plants, crops, young shoots; sometimes bark in winter. They may ruin pastures by eating the choicer grasses at the roots.   **Enemies:** carnivores, owls, buzzards

and hawks. **Breeding:** polygamous: one buck mates with several does. Litters, usually 2–8, at about monthly intervals from January to June. The young are capable of separate existence at one month. Nest in a blind tunnel off the main burrow. Doe will defend young against stoats. **Distribution:** formerly found in large numbers all over the British Isles, but reduced by about 90 per cent by myxomatosis. Numbers are now increasing, but have not yet reached pest proportions.

Rabbit

BROWN HARE   *Lepus europaeus occidentalis*
Description: body length 20–26″, tail 3–4″, black above, white at sides and below. Shoulders, neck and flanks are sandy-brown with a reddish tinge, darker in winter; the back is a mixture of greys and sandy-brown, chest and loins are sandy and the belly is white; long, erect ears have black tips; hind legs are long, soles of the feet are covered with hair. **Habitat:** grassland, arable; sometimes on sand-dunes and aerodromes; solitary; does not burrow, but rests on the surface in a slight depression, its 'form'. Leaps up to 15′ to break its scent trail. In spring males form groups to display and fight. **Food:** herbaceous plants, grain, roots and bark. **Enemies:** foxes and stoats. Hares escape by 'freezing' or by running at very high speed. **Breeding:** usually three litters of 2–4 a year; young (leverets) are born furred and are distributed between several forms. **Distribution:** found at altitudes of up to 2,000′ in England, Scotland and Wales.

Brown Hare   Alpine Hare

ALPINE HARE   *Lepus timidus*
Two sub-species are found in Britain.
   (i) **Scottish Hare** (Blue Hare)   *L.t. scoticus*
Description: body length 20″, tail 2″, white on top. In winter fur is white

except for ear-tips, in summer smoky-brown to smoky-grey above, and rear underparts are white; ears are shorter than those of the Brown Hare, and the tips are always black. **Habitat:** mainly on open moorland and rocks above the limit of cultivation, but may descend in winter; hides in rock crevices, but may sometimes scrape a shallow depression; solitary. **Food:** heather, grass and other herbaceous plants; sometimes bark. **Enemies:** birds of prey, foxes, wild cats, stoats. **Breeding:** two or three litters of 3–8 a year. **Distribution:** mountains and high hills of Scotland. Introduced into N. England and North Wales.

(ii) **Irish Hare** *L.t. hibernicus*
Description: body length 18–23″, tail 3″. Fur russet in summer, whiter in winter; ears are as long as the broad head. **Habitat:** open mountains and hillsides. **Food:** grasses and herbaceous plants. **Enemies:** birds of prey and foxes. **Breeding:** two or three litters of 2–3 a year. **Distribution:** indigenous all over Ireland, at all altitudes. Introduced into N. Wales and the Isle of Man.

Order RODENTIA

This is the most successful, numerous and widespread order of mammals. All species are characterised by specialised gnawing teeth. Most·of the species are wholly vegetarian. In the British Isles there are four species of voles, four of mice, two of rats, two of dormice and two of squirrels. In the last 50 years the Coypu Rat, the Musk Rat and the Chinchilla have all been introduced for fur-farming, while the Guinea Pig and the Golden Hamster have become popular as pets. Despite precautions escapes have occurred and both the Musk Rat and the Coypu have become pests, though the former has now been wiped out.

Sub-order Sciuromorpha

Family Sciuridae

RED SQUIRREL *Sciurus vulgaris*
Description: body length 8″, bushy tail 7″, laterally flattened. Fur brownish-red on the tail and above, white below; upper fur develops a greyish tinge in the winter. Muzzle has many whiskers; bright black eyes are prominent, and the long pointed ears bear tufts of hair; limbs are well adapted for climbing; hind legs are longer than the front; forefeet have four fingers and a rudimentary thumb, the hind feet have five toes; all feet have hairy soles and long, curved, needle-sharp claws. **Habitat:** woodlands; is truly arboreal, spending little time on the ground. **Food:** varied: pine cones, nuts, berries, young shoots, bark, insects, fungi, eggs and young birds. Food debris on the ground betrays its presence. It does not store food methodically, but merely buries the excess. **Enemies:** pine marten, stoat, buzzard and possibly the grey squirrel. **Breeding:** a litter of 2–6 is born in April or May. In the south a second litter may be born in late summer. The nest, or 'drey', is a bulky, neat ball of bark, twigs,

grass and leaves in a tree fork, or inside a hollow tree.   **Distribution:** formerly widely distributed in the woodlands of the British Isles, except the Isle of Man, but is now absent or rare in the Midlands and the south-east, where it has been replaced by the Grey Squirrel.

Red Squirrel   Grey Squirrel

GREY SQUIRREL   *Sciurus carolinensis*

Description: body length 10″, tail 8″, less bushy than that of the Red Squirrel. Fur grey above sometimes with a chestnut brown mid-dorsal stripe, white underparts; ears are large, but without ear tufts; four toes on the longer hind legs and four fingers and a rudimentary thumb on the forelimbs. More aggressive than the Red Squirrel.   **Habitat:** more open woodlands and parkland; truly arboreal.   **Food:** nuts, berries, beech mast, bark, roots, buds, grain, insects, eggs and nestlings.   **Enemies:** man, dogs, stoats, foxes and birds of prey.   **Breeding:** usually two litters of 2–5, between January and August. The nest, or 'drey', is larger and untidier than that of the Red Squirrel.   **Distribution:** introduced into Britain in the nineteenth century, it has now replaced the Red Squirrel in much of the south-east and Midlands, but not in East Anglia.

Sub-order Myomorpha

Family Cricetidae

BANK VOLE   *Clethrionomys glareolus britannicus*
Description: body length 4″, tail 1½–2″, ends in a pencil of hairs. Upper fur chestnut-red, underparts whitish, yellowish or buff, ears are oval, and the muzzle has white, inch-long whiskers; lips are pink, and feet are grey.   **Habitat:** shallow runs at depths of 1–4″, constructed in hedgerows and at the edges of woods; does not hibernate.   **Food:** herbage, roots, bulbs, seeds, nuts, berries, bark and sometimes snails and insects; does not store food for the winter. **Enemies:** chiefly owls, weasels and other predators.   **Breeding:** there are usually four or five litters, of between three and six, from April to October. **Distribution:** England, Wales and S. Scotland, but not Ireland, the Hebrides, Orkneys, Shetlands or the Isle of Man.

Subspecies *C.g. skomersis*, the Skomer Vole, is found on the Isle of Skomer off the Pembrokeshire coast; it is chestnut-brown in colour and somewhat larger than *C.g. britannicus*; unlike all the other voles it is very docile.

In the Scottish Highlands the Bank Vole is replaced by a larger and darker form. At least two subspecies of this have been reported from separate Western Isles: *C.g. alstoni*, Mull and *C.g. erica*, Raasay.

WATER VOLE   *Arvicola amphibius amphibius*
Sometimes incorrectly called 'the Water Rat'.
Description: body length 8″, tail 4″. Upper fur is thick and glossy, dark brown or reddish-brown in colour, sprinkled with grey or blackish-grey; underparts are yellowish-brown to brownish-grey; head is short and rounded, ears are rounded and just project above the fur; feet are naked with five pads on the sole. **Habitat:** near water, along streams, ponds or bogs; an expert swimmer and diver; its bankside burrow often has an underwater entrance.   **Food:** nuts, young willow shoots, sedges and other bankside plants, freshwater snails, caddis worms, insect larvae and freshwater crayfish. Holds food in the forefeet to eat.   **Enemies:** stoats, otters, weasels, owls and pike. Trout have been reported to eat young.   **Breeding:** several litters of 2–7 born between April and September in rush and grass nests in burrows and reed-beds.   **Distribution:** found widely in Great Britain, but not in the Scottish islands or Ireland. A smaller and darker form (*A.a. reta*) is found north of the Clyde.

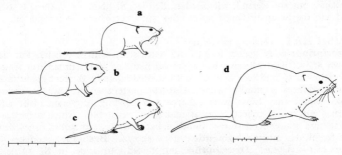

a, Bank Vole; **b,** Orkney Vole; **c,** Short-tailed Vole; **d,** Water Vole

ORKNEY VOLE   *Microtus arvalis orcadensis*
Description: body length 4–5″, tail 1½″. Upper fur dark reddish-brown, underparts greyish. In form it resembles the short-tailed southern vole, but is larger and darker.   **Habitat:** pastures, arable and heath. It has an extensive network of runs, which are about 3″ wide and link underground burrows. **Food:** grass, grain crops and the roots of heath rushes.   **Enemies:** birds of prey and carnivores.   **Breeding:** several litters a year, each of 3–6. The young are capable of separate existence at about three weeks.   **Distribution:** only in the larger Orkney islands. Other subspecies replace it on the other islands. *M.a. ronaldshaiensis* on South Ronaldshay, *M.a. rousaiensis* on Rousay, *M.a. westas* on Westray and *M.a. sandayensis* on Sanday.

SHORT-TAILED VOLE   *Microtus agrestis*
Also known as the Meadow or Field Vole.
Description: body length 4″, tail 1½″. Fur yellowish-brown to greyish-brown above, greyish-white below; short head is a blunt oval in outline, with the ends

Musk Rat

of the short rounded ears just visible above the fur. **Habitat:** ranges from open woodlands and bracken to damp pasture. The network of runways is at, or a little below, ground level. **Food:** grass, leaves, seeds and roots. Food may be stored in shallow burrows. **Enemies:** owls and other birds of prey, carnivores. **Breeding:** there may be up to eight litters, averaging 4–6, between February and September. Populations tend to increase to a peak every 3–4 years, then to decrease suddenly. **Distribution:** England, Wales and S. Scotland, but not Ireland, Isle of Man, Scillies, Shetland or Orkney. In Scotland and the Scottish islands seven other subspecies have been reported.

MUSK RAT   *Ondatra zibethica*
Description: body length 10–13″, tail 6–8″, scaly with few hairs. Fur dark brown above, lighter brown below; broad flattened head; broad feet fringed with stiff hairs, hind feet webbed; tail flattened laterally. A scent gland in the groin produces a musky scent. **Habitat:** extensive burrows in streambanks, which may cause bank collapse and flooding; prefers marshy sites. During autumn it collects a great mound of vegetation, which serves as a 'lodge' and winter food store. **Food:** aquatic plants; sometimes fishes, frogs and freshwater mussels. **Enemies:** none known. **Breeding:** produces 3–7 litters of 6–9 a year. **Distribution:** introduced into Britain in the 1920s for fur-farming; import now prohibited. Escapees established colonies which are now reported to have been eliminated.

Family Muridae

LONG-TAILED FIELD MOUSE   *Apodemus sylvaticus sylvaticus*
(Also called the Wood Mouse.)
Description: body length 3½″, tail 3½″. Fur dark yellowish-brown above, almost white below, sometimes with a buff or orange spot on the chest; grading to yellowish on flanks. Muzzle is pointed, with prominent eyes and large oval ears which project above the outline of the head. **Habitat:** runways in fields and woods, but may sometimes enter houses in the late autumn, where it may be mistaken for the House Mouse; gregarious, and a considerable number may occupy a single burrow. It moves quickly when alarmed, often zigzagging; can swim and climb well; nocturnal. **Food:** nuts, fruit, grass, leaves, bulbs, berries, snails, insects and eggs. **Enemies:** owls, foxes, weasels, stoats, hedgehogs and vipers. **Breeding:** between March and November, up to six litters, of 2–9. **Distribution:** all parts of the British Isles in suitable areas.

Many subspecies have been reported, including: Hebridean Field Mouse *A.s. hebridensis*, white underparts dotted with buff; Fair Isle or Shetland Field Mouse *A.s. fridariensis*, with yellow collar; St Kilda Field Mouse *A.s. hirtensis*, with brown underparts; Bute Field Mouse *A.s. butei*, darker in colour with shorter ears.

Left, Yellow-necked Field Mouse; *right,* Long-tailed Field Mouse

YELLOW-NECKED FIELD MOUSE   *Apodemus flavicollis wintoni*

Description: body length 4″, tail 4½″. Fur yellow-brown above and white below, with a yellow neckband in front of the forelimbs; ears large and oval. **Habitat:** woods, nesting in hollow trees or under tree-roots; much livelier than other field mice. **Food:** nuts, berries, fruit and leaves; sometimes slow-worms and eggs. **Enemies:** owls, other birds of prey, foxes, stoats and weasels. **Breeding:** several litters during the spring and summer; average litter five. **Distribution:** mainly in S. England.

HARVEST MOUSE   *Micromys minutus sorcinus*

Description: body length 2¼″, tail 2″, naked, scaly and pensile. Upper fur thick, greyish- to brownish-red, with a sharp line of separation from white underparts; eyes are bright, ears short and rounded, head is short and blunt; five toes on the hindfeet, four and a fleshy pad on the forefeet. **Habitat:** pastures and cornfields, where it uses its tail in climbing the stalks; common in untrimmed hedgerows, but in winter it may be found in corn ricks or shallow burrows. **Food:** seeds, grain, berries; sometimes herbage and insects; some seeds may be stored for winter use. It normally has a three-hour cycle of activity. **Enemies:** not known. **Breeding:** several litters of 5–9 are born each year. The young are greyish at birth, the reddish tinge develops later. The spherical nest is about 3″ across, made of loosely interwoven grass with a definite entrance, and is suspended from grass or corn stalks. **Distribution:** England, Wales and S. Scotland. Usually common in S. England, but less numerous in the north.

Left, Harvest Mouse; *right,* House Mouse

HOUSE MOUSE *Mus musculus*
Description: body length 3″, with tail 3″ tapering, flexible, scaly-ringed. Fur soft, grey or brownish-grey above and paler below; muzzle pointed, eyes bright and the large ears project above the outline of the head. **Habitat:** usually found in, or near, human habitation, but also in the woods, corn ricks and fields, where it may be more tawny in colour. Mainly nocturnal. **Food:** prefers grain, but will eat almost anything. **Enemies:** man, cats, dogs, carnivores and birds of prey. **Breeding:** breeds at any time of the year. Usually five or six litters of 5–10. The young are capable of separate existence at two weeks and can breed at six weeks. **Distribution:** throughout the British Isles.

BLACK RAT *Rattus rattus*
Description: body length 7½″, tail 8½″, almost hairless, scaly-ringed. Upper fur glossy blue-black sprinkled with grey, the underparts dark grey; long thin naked ears are about half the length of the head; feet are pink, with five pads on the sole, but the thumb on the forefeet is reduced to a tubercule. **Habitat:** it will live almost anywhere, but prefers human habitation, or port storage buildings; often found in the upper storeys of warehouses as it is a good climber, unlike the Brown Rat; very gregarious. **Food:** omnivorous. **Enemies:** man, dogs, cats, carnivores and birds of prey. **Breeding:** breeds at any time of the year; usually five or six litters of 4–8. **Distribution:** in Britain it is found in and around the ports and cities, but it has largely been replaced by the Brown Rat.
Several sub-species are known, including: The Alexandrine Rat, *R.r. alexandrius*, fur greyish-brown above, light grey below; brown feet. Tree or Roof Rat, *R.r. frugivorous*, fur light reddish-brown above and white or yellowish below; feet usually white.

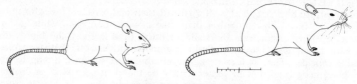

Left, Black Rat; *right,* Brown Rat

BROWN RAT *Rattus norvegicus*
Description: body length 9″, tail 7″, thick, scaly-ringed. The coarse fur is greyish-brown above, sometimes with a tawny tinge, and white below; ears, feet and tail are flesh-coloured; larger and more heavily built than the Black Rat; head is shorter, muzzle blunter and ears and eyes are smaller. **Habitat:** although found near human habitation, and especially near stored food, is less dependent on man than the Black Rat; established in the countryside and, as it is a good swimmer, is often found along rivers, canals and sewers. Gregarious, often burrows, but is a poor climber; mainly nocturnal. **Food:** omnivorous. **Enemies:** in towns, mainly man and dogs; in the countryside tawny owls, stoats, weasels and foxes. **Breeding:** breeds almost continuously, depending largely on the available food supply; three to six litters of 4–9 a year. Young can breed at 2–3 months. **Distribution:** throughout the British Isles.

Family Gliridae

DORMOUSE *Muscardinus avellanarius*
Description: body length 3″, bushy tail 2½″. Upper fur brownish-red, throat and upper chest white, the rear underparts yellowish-white; head comparatively large, muzzle blunt, eyes prominent, short ears rounded, long whiskers; short forefeet have four fingers and a rudimentary thumb, the hind feet have five toes; all claws are short, each foot has six pads. **Habitat:** essentially arboreal, living in copses, woods and hedgerows; nocturnal; sleeping nest is made of grass, moss and twigs forming a sphere about 3″ across. Winter hibernation nests are on or below the ground. **Food:** hazel-nuts, whitethorn haws, seeds; sometimes insects and eggs; holds food in its forefeet to eat. **Enemies:** birds of prey, badgers and foxes. **Breeding:** one or more litters of 2–7 a year. The breeding nest is similar to the sleeping nest but larger, sometimes measuring up to 7″ across. **Distribution:** S.W. England; infrequent in the Midlands, and absent from East Anglia, Scotland and Ireland.

EDIBLE DORMOUSE (Fat Dormouse) *Glis glis*
Description: body length 7″, tail 7″, bushy, squirrel-like. Fur light grey, tinged with brown above, white or nearly white below; head large, muzzle

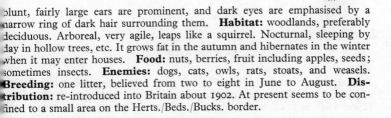

Above, Edible Dormouse; *below,*
Dormouse

blunt, fairly large ears are prominent, and dark eyes are emphasised by a narrow ring of dark hair surrounding them. **Habitat:** woodlands, preferably deciduous. Arboreal, very agile, leaps like a squirrel. Nocturnal, sleeping by day in hollow trees, etc. It grows fat in the autumn and hibernates in the winter when it may enter houses. **Food:** nuts, berries, fruit including apples, seeds; sometimes insects. **Enemies:** dogs, cats, owls, rats, stoats, and weasels. **Breeding:** one litter, believed from two to eight in June to August. **Distribution:** re-introduced into Britain about 1902. At present seems to be confined to a small area on the Herts./Beds./Bucks. border.

Family Echimyidae

COYPU (Nutria) *Myocastor coypus*
Description: body length 16–22″, tail 8–11″, bristly scaly-ringed. Fur darkish brown or reddish-brown, with many long coarse guard-hairs and dense yellowish underfur above, soft greyish below; muzzle squarish in front; hairy oval ears do not project above the head outline; eyes small; only the hind feet are webbed. **Habitat:** marshes and streams, burrowing into the bank, with

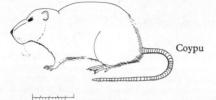

Coypu

inner chamber possibly 2′ across; an excellent swimmer and spends much of its time in the water. Largely nocturnal. It can be dangerous if trapped. **Food:** reeds, sedges and other aquatic plants. **Enemies:** weasels, otters, brown rats, owls and hawks. **Breeding:** breeding may take place at any time. There are usually two or three litters of 4–8 a year; young are furred and can swim at 24 hours. The teats lie along the flanks, enabling the young to suckle while the female is in the water. **Distribution:** escapees have established colonies in the waterways of East Anglia, where they have reached pest proportions. A few other small isolated colonies have been reported recently.

Order CARNIVORA

The flesheaters. Members of this order vary considerably in size, but all are well-armed with claws and teeth, the canines being especially well developed.

There are two sub-orders: (1) *Fissipedia* contains all the terrestrial species and have normal feet with a minimum of four toes. In Britain this division is represented by badger, fox, pine marten, polecat, otter, stoat, weasel and wild cat. (2) *Pinnipedia* contains the seals and sea-lions. This sub-order is represented by the grey and common seals.

Sub-order Fissipedia

Family Canidae

FOX   *Vulpes vulpes*
Description: body length 22–28″, bushy tail 12–18″, generally white-tipped. Height at shoulder 14″. Fur brownish-red above, pale grey below, forelegs and ear-backs are black; there may be some colour variations: a grey tinge is commoner in the north. The ears and muzzle are pointed, the body is slim

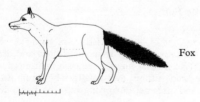

Fox

and the legs are long. **Habitat:** found in any type of country, including urban gardens, but prefers woodland. Solitary except at the breeding season. Normally nocturnal, lying up by day. **Food:** rabbits, rats, mice, hedgehogs, squirrels, voles, birds, poultry, frogs and some vegetable matter. Often kills more than it can eat. **Enemies:** man. **Breeding:** the vixen has one litter, usually four or five cubs, in April. They are taken hunting at one month. **Distribution:** throughout the British Isles, but not in the Scottish islands except Skye.

Family Mustelidae

PINE MARTEN *Martes martes martes*
Description: body length 16–20″, rather bushy tail 9–10″. Fur rich brown, except at the throat and breast, which are yellow to creamy-white; the middle of the back and the outside of the legs are darker and underparts are greyer. Muzzle sharp-pointed, head broad and triangular and the pale-edged ears are prominent; body slim, long legs terminate in five-toed feet with long sharp claws. **Habitat:** woods, mainly pinewoods. Arboreal, climbing trees easily and leaping across considerable spaces, but may also hunt on the ground; solitary and mainly nocturnal. **Food:** squirrels and birds, which it attacks in the nest in the trees or on the ground; also rabbits, hares, rats, voles, mice, berries and, it is suspected, poultry. **Enemies:** man; possibly foxes. **Breeding:** usually one litter, of 2–6 kittens, a year. The nest is hidden among rocks, tree-roots or in an old squirrel's or crow's nest. **Distribution:** wilder parts of N. England, including the Lake and Peak Districts, Scotland, the Hebrides, Wales and Ireland, now extinct, or almost extinct, in S. and Central England. The Forestry Commission and some other landowners protect it, as it destroys tree-damaging creatures.

a, Pine Marten; **b**, Stoat; **c**, Weasel; **d**, Polecat; **e**, American Mink

STOAT *Mustela erminea stabilis*
Description: body length 10–14″, furry tail 4–5″. Fur reddish-brown above, and white, tinged with yellow, below; reddish-brown tail tipped with a tuft of long black hairs; in the Scottish Highlands winter coat white, except for black tail-tuft. Body thin and elongated, legs short. **Habitat:** varied. Hills, woodlands, moors and cropland. Mainly nocturnal, hunting by scent, alone or in families. Usually moves in bounds. **Food:** truly carnivorous: all flesh, as

well as eggs, eels and fish. **Enemies:** man, birds of prey and the larger carnivores. **Breeding:** four or five young born in late April or May. **Distribution:** throughout the British Isles. In Ireland known locally as a 'weasel'. Two subspecies have been reported: Islay Stoat *M.e. ricinae*, which is smaller than the mainland species; Irish Stoat *M.e. hibernica*, found in Ireland and the Isle of Man, is of a darker colour which may extend to the underparts.

WEASEL *Mustela nivalis nivalis*

Description: body length 7–9″, furry tail 2″. Fur light reddish-brown above merging into white or cream below. The small narrow head, long neck, long slender body and short legs give it a snake-like appearance, similar to that of the stoat, but its tail is shorter, less bushy and without the black tip. **Habitat:** mainly on lower-lying land where food is abundant, also in woodlands and pastures. It moves in a series of bounds. **Food:** voles, mice, young rabbits, rats, frogs, small birds and eggs. **Enemies:** mainly hawks; also owls and the larger carnivores. **Breeding:** 4–6 kittens are born in spring, followed by a second litter in the late summer. **Distribution:** lower lying land in Great Britain, but is absent from Ireland and the islands, except Skye.

AMERICAN MINK *Mustela vison*

Description: body length 13–17″, bushy tail 5–8″. Fur dark chocolate brown, except for white patch on throat but many mutations exist. Body streamlined, legs short. Very vicious and impossible to tame. **Habitat:** wooded stream-banks or woods near marshy areas; spends much of its time in the water. **Food:** fish, all aquatic creatures including frogs, crayfish, freshwater mussels, snakes, poultry and small mammals. **Enemies:** none in Britain except man. **Breeding:** litters of 4–6 are born in the spring. The young leave their parents at seven weeks and breed at one year. The breeding nest is usually under a fallen bough or overhanging stream-bank. **Distribution:** in Britain mink are normally caged, but they have a reputation for escaping. Colonies have been established in areas near some of the fur farms.

POLECAT (Foul Marten) *Mustela putorius*

Description: body length 15–18″, bushy tail 7″. Fur long and coarse, dark brown above (buff underfur may show through), and black below; head blackish with white marks about the muzzle, between the eyes and the white-edged ears. The foul-odoured secretion is produced by glands under the tail. **Habitat:** woods and copses. Protected by foresters as it eats tree-damaging rodents, but hated by farmers as it kills for pleasure. In winter it may seek shelter inside buildings. Mainly nocturnal. A less able climber than the pine marten. **Food:** rats, mice, rabbits; sometimes birds including poultry, also eggs, frogs and snakes. **Enemies:** man. **Breeding:** pairs in February or March and the litter of 3–8 is born in April or May. A second litter may follow in the late summer. **Distribution:** formerly common in Britain, but now few remain except in the large woods, the remoter parts of Wales, the Lake District and the Scottish Highlands.

The ferret is a domesticated albino polecat. These have reverted to the wild state in the Isle of Mull.

Above, left, Red Deer.   *Right,* Roe Deer.   *Below,* Young Fallow Deer.

Young hare. The mother places one in each form for safety. It is not abandoned but would be if it were handled.

BADGER   *Meles meles meles*
Description: body length 30–36″, tail 4″. Rough fur appears dark grey above
and black below; long tapering muzzle and head marked with broad white
bands on either side of the small eyes from near each ear to the snout. Legs
short, and five-toed feet, especially the forefeet, are armed with strong claws.
Musky odour glands.   **Habitat:** mainly in wooded country, particularly on
hill slopes. Its burrows or 'sets' are a complicated series of tunnels which sometimes extend as much as ten feet below the surface and may reach 100 yards in
length. Normally nocturnal and solitary; in winter it sleeps longer but does not
hibernate.   **Food:** acorns, nuts, berries, fruit, grass, clover, earthworms, slugs,
young rabbits, mice, voles, insects and young birds which have fallen to the
ground.   **Enemies:** none known.   **Breeding:** the young, usually 2–3, are
born in February or March and remain inside the set for several months, often
leaving their parents in October.   **Distribution:** most of the suitable areas of
the British Isles, excluding the islands except Anglesey; rarely seen.

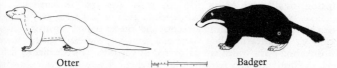

Otter   Badger

OTTER   *Lutra lutra*
Description: body length 26–35″, tail 17″. Fur appears to be dark brown (guard-
hairs have grey bases), lighter to silvery-grey below, often a light-coloured patch
on the throat. Body long and rather heavy; tapering tail is flattened horizontally;
broad head flattened from above, eyes bright and black and short, rounded, hairy
ears do not project above the head-outline; short powerful legs terminate in five-
toed webbed feet.   **Habitat:** along the smaller quite unpolluted rivers and may
visit or live along the sea-shore. Solitary and normally nocturnal, sleeps by day in
some convenient bankside hole, and at night may range several miles along a
stream or overland; does not hibernate.   **Food:** mainly fish; also eels, crayfish,
frogs, young birds and mammals.   **Enemies:** man.   **Breeding:** no fixed
season. Usually one litter a year. The two or three cubs remain with the mother
until she mates again.   **Distribution:** suitable areas of the British Isles.

Family Felidae

WILD CAT   *Felis silvestris grampia*
Description: body length 20–24″, thick tail 9–12″, usually marked with black
rings and tip. Fur thick and soft, yellowish-grey or yellowish-brown, and
lighter below. Often resembles the large domestic tabby. A pair of dark stripes
extend from the eyes to behind the ears; considerable variation of black or brown
markings on the body in the form of variable width stripes and spots. Un-

Wild Cat

approachable and untamable. **Habitat:** inaccessible mountain slopes; normally solitary and nocturnal. **Food:** rabbits and other small mammals and birds, also fish; has been reported to kill poultry, lambs and kids. **Enemies:** man. **Breeding:** little is known. Believed that litters of 2–5 are born in May. Nest is usually in a rocky cleft or hollow tree. **Distribution:** formerly only found in the Scottish Highlands and some of the Hebrides, but recently the numbers have increased and it has been reported in the surrounding lowlands.

Sub-order Pinnipedia

Family Phocidae

Body streamlined, forelimbs modified as flippers.

COMMON SEAL (Harbour Seal) *Phoca vitulina*
Description: total length 68–78″. Weight, males 400–550 lbs, females 220–350 lbs. Body covered with short hair, darkish grey or yellowish-grey on the back, with blackish or brownish small spots, and lighter below. Nostrils almost meet below **V**. **Habitat:** shallow water and estuaries, especially where there are sandbanks and rocks which are uncovered by the tide. **Food:** mainly fish, sometimes shellfish; normally feeds during high tide. **Enemies:** man, possibly killer whales. **Breeding:** one or two pups are born on sandbanks in June or July; they have white coats which are soon lost; swim at a few hours; normally weaned at six weeks and mature at three years. **Distribution:** suitable shallow areas on the east cost of England, the east and west coasts of Scotland, Hebrides, Orkneys, Shetlands and Northern Ireland.

Left, Common Seal; *right,* Atlantic Seal

ATLANTIC SEAL (Grey Seal) *Halichoerus grypus*
Description: total length, bulls 90–100″, cows up to 72″. Weight of bulls up to 800 lbs. Short hair light to dark grey, with dark spots. Nostrils distinctly separated below. **Habitat:** sea, off coves and at the base of exposed cliffs. **Food:** fish and shellfish. **Enemies:** man, possibly killer whales. **Breeding:** one pup is born in September–November on the flat rocks beneath high cliffs; white coat shed when weaned and deserted at three weeks. **Distribution:** off the west coast and the Farne Islands.

Order ARTIDACTYLA

Consists of the cloven-hoofed, even-toed mammals in which the original five-digit feet have been modified. In the case of pigs only the first digit has disappeared, but in the other members so have the second and fifth, leaving only the third and fourth.

Family Cervidae

RED DEER *Cervus elaphus scoticus*
Description: stag height at shoulder up to 48″, hind somewhat less, tail 6″. Summer coat reddish- to golden-brown above and white below, with a white patch around the short tail; in winter upper coat is brownish-grey. Only stags carry antlers, which are up to 42″ in length and consist of a single horn (the beam) with three lateral tines and terminal branches when fully developed at five years or more; shed in spring. **Habitat:** moors, although the vanished forests were its true home. Stags and hinds form separate herds except in rutting season. **Food:** grass, young tree shoots, heather, grain and vegetable crops. **Enemies:** man; foxes, eagles and wild cats may attack the young. **Breeding:** harems are collected in September at the beginning of the rutting season. The single calf is born away from the hind herd in May or June and is dappled like the fallow deer for four to eight weeks. Although it can run at a few hours, it does not feed itself until about eight months old. **Distribution:** Scottish Highlands, N. England, the New Forest and on the moors of Devon and Somerset.

ROE DEER *Capreolus capreolus thotti*
Description: height at shoulder of buck 25–30″, hind a little less. In summer the red-brown coat is short and smooth, but in winter is greyer and longer; underparts and rump are lighter and throat and muzzle tip white. Ears relatively large. Only the buck carries antlers, which are three-tined when fully grown at four years, but are only 8–9″ long; shed in the late autumn and new ones are clear of velvet by April. **Habitat:** dense woods and those adjoining grassland; moves with a bounding motion alone, in pairs or in small family groups but never forms large herds; usually remains hidden by day and forages by night. **Food:** grass, young shoots of trees, heather, berries, leaves and nuts. **Enemies:** man; foxes and eagles may take young. **Breeding:** roe rings, either circular or figure-of-eight, are trodden out during courtship; rutting starts in mid-August. The fawns, usually one or two, rarely three, are born in May and have white spots until autumn. At about 14 days they can follow the hind into the open. **Distribution:** S. Scotland, N. England, Norfolk-Suffolk border and in S. English counties from Devon to Sussex and Surrey.

FALLOW DEER *Dama dama*
Description: height at shoulder of buck 34″, tail 7″. Summer coat usually fawn to light reddish-brown speckled with smallish white spots, becoming greyish-brown; some variation in the base colour. Underparts yellowish, darker-fringed rump is white; short tail is black above and white below. Only the buck carries antlers and these reach full development at five years; upper end of the beam is flattened into a broad curved plate (palmate), with a number of small points, or 'spillers', along the posterior edge. **Habitat:** woods and grassland near woods. The sexes are found together during the winter, but separate in the spring. **Food:** young shoots, bark and nuts. **Enemies:** man. **Breeding:** rutting season is in the autumn, when the bucks give hoarse grunting roars. The fawns, usually one but sometimes two or three, are born in May or June in the bracken and can run at a few hours. **Distribution:** many deer

a, Red Deer; **b,** Fallow Deer; **c,** Roe Deer, **d,** Indian Muntjac Deer; **e,** Chinese Water Deer; **f,** Sika Deer; **g,** Indian Spotted Deer; **h,** Reindeer

parks, e.g. Bushy and Richmond Parks and Epping Forest. In addition, there are still many at large in various parts of the British Isles.

MUNTJAC DEER Two species, differing slightly in appearance only, are now breeding wild. Both are small and run with a crouching gait; the males carry short, two-tined antlers on long pedicles, parallel to the forehead; both sexes have tusk-like canine teeth protruding from the upper jaw. They may attack if provoked.

INDIAN MUNTJAC DEER *Muntiacus muntjac*
Description: height at shoulder 22″. Coat reddish-brown to yellowish-brown, with lighter underparts; no neck stripe.

CHINESE MUNTJAC DEER (Reeve's Muntjac Deer) *Muntiacus reevesi*
Description: height at shoulder 18″. Coat deep reddish-brown to red-brown, with a dark stripe at the nape of the neck; underparts lighter; ear-backs dusky, changing to olive-brown in winter. **Habitat:** fairly open woodland, with a good shrub-layer. They do not form herds but move alone, or in pairs, grazing in clearings. **Food:** grass, leaves, shrub shoots, fruit, roots and brassica crops. **Enemies:** none known in Britain, except man. **Breeding:** little known: one, rarely two, fawns are born in late summer or early autumn. **Distribution:** Woburn and other deer parks. There have been some escapes and they are now found wild in the south-east and as far west as Dorset.

CHINESE WATER DEER *Hydropotes inermis*

Description: height at shoulder about 22″. Summer coat light reddish-brown or fawn, becoming darker in winter; underparts lighter. Neither bucks nor does carry antlers, but the canine teeth have developed into short tusks. **Habitat:** long grass bottoms of river valleys, woods and grasslands. If alarmed it runs into long grass and lies flat. Normally solitary, it hunts by night and day. **Food:** grass, vegetable and root crops. **Enemies:** none known in Britain, except man. **Breeding:** rutting takes place in December and the young are born in May, usually two or three, but four or five are not rare. **Distribution:** Woburn and other deer parks. There have been some escapes and it is now established in the northern Home Counties.

INDIAN SPOTTED DEER (Axis Deer, Chital) *Axis axis*

Description: height at shoulder 36″. Coat bright reddish-brown with large white spots above, and white below. Similar in size and appearance to the fallow deer, but the buck's antlers are not palmate and are longer, extending up to 36″, and the spots are larger. **Habitat:** woodland or grassland near woods. **Food:** grass. **Enemies:** none known in Britain. **Breeding:** no fixed breeding season. **Distribution:** northern Home Counties, as a result of escapes from deer parks.

SIKA DEER *Cervus nippon*

Description: height at shoulder 32–38″, white tail 3–6″. Summer coat light reddish-brown with faint white spots, in winter greyish-brown; the prominent white rump, fringed with black, retains its colour throughout the year. Antlers average 24″ in length, with single tines and forked ends – four points in all at full development. **Habitat:** lies up in woods or sometimes in shrubs, bracken or reed-beds, by day, moving and feeding mainly at night alone or in small herds. **Food:** grass, bark, young shoots and herbaceous plants. **Enemies:** none known in Britain. **Breeding:** rutting takes place in November during which the buck's whistle is said to be audible for up to one mile. One calf is born in May. **Distribution:** found in small numbers in many of the more wooded parts of the British Isles as a result of escapes from deer parks.

REINDEER *Rangifer tarandus*

Description: height at shoulder 36″. Thick coat dark grey-brown in summer and lighter in winter; underparts white. Muzzle hairy, neck maned, ears and tail short. Both sexes carry antlers, in which the beam and the brow tine are branched, but the male's are more developed and are shed after rutting, while the female's are retained until after the calf is born. The hoof is broad and hard. **Habitat:** semi-arctic tundra, high moors or sparse woodland. **Food:** Reindeer moss. **Enemies:** none known in Britain. **Breeding:** each bull has a harem of several cows; rutting season is in September or October; the calf is born in spring and can walk at a few hours. **Distribution:** wild in Scotland until the twelfth century; a small herd was re-introduced in 1952.

Order SQUAMATA

Sub-order Lacertila (Sauria)

Family Lacertidae

COMMON LIZARD *Lacerta vivipara*

Description: total length 5″, of which about half is tail. Upper colour varies considerably: often yellowish-brown, but may be reddish-brown, greenish-brown or greyish-brown; three black or dark brown lines, or series of irregularly shaped spots, along the back and flanks; underparts of males are orange or red spotted with black, while females' are orange, yellow or pale green, sometimes with grey or black spots. The rather blunt head is brownish above, sometimes with lighter spots; throat is often white; no perceptible neck, legs are short. **Habitat:** sandy heaths, moors, meadows, fallow and sand-hills. It lives in cracks and old burrows. It often hibernates from October until March. **Food:** spiders, beetles, moths, ants, grubs and various small caterpillars. **Enemies:** snakes, birds of prey and other predators. **Breeding:** 4–9 young are deposited alive in a shallow pit in moist soil, still in the egg membrane which is soon broken. They begin to feed on insects at a few hours. **Distribution:** most suitable areas throughout the British Isles, except Skye, the Outer Hebrides, Orkneys and Shetland.

Left, Common Lizard; *right,* Sand Lizard

SAND LIZARD *Lacerta agilis agilis*

Description: total length 7″, of which half is tail; the female is a little shorter. Light brown or grey above, with longitudinal series of irregular-shaped dark brown or black light-centred spots along the back and either side; lower flanks sometimes purplish-brown in the female and greenish in the male; underparts whitish or cream, sometimes with black spots. The head is blunt, body heavier than the Common Lizard and legs are shorter. **Habitat:** burrows in sand or old mouse and vole burrows in the southern sandy heathlands and in the sand-hills of Cheshire and Lancashire. **Food:** insects, spiders, centipedes, worms, slugs and woodlice. **Enemies:** smooth snakes; also other snakes, birds of prey and hedgehogs. **Distribution:** mainly Dorset, Hampshire, Surrey and the coastal dunes of Cheshire and Lancashire; not found in Scotland or Ireland.

Family Anguidae

SLOW WORM *Anguis fragilis*

Description: total length 10–14″, tail longer than head and body. Background colour varies, usually pale yellowish-brown, yellowish-green or silvery when young, but becoming darker with age when it often becomes coppery-brown, or sometimes reddish, greyish or some tint of brown above; below, males black or dark grey and mottled, while females usually black; usually a dark line along either flank and another, especially in females, down the centre of the back. The head is narrower than the body; tongue notched not forked as in the snakes; it feels smooth despite its scales, has no legs and skin is cast whole, like the snakes. **Habitat:** spends much of its time underground, but may be seen hunting for food by day on commons, dry heaths, open woodlands and even gardens in the spring and summer. Movements are slow and deliberate unless discovered, when it will glide away rapidly or remain motionless; rarely bites. Normally hibernates from mid-October until March. **Food:** slugs, spiders, small worms, insects and their larvae. **Enemies:** vipers, foxes, hedgehogs, smooth snakes, badgers and birds of prey. **Breeding:** mates in May or June and 5–13 young are born in late August; these are able to fend for themselves from birth. It is ovo-viviparous. **Distribution:** throughout Great Britain, but not in Ireland; most common near the coast in S. and S.W. England.

The Blue-Spotted Slow Worm, *A.f.* var. *colchica*, which has spots or stripes ranging from light blue to ultramarine, is occasionally found in southern England.

Sub-order Ophidia (Serpentes)

Snakes have no limb-girdle and the ventral ends of their ribs are quite free. The angle of the jaw extends beyond the ear. The left and right sides of the jaw are capable of advancing alternately, dragging the prey backwards, while the backward-pointing teeth prevent it escaping. The tongue is long and forked, the eyes are always open, as there are no eyelids, only a transparent cover; there is no external ear.

Family Colubridae

GRASS SNAKE (Ringed Snake) *Natrix natrix helvetica*
Description: fully grown females are up to 48″ in length, while males are about 12″ less. Background colour uniformly olive-grey, olive-brown or olive-green; two rows of small black dots along the back, and a series of nearly vertical short black bars on either lower flank; underside chequered black, or grey, and white; rarely all black, just behind the head two large patches of yellow, pink, orange or white forms a collar, behind this are usually two black patches, often united to form a central line. Long narrow head ends in a blunt snout; upper lip yellow or white. The body tapers gently from its middle to a slender tail, which accounts for about one-fifth of its total length. **Habitat:** near ponds and ditches on chalk hills, sandy heaths, open woodlands, under hedgerows and in marshy places. Hibernates in a sheltered spot during the winter. **Food:** mainly frogs; also newts and sometimes fish, mice and small birds. **Enemies:** hedgehogs, badgers, flesh-eating mammals and birds of prey. **Breeding:** mates in April or May. Eggs are deposited in July and hatch out about eight weeks later. The young resemble their parents, but may be darker with less clear markings. **Distribution:** widely found in England and Wales and some have been reported in S. Scotland; absent from Ireland.

SMOOTH SNAKE   *Coronella austriaca*
Description: length 15–22″. Upperside grey, brown or reddish, with pairs
of small black, red or brown dots or cross-bars along the middle of back;
upper head is brown with a black patch at the back; underside is some tint of
orange, red, brown, grey or black, sometimes with white spots; sides may be
whitish. All scales are smooth.   **Habitat:** sandy heaths, stony ground and
wooded hillsides, often near water into which it slides and hides when alarmed;
spends much of its time underground. Usually hibernates from October until
spring.   **Food:** chiefly the sand lizard; also young snakes and slow worms;
sometimes mice, voles or shrews.   **Breeding:** mating takes place in the spring.
Eggs are retained until the 2–15 young are ready to hatch in August or September.   **Distribution:** broadly the same as that of its main food, the sand
lizard, especially the New Forest and other parts of Hampshire, Dorset,
Wiltshire and Surrey.

Slow Worm

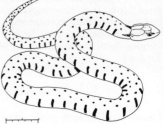

Grass Snake

Viper

Smooth Snake

Family Viperidae

VIPER (Adder)   *Vipera berus*
Description: females are about 24″ in length, males 3–4″ less. Considerable
colour variation: background colour is some tint of brown, olive or grey to
almost black; along the sides is a series of small whitish dots. The characteristic
mark is a dark zigzag line down the centre of the back; only rarely is this modified as a series of dots or infilled to form a continuous stripe; a dark bar in the
form of an **X**, or a **Λ**, can usually be seen on the back of the head.   **Habitat:**
sandy heaths, dry moors, open hillsides, hedgerows, nettle beds or stone walls.
May be seen basking in the sun.   **Food:** lizards, small mammals, birds, slow
worms, frogs, newts and large slugs. The viper paralyses its prey before swallow-
ing it, the poison acting within 30 seconds.   **Enemies:** man, birds of prey and
hedgehogs.   **Breeding:** pair in April. Eggs are retained until the young are
fully developed and appear in August or September; usually 5–20.   **Distribution:** all parts of Great Britain (it is the only snake found in any numbers
in Scotland), but not in Ireland.

AGRICULTURE

Introduction

Like many other industries agriculture continues to evolve and has achieved vastly increased production despite a considerable drop in manpower. The methods and ideas which were used in the past are being modified, and the extent to which this will change the face of Britain cannot yet be foreseen. Already battery hen-houses have almost replaced the clucking free-range birds; more and more pigs pass their entire lives in warm, draught-proof pig-houses instead of daily rooting in the fields and returning nightly to small, cold and often draughty sties; the in-wintering of sheep and cattle is an increasingly common practice, while on 'advanced' farms great storage silos contain feed-stuffs, which can be scientifically blended and fed to any number of animals by one man at a control console. In the fields also, changes have taken place: the horse has now been almost entirely replaced by the tractor, while farm machinery has become more complex, more extensively used and more expensive, leading to greater specialisation. Attitudes towards crops too are changing, and grass (dealt with in the section on Vegetation) is now firmly regarded as a crop, with as much care devoted to the selection of suitable seed mixtures and cultivation as to other crops. But, although methods have changed and are still changing, the basic farming cycle remains the same, and this too is part of the British landscape.

This section divides naturally into two: livestock and crops. The types of farm animals are easily recognisable, so there is no general identification key, each type being dealt with in separate descriptive keys. Crops are divided into cereals, roots, legumes and other field crops.

Identification key to cattle breeds

1. Cattle red and hornless.

The coat is uniformly deep red, frequently with a little white on the udder and a white switch (tail-tip). A rather large, dual-purpose animal, commonest in Norfolk and Suffolk. **Red Poll**

2. Cattle red, red and white or roan. Horned.

Large, with short, laterally flattened horns, not marked with black. The nose, lips and eyelids are flesh-coloured. Both beef and dairy types. **Shorthorn**
As Shorthorn, but the coat is a rich red all over.
Lincolnshire Red Shorthorn
Large, heavily-built, with a curly rich red coat, with white on the chest and the undersides and some white markings on the back and legs. The medium-length horns droop slightly. Beef. **Hereford**
Medium-sized, with a bright red coat, often dappled. The horns are tilted upwards. Beef. **Devon**

Large, with a smooth dark red coat and large spreading horns, usually dark-tipped. Beef.   **Sussex**

Medium-sized, with a brownish-red coat and white markings, especially a white stripe down the back and much white below. The drooping horns are long and forward-pointing. Dual-purpose.   **Longhorn**

Medium-sized, usually completely black, but sometimes completely red, with a heavy body and head, and short legs. The dark-tipped horns are forward-pointing. Dairy or dual-purpose. Irish.   **Dexter**

3. The cattle are black, sometimes with small white markings, and hornless.

Large, with a black coat, sometimes with a brownish tinge, and a few white patches below. The poll is rather sharply pointed. Beef.   **Aberdeen-Angus**

Large, with a thick, long, wavy brownish-black coat, a short head and a broad poll. Beef. Most common in south-west Scotland.   **Galloway**

Large, with a thick brownish-black coat and white patches forming a belt round the middle of the body. The head is short and the poll broad. Beef. Most common in south-west Scotland.   **Belted Galloway**

4. The cattle are black, with some white markings, and horned.

Large, with a coat of black and white patches. The small short horns curve inwards and forwards. Dairy   **British Friesian**

Medium-sized, with a black coat and sometimes white below and on the tail-tip. The large spreading horns are yellow with black tips. Dual-purpose. Originated in north and central Wales.   **Welsh Black**

Medium-sized, wholly black, with a heavy head and body, and short legs. The dark-tipped horns are forward-pointing. Dairy or dual-purpose. Irish.
                                                                          Dexter

Medium to small-sized with black and white patches. The large, widely set, horns are upward curving. Dairy.   **Ayrshire**

Small, with a black coat and often a little white on the udder. The legs are long. The medium-length thin horns curve upwards and inwards. Dairy. Irish.   **Kerry**

5. The cattle are brown to reddish-brown and horned.

Large, with a pale to deep reddish-brown coat. The medium-length horns are forward-curving. Dual-purpose. Largely restricted to Devon and Cornwall.   **South Devon**

Medium to small-sized, with a brown and white or black and white coat. The large, widely set, horns are upward curving. Dairy.   **Ayrshire**

Medium-sized, with a yellowish-brown coat, white below and with white markings. The horns curve upwards and forwards. The nose is usually buff-coloured. Dairy.   **Guernsey**

Medium-sized, with a brown coat and a white line running along the loins, over the tailhead and down the hind legs. Rare. Dairy.   **Old Gloucestershire**

Small, with a light brown coat; rarely grey or cream. The small horns curve inwards. The nose is black. Dairy.   **Jersey**

6. Medium-sized, with long and very shaggy coats of varying shades from cream and fawn, through red to black (rare). The spreading horns are very long. Beef. West Scottish coast and the Western Isles. **Highland**

7. White, except for a few red or black lines. The black-tipped horns are large and spreading. Dual-purpose. Few survive, and these are restricted to enclosed parks. **Park or British White**

8. Large, with blue, white and blue, or blue-roan and white coats. Rare. Dual-purpose. **Blue Albion**

Identification key to sheep breeds

1. The sheep has little or no wool. Horned.

Medium-sized. The little wool the animal may have usually falls out in the spring. The white skin is often black-spotted. The face is white and the nose pink. The horns are curled. Rare. Anglesey and Northamptonshire. **Wiltshire Horned (Western)**

2. The sheep is covered with wool and both sexes are horned.

Medium-sized and long-bodied, but the back is narrow. The wool is fine and fairly dense, extending to the knees. The broad head is woolled to just above the eyes, but the cheeks are bare. The face is white and the nostrils pink (flesh-coloured). Dorset, Somerset, Wiltshire and Hampshire. **Dorset Horn**
Small, with long dense wool extending to just above the knees. The face is a dull white, with a wool top-knot extending down between the eyes and there is wool on the cheeks. The nose is black. N. Devon and W. Somerset. **Exmoor Horn (Porlock)**
Small, with fine long dense wool, white or grey, black or brown, often with white patches. The tail is very short. Ewes (females) may be hornless. Shetland Islands. **Shetland**

3. The sheep is covered with wool. Only the rams (males) are horned.

Small to medium-sized, with long stringy locks of greyish wool, which nearly reach the ground. The horns form a flat coil. The faces and legs of lambs are a deep blue-black, but become grey or even white with age. Lake District. **Herdwick**
Small to medium-sized, hardy with long coarse wool. The ram's horns form an open spiral (corkscrew). The bare head is short and wide, and the nose convex. The face and legs are black, sometimes with white patches. Hills of Scotland and N. England. **Scottish Blackface**
Medium-sized, hardy, with fairly short dense wool, which stops well above the knees. The tail is long, almost reaching the ground, despite the long legs. The horns form an open spiral. The bare head is short, and the face black,

sometimes with white markings. S.W. and W. Yorkshire and N.W. Derbyshire.
Lonk

Medium-sized, with rough, fairly long wool, in stringy locks, which fall almost to the knees. The legs are mottled black and white, and are bare at least to the knees. The head is bare, the face black or dark grey, sometimes with light patches, and the nose is grey. The horns form an open spiral. Pennines in N. Yorkshire and Westmorland.
Swaledale

Medium-sized, hardy, with long, very coarse wool, reaching almost to the ground. The legs are mottled black and white. The horns form an open spiral. The bare head is black (sometimes with a brownish tinge), often with white markings, and the nose is grey. North Riding of Yorkshire and Westmorland.
Rough Fell

Small, with medium-length, dense wool. The legs are dark and almost clear of wool. The horns form an open spiral. The head is woolled over, except for a small tan area around the nose and mouth. Central Wales, but it is rather doubtful whether any pure-breds survive.
Radnor

Small, long-bodied, with fairly short dense wool, which stops at the knees. The legs are white, sometimes with tan patches. The horns form an open spiral. The bare head is white, sometimes with tan patches. The mountainous areas of Wales.
Welsh Mountain

Medium-sized, with fine dense white wool, which hangs below the knees. The white legs are bare, at least to the knees. Horns are uncommon and rarely exceed two inches in length. The short bare head is carried high. The ears are erect and bare. The nose is convex and the face is tan or white, covered with short wiry hair. S. Scotland and the Cheviot Hills.
Cheviot

4. The sheep is covered with wool, and is hornless. The face is white.

A. The head is completely bare of wool.

Medium-sized with a wide level back. The wool is long, lustrous and dense. The bare head is long, the nose convex, the face covered with soft white hair, while the nostrils and lips are black. The large erect ears are white, occasionally with black spots.
Border Leicester

Medium-sized with long, dense, fine white wool, which often hangs below the knees. The short bare head is carried high, the nose convex and the face covered with short wiry white hair. The ears are erect. S. Scotland and the Cheviot Hills.
Cheviot

Small, long-bodied, with fairly short dense wool, which stops above the knees. The legs are white, sometimes with tan patches. The bare white head sometimes has tan patches. The mountainous areas of Wales.
Welsh Mountain

Small to medium-sized, with long stringy locks of greyish wool, which nearly reach the ground. The lambs' deep blue-black faces become grey, and even white, with age. Lake District.
Herdwick

B. The top of the head is covered with wool, but the face is bare.

Large, massively-built, with wavy wool in thick locks (as wide as two fingers) which extends to the knees. The long head is carried high and the top-knot wool may hang over the face. The lateral white ears may be dotted with black.
Lincoln

Large, long-bodied, with fairly long, tightly curled dense wool. The head is broad and wool from the top-knot may hang over the face. The lateral white ears are often black-spotted. S. Devon and Cornwall.   **South Devon**

C. The top of the head is covered with wool and there is some on the cheeks.

Medium-sized, low-set, with long wool with curly ends. The wedge-shaped head is covered with white hair, sometimes with a bluish tinge, the nose is slightly convex, and the lips and nostrils are black.   **Leicester**

Medium-sized, long-bodied, with long dense wool. The wide forehead is covered with wool and there is some short wool on the face, including the cheeks. The nostrils are black.   **Romney**

Medium-sized with lustrous close, but not dense, slightly curly wool. The broad head is covered by wool extending from the top-knot to below eye-level and there is considerable wool on the cheeks.   **Devon**

D. The wool covers the whole head except for a small area around the end of the nose and the mouth.

Medium-sized with short, very dense wool, which extends to the knees on the forelegs, but to the feet on the hind legs. The uncoated parts of the face are white, and the nostrils light.   **Devon Closewool**

Small to medium-sized, with short, very close dense wool. The part of the face not woolled over is a dull white and the nostrils black.   **Ryeland**

5. The sheep is covered with wool and is hornless. The face is brown or brownish.

Medium-sized with fine dense white wool, which hangs below the knees. The legs are white and bare, at least to the knees. The bare head is short and carried high. The erect ears are bare. The nose is convex and the tan face is covered with short wiry hair. S. Scotland and the Cheviot Hills.   **Cheviot**

Small, round-bodied, with short, very fine, dense wool. The short legs are covered with wool down to the feet. The very wide head is woolled over, except for small grey-brown area around the nostrils and mouth. The ears are lateral. Southern Chalk Downs.   **Southdown**

Small, with dense, medium-length wool. The dark legs are almost clear of wool. The head is woolled over, except for a small tan area round the nostrils and mouth. Central Wales. (It is uncertain whether any pure-breds survive.)   **Radnor**

Medium-sized with short dense wool. There may be black patches on the white legs. The wool on the top of the head extends to between the eyes and there is wool on parts of the cheeks. The face is dark brown or tawny, as are the erect ears. Welsh border and the W. Midlands.   **Clun Forest**

Medium-sized with short dense wool, which extends down the legs to the knees. The forehead and cheeks are woolled, the face is pale brown, or brownish-grey, as are the lateral ears.   **Dorset**

Large with long dense wool, which extends to above the knees of the forelegs. The head is erect and the dark greyish-brown face is almost bare, but wool

from the top-knot reaches nearly to the eyes and there is wool on the cheeks·
The lateral ears are long and thin.   **Oxford**

6. The sheep is covered with wool and is hornless. The face is black and white.

Medium-sized, hardy, with fine soft short, fairly dense wool, which extends
down the black and white mottled legs to the knees. The bare head is black and
white, and the ears lateral. High Peak of Derbyshire. **Derbyshire Gritstone**
Small to medium-sized, hardy, with long coarse wool. The bare head is short
and wide and the nose convex. The face and legs are black sometimes with
white patches. The hills of Scotland and N. England.   **Scottish Blackface**
Medium-sized, hardy, with very long coarse wool, reaching almost to the
ground. The legs are mottled black and white. The bare head is black (sometimes with a brownish tinge), often with white markings, and the nose is grey.
The North Riding of Yorkshire and Westmorland.   **Rough Fell**
Medium-sized with rough, fairly long wool, hanging down almost to the
knees. The legs are mottled black and white. The head is bare, the face black
with white patches and the nose grey. The Pennines in N. Yorkshire and
Westmorland.   **Swaledale**
Medium-sized with coarse, rather short dense wool. The legs are black and
white and clear of wool to well above the knees. The head is bare, the face
black and white and the nostrils black. The ears are half-erect. Wales.
                                                                  Kerry Hill
Medium-sized with fairly short dense wool, which stops well above the knees.
The tail is long, almost reaching the ground, despite the long legs. The bare
head is short and the face black, sometimes with white markings. S.W. and W.
Yorkshire and N.W. Derbyshire.   **Lonk**
Large, long-bodied, hardy, with long curly wool. The face is bare, though
wool from the top-knot may reach below the eyes, and white with black spots
concentrated towards the end of the nose.   **Dartmoor**

7. The sheep is covered with wool and is hornless. The face is black, or nearly so.

Large, wide and stocky in build, with short dense wool. The legs are woolled
down to the feet. The broad head is covered with wool except round the eyes
and a small black area round the nose and mouth. The long lateral dark ears are
carried low.   **Hampshire Down**
Large with short, fairly dense wool. The long legs are black and clear of wool
to well above the knees. The rather long head is bare and black. The lateral
ears are long and black.   **Suffolk**
Medium-sized with short, fairly dense wool, which extends to below the knees.
The lower parts of the legs are soft black. The short broad head has wool
extending down the nose to below the eye-level and the cheeks are woolled.
The face is a soft black, as are the lateral ears.   **Shropshire**
Small to medium-sized, hardy, with long coarse wool. The bare head is short
and wide, and the nose is convex. The face and legs are black. The hills of
Scotland and N. England.   **Scottish Blackface**
Medium-sized with rough, fairly long wool in stringy locks falling almost to
the knees. The legs are mottled black and white. The head is bare, the face black

and the nose grey. Pennines in N. Yorkshire and Westmorland.   **Swaledale**

Medium-sized, hardy, with fairly short dense wool, which stops well above the knees. The tail is long, almost reaching the ground, despite the long legs. The bare head is short and the face black, sometimes with white markings. S.W. and W. Yorkshire and N.W. Derbyshire.   **Lonk**

Large, long-bodied, large-framed, with long, fine and lustrous wool in pencil-thick locks. The head is carried high and is crowned by a top-knot, but the deep blue-grey face is bare. The ears are lateral.   **Wensleydale**

8. The sheep is covered with fine long dense wool and is usually hornless.

Small, with white, grey, black or brown wool, often with white patches. The tail is very short. The rams and some ewes (females) are horned. The Shetland Islands.   **Shetland**

Identification key to pig breeds

1. The animal is all white.

Large with white hair and skin, although dark spots are occasionally possible. The head and body are long, as is the straight nose. The ears are erect or forward-pointing. Bacon or pork.   **Large White**

Similar to Large White, but the body is shorter and the long ears hang vertically down. Bacon.   **Large Ulster White**

Small, with a white skin and abundant white hair. The head is short and concave, the nose turned up and the cheeks heavy. The medium-sized ears are erect. Pork.   **Middle White**

Large, heavily-built, with abundant curly hair. The face is heavy and the ears drooping. Not common, except locally.   **Lincolnshire Curly Coated**

Large, heavily-built, but with a relatively short body, smooth skin and sparse white hair. A wide, but short concave face, and fairly short ears which droop over the eyes. Not common, except locally.   **Cumberland**

Large, of moderate length, with straight silky hair. The long ears hang over the face. Pork or bacon. Not common, except locally in parts of Devon and Cornwall.   **Long White Lop-eared**

2. The animal is black and white.

Small, with a rusty black, or pure black coat, white nose, feet and tail-tip. The head is fairly short and concave, but the nose is not up-turned, while the ears are erect or forward-pointing. Pork.   **Berkshire**

Large, black with a white 'saddle' over the shoulders, and white forelegs. The large stiff ears are erect and forward-pointing. Pork or bacon.
    Wessex Saddleback

Medium-sized, black with a white 'saddle' over the shoulders, white forelegs, hind feet and tail-tip. The medium-length ears are stiffly erect and forward-pointing. Pork or bacon.   **Essex Saddleback**

Medium-sized, long-bodied, black with white spots, or sometimes white with black spots. The head is of medium length, with long drooping ears, which hang over the face. Pork or bacon. **Gloucester Old Spot**

3. The animal is all black.

Large with a black skin and straight silky jet black hair, usually rather sparse. The head is of medium size, with long drooping ears. Pork or bacon. **Large Black**

4. The animal has flesh-coloured skin, with hair of varying shades of chestnut.

Medium-sized with a long, rather narrow body. The head is long and lean, with a straight nose and medium-length, pointed ears, set rather high. Bacon. **Tamworth**

Identification key to goat breeds

Large with a markedly convex nose and long ears, which hang down vertically. The short coat is usually a reddish-tan, sometimes with black along the spine and at the extremities, but almost any combination of reddish-tan and black is possible, though normally there are no white markings. Usually hornless. **Anglo-Nubian**

Large with long legs and muzzle. Usually all white. The nose-line is straight or slightly concave. Ears erect or forward-pointing. Sometimes bearded. Usually hornless. **British Saanen**

Medium-sized with a white coat, sometimes with black spots on the skin at the ears and eyelids, but no black hair. The nose-line is straight or slightly concave. Ears erect or forward-pointing. Sometimes bearded. Usually hornless. **Saanen**

Small with a short coat of light brown or fawn, a white muzzle and white strips up both sides of the face to above the eyes and round the ears. The rump and lower side of the tail are also white and there are sometimes white markings on the legs. There is a fringe of long hair down the spine and hind-quarters, and sometimes all round the body. The ears are erect or forward-pointing. The nose-line is straight or slightly concave. Sometimes bearded. Usually hornless. **Toggenburg**

Large with a short coat which varies in colour from light brown to a rich chocolate. The muzzle is often white and there are sometimes white strips up both sides of the face over the eyes and round the ears. There may also be white markings on the legs. Sometimes there is a fringe of longer hair. The nose-line is straight or slightly concave. The ears are erect or forward-pointing. Usually hornless. **British Toggenburg**

Most breeds show considerable variation, largely as a result of cross-breeding, and it is, therefore, somewhat difficult, even for an experienced person, to name the breed with absolute certainty in all cases. This table can only give some idea of the breed and is included for information and the sake of completeness.

Above, Stoat on snow. The winter coat is lighter but the black tail-tuft remains
Below, Weasel.

Wheat

Barley

Rye

Oats

Identification key to crop types

Tall and grass-like with narrow leaves, green ripening to pale yellow. **Cereals**

Slender, wiry stems, narrowly lance-shaped alternate leaves and blue, red, or rarely white, flowers.   **Flax or Linseed**

Short with a large swollen, conical to spherical tuber ('root'), which may be partly above ground. The stalked leaves are short and oval.   **'Root' Crops**

According to variety, the plant resembles either the swede or the turnip, but possesses a stem from which arise long-stalked leaves. There are no bulbous roots.   **Rape**

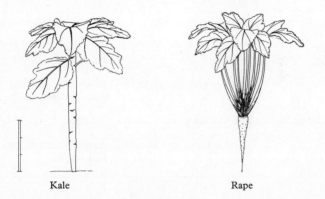

Kale   Rape

Short, loose-hearted with spreading leaves resembling broccoli when young, but growing to over 5 feet tall when mature.   **Kale**

Short, without bulbous roots, leaves are compound pinnate, or trifolate (three-leaved). Seeds in pods.   **Legumes**

Long, often prostrate, stems with compound pinnate leaves and long narrow green pods.   **Pulses (Peas and Beans)**

Slightly branched and the hairy stems bear coarsely-lobed pinnate leaves, bright green above.   **Mustard**

Note: Grasses are dealt with in the section on Vegetation, p. 149.

FIELD CROPS *Cereals* (Grains)

Common Name	WHEAT	BARLEY
Ear	Spiky, made up of snugly set spikelets; protrude in all directions, regular or irregular	Spiky, made of bearded se arranged usually in two ver rows, but sometimes in fou six rows
Whiskers	None usually, but bearded wheats have short spreading whiskers arranged in cylindrical clumps	Very long
Grains	Round profile	Double-pointed, cylindr short
Height	Fairly tall	Fairly tall
Stalk	Stiffly upright, unbranched	Droops so that the ears h down; unbranched
Auricle and leaf	Short and hairy	Very long
Uses	Flour for bread and biscuits	Animal feedstuffs, beer and a holic drinks

Wheat

Barley

	RYE	MAIZE
ppy, made up of 1–3 elets, mostly in ading panicles, either ound the stalk, or all one side	Spiky, made up of four rows of spikelets, giving a cross-shaped profile	A large cylindrical ear, with grains packed tightly upon stout stem (cob) and enclosed in a long green husk
rt, if present	Stiff hairs on spikelets, with long whiskers at the top of the ears	None
g, double-pointed ndle-shaped)	Short and ovoid or double-pointed	Rounded
	Tall	Very tall
ops a little; branched	Bends a little; unbranched	Thick and solid; un-branched
ie; projection right-led	No auricle	Broad juicy leaves
mal feedstuffs, por-e, etc.	Mainly animal feed	In Britain it is used as green fodder

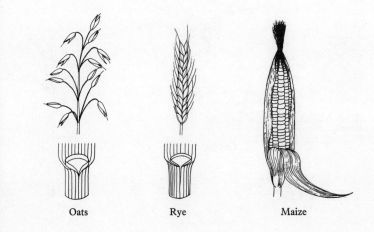

Oats   Rye   Maize

ROOT CROPS

Common Name	POTATO	TURNIP	SWEDE (Swedish Turnip)
Leaves	Dark green, compound, pinnate pairs of alternate leaves with pairs of small leaves, from lateral shoots on the stems. The main crop is not lifted until the foliage dies off	Pale green, rough and divided into distinct lobes; grow directly out of a greenish crown	Long smooth (exc first), thin lea grows from a s solid 'neck'
Root	White or nearly so, oval or rounded; entirely below ground which is normally ridged	White or yellow, plump and round; half above ground	Dull yellow, plu and round, with short but dist 'neck', which tinged purple, gr or bronze; one th or less, above gro
Uses	Human and animal food	Human and animal food	Human and ani food

Potato

Turnip

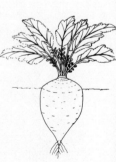

Swede

GOLD (Mangel-zel)	KOHL-RABI	SUGAR BEET	CARROT
k glossy green t-shaped leaves out of the n; may have red stalks	Irregular, long-stemmed, lance leaves grow out of top and sides of the root, but the latter fall out as the plant swells, leaving triangular scars	Smooth, bright green heart-shaped leaves grow out of the top of the root	Green feathery leaves grow out of the top of the root
te, tinged with yellow or orange. nd, straight-1 or spindle-ed; two-thirds of root is above nd	Greenish or purplish, large almost round, narrowing almost to a point; the 'root' is entirely above ground	White or pale yellowish, an inverted cone; entirely below ground, except for the rather greenish crown	Orange, a long tapering inverted cone; entirely, or almost entirely, below ground
nal feedstuff	Animal feedstuff	Extraction of sugar	Human and animal food

Mangold

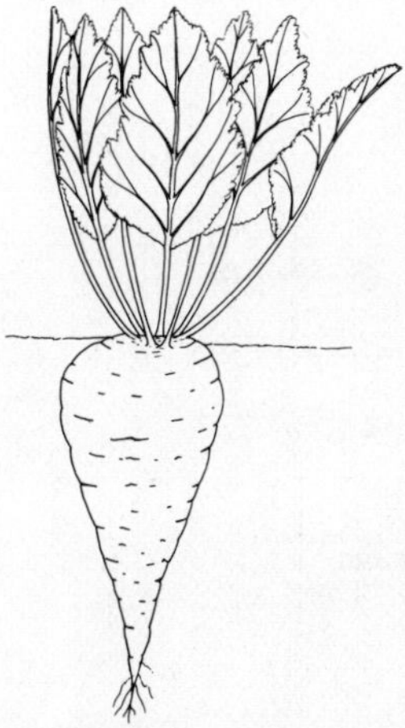

Kohl-rabi

Sugar Beet

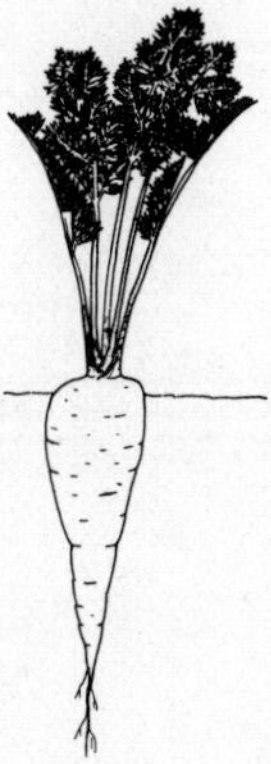

Carrot

Legumes (Family PAPILIONACEAE)

Common Name	SAINFOIN	VETCH
Stems	Branched	Trailing or climbing
Leaves	Compound, pinnate	Compound, pinnate; leaf tapering towards stalk, apex often notched; tendrils at end clinging to support
Flowers	A dense spike of deep rose-pink fls	Red or purple, pea-like
Seeds	Rough pods, each with a single kidney-shaped seed	Narrow pods, up to 2″, containing smooth seeds
Uses	May be grazed; important on dry chalk and limestone soils of the Downs and Cotswolds	Usually grazed

Sainfoin

Vetch

ERNE (Alfalfa)	TREFOIL	CLOVER
ched	Wiry	A low prostrate plant
pound, three-pointed ets, coarsely toothed the tips; ls may be y, but not stems	Compound, pinnate; leaflets taper towards stalk, sharply pointed, toothed; terminal leaflet long-stalked; broad stipules	Compound, three ovate leaflets, toothed or entire, and usually with marked stipules
nally blue or violet, y yellow	Flower-head composed of many small yellow fls	Thick round clusters of many small flowers, with narrow petals. Colour ranges from white to deep crimson
sted pods contain green-kidney-shaped seeds	Twisted black pods, when ripe	Pods contain 1–4 seeds
ed or cut for fodder	Grazed or cut for fodder	Grazed or cut for fodder

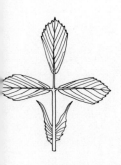

Lucerne

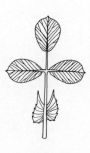

Trefoil

Clover

Other field crops

1. MUSTARD Family CRUCIFERAE

An annual with slightly branching, hairy stems, which may reach 24″. The coarsely-lobed pinnate leaves are pale green and rough below, but bright green and smooth above. The yellow flowers have notched petals. Two varieties are grown:

Black Mustard *Sinapis nigra*

Restricted to Norfolk, Cambridgeshire and southern Lincolnshire, where it is grown on contract for table-mustard makers. The seed-pod is short with a long slender beak, which turns black when ripe.

White Mustard *Sinapis alba*

Used as a green manure, or to feed sheep folded on it. The long seed-pod has a curving flat beak, which turns yellowish-green when ripe.

2. KALE Family CRUCIFERAE

A fodder crop on which animals are folded, the daily ration usually bounded by an electric fence. In the early stages its loose heart and spreading leaves resemble broccoli, but the wavy-edged, thicker leaves are longer than broad and often have a bluish tinge. When mature it may reach five feet. Two varieties are grown: Marrow-stem, which has a very thick stem; Thousand-headed, with a slimmer stem and more leafy heads.

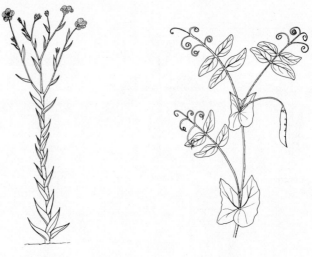

Flax   Pea

3. RAPE *Brassica napus* Family CRUCIFERAE

A fodder crop with oily seeds. Difficult to identify as, according to variety, it can resemble either the turnip or the swede. The chief distinctions are the lack of a bulbous 'root' and the presence of a stem with long-stalked leaves.

4. FLAX and LINSEED Family LINACEAE

These are two distinct varieties of the same species, *Linum usitatissimum:*

Flax. The stems are tall, often up to 40″, producing the long straight fibres needed to make linen. The wiry slender stems are usually unbranched when fully grown, although a few short branches may sometimes be retained. The alternate, lance-shaped leaves are narrow and hairless. The flowers are usually blue, rarely white.

Linseed. The slender wiry stems are much shorter than flax, usually not taller than 24″, and are branched at the top. The small, alternate, lance-shaped leaves are narrow and hairless. The flowers are usually red.

PEAS and BEANS ('Pulses') Family PAPILIONACEAE

	PEAS *Pisum arvense*	BEANS *Vicia faba*
Stems	Long and straggling	Stiff, upright and square-sided
Leaves	Compound, pinnate	Compound, pinnate
Flowers	Purple, mauve or white	White with black patches
Seeds	Long, narrow, green pods, containing many round green seeds	Long, narrow, knobbly green pods with many kidney-shaped seeds in white velvet lining
Uses	Human and animal foodstuffs	Human and animal foodstuffs

METEOROLOGY

The Beaufort Scale of Wind Force

Beaufort Number	Wind	Wind effect on land	Speed m.p.h.	km./hr.
0	Calm	Smoke rises vertically	Less than 1	Less than 1.6
1	Light air	Smoke drifts, but weather vanes not turned	1–3	1.6–6.3
2	Light breeze	Wind felt on face, leaves rustle gently, weather vanes move	4–7	6.4–12.8
3	Gentle breeze	Twigs and leaves in motion, light flags extended	8–12	12.9–20.8
4	Moderate breeze	Loose paper and dust raised, small branches stirred	13–18	20.9–30.5
5	Fresh breeze	Small trees in leaf start to sway, crested wavelets formed on inland water	19–24	30.6–40.1
6	Strong breeze	Larger branches swayed, whistling in telephone wires	25–31	40.2–51.5
7	Moderate gale (high wind)	Large trees in motion, it is difficult to hold an umbrella	32–38	51.6–62.7
8	Fresh gale	Twigs broken off trees, walking against wind difficult	39–46	62.8–75.5
9	Strong gale	Slight damage to buildings (chimney pots and slates blown off)	47–54	75.6–88.4
10	Whole gale	Unusual inland. Trees uprooted. Considerable damage to buildings	55–63	88.5–102.9
11	Storm	Very rare inland. Damage widespread	64–75	103.0–120.6
12	Hurricane		More than 75	More than 120.7

Visibility

DENSE FOG	Visibility less than	44 yards	(40 m.)
THICK FOG	Visibility less than	110 yards	(100 m.)
FOG	Visibility less than	220 yards	(200 m.)
MODERATE FOG	Visibility less than	440 yards	(400 m.)
MIST or HAZE	Visibility less than	1,100 yards	(1 km.)
POOR	Visibility less than	$1\frac{1}{4}$ miles	(2 km.)
MODERATE	Visibility less than	$4\frac{3}{8}$ miles	(7 km.)
GOOD	Visibility less than	$6\frac{1}{4}$ miles	(10 km.)
VERY GOOD	Visibility less than	$18\frac{3}{8}$ miles	(30 km.)
EXCELLENT	Visibility up to	25 miles	(40 km.)

Cloud forms

A. High clouds, 20,000 feet (6,000 m.), or more.

BROKEN

Delicate, feathery, without shading, generally white.

May be arranged in tufts, or bands, converging on the horizon. **Cirrus** (Ci)

White flakes, or small rounded masses, without shadows. May be in groups, lines or ripples. Rare. **Cirrocumulus** (Cc)

CONTINUOUS

A milky-white, thin veil. The sun and moon are not blurred, but a halo may be produced. **Cirrostratus** (Cs)

B. Middle clouds, between 6,500 and 20,000 feet (2,000–6,000 m.).

BROKEN

Large balls (resembling cotton-wool), sometimes rather flattened, **often** in groups or lines, but if crowded some edges may become joined. **Altocumulus** (Ac)

CONTINUOUS

A grey, or blue-grey veil, through which the sun or moon may gleam, but no halo is produced. May sometimes become rather thick. **Altostratus** (As)

C. Low clouds, between ground level and 6,500 feet (0–2,000 m.).

BROKEN

Large balls, or rolls, of soft grey cloud, with darker patches. Usually in waves or lines, giving a wavy appearance, which is still in evidence if the separate clouds combine to cover the whole sky. **Stratocumulus** (Sc)

CONTINUOUS

A uniform layer of fog-like cloud, not resting on the ground. **Stratus** (St)

A uniformly featureless cloud, dark grey in colour. **Nimbostratus** (Ns)

C. Low clouds (*contd.*)

BROKEN

A layer of fog-like cloud, broken
into ragged masses, but not resting on
the ground.   **Fractostratus** (Fs)

D. Clouds showing great vertical development.

Thick separate clouds, domed above, while the base appears to be almost
horizontal.   **Cumulus** (Cu)

A heavy cloud mass rising to form mountainous peaks. The upper parts are
fibrous and often spread out, resembling an anvil. Very dark below. May cause
local rain, hail or snow.   **Cumulonimbus** (Cb)

PART 2

MAN ON THE LAND

Introduction

Looking around, we can see ample evidence of man's influence on the landscape, in the sprawling towns with their ever-spreading suburbs, or in the pleasant rural scene and the wilder country of heaths, hills and fells. Fields and settlements, fences and roads, canals and railways are all clear signs of his action in changing the face of the land, so often dominated by glaringly-new blocks of flats, or mellower castle towers or church spires, while electricity cables on their high pylons may span the horizon. On a smaller scale drainage ditches cut lines across the fields, fruit trees stand in compact formations and drystone walls stretch into the moorland distances.

The change from wild forest and inhospitable marsh began long ago, as man slowly gained a foothold over nature and then continued to fight to retain what he had won. Over the centuries the pace gradually quickened; what we see today is an instalment, not the end of the story.

The first section is a brief account of our Prehistory, a story revealed by years of patient excavation to collect facts and then slowly piece them together – an unfinished task still with many blanks and vague outlines, which are slowly being filled in.

At first, prehistoric man made little impact on his landscape, as hunters and fishers live with nature rather than in opposition to it, but by the Neolithic Age these simple folk were displaced by farmers, gradually society grew more complex and if we know little of their primitive dwellings, they left their mark on the land in great burial grounds, henges and stone circles. Causewayed camps, the stone village of Skara Brae, Glastonbury's lake-village, brochs and the great Iron Age forts, such as that of Maiden Castle, all tell of man's spreading influence.

The story is continued in the next section which spans Roman Britain and the Dark Ages. This is followed by a section, which traces our development, and that of our buildings, from the Anglo-Saxons to the present day. The Romans, the Anglo-Saxons, Danes and Normans each added something new. The great castles show the disturbed nature of the Middle Ages just as open Tudor buildings indicate more settled times and the introduction of new ideas. Many of our towns and villages still contain delightful Georgian and Regency houses, although on closer inspection some of those in towns reveal new façades on older buildings.

But settlements are not only buildings. People live and work in them. Thus we must look also at social, cultural and technological changes. With the rapid growth of industry from the late eighteenth century, towns began to sprawl, aided by improved forms of transport – the quiet canals mainly for goods, then the railways which held sway until the internal combustion engine enabled the roads to become competitors and then leaders. But other technological changes also affected the landscape by altering the balance for or against any given place. Birmingham, for example, owed much of its early development to its freedom from craft guilds, so that new ideas and methods could be freely introduced, and to its position near the junction of three canals, while Crewe,

Swindon and to a lesser extent, Derby, expanded rapidly as railway towns. On the other hand the increasing size of ships killed many small ports with shallow entrances and the coming of railways to a few coastal towns caused the concentration of the fishing industry on a few large ports, though in some cases this was compensated for by the creation of seaside resorts which widened the possibilities for more people to take holidays. In the same way the change-over from water to steam-power meant that many factories, hitherto tied to river sites, could be built elsewhere while the later switch to oil or electricity again widened the choice further.

But the growth of industry and suburbs would have been much more restricted had not buses, trams and finally cars provided the necessary increase in transport within the urban areas. Better transport not only enabled houses to be built further away from town centres but also introduced a wider variety of building styles. The local materials then still in use over much of the country gave way to the cheaper mass-produced brick and Welsh slate which became characteristic of all parts of Victorian Britain, while later styles borrowed from civil engineering to produce the modern giant blocks, so similar in basic structure to timber framed houses of the sixteenth and seventeenth centuries. Of other buildings, mills certainly deserve a special mention. Not only are they prominent and interesting landmarks, but the evolution of their machinery provided the training ground for mill-wrights, the early engineers whose influence has so permeated our present-day life and landscape.

The section on agriculture provides identification keys for farm animals and crops. As in everything else, farming is now in a state of rapid change, but it can never escape its intimate association with landscape, and indeed is largely responsible for much of the rural scene, while the varying progress reflects our historic, social and economic fortunes (Page 233).

The final section deals with the elements commonly found in place-names, which form but one more link between the past and the present.

Above, Aberdeen Angus.   *Below*, Herefords.

Above, Highland cattle.   *Below*, Sussex.

PREHISTORY

We may never know when man first came to Britain. Our knowledge of early man has been painstakingly built up from the little he left or lost, for until comparatively recent times he remained a nomadic hunter, fisher and gatherer, living in small family groups in caves or simple shelters, leaving little trace, while the total population never exceeded a few hundreds. Chance played no small part in many discoveries, and even later when numbers increased, only the non-perishable items survived, mostly stone tools and it is on these, how they were fabricated and evolved, that the cultural classification is based. Stone Age man developed two varieties of tools, based on cores or flakes. Either he trimmed a large flint until it, the core, would serve his purpose, ignoring the fragments, or he worked the flakes and ignored the mass; few cultures worked both. Because we know so little of individual groups, Prehistorians speak of cultures – based on technology – rather than peoples, naming each after the site where it was first studied. For convenience, prehistory is divided into Ages, according to the material used for tool-making. The divisions represent no clear-cut lines, but rather the beginning of a period when the new material appeared in an area. The more distant in time, the more slowly innovations spread outward from their origins, so that it was possible for differing cultures to co-exist. But, with the passage of time, the number and pace of diffusion of ideas have accelerated at an ever-increasing rate, producing a more uniform culture over larger areas. Thus, major cultural changes indicate either an acceptance of new ideas from other groups, or a new and more advanced group replacing the earlier one.

One of prehistory's major problems was that of dating. Although newer deposits overlie older ones, this is comparative. Until 1948 no method of absolute dating existed. Then, by using the tiny but constant proportion of radio-active carbon (C_{14}) present in all living matter and which steadily decays an approximate date could be given. However, recent work indicates the time-scale may have been somewhat under-estimated; if this is so then accepted dates, and the broader inter-relationships of European prehistory may have to be modified.

For much of the last million years, a large part of the northern hemisphere was affected by the Pleistocene Ice Age, from which we emerged only some 20,000 years ago. However, this was not a continuous time of unrelieved cold, but at least four long cold periods (**Glacials**) separated by equally long warmer intervals (**Interglacials**) during which the climate often became hot, or even tropical. Even the glacials themselves were divided into phases by warmer spells (**Interstadials**), when valley glaciers were in retreat and ice-caps shrank, but did not disappear. All these immense changes took place over thousands of years, affecting palaeolithic man only marginally, for in a sparsely-populated world, he could move north or south easily, virtually staying in the same hunting environment.

Although only strictly applicable to Alpine glacials, the following names are widely used; being short and alphabetically arranged, they are easy to remember.

Gunz glacial

        Gunz – Mindel Interglacial

Mindel glacial

        Mindel – Russ Interglacial

Russ glacial

        Russ – Wurm Interglacial

Wurm glacial

        Post-glacial Period

In Britain the Palaeolithic, or Old Stone Age, began during the middle Pleistocene, for although chipped flints (Eoliths) occur in pre-Pleistocene deposits, these are generally believed to result from river pounding and not early man. The Gunz-Mindel interglacial offers surer ground, although the early finds at Cromer are still open to question, the later irregularly-edged **Abbevillian** (Chellean) hand-axes from the Thames gravels, and the flake tools and fire-hardened spear of the **Clactonian** are beyond dispute. The latter culture also appears in the Mindel-Russ interglacial, along with the **Acheulian**, whose better-worked smoother-edged hand axes are associated with the bones of Swanscombe Man, our earliest known ancestor. The improved **Levalloisian** technique of trimming flakes before detaching them from the core appeared late in this period, but its full development belongs to the Russ-Wurm interglacial, in the middle of which the **Mousterian** culture appeared. This culture is the first to be associated with an individual type, Neanderthal Man, who since he lived more in caves than the open, left a better sequence of artifacts and debris accumulated in one place. Formerly depicted as a beetle-browed half-man, this has now been shown to be local throw-back, recent discoveries showing he was much closer to modern man in appearance, while his skill and intelligence are seen in his better-worked fine-edged tools and the cave debris prove his hunting expertise of a wide range of animals. In Europe, he survived at least the first phase of the last glacial.

During the Wurm glaciation, the last and most extensive, Modern Man, who had almost certainly originated in the Middle East, developed improved techniques for working stone, bone and wood producing better tools – including spear-throwers, man's first mechanical aid – and the making of fire, a truly major advance. As climatic conditions improved, during the interstadials, he spread across large parts of Europe, in some cases leaving clear evidence of his way of life in cave paintings. The five main European cultures were:

a. **Chatelperronian** (formerly called Lower Aurignacian)

b. **Aurignacian** (formerly called Middle Aurignacian)

c. **Gravettian** (formerly called Upper Aurignacian)

d. **Solutrean**

e. **Magdalenian**

Of these, only the Aurignacian and Gravettian have been found in Britain, but the latter is represented by many cave deposits and later developed into the first British culture, named after Pin Hole Cave, Cresswell, Derbyshire, **Cress-**

wellian whose custom of burying tools with their red-ochre-covered dead indicates the beginning of a religion.

As climatic conditions continued to improve, hardy trees spread northwards and the survivors of the Cresswellian culture also extended over the southern part of the country, reaching Antrim by Late Boreal times. Meanwhile, the forest-dwelling **Maglemosians,** fishers and wild-fowlers, had crossed the deltaic marshes of the then North Sea area to settle along the east coast lowlands, bringing the tiny flint arrowheads or Microliths of the Mesolithic (Middle Stone Age) proper, as well as their long bows and large flint axes, with an oblique cutting-edge, which enabled them to fell trees for canoes and hut platforms on marshy ground, e.g. Star Carr, near Scarborough. By Early Boreal times, the **Sauveterrian** culture had spread from Flanders, but lacking the heavy axe, was restricted to the drier and more open uplands. Elements of the last two cultures had merged by Late Boreal times, giving the **Horsham** culture, characterised by equilateral heavy axes, stone 'maces', hollow-based flint arrow-heads which could be stuck on to a shaft instead of being slotted into it and the oldest artificial dwellings in Britain, pits three feet deep and up to thirty feet long, presumably roofed with branches and turf. The north-western sites, previously ascribed to the Azillians, are now considered to belong to a hybrid Cresswellian-Maglemosian culture, which developed as the **Obanian** and **Larnian** cultures, but with far wider distribution than the names suggest, about the beginning of the Atlantic period, around 5500 BC, when the land connection to continental Europe was broken.

The Neolithic (New Stone Age) did not bring merely a change in techniques, but a revolution in the whole pattern of life. While European communities still remained dependent on hunting, farming had begun with shifting cultivation in the Middle East and by about 7000 BC walled settlements had developed there. The greatest change brought by farming was not only the adequate and regular supply of food, but in the provision of a surplus which could support non-farming specialist craftsmen.

The revolution spread slowly, reaching Britain in late Atlantic times, about 3000 BC, when colonists from Flanders settled the southern Downs, and later built their distinctive **Causewayed Camps** – a compact area surrounded by a ditch and inner bank interrupted by several entrances of undisturbed ground in both. These appear to have been primarily enclosures for cattle, sheep and pigs rather than purely defensive sites, although in at least some cases the people lived inside, sheltered by the bank. Named the **Windmill Hill** people, after one of their larger camps, they felled trees with polished flint axes, a great improvement, before breaking the ground on small scattered plots with digging-sticks to plant wheat and barley which they harvested with flint sickles. Although some hunting was done, using leaf-shaped arrowheads, the rubbish-heaps (middens) mostly contain the bones of domesticated animals. Their dead were buried under long mounds of rock and earth. Eventually the culture spread west and north, where it often blended with older cultures, e.g. **Beacharra** in Kintyre and **Unstan** and **Pentland** on the west Scottish coast, but this must have led to increased trading in flint from mines on the South Downs and Grimes Graves, Norfolk.

About 2500 BC, a new and more formalised religion appeared in the west of Britain, where it remained strongest. Probably introduced by 'missionaries',

CLIMATIC, VEGETATIONAL AND CULTURAL CHANGES SINCE THE WURM GLACIATIO

Approximate commencement	British pollen zone	Climatic Stage	Vegetation
20,000 BC	—	Ice retreat began. Slow temperature rise began	
17,000 BC	—	*Milder Phase*	
Late Glacial			
13,000 BC	Ia	*Oldest Dryas Phase* Cold	Dryas (*D. octopetala*), some grasses and d birch
11,000 BC	Ib	*Bolling Oscillation* Sub-arctic; cool	Birch and pine, with s grasses and sedges
10,300 BC	Ic	*Older Dryas Phase* Colder	Tundra; dryas, with tered dwarf birch and A willow
10,000 BC	II	*Allerod Oscillation* Sub-arctic; cool	Thin 'islands' of forest hairy birch, aspen juniper; some Scots pin
8,900 BC	III	*Younger Dryas Phase* Colder	Tundra; dryas, dwarf b and Arctic willow; s hairy birch
Post-Glacial			
8,300 BC	IV	*Pre-Boreal* Temperature rose and annual range increased; rainfall decreased Cool Continental	Light forests of hairy silver birch with some as Followed by Scots spreading to central a of Scotland and Irel Shrubs, juniper and cherry, with willows arc lakes
7,700 BC	V	*Early Boreal* Temperature continued to rise and range to increase; rainfall decreased, giving: Warm Continental	Pine and hazel forest veloped, but birch rema dominant in North. oak, small-leaved lime common alder began appear
7,000 BC	VI	*Late Boreal* The Warm Continental climate continued but rainfall began to increase	Widespread pine and h forests. Common alder, and oak increasing

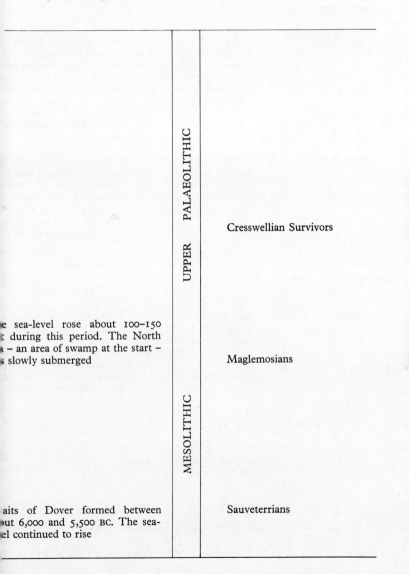

Physical Changes		*Cultures*
	UPPER PALAEOLITHIC	Cresswellian Survivors
...e sea-level rose about 100–150 ... during this period. The North ... – an area of swamp at the start – ... slowly submerged	MESOLITHIC	Maglemosians
...aits of Dover formed between ...ut 6,000 and 5,500 BC. The sea-...el continued to rise		Sauveterrians

Approximate commencement	British pollen zone	Climatic Stage	Vegetation
5,600 BC	VIIa	*Atlantic* Rainfall continued to increase, giving a warm and moist Coastal climate. Regarded by many as an 'optimum climate'	Oak and elm forests creased at expense of Sc pine, which retreated nor wards; lime also gain Great increase in shr layer of hazel, comm alder, wild cherry, ha thorn, holly, guelder r and ivy
3,000 BC	VIIb	*Sub-Boreal* Rainfall increased, temperature range increased, winters colder, giving: Continental climate	Oak dominated forests; e and lime declined, hazel creased; some ash prese Grassland and heath creased at expense of fores due to drier conditio Man began cultivation
500 BC	VIII	*Sub-Atlantic* Rainfall increased, summer temperature fell, winters a little warmer, giving: Cool Coastal climate	Hornbeam and beech creased, birch, aspen a juniper return, but o lost ground. Rapid grow of blanket peat on previou forested hills. Cultivat land continues to incre slowly
100 BC	—	Climate became drier and warmer	

Physical Changes		Cultures

...e last valley glaciers may have re-...ined in the Scottish Highlands ...til about 5,000 BC		Horsham
		Obanian
		Larnian
		Windmill Hill
		Peterborough
		Beaker Folk
	BRONZE	Wessex Food Vessel People (Urnfolk)
		Deverel-Rimbury
...ergence in north Scotland and ...th Ireland produced raised beaches		Iron Age A ('Hallstatt')
		Iron Age B ('La Tene')
... 100 BC the rising sea-level had ...merged coastal areas from East ...glia to the Scilly Isles	NEOLITHIC	Iron Age C (Belgic) I
		Iron Age (Belgic) II
		Roman Invasion

as there is no evidence of cultural changes, it is characterised by megalithic communal tombs covered by immense mounds which can still be seen, although the earth covering of some have been removed, often leaving only the capstone

Dolmen roofed by a single capstone from which the covering earth has been removed

supported by a few large blocks, **Dolmens.** The tombs, built of large blocks of drystone walling, with corbelled or slab roofs, are of two main types, with many regional variations:

Gallery Graves. These are long parallel-sided chambers, divided into sections by jutting slabs and sometimes with side-chambers, opening direct at the portal. The sides of the pear-shaped mound are retained by a drystone kerb.

Left, gallery grave; *right,* dummy portal type with side chambers

Severn-Cotswold Group. Found on hills from the Gower to the Mendips and Cotswolds. Often had corbelled transepts, which later became separate chambers. Curved wider end is stone-faced, with a forecourt in front. Central portal was later replaced by a dummy, a side-entrance being made. Some continued in use until about 1700 B C.

Clyde-Solway and Carlingford Groups. Oval or wedge-shaped mounds cover long galleries, transverse slabs nearly reach the corbelled roof, some with side-chambers. Externally the northern Irish ones offer more to see, as some façades have been extended (horned type) or inturned round the forecourt

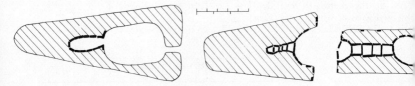

Left, lobster-claw type; *centre,* Clyde horned or forecourt coastal type; *right,* double horned type

(lobster-claw type), and others have forecourts at either end or straight façades with extra wide portals.

Scilly-Tranmere Group. A small round mound, retained by kerb of small stones, covers the gallery of slab or drystone construction.

Medway Group. A large elongated mound, surrounded by a kerb of large stones, covers a slab chamber. Most remain only as dolmens.

Passage Graves. A passage leads to a wider chamber, usually with three side-chambers. The covering mound is generally round.

Generalised section of a passage grave

Boyne Group. Originating along the River Boyne, it later spread to the lands surrounding the Irish Sea. A large round mound covered a long passage ending in a round chamber, with side-chambers arranged in a trefoil. Some continued in use until the Bronze Age. The mound of the finest example, New Grange, Meath, has an enclosing ditch encircled by standing stones.

Pentland Group. Found on both sides of the Firth. Most have a long passage leading to a rectangular chamber, covered by a huge mound encircled by a ditch. Forecourt usual, its absence associated with a shorter passage.

As the Neolithic colonists prospered, the earlier people learned from them, producing hybrid or Secondary Neolithic cultures. Two are particularly interesting. The *Peterborough* culture existed along rivers, marsh edges and the coast and although the people accepted farming, it was secondary to their hunting and fishing, but in addition they began trading finished and rough-outs from the 'axe factories' at Langdale (Lake District) and Penmaenmawr (North Wales). The *Skara Brae* culture, of the Orkneys, offers more to see. Essentially herders and shell-fishers, they are best known for their corbel-roofed rectangular houses, with a central hearth and built-in stone furniture, opening on to a stone paved and roofed alley, the village being preserved by a covering of wind-blown sand.

The **Bronze Age** began in Britain before 1900 BC with a series of landings by a warrior people, who quickly spread inland, making themselves a ruling aristocracy over the neolithic peoples. Known as the **Beaker Folk,** after their distinctive pottery, they had originated in Iberia where they had long used bronze. Mostly pastoralists, with arable farming playing only a minor role, the open uplands provided good grazing for their large herds. Their success and wealth is seen in the gold and other ornaments found in graves. Their dead

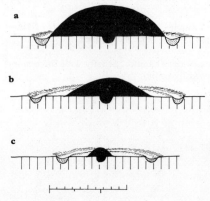

Principal types of round barrows: **a,** bowl; **b,** bell; **c,** disc

were buried under round bowl mounds, except in Ireland, where burials in Boyne megalithic mounds suggest they were absorbed into the existing way of life. Although little sign of house construction has been found, they were responsible for much of the work of building the huge religious monuments known as *henges*. Simple single entrance enclosures had previously existed, but they are responsible for the massive encircling ditch and outer bank at Avebury and the avenue of dissimilar paired stones leading to the sanctuary on Overton Hill. But this was soon eclipsed by the greater work at Stonehenge, where a ditch and inner bank existed. The work included building a similar avenue with flanking ditches and the erection of the Prescelly Bluestones in a double circle. Work on this scale needs large resources, social organisation and indicates the importance attached to religion.

In north-east Scotland, the Recumbent Stone Circles may be roughly contemporary. These are rings of upright stones, decreasing in height from those flanking the horizontal 'altar' stone. Other varying types of stone circles all over these islands may date from this period, although they have since become the centres of many strange local legends and myths.

The impact of the Beaker Folk invasion passed within two hundred years and there was a re-emergence of the former secondary neolithic people, especially those of Peterborough stock, whose culture had been modified by contact with, and possibly absorption of the Beaker Folk. Named the **Food Vessel** people, their culture spread over the whole country. In general they continued the same pastoral way of life, but their dead, buried in stone cists or under round mounds, were given a greater variety of metal tools and weapons and gold ornaments, indicating rising wealth among the expanding population.

A new invasion of the south-west by well-armed groups from Brittany spread over the Downs, producing a new warrior aristocracy, the **Wessex** culture, who buried their dead beneath Bell or Disc barrows. Although their more-advanced technology is best seen in their weapons, they were also important traders on a wide scale, ranging from the Baltic to the Mediterranean. Their greatest monuments are huge trilithons of Stonehenge erected in a double circle. The moving of the uprights, some weighing well over sixty tons, was a massive task while the carving of lintels show skill and knowledge, for these were not only tongued-and-grooved together, but mortised and tenoned to the uprights, besides being carved to fit the circle, with wider tops to eliminate the illusionary tapering when viewed from the ground, a concept usually ascribed to the Greeks.

By 1400 BC the power of the Wessex chiefs had waned and the remaining centuries of the Bronze Age were marked by a period of quiet prosperity, with more arable farming, although the only major change, which gives the cultural period the name of **Urnfolk,** was the burial of cremated remains in unmarked urnfields or the sides of earlier barrows. Only a few Bell barrows were constructed apparently for important chiefs. The use of metal greatly increased the work of itinerant smiths who appeared to have formed a special group, free of local ties. During this period a new group of settlers arrived. Pressure on continental Celtic people, descendants of the Battle-Axe and Beaker Folk, caused these land-hungry peasant-farmers to settle in the south. Having developed a well-balanced system of mixed farming, they introduced the Urnfolk to the two-ox plough. The newcomers, the **Deveral-Rimbury** people, lived in round huts on the sunnier south-sloping Downs, near to their square cornfields, but rain-water carried much of the lighter soil to the lower boundary, producing **Lynchets,** which often appear almost flat on the steep slopes. Their livestock were pastured on the colder northern slopes, the large fields bounded by earth banks and sometimes by narrow sunken ways, similarly bordered, along which animals could be driven with few drovers. In the later part of the period, the improvements in metal-working suggests the influx of more advanced smiths, rather than a fresh invasion, as the rest of the cultural pattern was not disturbed, but already a few iron goods were being imported.

The **Iron Age** in Britain began when the Hallstatt people of France and the low countries, who had been under increasing pressure from the east, made a series of landings along the east and south coasts and then began to spread inland. Besides their iron tools, they brought a new emphasis to arable farming, growing grain in small squarish fields, harvesting with iron sickles and then parching it and storing in deep mat-lined bell-shaped pits, which soon became mouldy and were then used for rubbish. The introduction of iron axes, billhooks and plough-shares enabled them to clear and cultivate more land around their small settlements, mostly little villages or single circular farmhouses with a central rectangle of posts around the hearth, and each surrounded by a fence and ditch. The fourth century BC saw an invasion threat by the La Tene people which led to the hurried building of many hill-forts as refuges, above the settlements. Although some remained unfinished – presumably the danger passed – others were permanently occupied. These followed one general plan, with a deep surrounding ditch and an inner bank topped by a palisade and wall walk, while the initial simple two-leaved gate, always the weakest point, was later greatly strengthened by a bridge over the gate linking inturned ramparts. Meanwhile, the highland zone was not penetrated, but the presence of iron goods suggests trading or raiding. A new type of village did develop with small groups of huts on raft-based artificial islands (**Crannogs**) near the sides of lakes and swamps.

The earlier threats developed at the end of the century with many incursions on the east and south-east coasts. Although most were repulsed, the frightening speed and mobility of their war-chariots, sometimes later buried entire with their chiefs, enabled the Iceni to establish supremacy quickly over the Urnfolk of Norfolk, as did the Parisi in Yorkshire, but in Sussex the two iron-age groups merged and penetrated the thick forest to work the Wealden iron-ores. While Wessex remained largely undisturbed, small Celtic bands occupied several Cornish sites in a quest for tin. For protection they built Cliff Castles or Ring Forts, e.g. Chun Castle, solid stone towers with a pronounced batter on the outside of the thick walls, but nearly vertical inside, where the base was radially partitioned into compartments, the whole enclosed by at least one deep ditch. Nearby nucleated villages, such as Chysauster, which was occupied between about 200 BC and AD 300, had courtyard houses flanking a paved way, while souterrains, underground chambers known locally as fogous, could have been used as refuges or storage cellars. Close trade ties with the Veneti of Brittany probably led to the introduction of the sling and its defence, multiple ditches and banks to keep the attackers at a distance. After their defeat by Julius Caesar, Veneti survivors appear to have sought safety in Cornwall. Over the whole country iron-working expanded, reaching the Forest of Dean, while the crannog sites of Glastonbury and Meare in Somerset have provided much evidence of the way of life, from complete smithies to dice. But the mining of metals remained the main basis of a wide-spread trade along the dry ridgeway routes.

In Scotland, the farming **Abernethy** culture spread from the Tay and Moray Firths to the west coast and south to Galloway. They built strong hill-forts faced with squared stones reinforced with timbers, but unlike those of southern England their outlines did not parallel the contours. Some were built of volcanic glasses and when these were attacked with fire, the timbers burnt, while the glasses fused together, producing the 'vitrified forts' which so puzzled the early prehistorians.

Teutonic expansion into continental Celtic areas had produced a hybrid culture, the **Belgae,** whose agriculture was based on the use of a heavy wheeled plough. This energetic people first created a settlement near Ashford, Kent, about 150 BC, but later moved the centre of their expansion to Wheathampstead. Ignoring hill-forts, they preferred to site their straggling settlements on the richer soils of cleared forest or valley bottom, where their iron-shared ploughs – equipped with coulter and mould-board, to cut and turn the sod – were well suited to the heavy clay soils. Being politically united, they outmatched the small earlier tribes and expanded their kingdom of *Catuvellauni*, besides maintaining their links with their continental kinsmen and aided them after their defeat by the Romans. This led Julius Caesar to invade in 55 and 54 BC, finally storming their capital and establishing a Roman trading port at London. The Gallic revolt of 50 BC and its suppression led to fresh Belgic landings in the south, where earlier hill-forts were enlarged and strengthened with more ditches and banks, but this threat proved to be less dangerous to most tribes than the renewed Catuvellauni expansion which began in the early years of the first century AD.

Although the non-Belgic areas were less affected by invasion, many of the iron-age and earlier peoples were influenced by Belgic culture and technology, especially their agriculture. Even the Brigantes of the six northern counties of England adopted it in a modified form. Meanwhile in Scotland, north of the

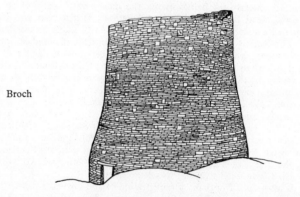

Maiden Castle, an Iron Age hill-fort

Abernethy people, a fierce warrior tribe had settled, showing many similarities to the Cornish Cliff Castle culture. Their distinctive stone towers, **Brochs,** were permanently occupied. The thick walls contained recessed chambers at ground level, but are hollow above. The height, some still stand over twenty

Broch

feet high, appears to be an answer to fire attacks against the two or three storey stone and timber buildings they contain. Probably they combined farming, fishing and piracy, unlike the peaceful farmers who occupied the contemporary **Wheelhouses,** large circular buildings, divided by radial partitions, each room accommodating a family.

The Roman invasion and occupation of southern Britain, affected the remoter and highland areas in varying degrees. Brochs continued to be used until the Viking invasion of northern Scotland; much of Wales remained outside the pale, while Ireland, more sheltered from continental raiders, benefited by increased trade, especially the export of gold. About the mid-fifth century, the Irish Scotti, who had often raided Britain's west coast, began to settle in Argyll at the invitation of the King of Strathclyde, who needed allies against the Picts. Meanwhile, the return of St Patrick in 432 AD as Bishop of Ireland, not only re-established Irish-Mediterranean links, but gave the multitude of small Irish Kingdoms a uniting bond.

ROMAN BRITAIN

Military Zone

Directed primarily against the war-like Belgae, and their Druid priests, hated for aiding their Gallic kinsfolk, the Roman Invasion (AD 43) over-ran their kingdoms, in a short, fierce campaign, delighting the longer-settled neighbouring tribes – fearful of Belgic expansionism – who accepted client-status in return for Roman protection, some tribal-kings gaining much as seen in Cogidumnus's Palace at Fishbourne. After two years' campaigning the legions controlled the area south-east of Exeter–Gloucester–Wroxeter–Lincoln and turned to consolidation, building a network of permanent roads for speedy troop movements, camps and towns, besides organising the provision of army supplies and exports, metal-ores being among the most-prized fruits of conquest. Silver-bearing lead from Mendips and Pennines, Welsh gold and Cornish tin remained a state monopoly under military control, but iron was later freed.

The legions advanced again in AD 49, but found tougher opposition in the hilly areas, while behind them was the ever-present danger of revolt, a fear realised when the Iceni rose (AD 60) under Queen Boudicca ('Boadicea') and savagely mauled one legion before razing the newly-established colonia Camulodunum (Colchester) and Londinium, besides ravaging a large area, before being crushed. An insurrection costing over 100,000 lives. To safeguard the northern frontier, legionary fortresses were transferred to Eboracum (York) and Deva (Chester) and, after occupying the Welsh lowlands, to Caerleon, but central Wales never came under full Roman control. Further northern campaigns followed, defeating the Brigantes and occupying southern Scotland to culminate in the defeat of the Highland tribes at Mons Graupius (AD 83), after which a Forth-Clyde defensive line was established.

With secure frontiers, administration of the lowlands passed increasingly to civil government, where many forts were dismantled as people accepted the benefits of Romanisation. But around AD 100, while southern defences were strengthened, the army withdrew to the Tyne–Solway line, where Hadrian built his wall (122-32) to control northward traffic. Fifteen feet high to its parapeted, patrolled roadway, with sixteen forts controlling the main routes, and two look-out towers between each pair of milecastles, it was a truly formidable work, secured by great ditches in front and behind (the Vallum) delimiting a zone of cleared country. A fresh advance into central Scotland and the building of the turf Antonine Wall (AD 142), was followed by a return to Hadrian's Wall thirteen years later, when a series of revolts broke out in the north. A later re-advance to the Antonine Wall again ended in retreat when the Picts broke through, taking advantage of army dissension over rival claimants for imperial power, which marked the last two decades of the century. The new Emperor, Severus, stabilised the position after a major campaign, before rebuilding Hadrian's Wall, with a screen of native frontier scouts and mobile forces, while in lowland Britain, a coastal fort built at Reculver was a portent of coming threats. But despite Roman reverses elsewhere, raiding remained insignificant until the late third century, when the position was again aggravated by officials weakening defences to further their political ambitions. Both York and Chester were destroyed in Pictish invasions, while the Scotti of Ireland raided the west coast. Again the damage was made good and defences improved. The ensuing peace lasted until 367, when a new Pictish invasion was combined with coastal raids by Scotti and Saxons, while armed bands of insurgents roamed parts of the country, but the speedy arrival of reinforcements prevented the situation getting completely out of hand. Various expedients were tried to meet the case, including the creation of semi-independent client-kingdoms north of the wall to act as buffer states. But though there was some prosperity, the situation was again damaged by politically-ambitious governors, large tracts were given up and, about AD 402, the remaining legions at York and Richborough were finally withdrawn. Despite appeals to Rome there is no evidence they ever returned.

Civil Zone

Unlike the army-controlled military zone, this was not ruled directly by the Governor from his provincial capital, London, after about AD 100. Divided into tribally-based cantons, these were administered from the old tribal capitals – or suitable nearby sites – and became the focal-points of the road system. These were Civitates, towns of non-Roman citizens, distinguished from the Colonia, including Colchester, Nervis Gleuensis (Gloucester) and Lindum (Lincoln), towns of ex-legionaries who had acquired land and citizenship after twenty-five years' service, and the Municipium towns granted a charter, e.g. Verulanium. To the Romans, organised towns contained the essence of civilised living, and were used as shop-windows displaying the advantages of Roman life to win over the native aristocracy and encourage competition amongst them. At first slow, Romanisation quickened as the post-occupation generation grew up accepting it, probably after that new status symbol, a Roman education, while a new wealthy merchant-class supplanted the former warrior aristocracy. By around AD 100, most cantonal capitals had their forum (market-place) with its Basilica (Town Hall) and flanking shops, surrounded by solidly-built houses with running water lining a grid-iron of paved, sewered streets, while towns of pretensions had public baths, the Roman social centres, and amphitheatres for public entertainments. Town houses varied greatly in size and style, but were mostly single-storeyed, half-timbered buildings, the larger built around a courtyard, but few having windows glazed with translucent glass, while the smaller were L-plan or rectangular, with the shorter side to the street, as were the open-fronted shops so displaying their combined saleroom and workshop. Besides established settlements, new villages developed outside forts to supply soldiers' needs and serving as markets. Many developed sufficient commercial momentum to continue after the military posts closed.

In rural areas, Iron Age round huts gave way to rectangular ones, sub-divided into rooms, but with increasing prosperity farms were replaced by substantially-built, half-timbered houses, plastered and painted inside and out. Later verandas were added and by the end of the second century many had been converted to enclosed corridors, while two-storeyed projecting wings were added to form the popular winged-corridor-house. Originally only Romans built large villas with courtyards surrounded by a ditch and wall, while a single-storeyed, aisled farm-building served as ventilated barn, stock shed and slaves' quarters. Whatever its size, each villa remained largely a self-sufficient farm, with its own forge and workshop and watermill, while the larger ones usually had a secondary industry, e.g. cloth-making or a saw-mill. Mosaics were common, but taste and workmanship varied from excellent to crude, while many of the reported hypocausts were really grain-drying floors. Later when some of the vast estates were split up, tenants again lived in rectangular houses, while managing bailiffs had winged-corridor-villas.

Besides those devoted to the official Emperor-worship, towns contained temples dedicated to the multitude of Roman deities, increasingly identified with comparable Celtic ones by Britons, while the army introduced others from the Empire, Mithras being especially popular. When Christianity arrived is unrecorded; Bede suggested mid-second century, but the martyrdom of St Alban and others (AD 301) proves prior establishment, and within fifteen years British bishops were participating in international synods. Although Christianity was strong in towns by mid-century, paganism remained a powerful force in the country.

The third century brought a major change with the building of town walls, hitherto forbidden. Their extent and workmanship show this was no panic measure, but the high costs account for the lack of other major building during the century, although proving invaluable during the strife of the last quarter. The next century saw these walls strengthened with ballistae towers, and although some house building was done, mostly on simpler lines, many villas continued production, especially those sited near towns which served as refuges and strongholds.

The Post-Occupational Period

It is now clear no dramatic collapse followed the final withdrawal, despite the loss of key political and administration staff and the severe economic blow. The country had never fully recovered its earlier prosperity after the 367 troubles, when the more highly-organised and profitable areas had suffered most. The semi-independent kingdoms almost certainly fared best, not only was their economy most closely related to the soil, but they already possessed a political structure closer to what was needed in the changed conditions, while in most of the Civil Zone considerable adaptations were needed quickly. In both areas Roman names and titles continued to be used as leaders struggled to retain their Roman standards of life learned in that past golden age, but of necessity changes came.

By about 425, a nationally-accepted leader, or king, Vortigen, had emerged, while the Scotti raids lessened after they had settled in western Scotland. But with the east coast still under attack, an attempt was made to emulate the Romans by employing mercenaries. This proved to be disastrous, for they quickly overran Kent, the flight of refugees marked by hurriedly-buried hoards of valuables. After some twenty years of indecisive warfare, the Anglo-Saxons were defeated by Ambrosius Aurelianius, and it seems likely that on the exploits of such leaders, the Arthurian legends were based. But there was a fresh Saxon landing at Selsey and it was not until about 495 that a second Anglo-Saxon defeat at Mons Badonicas stopped further expansion and an uneasy peace gave fifty years of relative prosperity. Little detail is known of this period as the repeated urban re-building has destroyed many sites, but about mid-century a renewed Saxon advance swept across country to the Exe and Severn, while before the century's end the north-eastern kingdoms too had fallen.

Above, Jerseys.   *Below*, British Friesians.

Above, Ayrshires.   *Below,* Dairy Shorthorns.

The Anglo-Saxons

Thus, raids and invasion turned to conquest and settlement and this greatly modified the landscape, for although the Romans were good organisers of vast projects, such as draining the Fens, they introduced few technological changes, but the small groups of Anglo-Saxons cleared and farmed the heavy clay woodlands for the first time, using heavy iron ploughs. The rural communities formed part of a larger, though loosely-knit, kingdom which in turn accepted the overlordship of a High King (Bretwalda). In 597 Ethelbert of Kent held the title and to him came St Augustine, bringing Christianity, learning and international recognition of the conquest, for the Celtic Church had ignored the invaders and, after 150 years of independence, the authority of Rome, a state of affairs which continued until the Synod of Whitby (664).

Briefly, at the beginning of the seventh century, Angles held the north-east (Bernicia and Deira), the Midlands (Mercia) and East Anglia; the Jutes Kent and Hampshire; while the Saxons occupied the south (Essex, Middlesex, Sussex and Wessex). Relations between the conquerors and the British ranged from outright clearance, through enslavement to co-operation, as evidenced by artifacts and place-names – the Celtic Afon for river becoming the River Avon – while it seems possible that Anglo-Saxon mercenaries had formed part of the fourth-century garrison of York, which, like London and Lincoln, appears to have remained in virtually continuous occupation throughout the conquest, although the Anglo-Saxon usually avoided town-sites.

Dominant power moved northwards, fluctuating between Bernicia and Deira, until these were united as Northumbria – a story recorded in detail, if somewhat angled, by the Venerable Bede – where Ethelfrith's realm prospered as he expanded over much of the north. But in Anglo-Saxon England everything depended on the individual king and following his death, Mercia became more dominant after the mid-century, while Wessex defeated Devon in 710. During the eighth century Mercia retained its strong position in a period of near equilibrium, with King Offa outstanding; though best remembered today for the dyke delimiting his western frontier, he was strong at home and influential abroad. After his death, Egbert of Wessex became High King following his successful campaigns extending from Northumbria and North Wales to Cornwall. But a new danger threatened. Vikings from Norway had been raiding the Scottish coasts since 798, and these spread southwards, growing in scale.

The crucial point came in 865, when a Danish army wintered in East Anglia. As with the Anglo-Saxons, raiding turned to invasion. By 870 much of eastern England had been conquered, besides many north-western islands and parts of Ireland, but despite temporary incursions, Wessex under Alfred held and eventually defeated the Danes at Edington. During the resulting short-lived peace, Alfred not only reorganised the militia (fyrd), established fortresses (burhs) – walled towns and refuges rather than personal castles – and roads, but encouraged ship-building and other crafts, together with learning, finding time himself to translate books into English. Although at this time society was divided into classes, these were extremely flexible, men could rise by their own efforts, while women enjoyed more freedom and equality than for centuries to come. Fresh hostilities resulted in further Danish defeats and the recapture of London (886). Peace brought Danish recognition of Alfred's overlordship, but they retained the north and east ('Danelaw'). By the time Alfred died (899),

Anglo-Saxon England was strong and during the next twenty years his children continued the fight, building new burhs as they cleared the country, despite an influx of expelled Viking colonists from Ireland, until by the time Edward the Elder's son, Athelston, succeeded to the throne, he was overlord of all Britain south of the Scottish Highlands. But although the next half century was marked by consolidation – during which the Danes in Danelaw continued to follow their own customs and accounting for the many Scandinavian place-names there – the end of the century saw a fresh series of Viking raids, which Ethelred the Unready could not stop, culminating in a campaign which put the Norwegian King Canute (Cnut) on the throne. Many welcomed a strong constitutional king, for the Scandinavians had always limited royal power, but Edward the Confessor (1042-66) found himself thwarted by this system when he tried to introduce new, Norman, ideas. Harold, the former Anglo-Saxon Earl of Wessex succeeded him, only to face two invasions within a year. The Norwegians were defeated at Stamford Bridge, but at Hastings he fell and the line of Saxon kings ended.

BUILDINGS

Whether Roman fort, 'wool' church, Georgian mansion or timbered cottage, buildings are among the more lasting of man's contribution to landscape, with houses not only the most numerous, but the most sensitive to changing tastes and conditions, both social and economic. Although this section is divided into churches, castles and houses, this is only for convenience as differing styles were usually common to all, though sometimes reflected in different ways. But, until recent years, ideas spread slowly geographically and through society.

Building has undergone many major changes of materials, techniques and style. The Renaissance saw entirely new designs, greater comfort and convenience, the wider use of brick and the rise of the architect, while the transport revolution of the eighteenth and nineteenth centuries opened the way to a nation-wide availability of brick and slate, even endangering the remaining local traditions.

Most areas, urban and rural, contain a priceless historical record in their buildings, but today this is all too often in peril of being swept away for new development, functional and yet too uniform and characterless, with an amazing disregard for the true local environment.

Churches

In most villages, the parish church is not only the oldest substantial building, but for centuries has remained the centre of the community. Besides its religious and spiritual role, the nave was the site for religious plays and even markets until the thirteenth century, while its tower and strong walls often served as a refuge in difficult times and many had a room or a cupboard for the parish arms until last century. It was also the centre of parish administration, the surviving reminder of this being the Official Notice Board. The cathedrals and monasteries merit a book to themselves, but here we are concerned with parish churches, whose history is often as long, but which have been an integral part of the evolving community.

Anglo-Saxon

These fall into two groups. The first, mostly built AD 600–800, were purely Anglo-Saxon, and the second, mostly built during the eleventh century, showed a strong Norman influence, probably due to the use of French masons. The rectangular naves and chancels of the former were short and narrow, with a very narrow chancel arch, although a few based on a Roman basilica were wider, with a round or polygonal chancel.

Walls. Early walls of mortar set with flints or pebbles, sometimes bonded with old Roman bricks, gave way to rough masonry.

Windows. Small, round-headed, often with a double splay to increase the amount of light, set high in the walls. A few triangular-headed ones can be seen.

ANGLO-SAXON

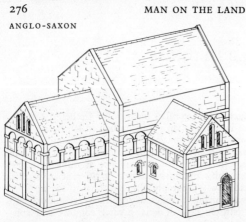

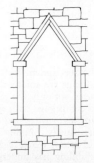

Triangular-headed window

St Lawrence's Church, Bradford-on-Avon

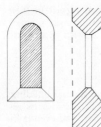

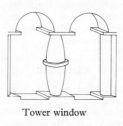

Small window with double splay

Tower window

Chancel arch

Double belfry windows, with round-arched heads cut from one stone and a baluster shaft between, were usual. Multiple openings were rare.

Arches. Round-headed. Doorways had a semi-circular arch of wedge-shaped stones or Roman bricks, but a few flat lintels can be seen.

Columns. Not common. Some were carved into a spiral.

Ornamentation. Thin stone strips (**pilasters**) as patterns or blind arches. Corners reinforced with long-and-short-work, long vertical stones separated by horizontal flat ones.

Norman *c.* 1066–1160

Few parish churches were built until the twelfth century. These were small, two-part, with a wider chancel arch than Saxon ones.

Walls. Up to six feet thick; built of mortar and pebbles or dressed stone casing a rubble core. Often no through stones except at openings.

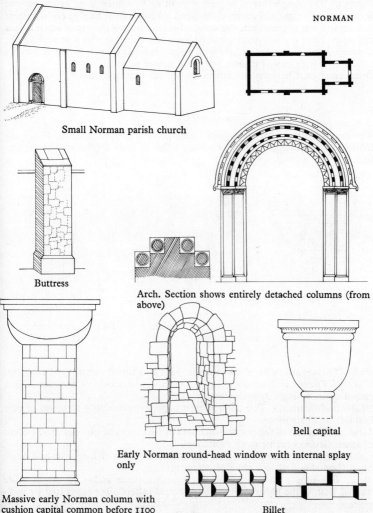

Small Norman parish church

Buttress

Arch. Section shows entirely detached columns (from above)

Bell capital

Early Norman round-head window with internal splay only

Massive early Norman column with cushion capital common before 1100

Billet

Windows. Initially round-headed slits, but became longer with an inside splay only.

Arches and Doorways. Round-headed, but larger and more complex than Saxon ones. Later became a series of concentric stepped-back arches, each with its own columns. Doorway heads were often infilled with a carved stone (**tympanum**), while a hood moulding or dripstone arch formed an outer ring.

Vaulting. The simple barrel or tunnel vaulting was often used in crypts, but because of its weight and outward thrust on walls was little used in naves, except in central-towered cruciform churches, where all four parts were of equal height and span. Here the intersecting vaults were strengthened with a projecting rib.

Columns. Early ones were massive with a plain capital; later became slimmer, of solid stone, with carved capital, but plain square abacus.

Ornamentation. Chevrons and billets; eagle beak introduced later.

Transitional c. 1160–1200

The heavy Norman style became a little lighter and more graceful. Many enlarged by lengthening the nave or adding aisles, to meet the increase of population.

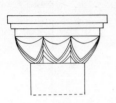

Scalloped capital use after 1100

Round flint and mortar tower, Norfolk

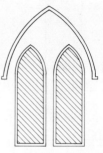

Two lancets under a single dripstone arch

Walls. Thinner, of better dressed stone; load and thrust carried by buttresses.

Windows. Pointed arch used and longer lancet windows became common. Often paired under a single dripstone arch.

Arches and Doorways. The pointed arch became increasingly common in new building and extensions.

Vaulting. The use of the pointed arch was important as height was independent of span. Groins became more prominent.

Columns. Bulk further reduced; sometimes a main shaft with four detached minor ones. Capital and abacus often ornately carved.

Roof. The simple tie-beam gave way to collar-beam and a variety of other curved beams; the lower ends of the principal rafters often supported by wall-posts.

Ornamentation. More mouldings used. Dog-tooth, eagle beak and lion claws replaced simple billet.

Early English c. 1200–70 (Gothic I)

Walls. Thinner, but heavier supporting buttresses in aisle walls, flying buttresses spanned aisle roofs to counter outward thrust of nave roof on its walls. Dressed stone with thin mortar, except in areas lacking building stone, where it was restricted to corners and openings.

Windows. Lancets arranged in 3s, 5s or 7s, with circles, trefoils or quatrefoils between their heads and the common dripstone arch. Each remained a separate opening piercing the full thickness of the wall. Known as 'Plate Tracery'.

Arches. Pointed arch used exclusively; often decorated with a variety of moulding, from simple chamfer to many-part profiles. Doorway columns were often completely detached.

Vaulting. Flexibility given by the pointed arch developed further, with extra load-bearing ribs replacing groins and lighter panels between.

Columns. Major and detached minor shafts common; abacus usually circular, with moulded edges; capitals often deeply cut into very stiff, formalised foliage.

Roof. Variations of the collar and other beams continued to be used.

Towers. West towers increasingly built; 'broach' spire appeared: named after the triangular broach pieces added at the junction of the square tower and octagonal spire.

Ornamentation. Complex moulding remained dominant, with dog-tooth, but ballflower introduced.

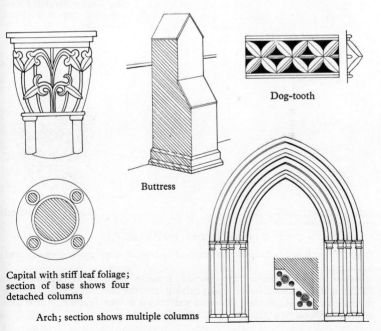

Dog-tooth

Buttress

Capital with stiff leaf foliage;
section of base shows four
detached columns

Arch; section shows multiple columns

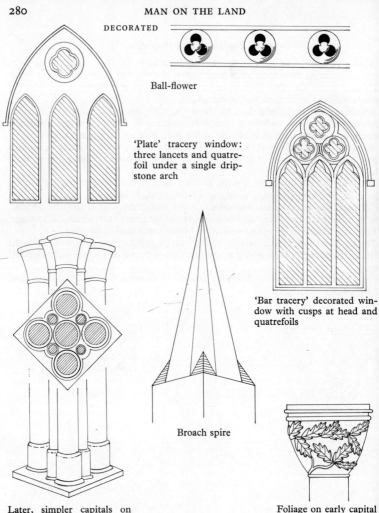

DECORATED

Ball-flower

'Plate' tracery window: three lancets and quatre-foil under a single drip-stone arch

'Bar tracery' decorated window with cusps at head and quatrefoils

Later, simpler capitals on multiple columns

Broach spire

Foliage on early capital

Decorated c. 1270–1350 (Gothic II)

Walls. Thin; outer buttresses often capped by conical or polygonal, ornamented pinnacles.

Windows. Now treated as one opening, separate lights being separated by slender stone mullions (vertical bars) curving from the base of the arch, forming simple geometrical patterns. The form was known as 'Bar Tracery'. A few flat-headed windows were also used.

Arches. The pointed arch still held sway, but the four-centred arch was introduced in the fourteenth century.

Vaulting. The number of ribs continued to increase, partly for decoration. Carved bosses at intersections became common.

Columns. Multiple or fluted columns; carving on capitals lost stiff formality, becoming more natural. Simple moulding common after *c.* 1320.

Towers. Broach spires often narrower, supported by flying buttresses to corner pinnacles, base increasingly hidden by a parapet.

Ornamentation. Cusps (curved points) and crockets (stone hooks) appear on spires, pinnacles and window mouldings whenever possible. Dog-tooth lost dominance to ball-flower. Tombs and font-covers often ornately decorated.

Perpendicular c. 1350–1540 (Gothic III)

In France, decoration became even more ornate, developing into the Flamboyant style, but in Britain the Black Death, which had killed over a third of the population, stopped further church building for a quarter century. When building resumed it was in the loftier, but simpler, even austere, perpendicular, with little or no decoration.

Walls. Dressed stone, capped by parapets, often crennellated.

Windows. Taller and wider, almost filling the space between buttresses. Main mullions continued to the top of the opening and were strengthened by horizontals (**transomes**), dividing the whole into a series of rectangles, each usually headed by its own pointed arch.

Arches. Pointed arch remained dominant, but the four-centred arch gained in popularity in the Tudor period, especially for doorways, where the space between it and the square dripstone arch was often carved. Some porches were enlarged, a second storey might be added to serve as school-room and meeting-place.

Vaulting. The pattern of principal and minor ribs was replaced by a system of equal ribs radiating from a centre to reach the ceiling in a half-circle. 'Fan Vaulting' grew until the whole ceiling was covered by its inverted cones.

Roof. The use of lead-sheeting meant that roofs could be lower pitched. Inside, timber ceilings reached their greatest peak with richly carved hammer-beams, and later the double hammer-beam trusses. In the south-west white panels of plaster were framed by dark rafters, forming the 'Wagon Roof'.

Towers. Many new lofty towers were built with slim spires supported by flying buttresses, especially in the rich wool districts.

Ornamentation. Little and simple, but the ball-flower still used.

Tudor 1540–1602

On the Reformation, confiscated monastic chapels were often sold as parish churches to the town or village; if unsold they were stripped and later 'quarried' for building materials. Few new churches were built.

Jacobean 1602–48

The full impact of the Renaissance, based on classical Roman buildings, was accompanied by the arrival of the architect. New churches showed a complete break with Gothic. Inside, they were basically a single room with emphasis on the congregation being able to see and hear, seen in the greater importance given to the pulpit.

PERPENDICULAR

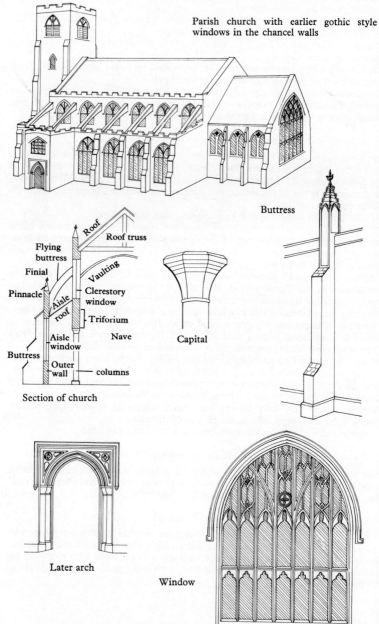

Parish church with earlier gothic style windows in the chancel walls

Roof

Roof truss

Flying buttress

Finial

Vaulting

Pinnacle

Clerestory window

Aisle roof

Triforium

Aisle window

Nave

Buttress

Outer wall

columns

Section of church

Capital

Buttress

Later arch

Window

Restoration 1660–1702

Many churches despoiled during the Commonwealth were restored, at least in part. New churches were built after the style of the Italian Classical, seen to best

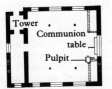

Tower

Communion table

Pulpit

Plan of post-restoration church

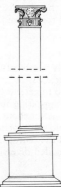

Post-restoration column *c.* 1680

effect in Wren's rebuilding after the Great Fire of London, 1666. Characterised by pediment, portico and slender spire, these were – despite the many awkwardly-shaped sites – basically simple rectangular rooms with galleries on three sides and a simple Communion Table against the east wall.

Georgian 1702–1820

The beginning of the eighteenth century saw a return from Wren's freer style to the stricter Italian Classical forms based on Inigo Jones' Palladian, although

Classical church *c.* 1735, Blandford, Dorset

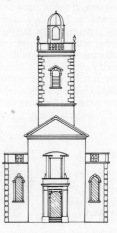

a few Baroque churches were built, mostly 1700–15, but soon designs began to
be based on genuine site-plans from Greece, rather than the current Italian
version of classical Roman, so that church exteriors resembled Greek temples.
Inside, Wren's principle of all being able to see and hear was followed, while his
designs enjoyed a wide popularity outside London. Although stone-facing was in
use, many churches were built in brick, with stone only used for decoration and
strength at corners and openings.

Victorian 1820–1914

By the early nineteenth century, the Romantic Movement was well under way,
manifesting itself in a swing to their version of the Decorated Gothic, but it
was allowed to get out of hand and decoration became excessive. By 1820 it was
dominant, appearing in the many new churches built in the expanding industrial towns. After about 1840 some of the worst excesses were avoided, but many
beautiful old parish churches in real Gothic had been disastrously 'restored'.
The end of the century saw a growing readiness to adapt to current needs, while
there was added diversity in Renaissance, Byzantine and many new ideas.

Twentieth Century 1918–

There was little church-building in the inter-war years, but the post-war
period with its urban bomb-damage and subsequent great population movements to suburban estates and New Towns gave great scope for the use of
modern design and techniques.

Castles and fortifications

Although it is suggested that the Anglo-Saxons may have built a few simple
castles, the evidence is not yet conclusive. Certainly they usually built fortified
towns (burhs) or refuges, rather than separate fortresses. However, with the
Conquest, the Normans needed castles to overawe a potentially hostile population and to provide secure bases from which their heavily armoured knights
could operate. The strong-point of these was a timber tower on a steeply-
sloping artificial mound (**motte**), flanked by a larger palisaded area (**bailey**),
containing the hall, stables and stores, the two linked by a narrow bridge and
fenced path, and each enclosed by a deep ditch. At this time there was little real
difference between a motte-and-bailey castle and a fortified manor, but this
widened when towers were re-built in stone, mostly in the twelfth century, but
a few royal castles were built in stone shortly after the Conquest. These stone
keeps (donjons) were of two basic kinds.

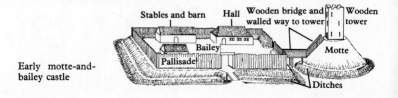

Early motte-and-
bailey castle

Stables and barn   Hall   Wooden bridge and   Wooden
                            walled way to tower   tower
                    Bailey
            Pallisade   Motte
                                                Ditches

Shell type consisted of a circular, or elliptical, outer wall topped by battlements and a wall-walk. Inside separate timber or stone buildings were erected against the wall, leaving open a central courtyard. Noted examples include Windsor and Launceston.

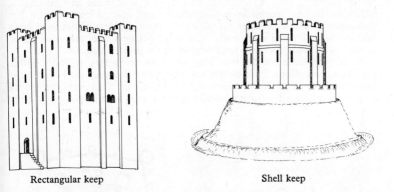

Rectangular keep   Shell keep

The *Rectangular type* was a solid block of three or four storeys, with thick corner buttresses and turrets on at least two corners linked by crenellated parapets. The approach was by an open stair to the second-storey hall, which like the first floor was usually stone-vaulted, but the upper floors were of timber. Later a fore-building was often added to defend the stairfoot. The most famous is The Tower of London (1067), but others include Newcastle-upon-Tyne, Canterbury, Rochester and Colchester.

Since the main defence of a castle was its sheer strength, increasing attention was focused on the gate, always the weakest point. The late eleventh century had seen the introduction of the portcullis; the new century saw the keep being built in line with the curtain walls, surrounding the bailey, dominating them and the gate. Meanwhile, arrow-slits were inserted in the outer wall, previously without any openings except the small slit-like tower windows. Initially a narrow six-foot vertical slit, with a recess behind for the archer, these became increasingly elaborated to widen the field of fire.

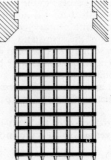

Portcullis; section shows vertical channels in which it moves

However, the dangers from attack by mining and battering-ram remained and this was first met by building square towers projecting beyond and above the walls, covering both the base and wall-walk. But, experience gained in the Crusades of heavier siege-engines showed the weakness of sharp corners when attacked with heavy missiles and later wall-towers were round or polygonal for greater strength. Two of these were often incorporated in the new gatehouses, which increasingly served as both residence and keep, while an extra fort (**barbican**) guarded the outer end of the drawbridge. New castles were often built on more isolated sites, while wide water defences were also constructed around older castles, to keep siege-engines at the greatest distance.

A further defence of the wall base was from temporary enclosed timber platforms (**hoardings**) built outside the battlements, but only the holes for the supporting beams remain. Towards the century's end, these were superseded by permanent stone balconies (**machicolations**) built over gateways and other

Machicolations: stone galleries over gateways and other weak points with floor openings for covering fire at wall base

Concentric castle (diagrammatic), early 14th century

danger points. Floor openings (**meutriers**) were also built into the ceiling of the gatehouse-passage, to attack intruders who had forced the up-drawn draw-bridge, portcullis and double doors, while a further portcullis closed the inner end, preventing access to the courtyard, but except for these and a few arrow-slits in the walls there was no direct way into the gatehouse proper.

New thirteenth-century castles were often characterised by a change of emphasis from massive static defence, with the risk of starvation, to a more active role, seen in the provision of posterns and sally-ports from which to raid the besiegers. Many castles were built in Wales to hold the land won: Conway, the solid bulk of Caernarvon to guard the new town, and the concentric castles of Harlech and Beaumaris, representing the peak of castle-building, with each ring dominating the walls and baileys outside, although details vary consider-ably.

The introduction of the cross-bow, with its greater range, made the parapet more dangerous, so heavy boards hung from iron pins, slotted into grooves in the merlons, closed the embrasures, while arrow-rolls were added to the top of the coping and mouldings around the arrow-slits to prevent bolts being deflected within.

Early drawbridges had been raised by a pulley-system or windlass and later were pivoted so that the inner end dropped into a pit, but by the thirteenth century they were moved more easily by counter-balanced arms, useful when speed was essential, while a water-chute from the first storey enabled the garrison to quench fires against the main doors.

Many fourteenth-century castles continued the practice of combining keep, residence and gatehouse, but there was a return to the earlier custom of a separate dominant keep, probably because of the increasing use of mercenaries, considered more open to bribes to surrender, than the former feudal retainers. But not all castles were re-built or modified and the landscape is dotted with castles of every style and variation. Many of the rectangular keeps, e.g. Dudley and Nunnery, were still in use, with the advantage of being easily held by a small garrison. But by the end of the century there was already a growing separation between the functions of fortress and residence, although a few gun-loops, horizontal apertures as opposed to the vertical arrow-slits, can be seen. The Battle of Bosworth (1485) saw not only the end of the Wars of the Roses and the virtual breaking of the barons' power, but the end of the personal fortress, although it is interesting to note that several castles successfully withstood long bombardment by the latest Roundhead artillery, Corfe Castle for three years. However, this led to their destruction when taken by the besiegers, who either razed or 'slighted' them – damaged to prevent their further use as fortresses.

In the northern counties of England and much of Scotland where the scene was marked by local raids, a smaller version of the rectangular keep, known as a Pele tower, was common. Built between the thirteenth and the seventeenth centuries, they followed a general pattern: three–four storeys high, with a battle-

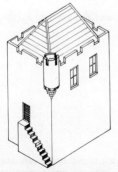

Pele tower, Scottish border. Windows enlarged and glazed in the late Georgian period

Scottish fortified tower house, later modified by the addition of larger windows and a Georgian wing

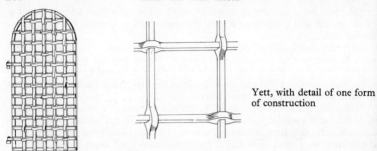

Yett, with detail of one form of construction

mented parapet and corner turrets. Like the keeps, the lower storeys were often stone vaulted and the entrance was to the second-storey hall by outside steps to a heavy door, usually protected by an iron door or yett. Some of the larger towers stood within a defended courtyard or barmkin with a gatehouse and drawbridge, but most relied on static defence against raiders, not a siege. With increased prosperity a purely house wing was added, and by the sixteenth century a second to form either an L-plan or a staggered line, with the old tower at the junction.

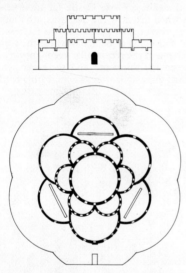

Coastal artillery fort, *c.* 1540

From the sixteenth century the building of private fortifications ceased over most of England and Wales and only national defences were constructed. Around 1540, Henry VIII built a series of artillery forts to guard the south coast, from Deal to Falmouth. Although varying in detail, each consisted of one or more solid round towers, with cannon on up to three levels, while Queen

Black-faced Ewe

Southdowns

Above, Border Leicesters. *Below,* Cheviots

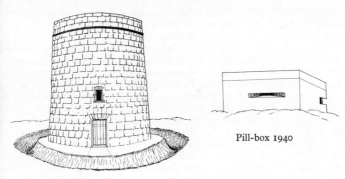

Martello tower, 1801-5

Pill-box 1940

Elizabeth had a strong wall, with projecting artillery towers, built around Berwick-on-Tweed.

The Commonwealth left only one fortification, a round tower on Tresco, but the Napoleonic threat led to the building of many Martello towers along southern coasts. These squat masonry towers were designed to contain a small garrison and 2–3 guns, and were set within a wide moat. The last war added yet one more type of defensive structure, round or oblong 'pill-boxes' set low into the ground, with wide lateral slits to protect vulnerable points.

Houses

Saxon and Norman Halls

Since the Saxons usually built in timber, few of their buildings have survived, but their form changed little in several hundred years and similar construction can be seen in the remaining great timber medieval barns. Basically a single all-purpose room, Saxon halls differed little, except in size, being made up of bays of about 16 feet long; a small farmhouse consisted of one bay, a palace of many. Each bay ended in a pair of stout vertical timbers (**posts**) carrying principal rafters, connected by a **tie-beam** bearing a central **king-post** to support the ridge or **collar-beam.** Horizontal timbers (**summers**) joined the posts, with minor verticals (**studs**) and the spaces between infilled with interwoven branches plastered with clay or mud mixed with straw (**wattle-and-daub**). Small high windows were protected with wooden bars and shutters. Roofs were of thatch

Three-bay aisled wooden hall. Reconstruction of type common from late Saxon until early mediaeval times. CP = crown post

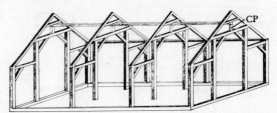

or turf laid on purlins and common rafters. Lacking a chimney, smoke from the central hearth escaped through louvres in the gable-ends, while in great halls cooking was often done outside to reduce fire-risk.

Extensions meant either adding more bays or carrying the roof out over side aisles, but leaving the posts to bear the weight of the main roof. In farmhouses, such extensions provided shelter for animals and stores. Across the upper end of great halls the high table, for family and guests, stood on a dais, while servants ate at trestle tables set lengthways and slept there on the straw at night. Few halls had detached huts (**bowers**) for the family to sleep. Later the upper end of the hall was partitioned off, providing a family room (**solar**), but this was rare until after the Norman Conquest, which made little change, as few of the new Lords-of-the-Manor could afford to re-build in stone.

By the twelfth century solars or parlours were common and the draughts from the main doors at the lower end had been reduced by screens. These developed into another partition (**speer-truss**) with two door openings and

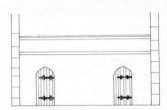

Speer-truss with screens separating the draughty cross-passage from the great hall proper

Solid screen in the 14th century hall with doors to the cross-passage beyond; ceiled over with a minstrel gallery above

then into a cross-passage, dividing the hall proper from the service rooms (buttery, milkhouse and kitchen), and in larger halls this was ceiled over to provide a minstrels' gallery. Until about this time the whole building had remained open to the rafters, but by ceiling over the end rooms, family chambers could be constructed above the parlour and a store above the service rooms, access being by a steep stair, sometimes built in a wall-cupboard, or ladder. This practice led to the ends of new houses built wider than the hall itself, producing the beginning of the H-plan house by the early fourteenth century, while higher walls enabled windows to be inserted in the upper storey.

Stone manor house, mid-13th century

Plan of 14th century manor house. CP = cross-passage; B =buttery; P =parlour; H =hearth; S =milkhouse or storage; K =kitchen

Stone-built manors date from *c.*1150, but were costly and few were built before the century's turn. Often known as 'King John's Houses', they comprised a solar and first-floor hall, approached by an external flight of steps, while the stone-vaulted ground floor provided storage and sometimes stabling, but was not connected to the hall.

In many small houses, pairs of curved timbers (**crucks**) acted as both posts and principal rafters, but gave an arched roof and sloping wall, which was either thatched to the ground or built of wattle-and-daub and protected by wide eaves. These were improved from about 1270 by using a longer tie-beam with ends projecting over the cruck base and then joining these with a short post to give a straight wall and allowing the use of more bent timber. Consisting of one room, known as 'the house', they were a small version of the hall.

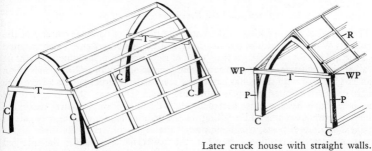

Early cruck house with sloping walls.
C = cruck; T = tie beam

Later cruck house with straight walls.
C = cruck; T = tie beam; P = post; R = rafter; WP = wall-plate

The Black Death, 1347–9, which had killed one-third of the population, produced many far-reaching effects on the landscape. The resulting farm-labour shortage led to the extension of wages and rents instead of feudal service in more areas and the emergence of yeomen farmers, who began to build farm-houses on their land instead of living in the village, clustered around the parish church. Elsewhere, villages and arable were cleared for large sheep farms, which needed few men.

Building styles continued to develop slowly, with H-plan houses becoming more popular, the projecting wings were slight, the whole being covered by a single roof, while in London tiles replaced thatch to reduce fire danger. Many houses were enlarged, with the emphasis on family rooms in the larger ones, where the parlours became purely receptional and were re-named 'withdrawing-rooms', while a separate family dining-room, or winter parlour, was added further reducing the importance of the hall. The increasing domestic division was also seen in the larger new houses, which boasted a stone-built axial chimney stack with a circular stair alongside for the family rooms. Troubled times were reflected in the provision of gatehouses, moats and drawbridges, while the major house windows only faced on to the enclosed courtyard. Smaller halls were increasingly partitioned, vertically and horizontally, richer farmers copying the manorial fashion, but parlours continued to serve as bed-rooms. Some cottages too were extended by the addition of a single aisle or lean-to as a separate room or 'outshot'.

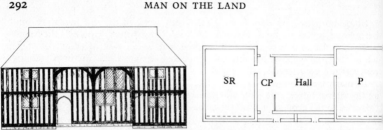

Yeoman's house, Kent, *c.* 1480. SR =service rooms, store above; H =hall, open to rafters; CP =cross-passage; P =parlour, main bedroom above

Tudors and the Renaissance 1485–1603

The arrival of a strong king marked not only the end of baronial power and the ruinous Wars of the Roses, but the demise of the feudal system, which resulted in the old nobility and the growing class of rich merchants building for comfort rather than defence. Early mansions were increasingly built in brick, mostly on an H-plan, but with the wings extending rearwards, internal passages were rare and rooms continued to open into each other. Doorways had four-centred arches, which became more flattened. Halls declined in importance, becoming merely entrance rooms and a setting for the great staircase, with heavily carved panels and newel-posts, which supported the inner corners of the three flights and landings between floors. In others the newel stair was built in the enlarged square porch, often richly sculptured and extending the height of the building to give an E-plan. Windows were larger with several casements, separated by slender mullions, under a flat lintel, while the projecting bays of oriel windows

Early Tudor stone mullioned window

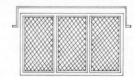

Later Tudor casement window of three lights

ran the full height of principal rooms. But continual extensions produced a rather haphazard appearance in older houses, best seen in the scatter of chimneys, but generally grouped from *c.*1500, although each flue retained its tall outlet, separately patterned in raised brick.

By mid-century the more settled and prosperous conditions had combined with an adventurous outlook to produce a climate of opinion more receptive to new ideas, including the change from Roman to Arabic numbers and Gothic to Roman script, resulting in the carving of names and dates and buildings, while the increased search for learning is seen in the foundation of many schools and colleges. H- and E-plan houses were still built, mostly in brick, but their

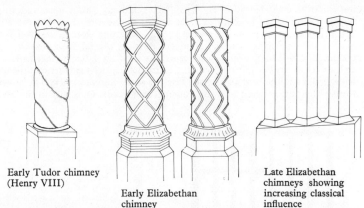

Early Tudor chimney
(Henry VIII)

Early Elizabethan
chimney

Late Elizabethan
chimneys showing
increasing classical
influence

symmetrical façades indicate more detailed overall design and culminated with wings being linked to form a square block (Longleat 1567), while a parapet hid the roof and the evenly grouped chimneys had their upper flues plastered as simple classical columns. Taller windows were divided by mullions and transomes into rectangles below and squares above. Some mansions were over-decorated, but the majority were solidly well-built for comfort. Inside, the emphasis turned to reception rooms, although many dining-rooms still resembled the medieval hall. In both, floor to ceiling panelling replaced tapestries, ceilings were plastered and later moulded, showing an Italian Renaissance influence. Outside, the enclosed courtyard gave way to a small formal garden.

Tudor stone window with mullions and transome

Tudor town house with each jettied storey over-hanging the one below

Some smaller houses were built in the new style, but the vernacular tradition remained strong and the introduction of the diagonal dragon-beam to support jettied corners without the need for free-standing corner-posts, meant that jettying could be extended to all floors and sides, although most town and village houses continued to be built at right angles to the street, so that the alleys between them became almost roofed by the projecting storeys. In most farmhouses, the kitchen became the dominant room as 2–3 service rooms were increasingly added to give an L-plan, especially in villages, while older halls were ceiled over to provide lofts and stairs to bedrooms replaced ladders, but the most widespread addition was an external brick or stone chimney stack. The growing timber shortage resulted in wider gaps between studs, especially in the south-

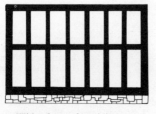

Wider form of studding

Timber-framing and types of infilling: **a,** timbers drilled for wattle; **b,** wattle (daub to be added); **c,** brick 'nogging'; **d,** pargetting

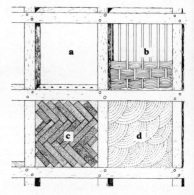

east *c.* 1550, and later a change to timber-framing, with the large panels infilled with wattle-and-daub or bricks, while the houses were strengthened by extending posts from sill to wall-plate instead for a single storey. New farmhouses in richer areas had axial stacks and stairs and by 1600 many, like the parsonages, had glazed windows in the principal rooms. Few cottages of the period remain. Most were one-roomed, although outshots became common and later external stone or brick chimneys began to replace the former clay-and-wattle flues. In the south-east, new two-roomed cottages with outshots were built as the rising population provided a better market for grain and other arable crops.

Small farmhouse with axial stack. P = parlour; K = kitchen; O = outshot

Stuart 1603–1714

Generally, Tudor expansion and Renaissance enlightenment continued to spread slowly, although this was checked by the Civil War and Protectorate, but by the end of the period there was a far greater readiness to try new methods and consider new ideas, except those under the strict control of local craft guilds. Although stage-coaches provided a service on main roads, and goods were carried by even slower wagons between towns, most villages remained largely self-supporting, and only a handful of large towns had populations of up to 10,000.

Mansions. Although some Jacobean (1603–48) great houses retained medieval features, such as the Great Hall and wings of Hatfield House (1603–11), the Italian Renaissance style became dominant with the rise of the professional architects, who followed many of Palladio's ideas. The accepted form was a rectangular block, with evenly-spaced tall windows, standing on a semi-basement podium and a central porticoed entrance approached by a wide flight of steps, while the roof was hidden behind a parapet or balustrade above a heavy cornice. But Palladio's ideas depended not only on external form and symmetry, but on the strict relationship of dimensions of a room, of one room to others and to the block as a whole, to the extent of reducing them to mathematical formulae. But while he had been flexible in applying these, his imitators were not, with the result that the style became increasingly rigid and inert.

The style was introduced by Inigo Jones, whose early works included Queen's House, Greenwich and the Banqueting Hall, Whitehall, both with a ground-floor storey instead of the later semi-basement podium. The former was plain except for columned loggias, while the latter had classical pilasters supporting the cornice along the façade, a feature which proved popular. Meanwhile the use of brick increased, seen in Kew Palace (1631), where the curved gables display

Dutch house, Kew Palace, 1631

Dutch influence, and Coleshill (*c.* 1650) where the balustrade around the flat top of the truncated hipped roof became another popular feature. A major technical innovation was in the use of internal load-bearing walls, enabling building in depth, while the introduction of inside corridors, instead of rooms opening out of each other, gave much greater privacy and comfort.

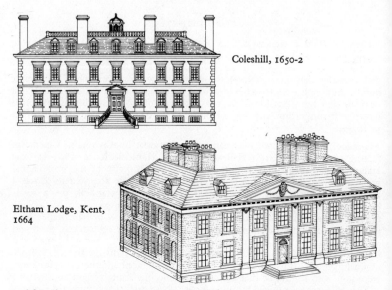

Coleshill, 1650-2

Eltham Lodge, Kent, 1664

After the severe stagnation under the Protectorate, largely because of heavy fines levied on Royalist landowners, the Restoration (1660) brought new ideas, such as the wide low pediment and giant pilasters on the brick-built Eltham Lodge (1662–3). Later, Wren's freer interpretation of Palladian principles opened many new avenues. Best known for the re-building of London's churches after the Great Fire (1666), although his plan for the City, involving wide streets and squares, was rejected, he was responsible for much good domestic building, while at Greenwich he leaned towards the grouped buildings and broad vistas of the Baroque. A style, never widespread, culminated in the work of others in vast central blocks connected by colonnades to flanking pavilions (notably Vanbrugh's Castle Howard, and Blenheim Palace).

The most constant feature was the tall narrow windows, with a single sliding sash appearing c. 1675 and by the end of the century the box-frame allowed both sashes to move, while glazing bars became lighter with the use of the new rolled sheet glass.

Smaller Houses. Changes developed more slowly than with the great houses, but one type – built in the Inigo Jones tradition at Chevening c. 1630 – stands out. A simple rectangular brick block, with quoined corners, a central front door, evenly-spaced windows and plain stacks at either end of the steeply-pitched roof, relieved by white-framed dormer windows. This basic form has since appeared in many designs from the larger Coleshill to the ever-popular Queen Anne house, for which it was so clearly a model. Outside the south-east, local styles remained strong, especially in the limestone belt, while timber-framed houses were still more usual in the West Midlands, Cheshire and southern Lancashire.

Smaller town house, Salisbury, *c.* 1701

Shell porch

The post-restoration house increasingly became double-span, two rooms deep, with either two separate roof-spans, the valley being made water-tight with the newly available lead sheeting, or a truncated hipped roof, with the flat top surrounded by a balustrade. Porticoes over front doors became smaller or were replaced by flanking pilasters and headed by a narrow pediment, while simple hoods – often shell-like below – began to appear.

Near London, many landowning families began to build speculative estates of plain brick terrace houses, mostly 2–3 storeys with a semi-basement and servants' attics lit by dormers, while the widening social custom of 'taking the waters' led to growth in many spa towns and the resulting travel further encouraged the enlargement of coaching inns.

Farmhouses. The differences between richer and poorer areas widened, with less building in the north, while in the south-east larger farmhouses with a second parlour, more service rooms and bigger attics for farm servants were common. Most had symmetrical façades with string courses at ceiling levels and stacks built within the walls, but gable-ends were retained. Throughout much of southern England, square towers to accommodate newel stairs were

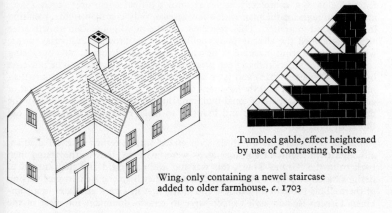

Tumbled gable, effect heightened
by use of contrasting bricks

Wing, only containing a newel staircase
added to older farmhouse, *c.* 1703

added to older buildings. New smaller farmhouses lost cross-passages, many being divided unequally into kitchen and parlour by the main stack, with an entrance lobby in front and a stair behind it. Regional styles remained strong, but façades became more symmetrical in the limestone belt along the eastern coast where pantiles became common, while brick at first (*c*.1635) used only for corners was later more widely used, as it was in the West Midlands. Double-span farmhouses first built in the home counties (*c*.1675) remained rare elsewhere.

Cottages. The two-storeyed form became increasingly common in the richer districts, but elsewhere a single storey remained the rule; however, external stone or brick chimneys were usually added to the latter.

Timber-framed cottage with outside stone chimney stack, 17th century. Bedrooms have been improved by raising the roof and replacing the original dormer windows

Georgian 1714–1810

Although the age was one of expansion, it began slowly in farming where improvements offered vastly greater yields, but demanded consolidated and fenced fields, not completely achieved until the final enclosures (1760–1830), at costs too high for the man with a few acres or only common rights, resulting in a townward migration. This, together with the rapid population growth after 1760, aggravated the already poor conditions in the growing industrial towns, where manufacturing machinery, developed to satisfy demands now outpacing cottage craft production, had been grouped in mills and factories to be powered by water (first used 1720) and later by steam (1760). But better transport than lumbering carts and pack-horse trains was needed to handle the rising flood of goods and led to a spate of canal building. But the most basic change lay in the drawing together of science and industry to make entirely new things or old things in new ways.

Mansions. The Baroque interlude soon ended with a return to the Palladian, although twin flights of entrance steps were favoured, but, to the young men back from the 'Grand Tour', this was too dull and rigid and they turned to designs based on plans of the classical sites, rather than the Renaissance version of them. This brought a freshness and grace, first in Greek and later in a combined Graeco-Roman style, which were to remain dominant for most of the period. But by mid-century new influences began to appear. The Romantic Movement beginning in literature, glorying in the past and the picturesque, now began to influence architecture, appearing in the exotic (Chinese Pagoda at Kew and Indian, Seizincote) and the knightly (Downton Castle), while even the formerly-despised Gothic was included (Strawberry Hill, Lacock and Fonthill Abbeys).

While these influences were at work, the majority of houses remained simple rectangular blocks, with the tall window-frames increasingly hidden by brick-work. The last decade saw the growing use of coloured brick patterns in façades, but this was quickly superseded by the use of stucco to cover at least the lower part of the façade, while parapets increasingly concealed the roof and dormers. Inside, stone treads built into the wall and delicate wrought-iron balusters and rails replaced the heavy staircases. The final move to simpler exteriors is seen in the works of the Adam brothers, although better known for their interiors, where by reversing Palladian principles, they brought individuality of form, size and decor to each room (Library, Kenwood House).

Smaller Houses. The well-proportioned seventeenth-century styles continued to be popular, especially the Queen Anne house developed from Chevening, but with many variations from a slight projection of the central façade, to adding such Palladian features as a small portico or segmented flat window arches, while there was a growing trend to conceal the roof behind a parapet or balus-trade. Later, doorways gained a fanlight with radiating glazing bars, but lost their columned portico for flanking pilasters and a shallow canopy or hood, the inside moulded like a shell. Inside, the loftier rooms with painted plaster walls were in keeping with the tall windows, while the old heavy staircase was re-placed by lighter ones as they had been in the great houses.

Terraced town house, late 18th century

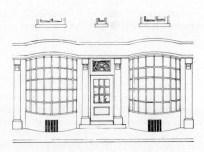

Late 18th century bow-windowed shop

Town houses were taller, 3–4 storeys, still built in terraces, often around squares or crescents which formed communal private gardens, but the semi-basement and approach steps allowed the entrance and reception rooms to appear as a 'first floor', following the example of Society. One change from Stuart style was the narrowness of smaller houses. Many had only two rooms and a side passage on each floor. The lower storeys still had tall windows, with frames now hidden by brickwork, but these became shorter above and almost square on the top floor. The use of stucco, following its use on larger houses, soon became popular and it was often applied to the older houses, but the Adam style was largely confined to copies of their fireplaces. One new feature in towns was the growing number of shops, many with large bow or barrel-shaped windows.

Farmhouses. The pace of building had slackened, but regained momentum with increasing prosperity. Many were double-span with symmetrical façades, often based on plan-book designs. By 1800 parlours had become common, while single workers still slept in the large attics, a practice made easier by the use of the Mansard roof, especially in East Anglia, while the old central stack gave way to chimneys built within the walls.

Double-span Georgian farmhouse in brick, *c.* 1740

Cottages. Two-storey cottages were built in more areas, often with an iron grate in the kitchen, while old farmhouses were sometimes converted into a row of cottages. Evidence of cottage crafts can be seen in the very long windows of one room. In towns, brick cottages were built from *c.* 1780, but the emphasis passed increasingly to courts of back-to-back houses, several rooms simply piled on top of each other, to give the maximum housing on a minimum of land, as close to the factory or mill as possible.

Regency 1810–1840

Britain prospered and changed. With over half the workers engaged in industry it was no longer an agricultural nation and the proportion increased as the population rose by a third (1811–31), while that of London, the first million-strong city, went up by a half. Industrial output soared as steam replaced water-power and muscle, overloading the new canals and the somewhat improved highways, while as yet the steam railways had little effect. The changing conditions and attitudes resulted in a widespread demand for education, met in part by the National and Sunday Schools, where by 1833 one child in three learnt at least the 3 Rs, while the Mechanics Institutes, from 1820, had begun to provide a broader education for the nineteenth-century technologists, often with much-needed library and cultural facilities. Science and technology were gaining general recognition, and by 1820 a town's canal-side gasworks was considered a status symbol of progress.

Large Houses. The few great country houses built owed much of their elegance and good proportions to the classical styles, but the emphasis had already begun to swing towards permanent large town houses, while the 'villas' of industrial and commercial magnates became a feature of town outskirts. Many impressive terraces were designed to give the illusion of a single massive house, the whole façade treated as a whole, with a central pediment, giant columns and flanking pavilions, all covered with painted stucco (Nash's Regent's Park Terraces). A brief revolt against the classical culminating in the Royal Pavilion, Brighton, soon died out as the Romantic Movement passed into the 'gothic' phase, but during the Regency the decorative battlements, towers and pinnacles remained only vaguely medieval, while interiors showed little change.

Regency house, *c.* 1815   Bow-windowed Regency house, *c.* 1812

Smaller Houses. Most retained many of the earlier features, but were usually taller, plainer and had flatter façades than the Georgian, although large bow windows were popular at first. Painted stucco was increasingly used to cover the whole front, often with that on the lower storeys roughened or marked by wide 'joints', while parapets generally hid the low-pitched roof, except in a very few cases where more steeply-pitched roofs were displayed above wide eaves. The plainness of some façades presented a clean, almost austere, appearance until the addition of elegant wrought-iron balconies to first-floor windows; canopies were often added (*c.* 1815), but later these tended to become bulbous (*c.* 1820). Others were relieved by arched recesses extending nearly to the eaves and including the principal windows (Keats' House, Hampstead). Although there was a brief return to the Palladian, this was engulfed in the Gothic Revival proper, which first appeared in pointed doorway and window arches, especially of country parsonages, about 1820. Towns, particularly London, were being surrounded by newly developed estates (e.g. Pimlico), but even by 1840, remained within the present ring of railway terminii, while the growth of wealthy areas in the west led to the principal shopping area moving from the City to the new Regent's Street.

Farmhouses. Most farmers in the better areas prospered and built new brick houses in their recently enclosed fields, increasingly following the styles of the towns rather than the local traditional ones.

Village and urban cottages, late 18th and early 19th centuries. B = bedroom (1st floor); K/L = kitchen/living room; S = scullery

Cottages. Although new cottages were now generally two-storeyed, the rooms remained small and low, with small casement windows or Yorkshire Lights. The kitchen remained the main room, but the iron grate sometimes included an oven.

In towns, the rapid population growth created a huge demand for accommodation within walking distance of the mine, mill or factory which could not be met. The fortunate lived in small brick cottages, while others had only the back-to-back houses or a single room in once good houses, but some better terrace houses were being built, mostly for the craftsmen and skilled mechanics.

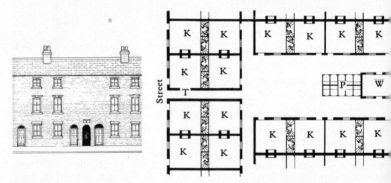

Urban workers' back-to-back, early 19th century, houses with tunnel entrance to court. K = kitchen/living room; W = wash-house; T = tunnel entrance; P = privies

Victorian 1840–1914

The many changes resulting from the industrial revolution gathered momentum, while wealth and influence increasingly passed to the rapidly-growing professional, manufacturing and commercial classes. Meanwhile steam reigned supreme, the symbol of growth and progress. The ever-widening range of goods was carried over the growing railway network, which offered faster travel to the wealthy besides opening new vistas to the day-excursionists (1844), many leaving their home towns for the first time. Later, the introduction of local public transport freed many from living near their work and caused a rapid development of better workers' houses in outer areas, while the better off moved westwards or to the higher ground, clear of windborne smoke and smells. But prosperity was uneven, concentrated mainly in London and the industrial towns of the Midlands and the North, while some rural areas stagnated, especially after the farming decline (1873), and former craft towns and small ports decayed.

As education continued to spread at all levels, aided by night schools and the strong Victorian belief in self-help, the rising standards resulted in a greater demand for books and newspapers, leading to a greater awareness and the more rapid spread of ideas throughout society.

Large Houses. By 1840 Regency frivolity and stucco sham were being rejected for Victorian Gothic, although the classical influence was not entirely lost (Cliveden 1851). Early Victorian Gothic was a mixture of Decorated pointed arches, towers and battlements and Tudor gables, twisted chimneys and mullioned windows (Scarisbrick Hall 1837). The former features permeated slowly throughout society, at least as decorations, but Victorian building is characterised by massive solidity, sense of permanence and respectability. Distinctions between country houses and the industrialists' villas became blurred, although the latter were built near towns of necessity. To the new rich trying to emulate and surpass the old nobility, the villa was a status symbol of position achieved, with the intensity of decoration emphasising their wealth. For some two decades the Gothic remained dominant, but with the choice of a classical style for the new Foreign Office it passed its peak (1860). Although it was still used for some large buildings, its decline opened the way to a wave of styles from the ever-popular Queen Anne, the Flemish with curved gables and leaded lights, to the Scottish Baronial with battlements and bartizans, among many others. Rooms became larger while the mass of pictures, bric-à-brac, heavy furniture and draperies declined, with the appearance of a lighter and simpler Neo-Georgian (Adam and Classical) of the nineties. There was also some Stockbroker Tudor, while a vigorous Baroque reached a peak during the more flamboyant Edwardian era, when red-brick public buildings with curved gables were enlivened by bands, quoins and keystones of light-coloured stone, but this too tended to become stylised.

Some 'modern' trends were also appearing in plain white walls, steeply-pitched roofs and tall functional stacks, but like the even more decorative Art Nouveau, it did not find wide acceptance; however, the introduction of steel-framing (1906) proved to be a greater indication of coming changes.

One new feature in the landscape pattern resulted from the rapid urban growth of the late nineteenth century, which had engulfed formerly wealthy districts. As these became less highly regarded and commuter train services improved, so the rich again built large houses in the country – convenient for stations with fast City services – although in London at least, many often retained a town house, increasingly replaced by a flat in a luxury block.

Urban Victorian 'Gothic villa' *c.* 1850

Urban terraced house, *c.* 1865. Party walls were often carried above roof level as a fire precaution

Smaller Houses. Here, the Gothic gained dominance more slowly and was usually restricted to pointed arches, small turrets and an absence of stucco, while decoration became increasingly heavy. By mid-century houses became larger and complex, with more passages and stairs, while continued urban growth forced new building further away from town centres, although the consequences of this were largely mitigated by the wider use of horse-buses. The Gothic had declined by the seventies, to be followed by a wide variety of simpler forms with flat-headed doorways and larger windows, mostly of 3–4 storeys plus a semi-basement in London, and generally one storey less elsewhere. Individually-built detached double-fronted houses, with a central stair and through hall, were preferred, but those built in pairs or terraces became more common.

The Garden Suburb concept first became a reality (1876–7) in Bedford Park, London, where substantially-built red-brick houses were grouped around a church and shopping area, the whole designed as a community from the outset. This was followed by Hampstead and taken a step further when work began in 1904 on the Letchworth Garden City, which was intended to provide good housing and work in pleasant surroundings for a broader spectrum of the population.

Urban workers' 6-roomed houses

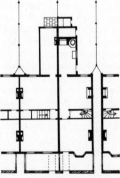

Above, Dorset Horn, with Southdown cross-bred lambs.   *Below*, Clun Forests.

Above, Landrace, an imported breed which is becoming increasingly popular as a bacon pig. *Centre*, Wessex Saddleback. *Below*, Large White boar.

Urban Workers. Enclosed courts and narrow alleys were prohibited under bye-laws during the forties, while clearance of jerry-built slums by the railways extending towards town centres was considered beneficial by civic authorities, whose powers had changed little since receiving their ancient charters. In the industrial areas, this resulted in monotonous streets of closely-packed two-storeyed houses. Mostly four-roomed, they were succeeded in the sixties by larger houses with gardens behind and sometimes by a nominal one in front, as a status symbol, and often named 'villas', a sad decline of meaning. Meanwhile, many central areas had declined to the point of being health hazards and local authorities were given powers to clear them, although commercial premises were often built on the sites. By the eighties, the six–roomed house had become the norm, usually with larger rooms and windows.

The provision of workers' accommodation by employers had originated at the beginning of the century with Robert Owen's New Lanark and the idea was followed in Middlesbrough, Saltaire, Bournville and Port Sunlight, while the railways did the same at their centres in Derby, Crewe and Swindon. The trend towards better housing continued into the new century, but many workers continued to live in the older houses among the factories and mills.

Shops. Retailing grew rapidly. Tradesmen opened additional sections as the range of goods increased, some becoming Emporiums, while many of the larger ones often provided board and dormitories for single employees until 1914. Others opened new branches, but the old pattern of making goods on premises declined in the face of mass-production, except in the case of luxury items.

Farmhouses. Building fluctuated with prosperity. The period of 'high farming' (1852–73), one of the most prosperous until then, saw many farmhouses improved or re-built, often in Tudor styles, with steeply-pitched roofs, gables, twisted chimneys and mullioned windows. But after a series of bad harvests and the succeeding cheap food imports, little was left save milk and vegetables, and farming slumped until 1914.

Cottages. With prosperity, these were increasingly built in pairs of brick and slate to urban designs. After 1875 the decline saw many of the older ones rot away as the townward migration continued, while community life declined.

Interwar Period 1918–1939

Despite a strong desire for a return to 'normal', peace brought greatly changed conditions. No longer the world's workshop, Britain faced increased competition and falling international trade. Established industries declined or formed larger and larger groupings, while new ones developed, often using the greater flexibility of electric-power and sited on Industrial Trading Estates, thus separating them from the residential areas, whether sprawling urban suburbs, council estates or ribbon development. The major change in transport produced by better roads and the ubiquitous motors offered greater opportunities of travel and escaping into the countryside, where the electric grid began to bestride the fields, while farming was allowed to slip back after its wartime revival.

Large Buildings. Economic conditions, rural decline and heavy death duties resulted in the building of few large private houses; on the contrary, many were sold for institutional or commercial uses, while parks went for building land. Large buildings were almost exclusively blocks of offices or flats and stood apart from the evolution in house styles. A few were given a trace of Neo-Georgian in their exteriors, but most followed the stark plainness of the modern movement, which had developed in the USA and arrived complete, with no intermediate stages. In time, as the potentialities were better understood, framework and cladding were contrasted to break up the sheer mass of the monotonously plain walls. Changes of material, balconies and more glass being used, so that by the late thirties the general effect was one of increasing lightness.

Smaller Houses. Two decades of building produced over four million houses' but quality and good design were sometimes sacrificed for speed and cheapness. The six-roomed semi-detached house was the most numerous, generally more square and lacking the rear kitchen extension of the pre-war counterpart, but the rooms were smaller and as costs rose so did building density, later houses occupying a higher proportion of each plot. Early types tended to be 'fussy' with timber decorations, projecting porches, thick window frames and leaded lights. By the mid-thirties, this had given way to a plainer façade, a recessed

Semi-detached houses, *c.* 1925   Semi-detached houses, *c.* 1936

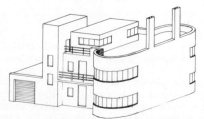

Interwar 'modern'

porch, slimmer window frames and a greater use of casements, although details varied considerably. Garages were frequently included in the designs of larger houses, but the side-garage was usual, while in some areas rear access roads with garages at the bottom of the garden saved valuable street frontage.

Municipal estates followed the same general form, but houses were usually in terraces, of a single basic design, which could extend to the whole road or even estate, giving a depressing uniformity. Council flats continued to be built in London and several Scottish towns, but were not widely popular elsewhere. The few 'modernistic' houses often had flat roofs, plain white walls, smooth curving bays and wide windows, but these were the exceptions.

Rural Housing. Because of the decline in farming little building was done, but in some villages urban-type council houses were an improvement on the older cottages and in the limestone belt the use of stone facing avoided the sharp contrast of red brick. Most new houses and bungalows were built for those willing to commute to neighbouring towns, or for retired people. While wireless lessened the sense of isolation, motor-buses and cars eased and speeded transport.

Post-War 1945–

When the war ended in 1945, not only had world conditions changed radically, but there was a yearning for Utopia rather than a return to the life of the thirties. Two new Acts were to have a marked effect on landscape. The first, New Towns Act (1946), carried forward the Garden City concept, while the second, Town and Country Planning Act (1947), sought to control development and urban sprawl. But in an atmosphere of austerity conditions improved slowly, and it was ten years before wartime controls disappeared, while industries moved forward into yet another phase of the industrial revolution, with the emphasis on both larger units in the heavy sector and more rapid development in the lighter, market-orientated ones. The railways lost more ground to the more flexible road transport, necessitating the provision of fast motorways, while a still rising population looked for better housing and better education to meet new challenges. But gradually, despite the growing technological emphasis in daily life, more and more people began to take an increasing interest in their environment and the natural world around them, and in the landscape as a whole.

Large Buildings. No large houses were built in the immediate post-war period, and the numbers continued to be small throughout the period, indeed many more passed into institutional and commercial use. Generally, the pre-war modern style had developed into an international one, often with the concrete-encased steel frame becoming an integral part of the façade, which was increasingly constructed of contrasting materials, with ever-larger windows until some resembled goldfish bowls. From the wide diversity two main forms emerged. The tall, narrow point block and the long slab, both receiving more light than the old hollow rectangles.

In badly bomb-damaged areas and the slums, local authorities initiated large-scale redevelopment schemes, clearing away the good and the bad regardless, to replace them by multi-storey blocks of flats. Nor are high-rise buildings confined to city centres, but are now appearing in towns of all sizes and in the suburbs, where lower costs prevail, while some universities have used the new forms and materials with startling originality.

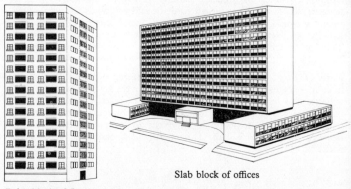

Slab block of offices

Point block of flats

Smaller Houses. The initial housing shortage was met by repairing bomb-damage and the factory production of small fitted pre-fabricated bungalows (pre-fabs), intended to last for ten years but many are still in use. Although this did little to relieve the position, it enabled industry to run-in, ready for the

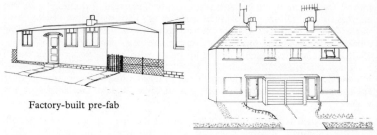

Factory-built pre-fab

Semi-detached houses of the late 1960s

estates and New Towns planned. Basically the New Towns were a series of neighbourhoods grouped around a shopping and commercial area, with an adjacent industrial estate. Blocks of flats soon supplemented the low density of housing, which had to be raised, and the open grassed areas before the houses, which had replaced gardens, were reduced.

At first severely restricted, private building gained ground rapidly in the fifties. Styles followed those of the late thirties, but gradually a new one developed, with the elimination of bay windows and the remaining decorations to leave a clean-lined rectangular block, marked by large paned-windows in metal frames and usually larger kitchens. Many new ideas were tried ranging from the ultra-modernistic to a return to terrace housing. Larger houses reflected the same general ideas, but had more individuality and often showed a faint hint of much earlier styles.

Rural Housing. The wartime upsurge of farming continued and increased, but the rapid rise in mechanisation offset the loss of farm-workers, while the continued townward drift was more than balanced by the inflow of commuters, the retired and the growing numbers employed in the light industries established in the market towns and larger villages, revitalising many, but swamping others until they had virtually lost their identity.

Other buildings

Watermills

The grinding of corn into flour was one of the earliest powered processes, and although the introduction of watermills into Britain is lost in the mists of time, some people believe that the Romans were responsible. The first known reference to them, however, dates from the late seventh century, but the change-over to inanimate power is important in itself. By the time the Domesday Book was compiled (1086), there were over 7,500 watermills in England. Now, few are left. Most have been demolished, allowed to decay or have been converted into houses, hostels or offices.

WATERWHEELS

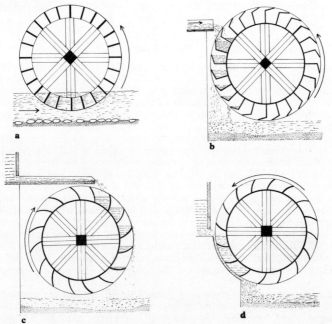

a, undershot wheel with straight paddles turned by the stream; **b,** pitch-back wheel with buckets; **c,** overshot wheel with curved blades; **d,** breast wheel

However, these few survivors provide an interesting link with the past, as it was with this form of power that Britain took the first stumbling steps on the road to 'industrialisation' and the factory system in the early eighteenth century. Even today, the term 'mill' is still used in many industries where water first supplied the power and, although mainly remembered in connection with textiles, we still talk of iron- and steel-rolling mills, whose fore-runners were water-powered hammers, which have left their mark on the old iron-working district of the Weald in the form of 'hammer ponds', reservoirs in which water was held back.

Irrespective of the material produced, watermills had to be sited where there was a reliable water supply and where either the river gradient was enough to provide the force to turn the water-wheel, or where this could be produced by building a dam or weir (a factor which became increasingly important as the industrial mills grew in size).

Water-wheels were of two types: those in which the water from the mill stream was directed on to the upstream side of the wheel and passed beneath are known as 'undershot', while those in which the water was carried above the wheel in wooden troughs to fall on the downstream side are called 'overshot'.

Finally, we must not forget the millwrights, who made first wooden mill machinery and later turned increasingly to iron, thus becoming the first mechanics and modern engineers. Many were sufficiently skilled and adaptable to build and develop the early industrial machines, some of which had been designed for human or animal power, e.g. Crompton's Spinning Mule.

Windmills

The windmill was introduced into Britain c.1191 and for a long time its form remained the same, that of the simple post-mill. This consisted of a rectangular cabin mounted on top of a stout wooden post, on which it could be turned into the wind by the miller, who pushed on a long projecting beam. The four sails were attached to a heavy wooden windshaft and turned the upper millstone through a series of wooden gears.

About the middle of the seventeenth century, the smock and tower mills began to make their appearance. The former consisted of a circular or polygonal wooden structure standing on a stone or brick base, while the latter were usually circular and built entirely of brick. Both had revolving caps, which carried the sails and windshaft, and were kept turned into the wind by a small set of sails (the 'fantail') at the rear of the cap. From about the same time post-mills were often given a permanent brick or stone circular base with a sloping roof, crowned by a larger cabin on its post. During the eighteenth and nineteenth centuries many improvements were made to mill machinery; one of these was the introduction, in the nineteenth century, of patent shutters in the sails, which could be opened or closed, thus controlling the speed of the sails without the need to stop them and adjust the canvas covering ('commons') formerly used.

While the uncertainty of the wind prevented the windmills from competing in the industrial field with watermills, there was one type of work in which they were supreme and they were used extensively in the Fens and other low-lying areas to lift water up from the drained fields into the man-made water-courses at a higher level.

Early post-mill dating back to mediaeval times

Later post-mill with brick base and fantail to keep the sails turned into the wind

Smock mill

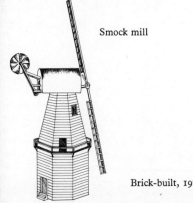

Brick-built, 19th century, tower mill

Few, if any, windmills are now working, their tasks having been taken over first by steam and then by internal combustion engines or electricity; but a number have been structurally preserved.

Oast houses for drying hops, Kent

BUILDINGS GLOSSARY

Abacus. The flat stone on top of a column capital.

Aisle. A lateral extension of a building, usually separated from it by a line of columns or posts.

Apse. A semi-circular or polygonal extension of a chancel or room.

Arch. A curved supporting structure at the head of an opening.

Dotted line = springing line

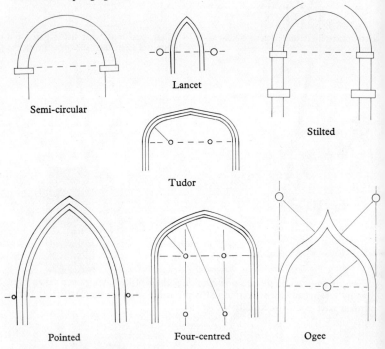

Semi-circular

Lancet

Stilted

Tudor

Pointed

Four-centred

Ogee

Semi-circular. A half-rounded form which remained dominant until about 1200. Height equalled half the span.

Stilted. A semi-circular arch raised on columns so that its top was level with that of another of greater span. Late Norman.

Lancet. A narrow pointed arch, arcs centred on springing line outside the arch, radii greater than span.

Pointed. A wider arch, arcs centred on springing line within arch, radii less than span.

Four-centred. An arch of four convex arcs, the lower and outer pair drawn from centres on the springing line; the upper and inner pair from centres below these.

Tudor. A four-centred arch, in which the upper and inner pair were only slightly curved; became progressively straighter.

Ogee. A four-centred arch, introduced in early thirteenth century. Lower pair of arcs convex and centred on the springing line, upper and inner concave drawn from centres above and outside the span.

Architrave. i. The moulded frame surrounding a doorway or window.
              ii. The lowest part of an entablature.

Ashlar. Stone blocks dressed to give a smooth surface and laid in courses with very thin joints.

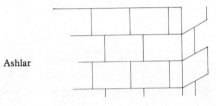

Ashlar

Bailey. The walled space within a castle; also known as a ward.

Ball-flower. A cut-away hollow sphere, representing a 3-petal flower containing a small ball. Introduced mid-thirteenth century.

Baluster. A short vertical member of a series, supporting a rail or coping. The whole forming a balustrade.

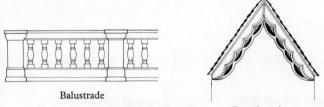

Balustrade

Bargeboards

Barbican. A separate outer defence work built in advance of a castle, or town; gateway.

Bargeboards. A pair of sloping boards, often decorated, on a gable roof to protect the ends of the roof timbers from the weather.

Barmkin. Walled courtyard of a Scottish or Border fortified house, often used as a cattle pound during troubled times.

Baroque. Late seventeenth- and early eighteenth-century style much favoured on the continent. Distinguished by the extravagant use of curves, lively decoration and the contrasting of mass with broad vistas on a grand scale. In Britain, modified by classicism, avoiding the worst excesses.

Bartizan. A small, usually enclosed turret projecting from an upper corner of tower or wall.

Batter. The inward slope of the face of a wall, or tower base.

Battlement. A defensive parapet, consisting of alternate raised (merlons) and lower (embrasures) portions. Later used solely for decoration.

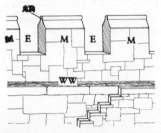

Battlements. AR =arrow-roll; M =merlon; E =embrasure; WW =wall walk

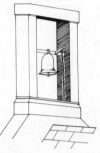

Bellcote

Bay. A structural division of a building, marked internally by columns, posts, etc.

Bay window. A window contained in an angled or curved projection, usually carried on foundations.

Bead moulding. A continuous Norman decoration carved to resemble a string of beads.

Beak. A Norman decoration, consisting of a series of heads of birds, animals or humans spaced along a half-round moulding.

Beam. A main horizontal timber supporting an upper floor or roof.

Bellcote. A framework of brick or stone built above the roof to support a bell.

Billet. A Norman moulding consisting of a band of squares, rectangles or part cylinders, and spaces in a regular sequence.

Bond. The method used in brickwork to ensure that all vertical joints are not in line. The three commonly used are:

English Bond. Bricks laid in alternate courses only of headers (ends) or stretchers (long sides).

English bond

Flemish bond

Flemish Bond. Bricks laid in courses, each consisting of alternate headers and stretchers.

Scottish or English Gardenwall Bond. Except the fifth, sixth or seventh courses, all bricks laid as stretchers.

Boss. Ornamental projection covering the intersection of groins or ribs.

Bow window. A window carried in a curved projection beyond the general line of the building.

Buttery. The service room in which ale and beer was brewed.

Buttress. A projecting stone or brick pier built against, or as an integral part of, a wall to strengthen it and counter an outward thrust.

Buttress, flying. A stone arch which carries the thrust against its upper end to a buttress at its lower, e.g. one carrying the thrust of the roof against the main walls of a cathedral over the aisle.

Byzantine style. Style which reached its peak in Byzantium (Istanbul) about AD 800. Characteristic form, a Greek cross (four equal arms) inside a square, with the principal block capped by a large dome.

Cap. The rounded top of a smock or tower windmill, which carries the sails and windshaft, turned into the wind by small sails, the fantail.

Capital. The stone block on the top of a column.

Cushion. Early Norman form with the lower edges of a square block rounded to fit the head of a circular shaft.

Scolloped. A later Norman development with the sides of the block carved into a series of flattened half-cones.

Bell. The whole rectangular block rounded, resembles an inverted bell.

Crocket. An Early English form with sides deeply cut into highly formalised leaves.

Casement. A rectangular light, usually one of a group, often hinged on one side to frame or mullion.

Chamfer. The sloping or concave surface produced when an edge is cut away.

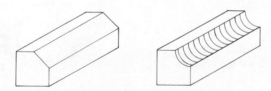

Chamfer and hollow chamfer

Chancel. The eastern part of a church, reserved for the clergy and containing the principal altar.

Chevron. A common Norman moulding or carving in the form of one or more series of zigzags.

Chimney breast. The chimney walls which project into a room and contain the fireplace and flues.

Chimney stack. The hollow brick or masonry column which extends through the building and projects above roof level, contains one or more flues, which may be topped by individual shafts or chimney pots.

Choir. The part of a large church or cathedral, usually between the chancel and nave, where the choristers' stalls are located.

Cladding. The non-loadbearing skin, between the framing of a modern building, which keeps out the weather.

Clerestory. The window storey in the upper part of the main walls of a church, above the level of the aisle roofs.

Cloisters. The vaulted passages surrounding a quadrangle or lawn, on to which it opens through a series of arches along one side.

Cob. A simple building material consisting of clay or mud mixed with straw and water and then tightly rammed; cheap but needing wide eaves to carry rain clear.

Collar beam. A horizontal strut connecting pairs of rafters above their mid-points.

Column. An upright stone cylinder which carries a weight; usually consists of an abacus, capital, shaft, base and sometimes a plinth. Term may be for the shaft only.

Coping. The upper course of a wall, or the top of a balustrade, usually a sloping or concave surface to throw off the rain.

Corbel. A block projecting from a wall face, to support a beam or other weight.

Cornice. i. A continuous moulding near the top of an external wall face to throw rainwater clear of the base.

ii. A continuous decorative moulding running round the upper walls of a room.

iii. The top projecting section of an entablature.

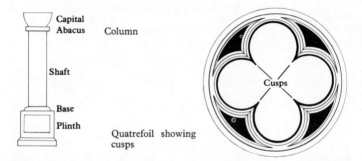

Capital
Abacus   Column

Shaft

Base
Plinth

Quatrefoil showing
cusps

Cusps

Cottage orné. An elaborately rustic house, usually thatched and half-timbered; picturesque phase of Romantic Movement, mostly 1790–1815.

Crocket. A decorative leaf carving, usually one of a series projecting from edges of window frames, pinnacles, spires, etc.

Cross-passage. i. The passage from the main door running behind the cross-screen of a medieval hall, dividing the hall proper from the service-rooms.

ii. Any passage from the main door extending the full depth of a house.

Crucks. Pairs of large curved timbers forming the principal roof trusses and wall supports at either end of each bay of some medieval houses.

Cupola. A dome, usually small, on a circular or polygonal base.

Curtain wall. i. The outer wall of a castle, around the bailey or ward.

ii. Modern. A non-loadbearing external wall which excludes the weather.

Cusp. The curved point formed at the intersection of arcs in tracery.

Dark Ages. The period from the end of Roman rule till the Norman Conquest.

Dog-leg stair. A stair of two reversed flights and a half-floor landing.

Dog-tooth. Early English pyramidal ornament, a diagonal 4-pointed star.

Dome. A hemispherical roof or vault.

Donjon. The Norman name for a castle keep.

Dormer window. A vertical window in a sloping roof lighting an attic.

Dripstone arch. An external moulding above an opening to shed rainwater.

Drystone wall. A rubble boundary wall, built without mortar from locally gathered stone.

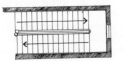

Dog-leg stair

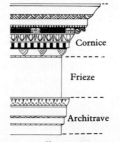

Cornice

Frieze

Entablature   Architrave

Embrasure. An opening in a fortified parapet, usually narrow.

Entablature. The upper part of a classical order, consisting of architrave, frieze and cornice.

Façade. The front of a building. Sometimes of a later date than the rest, especially when fronting a street.

Fanlight. i. Georgian and Regency. Usually a semi-circular window above the front door, often with radiating glazing bars resembling a fan.
ii. Post-Regency. Any window, irrespective of form, above a front door.

Fantail. The small set of sails which keep the cap of a smock or tower windmill turned into the wind.

Finial. The uppermost ornament on the top of a pinnacle, gable, etc.

Flamboyant. The final phase of the Gothic in France, with tracery in the form of long wavy bars. Few examples in Britain.

Flight. A series of stairs or steps uninterrupted by a landing.

Foil. A lobed opening in stone made up of a number of arcs (indicated by a prefix, e.g. quatrefoil), the intersection points forming cusps.

Folly: 'Greek temple'

Folly: 'castle ruins'

Folly. A tower, Grecian temple or sham ruin built in a landscaped park, solely for the picturesque effect. Popular in Georgian and Regency times.

Framed building. i. A modern building in which the load is carried by a steel girder framework and infilled with a light curtain wall.

ii. A timber framework; between the members are panels which are infilled with timber, wattle-and-daub, plaster or brick.

Freestone. A building stone which can be cut in all directions with equal ease.

Frieze. i. A decorative band round the upper walls of a room.

ii. The middle division of entablature.

Gable. i. The triangular portion of an external wall above the level of the eaves, framed by the ends of a pitched roof.

ii. The decorative section of an external wall, above the main eaves, often curved and with its own pitched roof which it conceals, Dutch Gable.

Giant order. A column or pilaster extending two or more storeys.

Girder. A steel support, or member of a steel framework of a modern building, usually an H-shaped section. (Technically Rolled Steel Joist.)

Gothic. The styles of building in stone which evolved from the Norman. In Britain, the three main phases were:

Early English, c. 1200–1270.

Decorated, c. 1270–1350.

Perpendicular, c. 1350–1540.

Gothic revival. The final phase of the Romantic Movement, loosely based on the Decorated period of the Gothic, reached its peak c. 1865.

Glazing bars. The wooden bars within a window which hold the separate panes.

Greek Cross. A cross with four equal arms.

Groin. The projecting and strengthening ridge found at the intersections of two tunnel vaults.

Hall. i. The principal room of a medieval house, or the house itself.

ii. Sixteenth century onwards, an entrance room or passage, usually containing the stairs.

Header. A brick laid so that only its end shows in the wall face.

Hip. The external angle formed by the intersection of two sloping roof surfaces of different sides of the building.

Hood-mould. See Dripstone arch.

Inglenook. A fireside seat, covered by the projecting chimneypiece.

Jettying. The projection of the second and higher storeys beyond the lower ones. Introduced thirteenth century, reached peak in Elizabethan times.

Joists. Horizontal timbers which support the floor-boards only.

Keep. The strongest wooden or stone tower of a castle and usually dominating it. During a siege it served as the last refuge.

Keystone. The central and often the largest member of an arch.

King-post. A vertical roof support from tie-beam to ridge.

Lancet. See Arch, Lancet.

Lantern. A small circular or multiangular cylinder or drum topped by a dome or sloping roof. Serves to light a dome or hall below.

Latin Cross. A cross with three equal and one longer arms.

Lights. The individual openings grouped to form a single window, e.g. two lancets and a trefoil, or a 3-casement Tudor window, each have 3 lights.

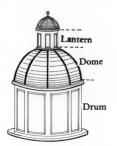

Drum, dome and lantern

Lych gate

Lintel. The horizontal stone or support spanning the top of an opening.

Long-and-short-work. Corner re-inforcement consisting of a series of long vertical stones separated by flat horizontal ones. Anglo-Saxon.

Long Gallery. A long narrow passage-room, usually found on the first floor at the rear of larger Tudor houses.

Lych Gate. A churchyard gateway with open sides and a pitched roof. Originally where the dead were removed from the parish coffin.

Machicolations. A projecting stone gallery carried on corbels outside castle walls, especially on gatehouses and towers, with floor openings to allow defenders to cover the gate or wall base.

Manor House. The principal house in a village, occupied by the Lord of the Manor, later by the Squire or chief landowner.

Medieval. The Middle Ages, roughly 1066–1485.

Merlon. The raised portion of a battlemented parapet.

Meutriers. Floor openings in machicolations and the ceilings of gateway passage, from which defenders could assail attackers below.

Mews. The rows of coach-houses at the rear of eighteenth- and nineteenth-century town houses. Now often converted into flats and garages.

Milkhouse. The medieval name for a dairy.

Motte-and-Bailey. Early Norman castles with a wooden tower on top of a steep-sided mound (motte) and an enclosure (bailey) surrounded by earthen bank and palisade, with an outer ditch.

Moulding. A continuous projecting narrow strip, varying in profile from square to complex with many flat or curved surfaces.

Mullion. The stone or wooden uprights which divide a window into lights.

Nailhead. Early English ornamental band of many low pyramids.

Nave. The main western part of a church, sometimes flanked by aisles, for the use of the congregation.

New Towns. Towns which were created, as opposed to those which grew up. In the post-war period those authorised under the New Towns Act (1946).

Orders. i. The columns and entablature in one of the acknowledged classical styles.

ii. The series of concentric arches and columns of a doorway, etc.

Anglo-Saxon long-and-short-work

Oriel window

Oriel window. A tall projecting three-sided window, carried on corbels; originally lighted the upper end of Tudor and medieval halls.

Outshot. A service-room or scullery of a small house or cottage, usually built under a roof extension continuous with that of the main building.

Palisade. A continuous defensive timber fence.

Pantile. A roofing tile, ∽-shaped in section.

Parapet. A wall built along the edge of a sudden drop, e.g. a roof.

Pargeting. External wall plaster which has been combed or moulded into designs or shapes, mostly found in East Anglia.

Parlour. i. A private family room in a medieval hall, often doubling as the principal bedroom; later called withdrawing-room (drawing-room).

ii. Sixteenth century onwards, often used for the workshop of a cottage craftsman.

iii. Nineteenth and early twentieth centuries used for a formal ground-floor sitting-room.

Classical   Open   Broken

Pediments

Pediment. A triangular ornament representing a classical entablature crowning a façade, door, porch or other opening usually 'carried' on columns or pilasters.

Pele tower. The fortified towers and tower houses of the Border and Scotland, mostly built between the thirteenth and seventeenth centuries, for defence against local raiding.

Picturesque. The first phase of architecture associated with the Romantic Movement in Arts and Letters. Mostly late eighteenth and early nineteenth centuries, when reaction to the formalised classical styles led to the introduction first of many exotic oriental forms and then to those of the Tudor and medieval which were to culminate in the Gothic Revival. It resulted in the deliberate creation of 'rustic' and scenic features.

Pier. A massive support of solid masonry or brick, squared section.

Pilaster. A decorative flat buttress or column, often of plaster.

Pillar. A free-standing vertical support, not necessarily circular section or of any particular style.

Pinnacle. A conical or pyramidal termination of a buttress, gable, etc.

Plinth. A pedestal for a column, statue, etc.

Podium. A flat platform on which a building or other structure stands.

Point block. An office or flats block in the form of a tall tower, length small in relation to height.

Porch. A cover projecting from a building over an entrance, open-sided, partly or fully enclosed.

Portcullis. A strong lattice of iron, or wood reinforced with iron, which can be slid down vertical grooves to protect a door or gateway.

Portico. A porch over the main entrance of a large building. Consists of a roof, often pedimented, supported by columns.

Portico

Post. A principal vertical wooden member of medieval or timber-framed houses.

Pre-fab. A general term used for small pre-fabricated bungalows of the early post-war years.

Purlin. A horizontal wooden roof support parallel to the ridge, supported by the principal rafters and carrying the common rafters.

Quadrangle. A square or oblong enclosed courtyard, lawn, etc.

Queen-post. One of a pair of parallel vertical timbers extending from a tie-beam to a collar-beam in the same roof truss.

Quoins. Large dressed stones used at the corners or openings of buildings, usually arranged so that a side alternates vertically with an end.

Rafters, common. Inclined wooden roof supports, extending from wall-plate or eaves, to ridge or hip and sometimes supported by purlins.

Rafters, principal. Pairs of large wooden roof supports which form the upper members of a roof truss and carry the purlins and weight of the roof.

Rainwater head. The metal junction-box, through which the water from the roof gutters passes into the down-pipe. Often dated until nineteenth century.

Rampart. A stone or earthen defensive wall.

Renaissance. The re-awakening in Arts and Letters at the end of the Middle Ages. Originating in Italy (*c.*1420) and strengthened by an influx of fresh knowledge after the fall of Byzantium (1453). Later extending to other countries with the Italian version of classical Roman styles and an insistence on a symmetrical façade.

Rib. A structural or decorative projection on a vault or ceiling.

Ribbon development. The inter-war extension of urban sprawl along main roads into the countryside.

Ridge. The horizontal line, or timber, at the junction of opposite sides of a roof.

Rococo style. The last phase of the continental Baroque (*c.* 1730–80). Characterised by its use of colour and excessive ornamentation, often as naturalistic trees, flowers and rural scenes. Uncommon in Britain.

Roof. The top surface of a building. The principal forms are:

Pitched or *Gable*. Two sloping surfaces meet along a ridge and cut the end walls to form triangular gables.

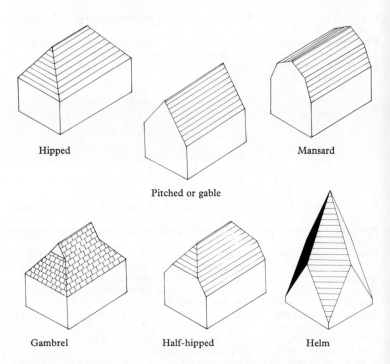

Hipped

Mansard

Pitched or gable

Gambrel   Half-hipped   Helm

Hipped. A pitched roof with two triangular sloping surfaces extending from the end walls to the ends of the ridge.

Gambrel. A pitched roof, with sloping surfaces from end walls to the base of a small gable at each end of the ridge.

Half-hipped. A pitched roof, with truncated gables on the end walls topped by short triangular sloping surfaces extending to the ridge.

Mansard. A pitched roof of two or more sloping surfaces on each side of the ridge. The lower surface being steeply-sloped allows more headroom in the roof-space than other types.

Helm. A tower roof with four equal sloping faces. The longer upper sides of each meet at the apex, the shorter lower ones of each face meet at a tower corner.

Flat. A roof with a slope of less than 10° to the horizontal. Rare before 1920s.

ROOF TRUSSES

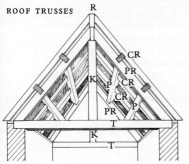

King-post and roof members: R = ridge; CR = common rafter; PR = principal rafter; P = purlin; K = king-post; T = tie-beam

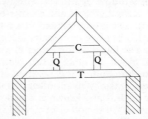

Queen-posts: C = collar beam; T = tie-beam; Q = queen-posts

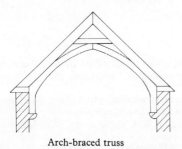

Arch-braced truss

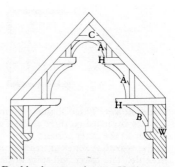

Double hammer beam: H = hammer beam; W = wall post; B = brace; A = arched brace; C = collar beam

Roof truss. The arrangement of wooden or metal members which form the principal support of the roof. Named after the characteristic member.

Rubble masonry. Walls built of roughly dressed stone, not laid in courses, with irregular mortar-filled joints.

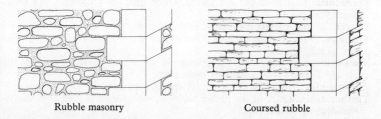

Rubble masonry   Coursed rubble

Rustication. Large stone blocks with deeply bevelled edges, or the same effect produced in stucco, sometimes with surfaces moulded to resemble roughly dressed stone.

Sash window. A window with two (originally one) glazed frames which slide in vertical grooves and counter-balanced by weights in the box-frame.

Shaft. The cylindrical part of a column between base and capital.

Sill. i. The stone or concrete block at the base of a window opening.

ii. The foundation member of a timber-framed house.

Slab block. An office or flats block, longer than depth or usually height.

Slate-hanging. A wall covering of overlapping slates.

Solar. A family room, often doubling as bedroom, in a medieval hall, manor or castle. Later known as a parlour.

Spire. A tall conical or pyramidal structure standing on a church tower.

Splay. The diverging sides of a wall opening, e.g. an arrow-slit.

Staircase (Stair). A series of horizontal treads, sometimes with landings between flights, which connect two floors or levels.

Newel stair

Stair, newel. Three flights of stairs with two intermediate landings between floors, arranged on three sides of an open square. Named after the supporting posts at the inner corners.

Stair, spiral. A series of treads or stone steps winding round a central column.

Steeple. The tower and spire or lantern of a church, taken as one.

Storey. A horizontal level within a building, with all the rooms on it. Counted from the ground floor.

Stretcher. A brick laid so that its long side appears in the wall face.

String course. A continuous projecting course of bricks in a wall.

Stucco. A plaster applied to outside of a building producing a stone-like surface.

Studs. The minor timber uprights of a half-timbered house, usually extend one storey only.

Terracotta. Clay fired but not glazed. Often used for mouldings and ornamentation.

Thatch. A thick roofing material of reeds or straw.

Through. A stone which extends to both faces of a drystone or coursed rubble wall to help bond it.

Tie-beam. The horizontal lower member of a roof-truss, connecting the principal rafters at or near their lower ends.

Tile-hanging. A wall covering of overlapping vertical tiles.

Timber-framing. A heavy timber skeleton, with panels infilled with wattle-and-daub or bricks.

Tracery. The arrangement of ornamental stonework, mullions of windows, etc.

Plate. Several lancets and foils grouped under a single hood mould but separated by the full thickness of the wall.

Bar. Introduced when windows were designed as a whole. Openings separated by mullions, which curve from the springing line.

Transept. A side extension of a cruciform church, usually joining the main line between the nave and chancel, below the central tower.

Transitional. Style between Norman and Early English Gothic, *c.* 1160–99.

Transome. The horizontal stone or wooden bar across a window opening.

VAULTING

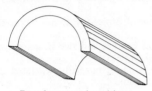

Cross vaulting

Barrel or tunnel vaulting

Norman ribbed vaulting

Norman ribs with extra ribs added

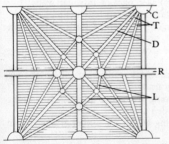

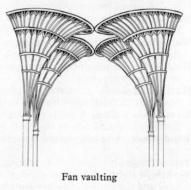

Vaulting ribs.   C = column;   D = diagonal rib; R = ridge rib; L = lierne ribs; T = tierceron rib

Fan vaulting

Turret. A small open tower, on a wall or larger tower, often extending above and beyond its parapet.

Tympanum. A stone, usually carved, filling the space between a flat-headed opening and a semi-circular arch above it.

Undercroft. A vaulted storage room, often at least partly underground.

Vault. An arched ceiling of stone or brick.

Tunnel. The simplest type, in effect a long semi-circular arch.

Groin. The form produced where two tunnel vaults crossed, with arcs of intersection strengthened by projecting arches (groins); later used as a separate form.

Rib. Basically as groin, but with the number of projecting arches increased for decorative and structural effect.

Fan. Many ribs originate from a column or bracket and rise in a concave half-cone, spreading over the ceiling in semi-circles.

Venetian window. A central round-headed window, normally separated by columns, from shorter flat-headed ones either side.

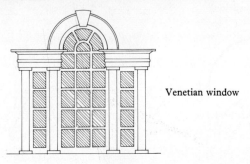

Venetian window

Villa. i. A Classical style country mansion, early eighteenth century.

ii. A large house near a town, usually belonging to someone of commercial importance, early to middle nineteenth century.

iii. A larger urban terrace house, *c.* 1860 onwards.

iv. Any urban terrace house today.

Wainscoting. The timber covering of the lower part of internal walls. Formerly up to four feet in height, now limited to bottom few inches.

Wall plate. A horizontal timber running along the top of walls and carrying the lower ends of the common rafters.

Wall walk. The top of the curtain walls of a castle, protected by battlements on the outer edge only.

Wattle-and-daub. A simple building material consisting of interwoven sticks (wattle) plastered with mud or clay usually mixed with straw.

Weather-boarding. A walling of overlapping horizontal planks on a timber framework. Found only in then well-wooded areas.

Wind brace. A usually curved strengthening strut in a timber-framed building.

Yett. A hinged iron grille door, often used to protect a pele tower door.

Yorkshire lights. A window divided vertically into two frames, one usually fixed and the other sliding horizontally.

PLACE-NAME ELEMENTS OF THE BRITISH ISLES

Introduction

The study of place-names can be fascinating, but it is one which is full of traps for the unwary, as both the form and spelling have almost certainly changed during the course of centuries. Thus Milton or Midton can both be either a corruption of a town (Anglo-Saxon *tun*) with a mill, or the middle town, while *bough*, or some other form of borough, usually refers to a defensively enclosed settlement (Anglo-Saxon *burh*), but it can also be a corruption of *burg* indicating a hill or mound.

This list of place-name elements should, therefore, be regarded as no more than a general guide. To discover the true origin, it is necessary to trace the place-name back to its earliest recorded use, a task requiring patient research and often the translation of ancient records. It is, therefore, advisable to compare the interpretation obtained from the present elements with an authoritative reconstruction by consulting one of the standard works listed in the bibliography, p. 333.

Some English place-name elements

Abbreviations

A-S Anglo-Saxon	O.N. Old Norman
M.E. Middle English (1150–1500)	Scand. Scandinavian.
O.E. Old English	

Ae (A-S): oak.

Anger (A-S): grassland.

Baer (O.E.): pasture for pigs in woods or waste.

Barnet (O.E.): areas cleared by burning.

Bere (O.E.): barley; also used during Middle Ages for outlying part of manorial estate.

Brad (O.E.): broad.

Brende } (M.E.): places cleared by burning.
Brente }

Burh, also in the forms **borough, borrow** and **burrough** (A-S): a fortified place, house or town. (M.E.): a court or manor house.

Burg } : a hill or mound.
Berry }

–by (Scand.): a farm or village.

Ceap, also **cheap** and **chep** (O.E.): a market.

Cester, also **ceaster** and **caester** (O.E.): a large fortified town.

Chy (Cornish): a house.

Cot(e) (O.E.): a cottage.

–combe (Cornish): valley.
Dale (Scand.): valley.
Denn (O.E.): the lair of.
Denu, also **dene** and **dean** (A-S): valley.
–dial (Scand.): farmstead and its buildings; later a village or town.
–don, also **–down** and **–dun** (A-S): hill.
Eg (O.E.): an island.
Eng (O.N.): meadow or pasture.
Eowestre (A-S): sheepfold.
Fealh (O.E.): ploughland.
Feld (O.E.): field.
Fell (Scand.): large hill.
Force
Foss } (Scand.): waterfall.
Foss (O.E. from Latin): ditch.
Gill (Scand.): valley.
Ham (A-S): farm or estate; from the eighth century, a village or town.
Hamm (A-S): fold or enclosed land.
Hamstede (A-S): chief house or manor.
–ing
–ingas } (A-S): the people or folk of.
Lan (Cornish): church.
Law (A-S): hill.
Lazar (M.E.): leper hospital.
Newton, also **Newington, Newnton, Naunton** and **Niton**: a new town. Often with the surname of founder added.
Pen (Celtic): height or hill.
–sea
–sey } (O.E.): island.
Slaughter (A-S): marsh or an alder.
Stock
Stoke } (A-S): holy place.
Stow (A-S): a site, especially with a saint's name.
–thrope (Scand.): hamlet.
–thwaite (Scand.): pasture or arable reclaimed from the waste.
Street, also **streat** and **strat** (A-S): place standing on a paved Roman road.
Toft (Scand.): homestead.
–ton
–tun } (A-S): enclosed lands, later land with buildings.
–ware (A-S): the dwellers of.
–wic(h) (A-S): a group of buildings, especially those at some distance from the manor.
–wick (Scand.): creek (on the coast), or a bog.

Some Welsh place-name elements

Aber: river mouth or confluence.
Afon: river.
Aran: high place.
Bach: small.

Bedd: grave.
Bettws: chapel.
Blaen
Blaenau } : summit.

Bod: dwelling.
Braich: an arm (of the sea).
Bron: rounded hill.
Bryn: small hill, or mound.
Bwlch: mountain pass, or gap.
Bychan: small.
Cader: seat.
Cae: meadow or enclosed field.
Caer: walled town or fortress.
Capel: chapel.
Careg: rock.
Carn ⎫
Carnedd ⎬ : cairn.
Cefn: ridge.
Celli: grove or bower.
Clogwyn: precipice.
Clwyd: gate.
Coch: red.
Coed: wood.
Craig: crag.
Crib: crest.
Croes: cross.
Croesffordd: cross-roads.
Cwm: corrie.
Cymmer: confluence.
Ddu: black.
Din ⎫
Dinas ⎬ hill-fort or fortified town.
Dol: dale.
Drosgl: hump.
Drws: pass.
Du ⎫
Dulas ⎬ : black.
Duffryn: valley.
Dwr: water.
Eglwys: church.
Esgair: long ridge.
Fach: little.
Fawr: great.
Ffordd: roadway.
Ffridd: forest.
Ffrsd: torrent.
Ffynnon: spring or well.
Fynydd: mountain.
Garth: hill or promontory.
Glan: bank or shore.
Glas: blue or green.
Gelli: grove.
Glyn: glen.
Goch: red.

Gogof: cave.
Groes: cross.
Gwen ⎫
Gyen ⎬ : white.
Hafod: summer dwelling.
Hen: old.
Hendre: winter dwelling.
Hir: long.
Isaf: lower.
Llan: church.
Llwyd: grey.
Llyn: lake.
Maen: stone.
Maes: field.
Mawr: great.
Melin: mill.
Moel: bare or bald hill.
Morfa: marsh.
Mynydd: mountain.
Nant: valley or a brook.
Newydd: new.
Ogof: cave.
Pant: hollow.
Pen: summit or a headland.
Pennant: the upper part of a glen.
Pistyll: spout.
Plas: hall or manor.
Pont: bridge.
Porth: port or gate.
Pwll: pool.
Rhaiador: waterfall.
Rhos: moorland.
Rhyd: ford.
Sarn: causeway.
Sych: dry.
Tan: under.
Traeth: sandy beach.
Tre– ⎫
Tref– ⎬ : house or town.
Twll: hollow or pit.
Twr: tower or heap.
Ty–: house.
Tyddyn: farmstead.
Uchaf: upper.
Y: of the, on the.
Yn: in, or at.
Ynys: island.
Ysgol: school.
Yspytty: hospital.
Ystrad: vale.

Some Scottish place-name elements

Aber: river mouth.
Ach: field.
Allt: stream.
An: of the.
–an: small.
Ard: height.
Aros: dwelling.
Auch: field.
Ault: stream.
Ay: island.
Bal: township (village).
Balloch: pass.
Ban: white.
Bar: height.
Beag / **Beg** : little.
Bealach: pass.
Beinn / **Ben** : mountain.
Blair: moor.
Brae: hillside or slope.
Buie: yellow.
Burn: hill stream.
Cam / **Cambus** : crooked.
Cairn / **Carn** : heap of stones.
Car: bend.
Carse: alluvial flat land beside a river.
Chulish: strait.
Clach: stone.
Clachan: small village.
Clunie: meadow.
Collie: wood.
Craig / **Creag** : crag.
Cruach: stack.
Dail / **Dal** : field.
Dearg: red.
Dour: water.
Druim / **Drum** : ridge.
Dubh / **Dhu** : black.
Dun: hill-fort.

Eaglais / **Eccle** : church.
Eilean: island.
Fail: cliff.
Fionn: fair.
Firth / **Frith** : an estuary, or an arm of the sea.
Fyne: fair.
Gart: enclosure.
Glas: grey or green.
Goe: creek.
Gorm: blue or green.
Gowan: blacksmith.
Haugh: the alluvial land by a river.
Holm: islet, or small island.
Hope: inlet, or small bay.
Howe: hollow.
Inch / **Innis** : island.
Inver: river mouth.
Kil: church, or hermit's cell.
Killie: wood.
Kin: head or headland.
Kinloch: the head of a loch.
Knoch: knoll.
Kyle: strait.
Lag: hollow.
Larig: mountain pass.
Law: conical hill.
Learg: hillside.
Leath / **Liath** : grey.
Linn: waterfall or rapids.
Lochan: small lake.
Machair / **Machar** : the low-lying fields or pasture by the sea.
Mains: the home farm attached to a manor.
Mam: rounded hill.
Meal: bare headland.
Monadh: moor.
Mor / **More** : great.
Mull: a bare headland.
Ob / **Oban** : bay.

Ochter: upper.
Ord: height.
Pit: township (village).
Pol: pool.
Policies: the private park of a large house.
Rath: fort.
Rhinns: peninsula.
Ross: forest.
Rudha: cape.
Scuir: steep rock.
Sgeir: skerry, sea rock covered at high tide.
Sgurr: steep rock.
Shieling: summer dwelling.

Strath: wide valley.
Tigh: house.
Tir: land.
Tober: well.
Tom: hillock.
Tor
Torr } : hill.
Tudloch
Tully } : knoll.
Ty: house.
Uam: cave.
Val: fell, or hill-side.
Vik: creek.
Voe: bay, creek or inlet.

Some Irish place-name elements

Agh: field.
Aherlow: valley.
Aill: cliff.
Annagh: marsh.
Ard: height.
As: waterfall.
Ath: ford.
Bal, also **bel:** an entrance or mouth.
Bal, also **bally** and **baile:** place or town.
Bal
Bally } : path.
Bane
Baun } : white.
Bawn: a fortified enclosure.
Beag
Beg } : little.
Ben, also **pin:** peak or mountain.
Bog: soft.
Boher: a road.
Boy: yellow.
Brag: a hill.
Cahir: a stone fort.
Callow: a landing-place or port.
Carrick
Carry } : a rock.
Cashel: an ancient stone fort.
Claddagh, also **clydagh:** a beach or sea-shore.
Clar(e): a level-space.

Clo(o)n: a meadow.
Clough: a shore.
Coon: a harbour.
Cor: round hill.
Creagh, also **cree:** boundary.
Crusha: cross or cross-roads.
Curra
Curragh } : marsh or low plain.
Dangan, also **dingle:** stronghold.
Dare, also **derry:** oak or oak grove.
Derg: red.
Don, also **down** and **dun:** a fort.
Donagh
Donny } : church, usually one
Donough thought to have been founded by St Patrick.
Doo, also **dub** and **duff:** black.
Droghed, also **drohjd, drehid** and **drought:** bridge.
Dron
Drum } : ridge.
Enis, also **inis:** island or water-meadow.
Espic also **aspick:** bishop.
Fee
Fid } : a wood.
Fith
Gal, also **goole:** river.
Glan, also **glen** and **glyn:** valley or hollow.

Glas: a riverlet.
Howth: head.
Imer, also **imor** and **ummey:** ridge.
Inch, also **inish** and **ennis:** island.
Iver: an estuary.
Kel, also **kil:** church.
Ken, also **kin:** head.
Knock: hill.
Kyle: strait.
Lee
Lei } : grey.
Lem: pass or leap.
Lis: enclosure.
Loch, also **lough** and **low:** lake.
Lusk: cave.
Ma, also **may, maw, mhagh** and **moy:** open plain.
Maam
Mam } : pass.
Men: small.
Mena: middle.
Moate: mound.
Mog: plain.
Mon, also **moon** and **mount:** peat bog.
Mor(e): big or great.
Muil
Mweel } : bare.
Mullagh: summit.
Mullen } also **mutty, vullen** and
Mullin } willin: mill.

Navan: grave.
Og: youth.
Oran: spring.
Oughter: upper.
Oul
Owe } : apple tree or orchard.
Owen: river.
Ower: pale grey, dun or light brown.
Pas: pass.
Rath
Ray } : circular fort.
Rea, also **reagh** and **revagh:** grey.
Reen, also **rin** and **ring:** point.
Risk: moor or marsh.
Rose, also **ross** and **rush:** promontory.
Sean, also **shan** and **shane:** old.
Skellig: high crag or rock.
Slieve: mountain.
Slighe: way or a pass.
Stra(i)d: street.
Stradbally: village.
Tass: green pasture.
Termon: sanctuary.
Thurles: strong fort.
Tipper, also **tober** and **tubber:** well.
Tom, also **toom** and **tuam:** tomb, tumulus or burial mound.
Tull, also **tulla** and **tully:** hillock.
Vally: path.

SUGGESTIONS FOR FURTHER READING

Most subjects have expanded so much in recent years that once the basic principles are grasped it becomes increasingly difficult to find an up-to-date book which adequately covers all branches of a subject. Yet it is far from easy to find one's way among the ever-growing mass of publications most of which are devoted to a single aspect of a narrow speciality. The list below should enable those interested to explore more thoroughly their chosen fields, the more so as most of the books named contain good bibliographies.

(P) denotes a book available in paperback.

Minerals. *Rocks and Minerals in Colour*, J. F. Kirkaldy; *Minerals, Rocks and Gemstones*, R. Sorner; *Rutley's Introduction to Mineralogy*, edited by H. Read; *Dana's Manual of Mineralogy*, edited by W. E. Ford; *Minerals and the Microscope*, H. G. Smith; *Elementary Crystallography*, J. W. Evans and G. M. Davies.

Rocks. *Pebbles on the Beach*, G. C. Ellis; *Principles of Petrology*, G. W. Tyrrel; *The Study of Rocks*, S. J. Shand; *Petrology of Sedimentary Rocks*, F. H. Hatch and R. H. Rastall (P); *Petrology of Igneous Rocks*, F. H. Hatch and A. K. Wells (P).

Fossils. *The Elements of Field Geology*, G. W. Himus and G. S. Sweeting; *An Introduction to Palaeontology*, A. Morley Davies; *Palaeontology*, H. Woods (P); British Regional Geological Handbooks of the Geological Survey.

Physical Evolution. *The Principles of Physical Geology*, A. Holmes; *An Outline of Geomorphology*, S. W. Wooldridge and R. S. Morgan; *Principles of Geomorphology*, W. D. Thornbury; *The Earth's Crust*, L. Dudley Stamp; *Geology and Scenery in England and Wales*, A. E. Trueman; *The English Coast and the Coast of Wales*, J. A. Steers (P); The Geological Survey Regional Handbooks; the Geologists' Association Guides, edited by A. K. Wells, Bentham and Co., Colchester, for areas around most university cities.

Geological History. *An Outline of Historical Geology*, A. K. Wells and J. F. Kirkaldy; *Britain's Structure and Scenery*, L. Dudley Stamp (P); *The Physiographical Evolution of Britain*, L. J. Wills; the handbooks and guides mentioned in the preceding paragraph.

Soils. *Good Soil*, S. Graham Brade-Birke; *The World of the Soil*, E. J. Russell (P); *Britain's Green Mantle*, A. G. Tansley.

Vegetation. *The Wild Flowers of Britain and Northern Europe*, Richard Fitter, Alastair Fitter and Marjorie Blaney; *Flora of the British Isles* and *Excursion Flora of the British Isles*, A. R. Clapham, T. G. Tutin and E. F. Warburg; *Britain's Green Mantle*, A. G. Tansley; and many volumes in the *New Naturalist* Series.

Trees and Shrubs. *A Field Guide to the Trees of Britain and Northern Europe*, Alan Mitchell; *Trees and Shrubs*, H. Vedel and J. Lange; *Trees in Britain*, R. Gurney; *British Trees*, E. H. B. Boulton; *Guide to Bark*, A. Schwankl.

Grasses, Sedges and Rushes. *Grasses*, C. E. Hubbard (P); *British Sedges*, A. C. Jermy and T. G. Tutin (P). Also see under 'Vegetation'.

Wild Animals. *The Handbook of British Mammals*, edited by H. N. Southern; *Mammals in the British Isles*, P. Street; *Field Guide to Mammals of Britain and Europe*, H. van der Brink; *British Mammals*, L. H. Matthews; *Living with Deer*, R. Prior; *A Field Guide to British Deer*, F. J. T. Page; *Collins Guide to Animal Tracks and Signs*, Preben Bang and Preben Dahlstrom; *British Amphibians and Reptiles*, M. Smith; *Reptiles and Amphibians*, edited by A. Leutscher.

Of the creatures not dealt with in the text, birds have already the most extensive coverage. *The Birds of Britain and Europe*, Hermann Heinzel, Richard Fitter and John Parslow; *Pocket Guide to British Birds*, R. S. R. Fitter and R. A. Richardson; *A Field Guide to the Birds of Britain and Europe*, R. Peterson, G. Mountfort and P. A. D. Hollom. The only mammals left out are dealt with in detail in *British Bats*, B. Vesey-Fitzgerald, while the sea-shore can offer a wide field of interest in a restricted area and is well catered for in *The Sea Shore*, C. M. Yonge; *Plants and Animals of the Sea Shore*, W. J. Prud'homme van Reine; *A Pocket Guide to the Sea Shore*, J. Barrett and C. M. Yonge.

Man on the Land. General. *The Making of the English Landscape*, W. G. Hoskins; *Man and the Land*, L. Dudley Stamp; *A Natural History of Man in Britain*, H. J. Fleure and M. Davies.

Prehistory. Ideas on Prehistory are continually modified as new archaeological 'digs' bring fresh evidence to light, while back-room research has revolutionised many other aspects. Nowhere is this more true than in the field of dating, with the use of radio-carbon and other techniques, which have drastically altered the time-scales compared with those used by earlier writers. For this reason, absolute or relative dates, as opposed to facts obtained from fieldwork, given in the older books must be treated with some caution.

Early Man. *Mankind in the Making*, W. Howell (P); *The History of the Primates* (P), and *Man-apes or Ape-men*, Sir Wilfred E. le Gros Clark; *Frameworks for Dating Fossil Man*, K. Oakley; *Dating the Past*, F. E. Zeuner; *Prehistoric Societies*, G. Clark and S. Piggot; *The Prehistory of European Society*, V. G. Childe; *Man the Toolmaker*, K. Oakley (P); *The Neolithic Revolution*, S. Cole (P).

British Prehistory. *Prehistoric Britain*, C. and J. Hawkes (P); *British Prehistory*, S. Piggot; *Prehistoric Communities of the British Isles*, V. G. Childe; *Prehistoric England*, G. Clark (P); *A Guide to Prehistoric England*, N. Thomas; *Scotland Before History*, S. Piggot and K. Henderson; *The Prehistoric Peoples of Scotland*, S. Piggot; *Prehistoric and Early Christian Ireland*, E. Evans; *Prehistoric and Early Wales*, Ll. Foster and G. Daniel; *Field Guide to Archaeology in Britain*, E. S. Wood; *Field Archaeology, some notes for Beginners*, Ordnance Survey; *Practical Archaeology*, G. Webster; *Archaeology from the Earth*, Sir Mortimer Wheeler (P); Series of Regional Archaeologies, edited by D. W. Wilson.

Roman to Norman Conquest. *Roman Britain*, A. Richmond (P); *Town and Country in Roman Britain*, A. L. F. Rivet; *From Caesar to Arthur*, Geoffrey Ashe; *Roman Britain to Early England*, P. H. Blair; *From Alfred to Henry II*, C. Brooke; *The Beginning of English Society*, D. Whitlock (P); *The Anglo-Saxons*, D. Wilson; *Anglo-Saxon England*, F. M. Stenton; *Roman Britain and the English Settlement*, R. G. Collingwood; *Celt and Saxon*, edited by N. F. Chadwick; *The Vikings*, Johannes Brondsted (P).

Post Conquest. *The Penguin History of England*, nine vols. (P); *History of the*

English-Speaking People, Sir Winston S. Churchill four vols. (P); *Nelson's History of England*; *Illustrated Social History*, four vols. G. M Trevelyan (P); *History of Scotland*, J. Mackie (P); *An Economic Geography of Great Britain*, W. Smith; *Historical Geography*, J. B. Mitchell.

Buildings. *A History of Architecture*, Sir Banister Fletcher; *An Outline of European Architecture*, N. Pevsner (P); *A History of English Architecture*, P. Kidson, P. Murray and P. Thompson (P); *The Historic Architecture of Scotland*, J. Dunbar; *The Architecture of England*, D. Yarwood; *A History of Architecture*, T. W. West; *England in Brick and Stone*, C. Trent.

Houses. *The Evolution of the English House*, Sir John Summerson; *The History of the English House*, N. L. Lloyd; *The English Home*, D. Yarwood; *Timber Buildings in England*, F. H. Crossley; *The Smaller English House, 1500–1939*, R. Turner; *The Welsh House*, I. C. Peate; *The English Farmhouse*, M. S. Briggs; *The English Farmhouse and Cottage*, M. W. Barley; *The Old English House*, H. Braun; *The English Country House*, R. Dutton.

Periods. *Looking for Elizabethan England* and *Looking for Georgian England*, R. Francis; *Georgian Architecture*, A. E. Richardson; *Nineteenth-Century Architecture*, R. Turner; *English Architecture since the Regency*, H. S. Goodhart-Rendel; *The Gothic Revival*, Sir Kenneth Clark (P); *Victorian Architecture*, R. F. Jordan (P); *Designed to Live in*, E. Beazley; *Architecture: the Indispensable Art*, W. R. Dalzell. *The Connoisseur's Period Guides* covering separately: Tudor, Stuart, Early and Late Georgian, Regency and Early Victorian periods.

Churches. *Exploring Parish Churches*, V. Bonham-Carter; *Parish Churches*, J. C. Cox and C. B. Ford (P); *An Introduction to Parish Church Architecture 600–1965*, T. M. Nye; *Pocket Guide to English Parish Churches*, John Betjeman.

Castles. *Castles of Great Britain*, S. Toy; *English Castles*, R. A. Brown (P); *The Scottish Castles*, S. Cruden; *Exploring Castles*, W. D. Simpson.

Mills. *British Windmills and Watermills*, C. P. Skilton; *Wind and Watermills* and *The English Watermill*, R. Wailes; *British Watermills*, L. Syson; *Windmills and Millwrighting*, S. Freese.

Other Buildings. *Industrial Archaeology of Southern England*, K. Hudson; *Industrial Archaeology of the East Midlands*, D. Smith.

Settlement. In addition to books listed under 'General' and 'History' above: *Urban Geography*, G. Taylor; *The Geography of Towns*, A. E. Smailes; *Borough and Town: a Study in Urban Origins in England*, C. Stephenson; *Britain's New Towns*, A. C. Duff; *Exploring Villages*, J. Finberg; *The English Village*, V. Bonham-Carter (P).

Transport. *An Economic History of Inland Transport*, C. I. Savage; *An Economic Geography of Great Britain*, W. Smith; *An Illustrated History of Civil Engineering*, J. P. M. Pannell; Longmans Industrial Archaeology Series (IAS).

Roads. *The Rolling Road*, L. A. G. Strong; *Roads and Road Vehicles*, A. Bird (IAS); *Packhorse, Waggon and Post*, J. Crofts; *Roads and Their Traffic, 1750–1850*, J. Copeland; *A History of British Bus Services*, J. Hibbs; *The History of London Transport*, T. C. Baker and M. Robbins.

Waterways. *British Canals*, C. Hadfield; *Navigable Waterways*, L. T. C. Rolt. (IAS); *The Canals of the British Isles*, edited by C. Hadfield (P).

Railways. *Railways of Britain*, J. Simmons; *The Railways of Britain*, W. H Boulton; *Railways*, J. B. Snel (IAS); *British Railway History*, H. Ellis; *A Regional History of the Railways of Great Britain*, five vols., edited by D. St John

Thomas; *British Steam Railways* and *British Steam Railways in Retrospect*, O. S. Nock.

Airways. *The Geography of Air Transport*, K. R. Sealy.

Agriculture. *Agriculture*, J. A. S. Watson and J. A. More; *Farming Dictionary*, D. H. Chapman; *The Smallholder Encyclopedia*, J. Hayhurst; *A Short History of Farming*, R. Whitlock; *The Evolution of the English Farm*, M. E. Seebohm; *Plough and Pasture*, E. C. Curwen; *Farming the Land*, V. Bonham-Carter; *Agriculture: Handtools and Mechanization*, L. A. West (P) (HMSO).

Place-names. *The Concise Oxford Dictionary of English Place-names*, E. Ekwall; *Introduction to a Survey of English Place-names*, Sir Allan Mawer and Sir Frank M. Stenton; *English Place-name Elements*, A. H. Smith; *The Place-names of England and Wales*, J. B. Johnson; *A Book of Welsh Names*, T. R. Davies; *Place-names of Scotland*, J. B. Johnson; *The Origins and History of Irish Names of Places*, P. W. Joyce; *Place-names of the Isle of Man*, J. J. Kneew.

Meteorology. *A Short Course in Elementary Meteorology* and *Cloud Forms*, (HMSO); *Meteorology*, D. Blunt; *The Restless Atmosphere*, F. K. Hare; *Climate and the British Scene*, G. Manley; *The Climate of the British Isles*, E. G. Bilham.

Index